Global Perspectives on Human Rights and the Impact of Tourism Consumption in the 21st Century

Maximiliano E Korstanje
University of Palermo, Argentina

Vanessa G.B. Gowreesunkar
Anant National University, India

A volume in the Advances in Hospitality, Tourism, and the Services Industry (AHTSI) Book Series

Published in the United States of America by
    IGI Global
    Business Science Reference (an imprint of IGI Global)
    701 E. Chocolate Avenue
    Hershey PA, USA 17033
    Tel: 717-533-8845
    Fax: 717-533-8661
    E-mail: cust@igi-global.com
    Web site: http://www.igi-global.com

Copyright © 2023 by IGI Global. All rights reserved. No part of this publication may be reproduced, stored or distributed in any form or by any means, electronic or mechanical, including photocopying, without written permission from the publisher.
Product or company names used in this set are for identification purposes only. Inclusion of the names of the products or companies does not indicate a claim of ownership by IGI Global of the trademark or registered trademark.

Library of Congress Cataloging-in-Publication Data

Names: Korstanje, Maximiliano E. editor. | Gowreesunkar, Vanessa G. B. editor.
Title: Global perspectives on human rights and the impact of tourism consumption in the 21st century / edited by Maximiliano E. Korstanje and Vanessa G.B. Gowreesunkar.
Other titles: Global perspectives on human rights and the impact of tourism consumption in the twenty first century.
Description: Hershey, PA : Business Science Reference, [2023] | Includes bibliographical references and index. | Summary: "The goals of the book are threefold: 1- Develop a rich conceptual debate around tourism consumption's impact on human rights. 2- The introduction to successful study cases where tourism contributes positively to the human rights 3- To lay the foundations for a new understanding of human rights involving hosts and guests"-- Provided by publisher.
Identifiers: LCCN 2023019746 (print) | LCCN 2023019747 (ebook) | ISBN 9781668487266 (hardcover) | ISBN 9781668487273 (paperback) | ISBN 9781668487280 (ebook)
Subjects: LCSH: Tourism--Social aspects. | Tourism--Political aspects. | Human rights.
Classification: LCC G156.5.S63 G56 2023 (print) | LCC G156.5.S63 (ebook) | DDC 306.4819--dc23/eng20230517
LC record available at https://lccn.loc.gov/2023019746
LC ebook record available at https://lccn.loc.gov/2023019747

This book is published in the IGI Global book series Advances in Hospitality, Tourism, and the Services Industry (AHTSI) (ISSN: 2475-6547; eISSN: 2475-6555)

British Cataloguing in Publication Data
A Cataloguing in Publication record for this book is available from the British Library.

All work contributed to this book is new, previously-unpublished material.
The views expressed in this book are those of the authors, but not necessarily of the publisher.

For electronic access to this publication, please contact: eresources@igi-global.com.

Advances in Hospitality, Tourism, and the Services Industry (AHTSI) Book Series

Maximiliano Korstanje
University of Palermo, Argentina

ISSN:2475-6547
EISSN:2475-6555

MISSION

Globally, the hospitality, travel, tourism, and services industries generate a significant percentage of revenue and represent a large portion of the business world. Even in tough economic times, these industries thrive as individuals continue to spend on leisure and recreation activities as well as services.

The Advances in Hospitality, Tourism, and the Services Industry (AHTSI) book series offers diverse publications relating to the management, promotion, and profitability of the leisure, recreation, and services industries. Highlighting current research pertaining to various topics within the realm of hospitality, travel, tourism, and services management, the titles found within the AHTSI book series are pertinent to the research and professional needs of managers, business practitioners, researchers, and upper-level students studying in the field.

COVERAGE

- Service Training
- Health and Wellness Tourism
- Destination Marketing and Management
- Customer Service Issues
- Casino Management
- Service Management
- Sustainable Tourism
- Travel Agency Management
- Hotel Management
- Service Design

IGI Global is currently accepting manuscripts for publication within this series. To submit a proposal for a volume in this series, please contact our Acquisition Editors at Acquisitions@igi-global.com or visit: http://www.igi-global.com/publish/.

The Advances in Hospitality, Tourism, and the Services Industry (AHTSI) Book Series (ISSN 2475-6547) is published by IGI Global, 701 E. Chocolate Avenue, Hershey, PA 17033-1240, USA, www.igi-global.com. This series is composed of titles available for purchase individually; each title is edited to be contextually exclusive from any other title within the series. For pricing and ordering information please visit http://www.igi-global.com/book-series/advances-hospitality-tourism-services-industry/121014. Postmaster: Send all address changes to above address. Copyright © 2023 IGI Global. All rights, including translation in other languages reserved by the publisher. No part of this series may be reproduced or used in any form or by any means – graphics, electronic, or mechanical, including photocopying, recording, taping, or information and retrieval systems – without written permission from the publisher, except for non commercial, educational use, including classroom teaching purposes. The views expressed in this series are those of the authors, but not necessarily of IGI Global.

Titles in this Series

For a list of additional titles in this series, please visit: http://www.igi-global.com/book-series/

Cases on Traveler Preferences, Attitudes, and Behaviors Impact in the Hospitality Industry
Giuseppe Catenazzo (ICN Business School, France)
Business Science Reference • © 2023 • 335pp • H/C (ISBN: 9781668469194) • US $215.00

Dark Gastronomy in Times of Tribulation
Demet Genceli (Istanbul Kent University, Turkey)
Business Science Reference • © 2023 • 283pp • H/C (ISBN: 9781668465059) • US $205.00

Inclusive Community Development Through Tourism and Hospitality Practices
Vipin Nadda (University of Sunderland in London, UK) Faithfull Gonzo (University of Sunderland in London, UK) Ravinder Batta (Shimla University, India) and Amit Sharma (Shimla University, India)
Business Science Reference • © 2023 • 361pp • H/C (ISBN: 9781668467961) • US $215.00

Sustainable Growth Strategies for Entrepreneurial Venture Tourism and Regional Development
Andreas Masouras (Neapolis University, Cyprus) Christos Papademetriou (Neapolis University, Cyprus) Dimitrios Belias (University of Thessaly, Greece) and Sofia Anastasiadou (University of Western Macedonia, Greece)
Business Science Reference • © 2023 • 247pp • H/C (ISBN: 9781668460559) • US $250.00

Measuring Consumer Behavior in Hospitality for Enhanced Decision Making
Célia M.Q. Ramos (CinTurs, ESGHT, University of the Algarve, Portugal) Carlos M.R. Sousa (ESGHT, CiTUR, University of the Algarve, Portugal) Nelson M.S. Matos (CinTurs, ESGHT, University of the Algarve, Portugal) and Rashed Isam Ashqar (CinTurs, ESGHT, University of the Algarve, Portugal)
Business Science Reference • © 2023 • 295pp • H/C (ISBN: 9781668466070) • US $225.00

Global Perspectives on the Opportunities and Future Directions of Health Tourism
Oğuz Doğan (Antalya Bilim University, Turkey)
Business Science Reference • © 2023 • 319pp • H/C (ISBN: 9781668466926) • US $270.00

701 East Chocolate Avenue, Hershey, PA 17033, USA
Tel: 717-533-8845 x100 • Fax: 717-533-8661
E-Mail: cust@igi-global.com • www.igi-global.com

To all those whose basic human rights have been violated in the tourism industry, we dedicate this book to you. Your struggles and experiences have inspired us to write on this pertinent issue.

We recognize that tourism has often been linked to various human rights abuses, including labor exploitation, child abuse, displacement of indigenous peoples, and environmental degradation. We hope that this book will serve as a tool to raise awareness about these issues and provide solutions that can help prevent further harm.

Our dedication also goes out to the countless individuals, organizations, and communities who have been fighting for human rights in the tourism industry. Your tireless efforts have been instrumental in creating a more just and equitable industry.

Finally, we dedicate this piece of work to future generations of travelers, tourism professionals, and activists who will carry on the fight for human rights. May this book inspire them to build a more sustainable, responsible, and respectful tourism industry that puts people and the planet first.

Vanessa & Max

Editorial Advisory Board

Oleg Afanasiev, *Russian State University of Tourism, Russia*
David Altheide, *Arizona State University, USA*
Ericka Amorin, *Polytechnic Institute of Tomar, Portugal*
Lwazi Apleni, *University of Zululand, South Africa*
David Baker, *Tennessee State University, USA*
Brian Berquist, *University of Wisconsin at Stout, USA*
Raoul Bianchi, *University of West London, UK*
Paul Brunt, *Plymouth University, UK*
Dimitrios Buhalis, *Bournemouth University, UK*
Richard Butler, *University of Strathclyde, UK*
Erdinc Camak, *Breda University, The Netherlands*
Neil Carr, *University of Otago, New Zealand*
Anthony Clayton, *The University of West Indies, Jamaica*
Erik H. Cohen, *Bar Ilan University, Israel*
Jean Costa Henriquez, *University of the State of Rio Grande do Norte, Brazil*
Gerry Coulter, *Bishop´s University, Canada*
Mahmoud Eid, *University of Ottawa, Canada*
Elspeth Frew, *La Trobe University, Australia*
Alan Fyall, *University of Central Florida, USA*
Babu George, *Fort Hays State University, USA*
Vanessa G. Gowreesunkar, *University of Africa, Toru Orua, Nigeria*
Ulrike Gretzel, *University of Southern California, USA*
Tony Henthorne, *University of Nevada, USA*
Freya Higgins-Desbiolles, *University of South Australia, Australia*
Luke Howie, *Monash University, Australia*
Rami Isaac, *Breda University of Applied Sciences, The Netherlands*
Stanislav Ivanov, *Varna University of Management, Bulgaria*

Metin Kozak, *Dokuz Eylul University, Turkey*
Sharad K. Kulshreshtha, *North Eastern Hill University, India*
Dominic Lapointe, *University of Quebec at Montreal, Canada*
Duncan Light, *Bournemouth University, UK*
Claudio Milano, *The Autonomous University of Barcelona, Spain*
Cesar Augusto Oliveros, *University of Guadalajara, Mexico*
Daniel Olsen, *Brigham Young University, USA*
Andreas Papatheodorou, *University of Aegean, Greece*
Alexandros Paraskevas, *Oxford Brookes University, UK*
Lorri Pennington Gray, *University of Florida, USA*
Abraham Pizam, *University of Central Florida, USA*
Arie Reichel, *Ben-Gurion University of the Negev, Israel*
Claudia Seabra, *University of Coimbra, Portugal*
Anukrati Sharma, *University of Kota, India*
Richard A. Sharpley, *University of Central Lancashire, UK*
Jonathan Skinner, *University of Roehampton, UK*
Geoffrey Skoll, *Buffalo State College, USA*
Marta Soligo, *University of Nevada, USA*
Peter Tarlow, *Texas A&M University, USA*
Dallen Timothy, *Arizona State University, USA*
Marcelo Tomé de Barros, *State University of Fluminense, Brazil*
Diego R Toubes, *University of Vigo, Spain*
Rodanthi Tzanelli, *University of Leeds, UK*
Ghialy Yap, *Edith Cowan University, Australia*

Table of Contents

Foreword *by Salah S. Hammad*... xv

Foreword *by Kheswar Jankee* xvii

Preface.. xix

Acknowledgment xxiv

Introduction... xxvi

Chapter 1
Tourism, Poverty, and Human Rights: An Unspeakable Relationship 1
    Maximiliano Emanuel Korstanje, University of Palermo, Argentina

Chapter 2
Tourism and Water: A Human Rights Perspective to Enhance Sustainable
Tourism 13
    Yesaya Sandang, Universitas Kristen Satya Wacana, Indonesia
    Stroma Cole, University of Westminster, UK

Chapter 3
Expanding and Updating Human Rights: Tourism as a Social Right in
Contemporary Societies 36
    Thiago Duarte Pimentel, Federal University of Juiz de Fora, Brazil
    Mariana Pereira Chaves Pimentel, Federal University of Juiz de Fora, Brazil
    Marcela Costa Bifano de Oliveira, Federal University of Juiz de Fora, Brazil
    João Paulo Louzada Vieira, Federal University of Juiz de Fora, Brazil
    Paulo Rodrigues Cerqueira, Federal University of Juiz de Fora, Brazil

Chapter 4
Dark Tourism and Human Rights: A Philosophical Quandary?............................59
  Maximiliano Emanuel Korstanje, University of Palermo, Argentina

Chapter 5
Revenge Travel: A Case of Pandemic Fatigue and Boredom 72
  Charul Agrawal, Amity University, India
  Taranjeet Duggal, Amity University, India
  Parul Gupta, I.T.S. Ghaziabad, India

Chapter 6
The Migrantour Experience at Porta Palazzo and Barriera di Milano:
Tourism Consumption in Intercultural Neighborhoods......................................92
  Adriana Maria Offredi Rodriguez, Universitat Autónoma de Barcelona,
    Spain

Chapter 7
Human Rights and Workforce Conditions in the Tourism Sector 129
  Osama Khassawneh, The Emirates Academy of Hospitality
    Management, UAE
  Zeynep Gulen Hashmi, National University of Science and Technology,
    Islamabad, Pakistan

Chapter 8
Corporate Social Responsibility and Analysis of Its Social Dimension in
Hotels in Malaga...153
  Miriam Stopiakova, EADE University, Spain
  Marina Haro-Aragú, University of Malaga, Spain
  Alicia Martin Garcia, EADE University, Spain

Glossary 194

Compilation of References 198

Related References...225

About the Contributors 256

Index..262

Detailed Table of Contents

Foreword *by Salah S. Hammad* xv

Foreword *by Kheswar Jankee* xvii

Preface xix

Acknowledgment xxiv

Introduction xxvi

Chapter 1
Tourism, Poverty, and Human Rights: An Unspeakable Relationship 1
Maximiliano Emanuel Korstanje, University of Palermo, Argentina

Over recent years, the philosophical dilemma of human rights has occupied a central position in the academic debate worldwide. Of course, tourism seems not to be an exception. Despite the promising economic benefits and multiplying effects of tourism, some voices have alerted on the problems and limitations of tourism management to achieve a fairer wealth distribution in local communities. Having said this, the idea of tourism as a key force towards a more democratic and prosperous society began to be placed under the critical lens of scrutiny. This chapter, in this context, discusses critically how tourism potentiates economic growth but under some conditions deteriorating (if not vulnerating) the basic rights of locals. The opposite is equally true. Local communities embrace tourism to boost their economies while paradoxically making them more dependent and vulnerable to external economic actors.

Chapter 2

Tourism and Water: A Human Rights Perspective to Enhance Sustainable Tourism 13

Yesaya Sandang, Universitas Kristen Satya Wacana, Indonesia
Stroma Cole, University of Westminster, UK

This chapter explores how acknowledging water as a human right affects government, business, and local communities in tourism. Tourism businesses have the responsibility to respect and protect the right to water, which aligns with the SDGs, particularly SDGs 5, 6, and 10. When the human right to water is not protected and respected, multifaceted violations occur and the potential for tourism to contribute to sustainable development will be undermined. The chapter suggests ways to improve tourism water management and prevent human rights abuses. By adopting responsible water management practices and engaging in partnerships with local communities, the tourism industry can help to promote the realization of the human right to water while also contributing to sustainable tourism.

Chapter 3

Expanding and Updating Human Rights: Tourism as a Social Right in Contemporary Societies 36

Thiago Duarte Pimentel, Federal University of Juiz de Fora, Brazil
Mariana Pereira Chaves Pimentel, Federal University of Juiz de Fora, Brazil
Marcela Costa Bifano de Oliveira, Federal University of Juiz de Fora, Brazil
João Paulo Louzada Vieira, Federal University of Juiz de Fora, Brazil
Paulo Rodrigues Cerqueira, Federal University of Juiz de Fora, Brazil

This chapter argues that tourism should be included as a social right because it synthesizes and represents the zeitgeist of contemporaneity. This idea is supported by three main arguments: (1) That there is a shift from a work-oriented society to a new consumption-oriented one, implying the revision of the meaning of current practices. (2) As a social force, tourism is a privileged category to represent, understand, and explain contemporary societies because it goes beyond the market and can heuristically express a complex and multifaceted human practice. (3) The references based on the previous societies' ideals, such as the right to work, must be revised and expanded to include tourism as a fundamental right, because (a) it can internationally represent a new kind of global citizenship, (b) basic material and economic human needs must be met for tourism to happen, and (c) it contributes to personal development, cultural exchange, and systemically update societies' development.

Chapter 4
Dark Tourism and Human Rights: A Philosophical Quandary?..........................59
  Maximiliano Emanuel Korstanje, University of Palermo, Argentina

Over the recent years, scholars have focused their attention on dark tourism as a newly emerging and global trend. Without any doubt, dark tourism remains a more-than-interesting object of study for social scientists and academia. At first glimpse, dark tourism exhibits a new morbid taste generated in post-disaster contexts, as well as environments of mass death and suffering. Paradoxically, dark consumption opens a much deeper question revolving around human rights. This chapter interrogates the intersection of dark consumption (as a type of commoditizing process) and human rights. As Zygmunt Bauman puts it, one of the paradoxes of memorizing the tragedy is that its roots are ultimately forgotten. In consonance with this, the authors hold the thesis that dark tourism enhances resiliency and local community, but at the same time, it generates a biased story of what should be memorized.

Chapter 5
Revenge Travel: A Case of Pandemic Fatigue and Boredom 72
  Charul Agrawal, Amity University, India
  Taranjeet Duggal, Amity University, India
  Parul Gupta, I.T.S. Ghaziabad, India

With the onset of the coronavirus pandemic, the people and their lives have been affected. The social distancing norms and the hygiene issues completely broke down the travel and tourism sector and people forgot what holidays and vacations were. Then came the period when the clutches of virus loosened and so did the lockdown, and people got an opportunity to open their windows and step out of their homes. Trapped under boredom and fatigue due to pandemic, people wanted to visit more, spend more on their holidays and trips, and thus emerged the concept of revenge tourism. Not only domestically, this phenomenon was observed globally when people flocked to nearby tourist destinations to ease their psychological stress as and when restrictions on lockdown were lifted. Revenge tourism is a recent phenomenon that is fueled by the monotony and the boredom faced by the people during the lockdowns imposed on them. The desire to participate in such a practice has been accentuated by the strict health rules and prolonged home traps.

Chapter 6
The Migrantour Experience at Porta Palazzo and Barriera di Milano:
Tourism Consumption in Intercultural Neighborhoods 92
  Adriana Maria Offredi Rodriguez, Universitat Autónoma de Barcelona,
    Spain

Migrantour contributes to spreading a culture of respect for the human rights of migrant communities in European cities by encouraging interactions of mutual respect between people with different origins. Since 2009, it has involved over 11,000 participants in the intercultural itineraries and more than 300 people as intercultural companions. Currently, new projects are under implementation to promote its methodology in rural areas and new cities. Thus, as it will be explained in the chapter, it can represent a successful study case where tourism contributes positively to human rights within the frame of interculturalism. The contribution is a part of a broader study examining the experience of Migrantour in Porta Palazzo and Barriera di Milano, two neighborhoods of the Italian town of Turin, under different grounds. The aim is to further contribute to the debate about the implications of the transformation of intercultural neighbourhoods into places of leisure and consumption for migrant communities.

Chapter 7
Human Rights and Workforce Conditions in the Tourism Sector 129
  Osama Khassawneh, The Emirates Academy of Hospitality
    Management, UAE
  Zeynep Gulen Hashmi, National University of Science and Technology,
    Islamabad, Pakistan

In this chapter, the focus is on the various challenges related to workforce conditions in the tourism industry and how human rights can play a role in alleviating these challenges. The chapter draws from a review of literature and offers a global perspective. Topics covered include the treatment of employees in the tourism sector, adherence to human rights and labor standards in the industry, the prevalence of mandatory and forced labor, collective bargaining, the use of child labor, fair treatment for all workers, and employee discrimination. The chapter will feature examples from different countries and conclude with recommendations for improvement.

Chapter 8
Corporate Social Responsibility and Analysis of Its Social Dimension in
Hotels in Malaga 153
    Miriam Stopiakova, EADE University, Spain
    Marina Haro-Aragú, University of Malaga, Spain
    Alicia Martin Garcia, EADE University, Spain

The main purpose of this research is to emphasize the importance of corporate social responsibility (CSR) within any hotel in operation. The main objective has focused on the analysis of social activities of CSR of accommodation in the city of Malaga. The basis of this project has been the investigation of the term CSR and its presence in tourism. At the same time, it has focused on the fact of the presence of the Covid-19 pandemic, which has caused many changes in tourism in recent years. As part of the investigation on the current situation of CSR activities in hotels Malaga city, interviews have been carried out with active professionals in the sector, in order to draw correct conclusions. Additionally, this project contributes with the proposal of activities within the social dimension of CSR of a hotel supporting the local community in different areas. It has been possible to reach various conclusions about the positive impact and importance of CSR in the hotel sector together with future lines of research, which can be supported by the results of this work.

Glossary 194

Compilation of References 198

Related References 225

About the Contributors 256

Index 262

Foreword

It is a great moment of achievement when scholars are deeply involved in shaping the destiny of our world. This book on "Global Perspectives on Human Rights and the Impact of Tourism Consumption in the 21st Century" edited by Dr. Maximiliano E Korstanje and Dr. Vanessa GB Gowreesunkar, is timely and a milestone in raising issues related to tourism, human rights and our collective development concerns.

The promotion and protection of Human Rights are keys for sustainable development globally and are an integral part of the universal human rights system core values. The principles and objectives of the Universal Declaration on Human Rights and all other global and continental instruments emphasise the need to priorities human rights in the context of business operations as inspired by the UN Guiding Principles on Business and Human Rights (UNGPs). Adopted in 2011, the UNGPs is a global framework grounded in the recognition of state duty to protect human rights; business responsibility to respect human rights; and appropriate and effective remedies.

The role of businesses, including tourism, in the developmental landscape of the developing countries has become significant. While business-related activities have contributed to the economic growth of states, some of these activities have also resulted in adverse human rights impacts such as environmental degradation, arbitrary displacement, labour right abuses and health issues. Specific groups including women, children, older persons, indigenous peoples and persons with disabilities have increasingly become vulnerable to these impacts.

In some parts of the world, particularly developing countries, there have been tensions, conflicts and protests related to the adverse impacts of business operations, including tourism, on human rights. These impacts highlight the need for states to strengthen their commitments to business strategies that as mindful of the protection of human in their operations. Some of these conflicts are protracted, affecting human development and significantly hampering the economic development of states.

The need for peace, sustainable development and the enjoyment of human rights make it imperative to address adverse impacts of business operations, including tourism, on human rights. That is why, I wish to take this opportunity to praise this book, which raises a rich conceptual debate around tourism consumption's impact on human rights by sharing successful study cases and best practices where tourism contributes positively to the human rights.

This book is a pioneering contribution to sustainable development, human rights promotion and protection and innovation globally.

Salah S. Hammad
African Governance Architecture, African Union Commission, Sudan

Foreword

The rapid growth in the tourism and hospitality industry has propelled a number of human rights issues in the forefront of academic research and policymaking. Changes in the international economic and geopolitical order, climatic changes and the recent covid 19 pandemics have brought new dynamics in the interface between tourism activities and human rights. Human rights are those basic standards without which people cannot live in dignity (Donnelly 2003). The rapid growth in the global tourism activities has raised a lot of concern on the violation of human rights in academic circles, NGOS, pressure groups and other related organisations. It became imperative for stakeholders in the tourism industry to assess the implications of their activities from a human rights perspective. The United Nations Universal Sustainable development goals (SDGs) reiterated the cross-cutting relationships between human rights and tourism development. Though the positive and negative effects of tourism activities in the host countries have been well documented, integrating human rights in the tourism practice is quite a novel phenomenon. The analysis of the tourism activities from human rights perspective has led to an evaluation of the costs and benefits from tourism development. The adverse impact of climate change has warranted for sustainable tourism policies. Human rights are violated when tourism industry gains too much importance in the host economy that local community is displaced, access to public beaches or touristic spots is reduced, rise in the prices of land for locals given at times agricultural lands and coastal lands are transferred to the tourism industry for hotels and infrastructural development, impact of tourism on fishing community and local suppliers of services like taxi cars when the package is all inclusive. Moreover, the employer -employee relationship may also affect human rights when the big share of the profit goes abroad with foreign owners and in terms of the resources invested including environmental, the employees are exploited. Ethics are also associated with tourism and human rights in the cases of sex tourism, displacement, rights of indigenous people, discrimination, freedom of movement, privacy amongst others.

Foreword

Tourism development remains an engine of growth for many countries but in many cases human rights are violated. Policy makers and the government should not be controlled by these powerful multinational companies which can even start blackmailing for incentives and susbsidies using the employment creation argument. Training of staff as well as special government agencies are set up for tourism promotion. During Covid 19 pandemic for example in many countries, financial resources at the cost of tax payers were granted to tourism industry as it has become to big to close down given the employment argument. A lot of research is being undertaken to address all the human rights issues relating to different tourism activities such medical, cultural as well as ecotourism. This is a timely and welcome book written by experts with examples and case studies on the interface of tourism activities and human rights. This book fills up a major much filling gap on the debate on tourism development from a human rights perspective bringing a number of new dimensions. An innovation is to also highlight the positive effects of tourism consumption on human rights supported with case studies as compared with earlier attempts to emphasize only the adverse effects. It is a successful attempt to develop a conceptual debate around tourism consumption from a human rights perspective and lay the foundations for a better understanding of human rights in the tourism ecosystem.

Kheswar Jankee
Ambassador of Mauritius to Russian Federation

Preface

HUMAN RIGHTS AND TOURISM: A DIFFICULT RELATION?

The concept of human rights has certainly gained considerable traction in the mid of former twentieth century, to be more exact, just after the crimes perpetrated by Nazi Germany during the WWII. From that moment onwards, human rights have occupied a central position in the academic debate in social science, philosophy and humanities (Fraser 1999; Headley 2008). Beyond any controversy, one must speculate, human rights have supporters and detractors. While some voices allude to human rights as basic conventions or moral standards oriented to protect the individual subject and its privacy (Marks, 1980; Sengupta 2004), others emphasize on its idolatry nature which leads to political manipulation (Kennedy 2002; Ignatieff 2011). What is more important, some acts of political violence as well as atrocities without mentioning ethnic cleansing have been made on behalf of "human rights" (Comaroff & Comaroff 2006). Having said this, human rights are a global and universal movement (force) that particularly takes different meaning and interpretation according to each cultural background. In fact, the cultural relativism, a movement emerged in the fields of social science, punctuated that what is condensable in one human group may be not in others and vice versa. Hence, supporters of human right conventions strove historically for reaching universal consensus on how basic rights should be applied for all citizens globally no matter religion, class, race, culture or ideology (Teson 1984; Merry 2001).

As the previous backdrop, in the constellations of tourism and hospitality, human rights have taken a broader connotation. As McCabe & Diekmann (2005) put it, scholars have toyed with the belief that the tourism industry enriches social life through positive impacts on health, culture, well being and quality of life for locals. For that, tourism is seen as a necessary force that democratizes local culture and institutions while improving local interaction with visitors. At the same time, tourism boosts local economies while sanitizing or correcting some material asymmetries culturally enrooted into under-developing economies. This plausibly leads to two connected debates. On one hand, to what extent tourism opens the doors that ensure

Preface

the participation of all stakeholders and actors and on another, why tourism should be considered as a basic right. In consonance with this, Cole & Eriksson (2010) alert that despite of the benefits of tourism which act as a key driver to social transformation, the industry, unless duly regulated, recreates the conditions for new inequalities or asymmetries. The point of convergence, these authors discuss, associates to the right or freedom to travel vs. the rights of local people (most of them doomed to immobility). Per their standpoint, there is an ethical quandary between the leisure behavior emulated in the First World and the right to water, and housing in local communities, which needs further revision. At a closer look, tourism should be understood as an agent of positive transformation which ensures some basic rights in locals while fostering community-based development. However, since a major portion of tourism enterprises are controlled by multinationals operating in poor nations further attention should be paid to local legislation protecting workers´ integrity and their basic rights. Under some conditions, when the rights of tourists are valorized over the locals, guest-host relations are marked by financial inequalities. This is particularly true in former colonies or nations oppressed by colonial powers in the pastime. When this happens, local cultures face social maladies which include: mass migration, exclusion of locals who are banned from basic access to water and housing, human trafficking, or children abuse, alcoholism and drug addiction, the acceleration of gentrification process or overcrowding, non-secure labor contract, long working hours and high work intensity (only to name a few). In the other corner of the square, R. Bianchi calls the attention to the censorship exerted by some nations cautioning not to travel to countries where human rights are not respected. Not only the aversion for risky destinations, but also the travel reports issued by embassies which discourage the visit to destinations framed as "rogue states" creates a climate of censorship which is inexpugnable to the critical eye. For Bianchi, the right to travel globally accepted simply collides with the autonomy of nations to be self-regulated (Bianchi & Stephenson, 2014). An interesting additional debate have been placed on the tapestry in the recent COVID-19 pandemic where nation-states suspended the right to travel to preserve the public security and safety (Bianchi, Stephenson & Hannam 2020; Baum & Hai, 2020). With the benefits of hindsight, Korstanje & George argue that the COVID-19 pandemic shows two important things. At a first look, the rights endorsed by states are constructed on a temporal basis. This means that nation-states reserve the legitimacy of law and the public force to endorse or remove assigned rights. And of course, this can be done without intervention of an external state. Secondly, as the history witnessed, basic rights are systematically suspended during the states of emergency. The tourism industry was the main spreader and victim of COVID-19 pandemic. Governments, which disposed of strict measures to the stop the contagion, adopted strategies to close the airspace and airports, as well as bus stations and any modern transport mean. At the same time, school and

Preface

public building have been closed as well as serious restriction to circulation during the day. All this ignited a climate of fear and mistrust in some groups that ultimately aligned with protests worldwide. The right to travel was invoked as the main tug of war of some militant groups that condemned the restrictive steps instrumentalized by some governments (Korstanje & George 2021; 2022).

As the previous argument is given, the human rights and tourism still has a more than interesting relationship, this book looks to decipher. Having said this, chapters accepted in this book contains an interesting debate originated from empirical study-cases or conceptually-based papers that interrogate critically on the interplay between tourism and human rights.

In the first chapter, Maximiliano Korstanje (one of the editors) offers an interesting diagnosis on the connection of poverty and human rights. This diagnosis is mainly based on a much deep conceptual debate that puts the economic-centered paradigm under the critical lens of scrutiny. Over years, tourism has been considered a key force that sanitizes economies boosting local consumption. The chapter, rather, goes on the opposite direction reminding how tourism generates positive economic empowerment but under some conditions increasing the state of vulnerability and dependency in locals. In this way, tourism creates serious material asymmetries that vulnerate locals´ rights. In consonance with this, the second chapter which is authored by Y. Sandang & S. Cole, gives a fresh description that explains how tourism affects local human rights, above all the access to water and housing. The healthy access to water affects not only to governments but also local communities and businesses. For that, tourism businesses open the doors towards more tolerance respecting the duty to protect local water in sync with SDGs. Authors offer a good description of how sustainability and tourism consumption can be ethically articulated to protect locals´ rights. T. Duarte Pimentel et al. (in the third chapter) debate to what extent tourism should contemplated as a social or human right. The chapter toys with the belief that significant underlaying changes are creating new working conditions that alter tourism consumption. At the same time, tourism should be defined as a social institution that precedes human action and leisure practices. Therefore, some basic rights should be met earlier than the tourist practice emerges. This behooves us to consider tourism as a social right resulted from the expansion of global capitalism. M. Korstanje -in the fourth chapter- interrogates furtherly to what extent dark tourism practices align with human rights. Although dark tourism consumption not only has innumerable benefits helping locals to accelerate their recovery timeframes just after a disaster takes hit, there is some risks to enter in what Korstanje dubbed as "the Spectacle of Disaster", in which case, the roots and real reasons that preceded the event are replicated. In the fifth chapter, C. Agrawal, T. Duggal & P. Gupta explore the effects of the COVID-19 pandemic in the human geographies, the right to travel as well as the tourism industry. Although subservice sectors went

Preface

through similar risks in the past (including the H1N1 pandemic, or even SARS) nothing was so devastating for the industry like COVID-19. Per their stance, revenge tourism, a post-modern phenomenon derived from the long and strict lockdown where people have been chronically subject to fear, anxiety and boredom, paved the ways for a new re-engagement of consumers with touring. As a result of this, in the new normal the tourism consumption and touring experienced several (radical) changes which capitated the attention of scholarship and policy-makers. In next, A. Offredi Rodriguez (in the sixth chapter), shares the experience of Migratour and Porta Palazzo and Barriera di Milano, Italy. She argues that Migratur was a helpful project that assisted many migrants for spreading their mainstream cultural values in Europe. In the spheres of globalization and multiculturalism, as the author puts it, the chapter describes a successful study-case aimed at protecting migrants´ rights before the rise of xenophobia and discrimination. The rest of the book is formed by two interesting (if not intriguing chapters) that remind the importance to evaluate the working conditions on front-desk staff in the tourism and hospitality industries. Under some contexts, workers are pressed to move a distressing atmosphere as well as excessive working hours. Chapters seventh and eighth gives a critical reflection on the role played by CSR Corporate Social Responsibility not only in improving working conditions but also endorsing workers´ rights. Lastly, let´s conclude this preface acknowledging overtly that all the gather chapters take part of a high-quality product that discusses critically the future of human rights and its impacts in the tourism and hospitality industries.

Maximiliano E. Korstanje
University of Palermo, Buenos Aires, Argentina

Vanessa Gowreesunkar
Anant National University, Ahmedabad, India

REFERENCES

Baum, T., & Hai, N. T. T. (2020). Hospitality, tourism, human rights and the impact of COVID-19. *International Journal of Contemporary Hospitality Management, 32*(7), 2397–2407. doi:10.1108/IJCHM-03-2020-0242

Bianchi, R., & Stephenson, M. (2014). *Tourism and citizenship: Rights, freedoms and responsibilities in the global order*. Routledge. doi:10.4324/9781134594535

Preface

Bianchi, R. V., Stephenson, M. L., & Hannam, K. (2020). The contradictory politics of the right to travel: Mobilities, borders & tourism. *Mobilities, 15*(2), 290–306. doi:10.1080/17450101.2020.1723251

Cole, S., & Eriksson, J. (2010). Tourism and human rights. In S. Cole & N. Morgan (Eds.), *Tourism and inequality: Problems and prospects* (pp. 107–125). Cabi. doi:10.1079/9781845936624.0107

Comaroff, J., & Comaroff, J. (2006). *Ethnicity Inc.* University of Chicago Press.

Fraser, A. S. (1999). Becoming human: The origins and developments of women's human rights. *Human Rights Quarterly, 21*(4), 853–906. doi:10.1353/hrq.1999.0050

Headley, J. M. (2008). *The Europeanization of the world: On the origins of human rights and democracy*. Princeton University Press. doi:10.1515/9781400880249

Ignatieff, M. (2011). Human rights as politics and idolatry. In *Human rights as politics and idolatry*. Princeton University Press.

Korstanje, M. E., & George, B. (2021). *Mobility and globalization in the aftermath of COVID-19: Emerging new geographies in a locked world*. Palgrave Macmillan. doi:10.1007/978-3-030-78845-2

Korstanje, M. E., & George, B. (2022). *The nature and future of tourism: A post-COVID-19 context*. CRC Press. doi:10.1201/9781003277507

Marks, S. P. (1980). Emerging human rights: A new generation for the 1980s. *Rutgers Law Review, 33*, 435.

McCabe, S., & Diekmann, A. (2015). The rights to tourism: Reflections on social tourism and human rights. *Tourism Recreation Research, 40*(2), 194–204. doi:10.1080/02508281.2015.1049022

Merry, S. E. (2001). Changing rights, changing culture. *Culture and rights: Anthropological perspectives, 31*, 38.

Sengupta*, A. (2004). The human right to development. *Oxford development studies, 32*(2), 179-203.

Tesón, F. R. (1984). International human rights and cultural relativism. *Va. j. Int'l L., 25*, 869.

Acknowledgment

The book *Global Perspectives on Human Rights and the Impact of Tourism Consumption in the 21st Century* is a precious piece of work which was brought to fruition by a great team. The publication of this book would not have been possible without their contributions. We wish to offer our gratitude to all those creative minds behind - the contributors, the reviewers, the publisher, the endorsers and all those who indirectly accompanied us during this wonderful journey.

First, we would like to thank the authors who have dedicated their time and expertise to produce insightful and thought- provoking chapters for this book. Tourism being an industry run by the people for the people and though the people, human rights becomes a crucial topic that need address. The quality of chapters written by authors have shed considerable light in the status of human rights in tourism. With socio-economic progress and better standard of living, the 21st century has certainly witnessed a paradigm shift in tourism consumption. However, alongside, pleasant and unpleasant impacts have also accompanied this trend. The content provided by authors and editors have helped to fill a gap in the specialized literature discussing human rights, not only in tourists but also in some marginalized groups which are subordinated to the dynamics of the tourism industry. We are grateful for their dedication and commitment to advance understanding of the impact of tourism consumption on human rights.

We also extend our gratitude to the reviewers who have provided constructive Feedback and guidance throughout the review process. Their expertise and attention to detail have helped to shape the content of this book and ensure its quality.

We would like to acknowledge the support of our publisher, who has worked closely with us to bring this project to fruition. Their guidance and assistance have been invaluable, and we are grateful for their commitment to support authors and editors in producing high-quality work academic work. The IGI Global is an international academic publisher committed to expand the body of knowledge available to the research community. Headquartered in Pennsylvania, IGI Global works in close

Acknowledgment

collaboration with expert researchers and professionals from leading institutions and publishes quality peer-reviewed content across several discipline.

This book is a valuable resource for those seeking to understand the complex relationship between tourism and human rights and to develop effective policies and practices to promote human rights in tourism. We would therefore take this opportunity to acknowledge our target audience who shared their appreciation and Feedback during the writing phase of the book. This includes research scholars, scholars, fieldworkers, policymakers, and practitioners engaging in tourism consumption, social justice, and human rights.

In conclusion, we would like to express our deep appreciation to all those who have contributed to this book's production. We believe that this book will make an important contribution to the literature on human rights and tourism and help raise awareness of the critical issues facing the industry. We hope that this book will inspire further research and action to promote human rights in tourism and contribute to a more just and sustainable tourism industry.

Maximiliano E. Korstanje
University of Palermo, Argentina

Vanessa G.B. Gowreesunkar
Anant National University, India

Introduction

HUMAN RIGHTS AND TOURISM: A CONCEPTUAL COMPANION

A Short Companion

Over the centuries, philosophy has interrogated historically the limitations and problems of authorities to protect their citizens. The question of war, as well as invasions, slaughters, and civil wars have been theorized by great ancient thinkers such as Socrates, Plato, Anaximander and even Plutarco. What is more evident, ancient mythology is a fertile ground of stories where disasters (disposed of by Gods) take place once innocent are cowardly assassinated by army forces (Auffarth 1992). All this suggests that though human rights are a modern invention, resulting from the crimes perpetrated by Nazi Germany after WWII ended, no less true seems to be that ancient theorists have been concerned with dissociating the figure of mankind, which means all men equal before the law, the "otherness" or the stranger (some of them dispossessed from any right) and the cruelties and crimes committed by states (Weissbrodt, 2008; Kekes 2005). A modern definition of human rights comprises a set of moral values, norms and regulations oriented to protect human autonomy as well as its integrity. The literature acknowledges that human rights are inalienable simply because they are consigned to all men as human beings no matter ethnicity, religion, class or affiliation. Whatever the case may be, human rights are widely supported by a vast legal jurisprudence worldwide, but fundamentally they are enthusiastically enthralled in 1948, just after the promulgation of the Universal Declaration of Human Rights. This document, which was originally issued by the United Nations General Assembly, consisted of 30 articles discussing the fundamental basic rights and freedoms applicable to all human beings. Nowadays, the discrepancy is certainly given by the duality of human rights (Mutua 2001). This can be very well expressed better in the form of an axiom: since there is nothing like international law or jurisprudence applicable to all nations on equal feet, nation-states are the watch guards of human rights. History witnessed how the citizens´ rights are often vulnerated or violated by the same states that should honor them. This paradox has

Introduction

been widely criticized by detractors of human rights (Ignatieff, 2011a; 2011b; Brown 2004). There is a list of points or discrepancies scholars have objected to regarding the unrestrictive application of human rights to all global contexts. In a seminal book, entitled *Justiciability of Economic and Social Rights,* Fons Coomans (2006) calls attention to how international declarations often collide not only with local law but also with the interpretation of judges. In some countries, human rights are legislated by the law and hosted in the constitutions while in others they are part of the signatures or specific political agreements. Besides, Human Right Declaration poses some challenges and opens questions about the private interests of some pressure groups. The property right or to protect economic interests can be opposite to the collective rights. Here some questions surface: what is the basis to endorse rights to vulnerable people? how can domestic courts deal with cases brought by individuals who claim social rights? Are economic rights applicable in all cases? What happens when the collective right vulnerates the right of a minority? We may very well start the discussion from the liberal tradition which holds eloquently that any right involves duties or responsibilities. If this is correct, what are the liabilities or compromises for collective rights?

As the previous questions are given, Coomans go on to answer that developed countries geographically situated in the Global North are more reluctant to change their well-fare system or transform their economies because of human right legislations. In these countries, local courts play a leading role in exploring or undermining the possibilities of stronger protection for vulnerable citizens. In this respect, under-developed countries, rather, appeal to constitutional legislatures to set a system of social protection. Some nations consider socioeconomic rights as part of human rights while others simply reject or put them simply secondary rights. Furthermore, it is very hard to denounce a violation of an economic or social right before a local court in which case the justiciability is an object of dispute. In sum, the application of human rights faces legal and non-legal (political) setbacks which need to be discussed. For example, some studies have approached the rise of xenophobia or discrimination in the case the protection is applied to strangers -above all asylum-seekers or forced migrants- (Weiler 1992; Vorster 2002). Noting this, if we start holding that human rights are collective rights, some voices question to what extent collective rights can be subordinated to the individuality of strangers who does not live in the country. The opposite is equally true, in some conditions, strangers (or even tourists) violate local rights (Baum & Hai, 2019; Panko & George 2012). For example, when the tourist services include child abuse, human or organ trafficking, or even in acts of violence against locals. In perspective, Panko & George (2012) alert that Child Sex Tourism (CST) represents today a kind of new nice in the tourism industry which offers services to satisfy the need of certain customers practising sexual commerce with children. This criminal act not only is a sign of modern

xxvii

Introduction

slavery but a major challenge for human rights legislation globally. As the authors conclude, the trauma generated by these victims endures for years and sometimes is irreversible. Other examples can be found in organ traffic. Citizens who are excluded from the economic system sell their organs to dark corporations to meet the need for health tourism. Doubtless, transplant tourism offers a fertile ground for these criminal associations (Delmonico, 2009). Tourism is a legal activity that engenders reciprocity and friendships even straddling cultures but this does not authorize to assert that all tourists are good. Some tourists pay exorbitant amounts of money to commit criminal acts strictly punishable in their countries. Korstanje & Tarlow (2013) and Korstanje & Olsen (2012) have reviewed the plot of Hostel, a well-known film directed by Eli Roth, where three young American tourists are kidnapped in Eastern Europe to be offered to sadist millionaire tourists. This film evinces not only what Korstanje dubbed as Dark Hospitality, which is the corruption of the sacred law of hospitality, but also gives a clear description of how rich tourists move beyond the local law. Per Korstanje (2023), hospitality should be defined as an ancient (social) institution that makes familiar the figure of the stranger. Since the act of travelling engenders a climate of mistrust and anxiety, hospitality provides both guests and hosts equal (and just) treatment under the auspices of the law. Hence, hospitality not only puts guests and hosts in equal condition but also emanates from divine power. Gods punish those tribes or cultures who do not honor hospitality or good treatment to strangers. The modern tourism industry is part of this social system based on a much deep agreement of non-aggression among the involved parties. It is important to mention hospitality is a sign of goodwill where hosts and guests remain unfamiliar with the intention of each other. Having said this, ancient mythology shows interesting stories where the pact of hospitality is breached. From Aquiles´ adventures to Helen of Troy, the disaster takes place when the sacred law of hospitality is broken. Quite aside from this, Korstanje coins the term dark (or black) hospitality to a sinister driver resulting from greed, the quest for fame or glory, the conquest, and even political or economic interests, where hosts´ integrity is vulnerated by guests in secrecy. Dark hospitality is part of the essence of evilness which -anthropologically speaking- corrupts the human soul. Of course, echoing Derrida, hospitality can be offered or not, but once accepted, it follows the dynamic of gift-and-exchange rites. Following this reasoning, hosts are often attacked or killed when eating, sleeping, unarmed or in vulnerable conditions. Dark hospitality centers on the degradation of social ties or when individual goals are interposed with collective well-being. This applies not only to criminal activity in tourism -above mentioned- but also to human rights violations. At the time hospitality is broken guests´ rights are hurt. This moot point will be reviewed in the next sections.

xxviii

Introduction

Human Rights and Tourism

In the same line of inquiry, human rights occupy a central position as an object of necessary discussion within the academic circle of tourism research. The expansion of the globalization process, associated with a notable improvement in working conditions, has invariably derived in the growth of tourism and the multiplication of leisure travel. The right to travel has been situated as a right for many Western cultures. Tourism and leisure practices are mostly seen as activities that enrich tourists´ lives while impacting positively health, life span, happiness and quality of life (Cole & Eriksson, 2010; George & Varghese, 2007; Breakey & Breakey 2013). However, a closer look reveals that the globalizing force, which was coincident with the capitalist expansion, has generated a double-edge effect in Western culture. On one hand, a privileged group seems to be legally endorsed to travel across the globe without restrictions. On another, an underclass is restricted to move or subject to strict surveillance at the time it tries to cross established borders (Bauman, 2017). In his book, which is entitled Mobilities Paradox, M. Korstanje (2017) overtly accepts that the right to move is a basic symbolic core of Western culture, but it serves as an ideological discourse. As he notes, only a small portion of mankind is really in a condition to travel without restrictions. Korstanje builds a lost conceptual dialogue between classic Marxism and the mobilities theory (above all in the hands of John Urry). The mobilities paradox starts from a premise that ideological message should not be evaluated by what it says, but by what they ultimately silences. In consonance with this, mobilities offer an illusion to be free or having the freedom to move, but this action leads us to a culture of immobility. In a Derridean sense, there is a much deep dichotomy between absolute and conditional hospitalities. While first-world tourists -who had the necessary resources to pay for the lodging services- are encouraged to travel worldwide, migrants and asylum seekers are surveilled and deported as undesired guests (Korstanje 2017). As McCabe & Diekmann put it, this reality applies only to rich nations; under some conditions there is a pending debate revolving around the right to travel can be entitled to Third World citizens. The literature needs to discuss to what extent the capitalist system ensures the same opportunities for all citizens to take an active part in leisure practices. At the same time, there is no clear basis to what extent tourism is a basic right or not (McCabe & Diekmann, 2015). It is safe to say that the legal doctrine that holds the act of travelling should be considered a fundamental right has received a caustic critique in recent decades (Bianchi & Stephenson, 2013; 2014). What is more important, recent interesting research has lamented the negative impacts of tourism on local culture, in some cases curtailing basic rights in communities like access to water, housing, energy and food (Cole 2014; Sandang & Cole 2022; Cole & Morgan 2010). In this context, Breakey & Breakey (2013) argue convincingly that much

Introduction

of the academic debate overlooks to justify a fundamental question: why do we think is the right to tourism ethically justified? Based on the text and legacies of liberal thinkers such as J. Locke, Jefferson, and S. Mill, the authors said that the right to move is ethically justified by major international human rights treaties and declarations. Not surprisingly, the ethical argument in favor of tourism is mainly based on earlier philosophical treatments which legitimated the right to hospitality -a la Kant- which means the right to be protected as a stranger who not only moves abroad but is unfamiliar with the visited territory. The right to hospitality, which is continued by tourism, is part of the essential core of Western Europe. Having said this, no less true is that this debate takes place once Europe expands to colonize the world. In this vein, the ontological connection between hospitality and tourism should not be ignored, as the authors adhere. The tourism right is an essential part of the right to hospitality (in equal juridical status to the right to labor or freedom of speech). As the authors go on to write: *"In other words, the tourism right has become an indispensable aspect of our current list of human rights because people have voted with their feet. Their choices to find fun, relaxation, and fulfilment in this activity are a perfect example of the restless human spirit and its quest for the good life—a quest that is protected by the right to the pursuit of happiness"* (Breakey & Breakey 2013: 746). This does not mean that tourists are not harassed, attacked or discriminated against abroad, nor does the local law protect them as necessary. Here is where a new debate commences: Does international law protect tourists from local abuses? Or the opposite appears to be equally valid: we can do states when tourists violate human rights?

To answer the above-noted questions, we shall review four clear-cut axes: the right to travel -as least as it is imagined in Western cultures-, the rights of locals, the state of emergency and rights, and the right to circulate in the context of COVID-19.

The Right to Travel

As discussed, the right to travel has support and detractors globally. In this section, we will share a mix-balanced discussion of their strengths and weaknesses. The tourism right appears to be discussed in academic instances with considerable depth. At best, the right to travel or to tourism has been framed within the right to move freely, or mobility rights (in other terms) (McCabe & Diekmann, 2015). Freedom of movement is certainly inscribed as a basic right that entitles the subject to move freely from one point to another in a specific territory. This means that the citizens are also free to abandon the country and return to it unless penal restrictions. This right alludes to the freedom to change a city of residence without further notice to authorities. Of course, this freedom is temporarily granted by authorities and it can be reversed in times of war, political instability or even states of emergency (Baum

Introduction

& Hai 2019; Milano & Coens, 2022). The tourism right has received support and criticism within academic circles. Supporters argue that the right to travel is not only present in the philosophical treaties of liberal thinkers but also in the constitutions. What is equally important, is the tourism right is part of the inalienable access to hospitality each citizen holds (Breakey & Breakey, 2013). Other voices assume that beyond this right lies an ideological discourse oriented to reaffirm a post-colonial dependency between center and its periphery. As Bianchi & Stephenson (2014) lament, mobilities offer a sign of status and privilege leaving millions of citizens out. Tourism is over-valorized as a key force towards prosperity, political stability and democracy, and even an unquestionable right, but paradoxically millions of persons are doomed to immobility. The modern nation-state fabricated different narratives revolving around mobilities, which allowed European expansion (in the colonial period). Now newcomers arriving from former colonies are unwelcomed or plausibly subject to restrictive migratory scrutiny. For authors, the right to travel legitimated ideologically not only the European expansion but also the global capitalism which imposed the liberal market as its tug of war. Sooner or later, the freedom of travel has become the freedom of trade. In a nutshell, Bianchi & Stephenson conclude that international tourism has been valorized as a basic right, instead of what it indeed is, a privilege (Bianchi, Stephenson & Hannam 2020). Other studies allude to the censorship exerted by countries in Global North alerting their citizens not to visit "risky destinations" or countries associated with terrorist activity (Frary 2018; Lash & Urry 1993). Last but not least, Jordi Gascon (2016) describes how the right to travel has been historically sustained by UNWTO (World Tourism Organization) to justify its presence in the United Nations, some specific investment programs or economic interests as well as its financial budget. In the next section, we will debate the travel restrictions in the times of the COVID-19 pandemic. Detractors and supporters, far from reaching an agreement, have left an open point. Another emerging platform of theories has emphasized the right of locals (counterposing them to the right to move).

The Basic Rights of Locals

To date, the debate has been circumscribed to the tourists´ right or the right of citizens to move freely elsewhere. Anyway, some studies have recently claimed the need to evaluate the impacts of tourism on the hosts´ quality of life (Moscardo 2009; Beckendorff et al. 2009). This means that local communities have rights which should be protected and respected by policymakers. It is not difficult to resist the impression these rights are different in urban than rural areas. In urban cities, locals claim the negative effects of pollution, overcrowding, and mass tourism which very well affect their quality of life. The new business supported by AI and digital

xxxi

technologies has paved the way for the rise of new informal accommodations such as Couchsurfing or Airbnb. These changes altered not only the classic hospitality industry but also the carrying capacity of visited destinations (Nilson, 2020). At the same time, some militant groups and grassroots movements have resisted the adoption of mass tourism in urban areas. Some reports have focused on the figure of tourist phobia or anti-tourism movement. Doubtless, over-tourism has gained traction as an object of study in recent years (Milano, Cheer & Novelli, 2018; Moreno-Gil & Coca Stefaniak, 2020). In some off-the-beaten-track destinations, one might see graffiti saying "Tourists go home! Or tourists you are the real terrorists!" This happens simply because over-tourism is very hard to legislate by local courts. The opposite is equally true, in rural areas tourism is gradually relegating some dwellers to peripheral positions hurting their quality of life or even limiting their access to housing and water (Cole & Eriksson, 2010). The urgency is mainly given to the opportunity to create new businesses that protect non-renewable resources and the locals´ quality of life. There are serious concerns in the literature about the concept of economic growth which is centered on the neoliberal agenda. This suggests that tourism should be seen as a vehicle towards economic progress and development subordinating other aspects to material production. As a result of this, tourism invariably leads to overcrowding, tourism or the curtailing of locals´ rights Concepts such as degrowth tourism and small-scale tourism are being gradually put on the tapestry (Higgins-Desbiolles et al. 2019).

The Right to Travel After the COVID19 Pandemic

A state of emergency is defined as any outstanding condition or crisis that empowers the government to introduce policies for the protection of citizens normally unaccepted. The state is often declared in case of invasion, disasters, medical pandemics, or riots. During this period, basic rights are limited or temporally suspended. The right to tourism or move freely is seriously affected during a state of emergency (Beirman 2011; Korstanje & George 2022). Without any doubt, the best example to explain this was the lockdown and travel restrictions unilaterally imposed by governments during the COVID-19 pandemic (Altshuler & Schmidt, 2021). As Baum & Hai (2020) notably adhere, the COVID-19 pandemic was originally reported in Wuhan, China but rapidly disseminated through tourism and flights globally. At a closer look, governments have desperately adopted different restrictive measures that included the closure of borders, airspaces or even the lockdown and prohibitions to celebrate feasts, festivals or sporting events. Persons have been confined at their homes (under the lemma stay at home) to preserve public health. This shows two important assumptions. On one hand, the right to travel can be suspended in an emergency context by authorities without previous consent. On another, tourism has been the

xxxii

Introduction

main victim and spreader of COVID-19. Whatever the case may be, the pandemic accelerated not only the employment of digital technologies to monitor (potential) sick passengers but also the creation of new forms of identity validation (such as the sanitary or health passport) which changed travel behavior. The philosophical limitations of health passports will be discussed and assessed with cold-blood detachment at the conclusion of this book. For instance, let´s return to the effects of COVID-19 and the suspension of the right to tourism. In emergencies or crises, some practices which may be prohibited are accepted. For example, in a fire or a disaster, breaking a vending machine of food to assist victims is a valuable act of heroism while in normal conditions it is not. The opposite is true, the state of emergency -of course- inverts the rules and procedures making for acceptable practices punishable crimes. The COVID-19 pandemic not only generated devasting effects in tourism but also changed substantially our travel behavior in a fractured world (Higgins-Desbioles, Bigby & Doering, 2022; Korstanje, Seraphin & Maingi, 2023). The surveillance technology -disposed originally to monitor illegal migration- has been used to follow up on potential spreaders. In the mid of the pandemic, many tourists have been arrested and deported abroad because of their resistance to staying at the hotel, as authorities punctuated. At the same time, thousands of tourists have been stranded abroad without food, money or shelter (most of them sleeping in bus stations and airports for weeks). The embassies repatriated gradually some of their citizens utilizing their flag carriers. As Korstanje & George (2022) put it, the mobile culture and the tourist gaze, well described by J Urry, has been replaced by a new feudalized (and immobile) landscape, where the stranger, the Other, the tourist is demonized as an "undesired guest". The right to make tourism is temporarily suspended, and its only valid right is to stay at home. It is important not to lose sight of the fact that "vaccine tourism" has been an emerging (interesting) social issue in the global North. Developed economies, far from assisting poor countries, unilaterally appropriated a major portion of doses leaving underdeveloped economies in a difficult position (Okafor & Yan 2022). Paradoxically, since a significant number of their citizens refused the vaccine because of conspiracy theories, tourists coming from Latin America and Africa travelled to the "Global North" to be inoculated (Adongo et al. 2021; Korstanje 2022; Hom, 2022). Some governments (following ideological reasons) closed their borders leaving their conational citizens stranded without any type of assistance. This incident has been documented by Korstanje in the case of Alberto Fernandez´ administration (Korstanje 2021; 2022).

Last but not least, the long-lasting effects of the pandemic worldwide have created a condition towards what experts dubbed degrowth tourism, a unique opportunity to embrace successful sustainable practices in the sector (Higgins-Desbiolles, 2020). This point has been applauded by considerable studies in Academia, but to what extent this happens is a matter of debate (Prayag, 2020; Sigala, 2021; Rastegar,

Introduction

Higgins-Desbiolles & Ruhanen, 2021). To wit, Benjamin, Dillette & Alderman (2020) question whether the tourism transformation should adapt to the new normal while laying the foundations for equity and solidarity. Since the new normal exhibited the inherent tensions between the capitalist system and inequality, post-pandemic tourism should move in more equitable terms.

Final Remarks

To here, we have ignited a hot debate revolving around human rights (or tourism right) and the effects of COVID-19. The specialized literature can be divided into two opposing poles. Those studies emphasize the tourists´ right (not to be attacked) or even the right to move freely and those alerting on the rights restrictions in local communities. The present introduction has been reviewed by both academic waves to offer readers a mix-balanced argumentation. Of course, we cannot close a conclusion without discussing the implementation of health passports (during the COVID-19 pandemic) and the right to privacy. In fact, many governments stimulated their citizens to be vaccinated, though in some countries there was a high rejection rate. At the same time, governments issued documents and digital vaccination certificates to allow their citizens to travel. In Europe and the US foreign tourists should present vaccination certificates at their arrival. What seems to be more polemic, those passengers inoculated with Russian (Sputnik-V) or Chinese vaccines (Sinopharm & Sinovac) have been retained and deported. Doubtless, the question of vaccines opens the doors to new emerging political tensions between Russia and the US. In many Western countries, the tourist visas were issued taking the vaccine origin as the main requisite of the migratory entrance. As never before, the COVID-19 pandemic changed migratory regulations as well as travel behavior. Health or vaccine passport is a term reserved for digital certificates that validates the levels of immunity of holders showing to be proof of non-contagion. This certificate was originally made to be presented in museums, festivals, cinemas or swimming pools and has lately been adopted by air companies. In some countries like France, the US and Germany this measure woke up several criticism and protests because it curtails the basic right to privacy and the fundamental freedoms legislated in the respective constitution. The system was successfully applied in other countries like Norway, China, and Switzerland. Ultimately, COVID-19 accelerated the crisis of Western hospitality, and changed the ways to understand the "alterity". The figure of a stranger, who was an object of curiosity for former centuries, is now an object of fear. In this context, the present book intends to shed light on the strengths and weaknesses of the specialized literature in human rights positing as a must-read text for those who are concerned by the tourism future.

Introduction

Maximiliano E. Korstanje
University of Palermo, Argentina

Vannesa Gowreesunkar
Anant National University, India

REFERENCES

Adongo, C. A., Amenumey, E. K., Kumi-Kyereme, A., & Dubé, E. (2021). Beyond fragmentary: A proposed measure for travel vaccination concerns. *Tourism Management, 83*, 104180. doi:10.1016/j.tourman.2020.104180 PMID:32952254

Altshuler, A., & Schmidt, J. (2021). Why does resilience matter? Global implications for the tourism industry in the context of COVID-19. *Worldwide Hospitality and Tourism Themes, 13*(3), 431–436. doi:10.1108/WHATT-01-2021-0015

Auffarth, C. (1992). Protecting strangers: Establishing a fundamental value in the religions of the ancient Near East and ancient Greece. *Numen, 39*(2), 193–216. doi:10.1163/156852792X00032

Baum, T., & Hai, N. T. T. (2019). Applying sustainable employment principles in the tourism industry: Righting human rights wrongs? *Tourism Recreation Research, 44*(3), 371–381. doi:10.1080/02508281.2019.1624407

Baum, T., & Hai, N. T. T. (2020). Hospitality, tourism, human rights and the impact of COVID-19. *International Journal of Contemporary Hospitality Management, 32*(7), 2397–2407. doi:10.1108/IJCHM-03-2020-0242

Bauman, Z. (2017). Tourists and vagabonds: Or, living in postmodern times. In *Identity and social change* (pp. 13–26). Routledge. doi:10.4324/9780203789339-3

Beirman, D. (2011). The integration of emergency management and tourism. *Australian Journal of Emergency Management, 26*(3), 30–34.

Benckendorff, P., Edwards, D., Jurowski, C., Liburd, J. J., Miller, G., & Moscardo, G. (2009). Exploring the future of tourism and quality of life. *Tourism and Hospitality Research, 9*(2), 171–183. doi:10.1057/thr.2009.7

Bianchi, R., & Stephenson, M. (2014). *Tourism and citizenship: Rights, freedoms and responsibilities in the global order*. Routledge. doi:10.4324/9781134594535

Bianchi, R. V., & Stephenson, M. L. (2013). Deciphering tourism and citizenship in a globalized world. *Tourism Management, 39*, 10–20. doi:10.1016/j.tourman.2013.03.006

Breakey, N., & Breakey, H. (2013). Is there a tourism right? *Tourism Analysis*, *18*(6), 739–748. doi:10.3727/108354213X13824558470943

Cole, S. (2014). Tourism and water: From stakeholders to rights holders, and what tourism businesses need to do. *Journal of Sustainable Tourism*, *22*(1), 89–106. do i:10.1080/09669582.2013.776062

Cole, S., & Eriksson, J. (2010). Tourism and human rights. In *Tourism and inequality: Problems and prospects* (pp. 107–125). CABI. doi:10.1079/9781845936624.0107

Cole, S., & Morgan, N. (2010). *Tourism and inequality problems and prospects.* CABI. doi:10.1079/9781845936624.0000

Commans, F. (2006). *Justiciability of Economic and Social Rights: experiences from the domestic system*. Intersentia.

Delmonico, F. L. (2009). The implications of Istanbul Declaration on organ trafficking and transplant tourism. *Current Opinion in Organ Transplantation*, *14*(2), 116–119. doi:10.1097/MOT.0b013e32832917c9 PMID:19300258

Frary, M. (2018). Freedom to travel v travel towards freedom: Exclusive new data analysis for the magazine on whether tourists worry about a holiday resort's reputation for media freedom. *Index on Censorship*, *47*(2), 39–44. doi:10.1177/0306422018784529

Gascón, J. (2016). Deconstruyendo el derecho al turismo/Deconstructing the right to tourism. *Revista Cidob d'afers internacionals*, 51-69.

George, B. P., & Varghese, V. (2007). Human rights in tourism: Conceptualization and stakeholder perspectives. *EJBO. Electronic Journal of Business Ethics and Organization Studies*, *12*(2), 1–15.

Higgins-Desbiolles, F. (2020). The "war over tourism": Challenges to sustainable tourism in the tourism academy after COVID-19. *Journal of Sustainable Tourism*, *29*(4), 551–569. doi:10.1080/09669582.2020.1803334

Higgins-Desbiolles, F., Carnicelli, S., Krolikowski, C., Wijesinghe, G., & Boluk, K. (2019). Degrowing tourism: Rethinking tourism. *Journal of Sustainable Tourism*, *27*(12), 1926–1944. doi:10.1080/09669582.2019.1601732

Hom, S. M. Pandemic Postscript: Tourism, Migration, and Exile. In Intersections of Tourism, Migration, and Exile (pp. 238-251). N. Bloch & K Adams. Abingdon, Routledge.

Ignatieff, M. (2011a). Human rights as idolatry. In *Human rights as politics and idolatry* (pp. 53–98). Princeton University Press.

Introduction

Ignatieff, M. (2011b). Human rights as politics and idolatry. In *Human rights as politics and idolatry*. Princeton University Press.

Kekes, J. (2005). *The roots of evil*. Cornell University Press.

Korstanje, M. E. (2017). *Mobilities Paradox: a critical análisis*. Edward Elgar.

Korstanje, M. E. (2021). Habeas Corpus: Argentinean Tourists Stranded. *Tourism and Hospitality, 2*(4), 327–331. doi:10.3390/tourhosp2040021

Korstanje, M. E. (2022). Asymmetries between the Global North and South in leisure practices: Vaccine tourism reconsidered. *International Journal of Tourism Anthropology, 9*(1), 40–51. doi:10.1504/IJTA.2022.128052

Korstanje, M. E. (2023). *Questionable Hospitality: New Relations and Tensions Between Hosts and Guests After Covid-19. Changing Practices of Tourism Stakeholders in Covid-19 Affected Destinations, 181-191.* Channel View.

Korstanje, M. E., & George, B. (2022). *Mobility and globalization in the aftermath of COVID-19: Emerging new geographies in a locked world*. Palgrave Macmillan.

Korstanje, M. E., & Olsen, D. H. (2011). The discourse of risk in horror movies post 9/11: Hospitality and hostility in perspective. *International Journal of Tourism Anthropology, 1*(3-4), 304–317. doi:10.1504/IJTA.2011.043712

Korstanje, M. E., Séraphin, H., & Maingi, S. W. (Eds.). (2022). *Tourism Through Troubled Times: Challenges and Opportunities of the Tourism Industry in 21st Century*. Emerald. doi:10.1108/9781803823119

Korstanje, M. E., & Tarlow, P. (2012). Being lost: Tourism, risk and vulnerability in the post-'9/11'entertainment industry. *Journal of Tourism and Cultural Change, 10*(1), 22–33. doi:10.1080/14766825.2011.639455

Lash, S. M., & Urry, J. (1993). *Economies of signs and space* (Vol. 26). Sage.

McCabe, S., & Diekmann, A. (2015). The rights to tourism: Reflections on social tourism and human rights. *Tourism Recreation Research, 40*(2), 194–204. doi:10.1080/02508281.2015.1049022

Milano, C., Cheer, J. M., & Novelli, M. (2018). Overtourism: A growing global problem. *The conversation, 18*(1), 1-5.

Milano, C., & Koens, K. (2022). The paradox of tourism extremes. Excesses and restraints in times of COVID-19. *Current Issues in Tourism, 25*(2), 219–231. doi:10.1080/13683500.2021.1908967

Moreno-Gil, S., & Coca-Stefaniak, J. A. (2020). Guest editorial": Overtourism and the sharing economy–tourism cities at a crossroads. *International Journal of Tourism Cities*, *6*(1), 1–7. doi:10.1108/IJTC-03-2020-174

Moscardo, G. (2009). Tourism and quality of life: Towards a more critical approach. *Tourism and Hospitality Research*, *9*(2), 159–170. doi:10.1057/thr.2009.6

Mutua, M. (2001). Savages, victims, and saviors: The metaphor of human rights. *Harv. Int'l LJ*, *42*, 201–207.

Nilsson, J. H. (2020). Conceptualizing and contextualizing overtourism: The dynamics of accelerating urban tourism. *International Journal of Tourism Cities*, *6*(4), 657–671. doi:10.1108/IJTC-08-2019-0117

Nilsson, J. H. (2020). Conceptualizing and contextualizing overtourism: The dynamics of accelerating urban tourism. In J. Oskam (Ed.), *International Journal of Tourism Cities* (pp. 151–170). Emerald. doi:10.1108/IJTC-08-2019-0117

Okafor, L., & Yan, E. (2022). Covid-19 vaccines, rules, deaths, and tourism recovery. *Annals of Tourism Research*, *95*, 103424. doi:10.1016/j.annals.2022.103424 PMID:35600093

Panko, T. R., & George, B. P. (2012). Child sex tourism: Exploring the issues. *Criminal Justice Studies*, *25*(1), 67–81. doi:10.1080/1478601X.2012.657904

Prayag, G. (2020). Time for reset? COVID-19 and tourism resilience. *Tourism Review International*, *24*(2-3), 179–184. doi:10.3727/154427220X15926147793595

Sandang, Y., & Cole, S. (2022). Using a human rights approach to improve hotels' water use and sustainability. *Journal of Sustainable Tourism*, 1–19. doi:10.1080/09669582.2022.2108041

Sigala, M. (2021). A bibliometric review of research on COVID-19 and tourism: Reflections for moving forward. *Tourism Management Perspectives*, *40*, 100912. doi:10.1016/j.tmp.2021.100912 PMID:34804787

Vorster, J. M. (2002). Racism, xenophobia and human rights. *The Ecumenical Review*, *54*(3), 296–310. doi:10.1111/j.1758-6623.2002.tb00155.x

Weiler, J. H. (1992). Thou shalt not oppress a stranger: On the judicial protection of the human rights of non-EC nationals-a critique. *European Journal of International Law*, *3*(1), 65–75. doi:10.1093/oxfordjournals.ejil.a035808

Weissbrodt, D. (2008). *The human rights of non-citizens*. Oxford University Press. doi:10.1093/acprof:oso/9780199547821.001.0001

Chapter 1
Tourism, Poverty, and Human Rights:
An Unspeakable Relationship

Maximiliano Emanuel Korstanje
ⓘ https://orcid.org/0000-0002-5149-1669
University of Palermo, Argentina

ABSTRACT

Over recent years, the philosophical dilemma of human rights has occupied a central position in the academic debate worldwide. Of course, tourism seems not to be an exception. Despite the promising economic benefits and multiplying effects of tourism, some voices have alerted on the problems and limitations of tourism management to achieve a fairer wealth distribution in local communities. Having said this, the idea of tourism as a key force towards a more democratic and prosperous society began to be placed under the critical lens of scrutiny. This chapter, in this context, discusses critically how tourism potentiates economic growth but under some conditions deteriorating (if not vulnerating) the basic rights of locals. The opposite is equally true. Local communities embrace tourism to boost their economies while paradoxically making them more dependent and vulnerable to external economic actors.

INTRODUCTION

Different experts and pundits of all stripes have considered tourism not only as an economic multiplying factor but also as a key driver towards economic prosperity and fairer wealth distribution (Pablo-Romero & Molina, 2013; Ivanov & Webster, 2007). Doubtless, tourism only is successfully proliferated in the context of strong

DOI: 10.4018/978-1-6684-8726-6.ch001

Copyright © 2023, IGI Global. Copying or distributing in print or electronic forms without written permission of IGI Global is prohibited.

democratic institutions which lead invariably towards political stability (Harrison & Schipani 2009). Having said this, tourism contributes positively and of course directly to the development of the local community, at least as the specialized literature holds. Anyway, some emerging voices have alerted on the problems as well as conceptual limitations economic growth has. At a closer look, some under-developing economies come across higher levels of dependency which impedes a fair wealth distribution (Fayissa, Nsiah & Tadasse 2008). In other cases, tourism paves the way for the rise of much deep sentiment of resentment and inter-class conflict which ultimately turns out of any governmental control (Comaroff & Comaroff 2009). The present book chapter interrogates furtherly on the paradox of economic growth [at least stimulated by tourism] where [under some conditions] some basic rights of local people or ethnic minorities are simply vulnered. The opposite is equally true, local stakeholders strive for adopting tourism as the main source of growth, and in so doing they develop a strong dependency on foreign investment.

THE ASHES OF POVERTY AND TOURISM

The history of poverty as well as the intention of international financial corporations to employ tourism as an efficient poverty relief seems far to be new. As Andrew Holden (2013) eloquently documents, once situated as a WatchGuard of economic stability (just ended WWII) the US instrumentalized the development program to assist developing economies since the 70s decade. Over years, the concept of development stimulated by the World Bank was invariably synonymous with economic progress. In these terms, development theory conceptualized economic progress through quantifiable factors and indicators which overlooked other types of wealth. At the time Truman`s speech divides the world into two, developed and underdeveloped economies, the debates revolving around the notion of poverty are simply introduced to the legitimate economic intervention of some nations over others. Beyond any ideological dispute, it becomes evident that the financial asymmetries between the global North and South call attention to a radical shift in the economic paradigms. Unless these dichotomies are previously resolved, tourism tends to perpetuate exploitative relations between development-generating countries and peripheral destinations. In consonance with this, Emanuel de Kadt (1979) describes the role played by culture in the configuration of exploitative institutions which impede genuine development. Per his viewpoint, those peripheral destinations mainly marked by a state of subordination or domination by the side of external powers have little probability to adopt successful development programs. De Kadt holds the thesis that tourism development works in the context of economic dependency and political

Tourism, Poverty, and Human Rights

stability (de Kadt 1979a; 1979b). The impacts of tourism on the local economy are complex and very hard to describe the long-lasting effects.

As the previous argument is given, Blake et al. (2008) argue convincingly that the effects of tourism on the economy vary on the country or culture. Anyway, the effects of tourism are as a whole positive but higher-income groups have further possibilities to amass further profits and wealth than lower-income groups. This evidence which is based on the case of Brazil, suggests that far from being homogenous impacts on the local economy gravitate differently among each stakeholder. Croes & Vanegas (2008) acknowledge that one of the main limitations of applied research rests on the lack of empirical information on how tourism impacts low-income actors or poor people. Beyond the panacea of tourism fighting to reduce poverty, experts agree there is no firm evidence that describes clearly the relationship between tourism and poverty. Originally, some studies have emphasized the promises of tourism to alleviate and eradicate poverty efficiently. There is a direct correlation between tourism expansion and poverty relief simply because modernization and development open the doors to new opportunities for relegated groups. As the authors put it, tourism seems to work for the poor but this does not mean that tourism generates local development in all cases. Above all, poor classes often adopt tourism ignoring sustainable practices in which case it leads the environment to degradation. At first glimpse, tourism expansion should be associated with a fairer wealth distribution, direct local engagement as well as a coherent development strategy which ensures poverty reduction and social equity. In a seminal book entitled Stuck with Tourism, Matilde Cordoba-Azcarrate (2020) reveals how the industry not only generates social maladies but also asymmetric inter-class labor relations associated with real-estate speculation as well as the acculturation process. To put this simply, tourism should be studied as a global force more complex than a simple industry, it rather pervades social relations while imposing stereotyped discoursed designed to mould politics. Some local groups experience spatial segregation because of international direct investment but far from struggling for their rights local communities internalize a so-called state of inferiority and vulnerability which is explained through the development theory. Based on a critical lens, she holds that tourism interrogates a sense of belonging that paradoxically engages with a collective level of consciousness and reciprocities where some exploitative practices are ideologically legitimated. Per her stance, tourism affirms some exploitative and strict practices that originated in the colony. Locals internalize their need to be more developed but renounce to administer their resources. What is more important, these practices not only segregate locals to a peripheral position but also impose enclave tourism while affecting seriously the autonomy of some vulnerable groups (without mentioning curtailing their basic rights). The opposite is equally true, under some contexts, poverty is commoditized and offered as a spectacle to global North tourists. These types of high-income segments seem to be mainly moved by consuming spaces of poverty and slumming not only to valorize their nations but also to keep empathy with "the suffering Other". These segments are formed by educated and mid-class citizens coming from developed nations, above all from Europe and the US. It is not difficult to resist the impression that slum tourism emerges as a valid and efficient strategy in poor zones to alleviate the economic conditions. These areas are part of countries which have been former exploited colonies (Tzanelli 2018; Hoogendoom et al. 2020; Tzanelli & Korstanje 2016). As Bianca Freire Medeiros (2016) eloquently observes, slum tourism not only situates as a novel form of consumption which bridges a new relationship between hosts and guests but also poses a philosophical dilemma. How can slum-dwellers eradicate their source of wealth?

The above-noted question has not an answer. Echoing Medeiros, while laying the foundation for a new condition where poverty is perpetuated, slum tourism makes poverty the main commodity to exchange with rich visitors. Whatever the case may be, slum tourism generates some positive effects and social upward in the local economy (Seraphin & Korstanje 2020; Seraphin & Korstanje 2021). Last but not least, Seraphin and Korstanje (2021) argue that slum tourism has captivated the attention of Academia in recent years. The impossibility of local governments to enhance their citizen living conditions, associated with political instability has invariably led locals to accept poverty as their main asset. However, this paradoxically entails that their basic rights would have never been met. Based on Haiti as the main study case, the authors said overtly that in former colonies enclave tourism may very well generate resentment and hostility against tourists. This sentiment of resentment can be successfully reduced when local tourists are engaged and empowered by the new economic conditions brought by tourism.

TOURISM, POVERTY, AND HUMAN RIGHTS

Put the problem in binomial terms, tourism alleviates poverty while assisting local stakeholders to be a source of wealth and profit. Anyway, poverty is never eradicated but perpetuated under some conditions. To some extent, this suggests a dilemma because the economic growth and social upward are not enough for locals to have ensured their basic rights (at least the universal right to water and food access). To wit, Cole and Eriksson (2010) have certainly called attention to the fact tourism may potentiate the existing asymmetries among classes or groups, or what is worse, affirm existing exploitative conditions and relations in the poorest members of the community. Higgins-Desbiolles and Blanchard (2010) describe how the constant

Tourism, Poverty, and Human Rights

failures of the neoliberal agenda to expand social justice to all classes have ushered some local cultures to adopt tourism as an efficient instrument to reduce poverty. Notwithstanding this fact, their local citizens are deprived of the right of traveling or moving. Tourism is an alienable right but it does not extend to all citizens. Most of the developing economies are today unfit to meet their citizens´ basic rights. Under these conditions, social tourism implementation sounds at least impossible. The authors go on to write:

Tensions are clear. While neo-liberalism demands that the benefits of tourism are allocated according to the invisible hand of the market, the discourse of tourism as a human right demands a social tourism agenda, which requires continued intervention by governments and communities to ensure that tourism contributes to a better quality of life and equitable sharing of tourism bounties. However, vigilance is required to uncover such tension. (Higgins-Desbiolles & Blanchard, 2010, p. 40)

Human rights convene a set of rights which are bestowed simply because the holder is a human being. These universal rights are inherent to all human beings no matter age, gender, nationality, ethnic group or religious affiliation. Having said this, human rights has been adopted by the UN just after WWII ended (in 1948 to be exact). These universal and inalienable rights include freedom from any type of discrimination, the right to equality, the right to life, access to water and food, the right to security and liberty, as well as the right to movement. Over recent years, some voices have questioned the right of movement as a limited and reserved right for a small group. The right to travel falls often into some misinterpretations which need to be decoded. Since human rights are vital to life, it is very hard to understand the right to travel (a liberal mandate emanated from the success of globalization) as an inalienable right equable to access to food and water. The liberty to mobility is mainly based on the standardization of modern work which does not apply in all countries (above all to former colonies which suffered European oppression). The working conditions in the Global North simply differ from the South. In this respect, the right to travel derives from old neocolonial discourses oriented to cement a new center-periphery dependency. Paradoxically, this European expansion (which occurred in the 18th century) was orchestrated by the violation of many alienable rights in local communities. What being a tourist means, suggests two important assumptions. On one hand, some groups are legally encouraged to move freely while others are circumscribed to a state of immobility. On another, mobility is today a symbol of high-status classes reinforced by the action of capital. To wit, the right to travel envisages that only a small portion of people move (Bianchi & Stephenson, 2013; 2014; Korstanje 2017). This was exactly manifest after the COVID-19 regulations imposed by governments to stop mobilities and free circulation (Korstanje & George 2021; Bianchi, Stephenson & Hannam 2020). The opposite is equally true, the human rights of local communities are sometimes not potentiated (if not deteriorated) by the action of mass tourism. This gradual process of degradation is associated with real-estate speculation, the displacement of locals to peripheral zones, or inflation which make the local lives a real nightmare (Higgins-Desbiolles & Whyte, 2015; Butt 2016). The figure of poverty occupies a central position in academic debates. Echoing Bianchi and Stephenson (2013), discussions revolving around human rights are incorrectly placed. At the best, modern tourism derives from the European expansion that occurred in the former centuries. The consolidation of human rights -invented in the core of European nations- to protect ethnic minorities crystallizes the end of the Second World War as well as the rise of the Cold War. At the time the European civilization flourished in the colonial period, the oppressed colonies were impoverished. To put this bluntly, the financial asymmetries mark the pace to those who can access or do not to the right to travel but says little about the injustice and crimes perpetrated by Colonial Powers in the pastime. The right to travel coincides with an ideological disposition (ideal) not all agents can follow up, above all in the former colonies. The poverty generated in a constant state of exploitation conducted by colonial powers (over the colonized nations and cultures) has been invariably silenced while the right to travel enthralls as the only feasible and idealized goal.

A NEW AGENDA FOR HUMAN RIGHTS AND TOURISM

As discussed, human rights encompass a set of complex and broad aspects that this book chapter simply overlooks. Anyway, we have placed the concept of a right to travel (as well as the problem of poverty) under the critical lens of scrutiny. It is safe to say that a new agenda for human rights is at least desired and necessary. What is more important, unlike other human rights violations which are legally sanctioned (such as human enslavement, child abuse, or even discrimination), poverty remains a voluntary option for many displaced groups and communities. In other cases, poverty and immobility are seen as a type of cultural barrier that prevents some ethnicities to embrace development. The question of development and human rights are inextricably intertwined. To put this simply, some rights cannot be homogenized not only because of legal restrictions culturally enrooted in religion or cultural attachment to certain mainstream values but also by the impossibility among states to yield global agreement and shared conventions. To be poor in the US seems not to be the same as in any other under-developed nation (Hashimoto, Harkonen & Nkyi 2020). Critical research in the field of the human right convention should be centered on these three main axes:

1. Cultural barriers and human rights
2. Violence and human rights
3. Security and tourism

Cultural Gaps and Relativism

Far from being new, the problem of relativism has gravitated further toward the emerging debate revolving around human rights and tourism. What is desired for some groups is rejected by others. The dilemma is put in the following direction. Since envisioned human rights tend to have global and universal applications, but here two problems arise. On one hand, the state, which should protect its citizens, is the first in breaking fundamental rights when homeland security is in danger. On another, universalism leads to arbitrary applications where local autonomy is never respected. This means that what is allowed or promoted in a culture (like drinking alcohol in England) is strictly prohibited in others (like Muslim countries) (Donnelly 1984). Hence, cultural barriers are of significant importance to understand how human rights enhance local lives. To put the same in other terms, universalism -unless duly regulated- engenders the risks to reach a moral imperialism where the local laws and rights are ignored. The opposite is true in tourism. For example, some countries have customs (like drug consumption, alcohol drinking or even prostitution) that ultimately offend locals. When this happens negotiations between hosts and guests or the adoption of a shared code of ethics are strongly recommended. The recent FIFA WORLD Cup in Qatar showed how alcohol drinking in stadiums, as well as women dressing in revealing or tight clothes or kisses in public, are strictly prohibited. At the same time, some attendants and fans were arrested while protesting for LGBT rights in stadiums. In sum, the clash between universalism and relativism is far from being closed and now revives a hot debate in tourism research and Academia.

Human Rights and Violence

The second point of entry in this discussion is the question of violence (above all in successful projects where tourism is adopted). In a trailblazing book, entitled Ethnicity Inc, Comaroff and Comaroff (2009) narrate the cases where local populations appeal to empower tourist undertakings to enhance their living conditions. Tourism seems to be a fertile ground for economic prosperity as well as a financial investment. Historically relegated from the wealth distribution, these ethnic minorities adopt successfully tourism for gaining social upwards. In that instance, higher taxes imposed by local administration over these amassed profits make local communities angry paving the pathways for the rise of extreme conflict (and even war). Like the case of some African nations, Comaroff and Comaroff lamented, tourism represents a

Tourism, Poverty, and Human Rights

valid economic source in the short run, but invariably it aggravates long-dormant ethnic conflicts when the administration attempts to retain local gains. In some other contexts, violence emerges as a sentiment of resentment developed by the inequalities between locals and first-world tourists (Korstanje 2017).

Safety-Security Tourism

We have discussed not only how violence but also cultural relativism impacts the fields of human rights. The safety-security in tourism remains a cornerstone to promoting firm institutions that cement political instability. As Peter Tarlow (2014) brilliantly observes, those countries where democratic institutions are not firmly construed, are prone to human rights violations. In this context, the security of locals and visitors is far from being granted. For the correct evolution of the industry, the living conditions of locals and visitors as well as their ontological security should be warranted by the state. Possibly, some radical cells (like the case of terrorism) or local crime tend to attack foreign tourists to destabilize the government. For that, governments and authorities should work together not only to celebrate extradition programs but also to achieve shared security-safety policies that protect citizens and tourists alike. As Tarlow acknowledges, the quest for a risk-zero society is a utopia almost impossible to accomplish. By its nature, tourism needs mutual reciprocity to exist. Hosts and guests should compromise not to harm each other. Although in recent years, technology has made from destination a safe place, no less true appears to be that tourists avoid familiar places. Any tourist travel combines (here) two opposed tendencies: the quest for novelty which pushes us to new landscapes and the need for safety and protection. Having said this, Tarlow alerts that cultural relativism, which suggests that each actor or culture develops its own interpretation of risks, conditions policymakers to elaborate all-encompassing models to mitigate risks. Safety-security programs in tourism should be worked on a global and international platform that invites multicultural specialists as well as nations coming from the four corners of the globe.

CONCLUSION

In this book chapter, we have certainly discussed the problem of human rights as they are applied in the constellations of tourism and hospitality. The specialized literature emphasizes the importance to balance the rights of all stakeholders. However, this is a goal very hard to meet. We have scrutinized the dilemma of poverty as well as the urgency for slum tourism as a replicator of poverty. It is impossible to eradicate what is the main commodity to exchange. At the same time, we lay the foundations

Tourism, Poverty, and Human Rights

for a model based on three axes which are vital to this deep-seated issue: a) the cultural barriers, b) human rights and violence, c) safety-security tourism. While the problem of culture poses an interesting debate between universalism and relativism, violence emerges as a precondition of the failure of local authorities to adopt a sustainable plan for poverty relief. Lastly, under some conditions, the resentment against foreign tourists leads local cultures to coexist with radicalized groups that appeal to violence as a form of expression.

REFERENCES

Bianchi, R., & Stephenson, M. (2014). *Tourism and citizenship: Rights, freedoms and responsibilities in the global order*. Routledge. doi:10.4324/9781134594535

Bianchi, R. V., & Stephenson, M. L. (2013). Deciphering tourism and citizenship in a globalized world. *Tourism Management*, *39*, 10–20. doi:10.1016/j.tourman.2013.03.006

Bianchi, R. V., Stephenson, M. L., & Hannam, K. (2020). The contradictory politics of the right to travel: Mobilities, borders & tourism. *Mobilities*, *15*(2), 290–306. doi:10.1080/17450101.2020.1723251

Blake, A., Arbache, J. S., Sinclair, M. T., & Teles, V. (2008). Tourism and poverty relief. *Annals of Tourism Research*, *35*(1), 107–126. doi:10.1016/j.annals.2007.06.013

Butt, B. (2016). Conservation, Neoliberalism, and Human Rights in Kenya's Arid Lands. *Humanity*, *7*(1), 91–110. doi:10.1353/hum.2016.0009

Cole, S., & Eriksson, J. (2010). Tourism and human rights. *Tourism and inequality: Problems and prospects*, 107-125.

Comaroff, J. L., & Comaroff, J. (2009). *Ethnicity, Inc*. University of Chicago Press. doi:10.7208/chicago/9780226114736.001.0001

Cordoba-Azcarrate, M. (2020). *Stuck with Tourism: space, power and labor in contemporary Yucatan*. University of California Press. doi:10.1525/9780520975552

Croes, R., & Vanegas, M. Sr. (2008). Cointegration and causality between tourism and poverty reduction. *Journal of Travel Research*, *47*(1), 94–103. doi:10.1177/0047287507312429

De Kadt, E. (1979a). *Tourism: Passport to Development. In Perspectives on the social and cultural effects of tourism in developing countries*. Oxford University Press.

De Kadt, E. (1979b). Social planning for tourism in the developing countries. *Annals of Tourism Research*, *6*(1), 36–48. doi:10.1016/0160-7383(79)90093-8

Donnelly, J. (1984). Cultural relativism and universal human rights. *Human Rights Quarterly*, *6*(4), 400. doi:10.2307/762182

Fayissa, B., Nsiah, C., & Tadasse, B. (2008). Impact of tourism on economic growth and development in Africa. *Tourism Economics*, *14*(4), 807–818. doi:10.5367/000000008786440229

Freire-Medeiros, B. (2014). *Touring poverty*. Routledge. doi:10.4324/9780203840719

Harrison, D., & Schipani, S. (2009). Tourism in the Lao people's democratic republic. *Tourism in Southeast Asia: Challenges and new directions*, 165-188.

Hashimoto, A., Harkonen, E., & Nkyi, E. (2020). *Human Rights Issues in Tourism*. Routledge. doi:10.4324/9781351033862

Higgins Desbiolles, F., & Blanchard, L. (2010). *Context of Human Rights, Justice and Peace. In Tourism, progress and peace*. CABI.

Higgins-Desbiolles, F., & Whyte, K. P. (2015). Tourism and human rights. In *The Routledge handbook of tourism and sustainability* (pp. 123–134). Routledge.

Holden, A. (2013). *Tourism, poverty and development*. Routledge. doi:10.4324/9780203861547

Hoogendoorn, G., Letsatsi, N., Malleka, T., & Booyens, I. (2020). Tourist and resident perspectives on 'slum tourism': The case of the Vilakazi precinct, Soweto. *GeoJournal*, *85*(4), 1133–1149. doi:10.100710708-019-10016-2

Ivanov, S., & Webster, C. (2007). Measuring the impact of tourism on economic growth. *Tourism Economics*, *13*(3), 379–388. doi:10.5367/000000007781497773

Korstanje, M. E. (2017). *Terrorism, Tourism and the end of Hospitality in the West*. Palgrave Macmillan.

Korstanje, M. E. (2018). *The mobilities paradox: A critical analysis*. Edward Elgar Publishing. doi:10.4337/9781788113311

Korstanje, M. E., & George, B. (2021). *Mobility and globalization in the aftermath of COVID-19: Emerging new geographies in a locked world*. Palgrave Macmillan. doi:10.1007/978-3-030-78845-2

Tourism, Poverty, and Human Rights

Pablo-Romero, M. D. P., & Molina, J. A. (2013). Tourism and economic growth: A review of empirical literature. *Tourism Management Perspectives, 8*, 28–41. doi:10.1016/j.tmp.2013.05.006

Séraphin, H., & Korstanje, M. E. (2020). Ethical comments revolving around post-disaster marketing. In *Sustainable destination branding and marketing: strategies for tourism development* (pp. 73–81). CABI. doi:10.1079/9781786394286.0073

Seraphin, H., & Korstanje, M. E. (2021). Neither Passive nor Powerless: Reframing Tourism Development in a Postcolonial, Post-conflict and Post-disaster Destination Context. In *Progress in Ethical Practices of Businesses* (pp. 117–135). Springer. doi:10.1007/978-3-030-60727-2_7

Tarlow, P. (2014). *Tourism security: strategies for effectively managing travel risk and safety*. Elsevier.

Tzanelli, R. (2018). Slum tourism: A review of state-of-the-art scholarship. *Tourism, Culture & Communication, 18*(2), 149–155. doi:10.3727/10983041 8X15230353469528

Tzanelli, R., & Korstanje, M. E. (2016). Tourism in the European economic crisis: Mediatised worldmaking and new tourist imaginaries in Greece. *Tourist Studies, 16*(3), 296–314. doi:10.1177/1468797616648542

ADDITIONAL READING

Breakey, N., & Breakey, H. (2013). Is there a tourism right? *Tourism Analysis, 18*(6), 739–748. doi:10.3727/108354213X13824558470943

Cole, S. (2014). Tourism and water: From stakeholders to rights holders, and what tourism businesses need to do. *Journal of Sustainable Tourism, 22*(1), 89–106. do i:10.1080/09669582.2013.776062

Cole, S., & Morgan, N. (Eds.). (2010). Tourism and inequality: Problems and prospects. Wallinford, CABI. doi:10.1079/9781845936624.0000

George, B. P., & Varghese, V. (2007). Human rights in tourism: Conceptualization and stakeholder perspectives. *EJBO. Electronic Journal of Business Ethics and Organization Studies, 12*(2), 1–15.

Hemingway, S. (2004). The impact of tourism on the human rights of women in South East Asia. *International Journal of Human Rights, 8*(3), 275–304. doi:10.1080/1364298042000255216

Jamal, T. (2019). Tourism ethics: A perspective article. *Tourism Review*, *75*(1), 221–224. doi:10.1108/TR-05-2019-0184

Korstanje, M. E. (2016). *The rise of thana-capitalism and tourism*. Routledge. doi:10.4324/9781315457482

Korstanje, M. E. (2016). The spirit of terrorism: Tourism, unionization and terrorism. *Pasos (El Sauzal)*, *14*(3), 239–250.

Korstanje, M. E., Raj, R., & Griffin, K. (Eds.). (2018). *Risk and safety challenges for religious tourism and events*. CABI. doi:10.1079/9781786392282.0000

Korstanje, M. E., Tzanelli, R., & Clayton, A. (2014). Brazilian World cup 2014: Terrorism, tourism, and social conflict. *Event Management*, *18*(4), 487–491. doi:1 0.3727/152599514X14143427352391

Sharpley, R., & Telfer, D. J. (Eds.). (2014). *Tourism and development: Concepts and issues*. Channel View. doi:10.21832/9781845414740

KEY TERMS AND DEFINITIONS

Human Rights: Comprise basic rights that belong invariably to every person who is a human being.

Poverty: Is a state of having few material possessions or facing low income.

Safety-Security Tourism: Is a set of conditions, prerequisite, legal dispositions, and instruments orchestrated to protect tourists and their integrities.

Tourism Consumption: Includes the consumption of tourist experiences and products located in a specific destination or territory.

Violence: Is an atypical behavior oriented to hurt, harm, or kill someone or something.

Chapter 2

Tourism and Water:
A Human Rights Perspective to Enhance Sustainable Tourism

Yesaya Sandang
(iD) https://orcid.org/0000-0002-2902-6859
Universitas Kristen Satya Wacana, Indonesia

Stroma Cole
University of Westminster, UK

ABSTRACT

This chapter explores how acknowledging water as a human right affects government, business, and local communities in tourism. Tourism businesses have the responsibility to respect and protect the right to water, which aligns with the SDGs, particularly SDGs 5, 6, and 10. When the human right to water is not protected and respected, multifaceted violations occur and the potential for tourism to contribute to sustainable development will be undermined. The chapter suggests ways to improve tourism water management and prevent human rights abuses. By adopting responsible water management practices and engaging in partnerships with local communities, the tourism industry can help to promote the realization of the human right to water while also contributing to sustainable tourism.

INTRODUCTION

It is well documented that tourism is a "thirsty industry" regardless of the fact it is dwarfed by use in other sectors such as agriculture (Hadjikakou et al., 2012). In an entry of Encyclopedia of Tourism, Tirado Bennasar (2014) recorded factors that

DOI: 10.4018/978-1-6684-8726-6.ch002

Copyright © 2023, IGI Global. Copying or distributing in print or electronic forms without written permission of IGI Global is prohibited.

make tourism a significant water consumer. First, the consumptive uses provided by local supplies for numerous tourism activities and attractions such as swimming pools, golf courses, gardening/landscaping, meals, drinking, washing, and cleaning. Second, non-consumptive water use that is integral to the ecosystem, such as nature tourism activities (enjoying wildlife at beaches, and a variety of water sports). Third, intermediating water use generated by tourism related products such as agriculture and migration related to tourism development. In addition, we must consider the climate disaster affecting the hydrogeology cycle that jeopardizes water availability, particularly in semi-arid and arid destinations (Kiper et al., 2022).

As a result of high and unsustainable water consumption, tourism activities are negatively impacting the environment and human beings, particularly local people, through water depletion, water pollution and social conflicts (Cole & Browne, 2015; Epler-Wood, 2017; Strauß, 2011). However, securing water for the tourism industry is much more dominant in the literature (Cole et al., 2020). Taking a "tourism first" stance, how to manage the water supply for the tourism industry when their water security is threatened is most frequently investigated. Despite struggles in all continents, the community's perspectives have been the subject of far fewer studies. Studies have suggested that private concessions have been used to guarantee the supply of water in tourist areas as a mechanism of accumulation and reproduction of capital (Hernández Peñaloza et al., 2017); such as in Bali, Costa Rica, Honduras, and Nicaragua where there has been rapid and unchecked growth of tourism at the expense of the environment. Commodification and privatization of the water supply when water is constrained is common in tourist destinations (Cole, 2017; Cole & Ferguson, 2015; Hof & Blázquez-Salom, 2015). Furthermore, weak governance, and lack of law enforcement, was evident in Bali, Costa Rica, and Yogyakarta (Cole, 2012; Cole & Ferguson, 2015; Sandang, 2022). These approaches, that treat water as a commodity, are likely to reinforce disparities between those who can afford to pay for water compared with those who find water prices prohibitive, and thus infringe the human rights to water, often of the most vulnerable.

Based on our previous work and literature, this chapter explores the multifaceted relationship between tourism and water through a human rights lens. Throughout the years of our research and activism, we have found that tourism activities raise serious concerns about the right to water for local communities, together with the sustainability of the environment. Because ultimately, tourists come and go but the community and environment remain in whatever state they are left (Cole & Browne, 2015). We believe that human rights principles must work as a guarantor for fulfilling basic rights and protections against abuses that arise from tourism activities. This argument is based on a firm understanding that the globalization of tourism has created governance gaps that require both states and tourism businesses to engage more proactively in preventing human rights abuses (Cole, 2014; Eriksson et al., 2009; Ruggie, 2008).

We explore the implications of acknowledging water as a human right for government, business, as well as local communities in relation to tourism. We emphasize that respecting and protecting the right to water is part of tourism businesses' obligations. Simultaneously, taking human rights to water into consideration links to the Sustainable Development Goals (SDGs) that currently provides a framework for the future of sustainable tourism. In particular, SDG 5 (Gender equality and women's empowerment), SDG 6 (Clean water and sanitation), and SDG 10 (Reduced inequality). The final part of the chapter examines remedies and ways forward that could improve tourism water management and prevent further abuse of the human rights to water.

DISCUSSION: THE HUMAN RIGHTS TO WATER AND ITS IMPLICATIONS FOR TOURISM

State Duties

In 2010, the United Nations (UN) General Assembly passed a resolution (A/RES/64/292 of 28 July 2010) recognizing the importance of water in sustaining both life and livelihoods. This resolution led to the acknowledgment that access to adequate, secure, available, and affordable water is a basic human right. Subsequently, the UN Human Rights Council confirmed that it is the responsibility of states to uphold this right without discrimination, and to respect, protect, and fulfill it (Human Rights Council, 2010; Winkler, 2014). This is based on the fundamental principle that safeguarding human rights is not simply an act of charity, but rather a universal ethical duty, resulting in the state being held accountable as the duty-bearer (Winkler, 2014).

The state holds primary responsibility for ensuring that human rights are implemented and protected, as it is one of the legal subjects of international law (Donnelly, 2013). Specifically, in relation to the human right to water (HRtW), the state is viewed as the main authority in managing freshwater resources in a just, efficient, and sustainable manner (Andreen, 2011; Bohoslavsky et al., 2015). However, critics argue that the UN and international law lack the ability to compel a country to take action that it would not otherwise take (Staddon et al., 2012). Additionally, even if a government enacts laws recognizing the right to water, marginalized individuals may face significant obstacles in accessing justice and upholding the rule of law. Ultimately, the success of addressing the right to water is heavily reliant on the state's trustworthiness and governance approach (Brooks, 2007).

When it comes to the tourism industry, it is crucial that governments prioritize the protection of the HRtW. They should establish clear regulatory frameworks for managing water resources in the context of tourism development, which should be based on integrated and participatory planning. This entails setting expectations that all tourism businesses operating within a state's jurisdiction will respect the right to water, and can be accomplished through effective policies, legislation, regulations, planning, and infrastructure related to the right to water (Noble et al., 2012). It is also important to assess water resources and determine the carrying capacity of tourist activities. Other factors such as population growth, climate change, and watershed degradation should also be taken into account, and measures should be put in place to protect agriculture and freshwater fishing from overconsumption, pollution, and land appropriation caused by tourism development (Noble et al., 2012).

BUSINESS RESPONSIBILITIES

In addition to the state's duty to protect and uphold the human right to water, the UN Guiding Principles on Business and Human Rights (GPs) also require tourism businesses of all sizes, sectors, operational contexts, ownership structures, and geographical areas to respect this right. While the GPs are considered "soft law," meaning they are not legally binding, their goal is to establish a global standard for preventing potential human rights violations associated with business activities. They also serve as an internationally recognized framework for improving practices and standards related to business and human rights. The GPs are seen as a driving force in advancing the business and human rights agenda by aligning the state's obligations and business responsibilities within the same guidelines (Deva, 2020; Pitts, 2016; Santoro, 2015).

By fulfilling their obligation to respect human rights, as outlined in the GPs, tourism businesses can improve their water usage and sustainability (Sandang & Cole, 2022). The GPs, particularly principles 15-21, emphasize the importance of due diligence in areas where water is scarce or of low quality, or where business activities affect the water supply of disadvantaged communities. Due diligence involves identifying, preventing, mitigating, and accounting for a business's impact on human rights. In particular, a human rights impact assessment (HRIA) is necessary to assess policies, laws, programs, and projects and determine their effects on human rights (Götzmann, 2017).

In order to identify and address the impacts on the HRtW, tourism businesses could follow the recommendations of the Institute for Human Rights and Business (2011). Firstly, by implementing effective water resource management as a standard practice. This means that, as part of their human rights due diligence, businesses determine if their operations affect the public's access to water for domestic purposes. Secondly, having reliable data and information about water usage is crucial to fully understand the impact of business water usage. Finally, conducting an HRtW impact assessment can be a useful starting point for tourism businesses to improve their water management practices. This approach will provide a comprehensive view of their water impact and help them take appropriate action in all aspects of their water management.

COMMUNITY AGENCIES

Furthermore, the acknowledgement of the HRtW can give a foundation for advancing a claim on water equity. As demonstrated by Morinville & Rodina (2013) the victory for the indigenous peoples in Botswana, in terms of water access in their ancestral land, illustrated the strategic potential of the HRtW i.e., "to not only ensure physical access to water, but also to advance claims in broader social justice contexts" (p.157). Whilst in terms of tourism development, Cole's (2021) longitudinal study in Bali has shown that a human rights lens can become a significant starting point for social mobilization for expanding struggles for water equity and water security simultaneously; underlining the importance of balancing human and environmental water needs. Academics and civil society organizations have triggered a series of actions to deal with the pending water crisis among key stakeholders. Following up on Cole's research findings, local NGOs have begun working on public education to act in saving and protecting Bali's freshwater.

According to Principle 15 of the GPs, the integrated cooperation among governmental bodies, tourism businesses, and community groups is of paramount importance. The effective implementation of a human rights-based approach to tourism water management requires the active participation of local communities and a robust system of community governance. This approach necessitates the confluence of political will and good governance to enable substantive community engagement, while simultaneously addressing intricate trade-offs in a transparent and accountable manner (Baillat, 2013; Harris et al., 2017).

The GPs emphasizes the importance of inclusive participation as a fundamental principle, extending beyond mere consultation or technical additions to project design (Götzmann, 2017). The GP also recognizes the significance of meaningful dialogue with rights holders, paying particular attention to disadvantaged communities and the various risks faced by women and men (Principle 18). To operationalize principle 18 of the GPs, it is imperative that rights holders are afforded the opportunity to meaningfully participate in shaping and influencing the HRtW impact assessment process, as well as the associated findings and decisions. As pointed out by Cole

(2014), fostering open relationships with rights holders through an HRtW impact assessment has the potential to promote trust and rapport with local communities and NGOs, while allowing tourism businesses to address local needs and improve the quality of life for local inhabitants.

Multifaceted Impacts

Thus far, we have established implications of the HRtW for government, business and communities in relation to tourism. In the following section we explore multifaceted impacts of unchecked tourism development on the HRtW. These include impacts on the right for a healthy environment of those most impacted, i.e., women and vulnerable groups such as children.

Right for a Healthy Environment

The right to a healthy environment and the right to water are closely related. Access to safe and sufficient water is essential for maintaining a healthy environment and ensuring that people can live healthy and dignified lives. In turn, a healthy environment is necessary for protecting and sustaining water resources. Article 24.2 of the Convention on the Rights of the Child (1989) explicitly states that the provision of adequate clean drinking water is a prerequisite to the right to health (Fantini, 2019). Moreover, according to guidelines from the World Health Organization (WHO), a minimum of 50 to 100 liters of water per person per day is required to ensure that basic human needs are met and to prevent health concerns from arising (UN-Water Decade Programme on Advocacy and Communication and Water Supply and Sanitation Collaborative Council, n.d.).

We can see the connection between injudicious use of water by the tourism sector and the infringement of rights for a healthy environment in water conflicts between hotels and communities in Yogyakarta, Indonesia. In their lawsuit filed against a condotel, the neighboring resident highlighted that the community's struggle for a good and healthy environment was tied to their human rights to water (Apriando, 2015). Symbolically, they filed the lawsuit on Human Rights Day (10th December 2015). Another example occurred in Guanacaste, Costa Rica. The tourism industry in this region, which relies heavily on water for golf courses, hotels, and other activities, led to severe water shortages and contamination of local water sources, negatively impacting the health and livelihoods of local communities. Studies have highlighted the inadequate regulation of water usage by the tourism sector, resulting in overexploitation of groundwater resources and a lack of access to clean and safe water for local communities (Bolaños, 2019; Cañada, 2019).

Inspired by the GPs, Sandang (2022) argues that the hotel industry's responsibility to preserve the environment corresponds to its obligation to respect the community's right to a healthy environment and implies the responsibility to respect the HRtW. This argument is based on the premise that environmental damage can and does infringe on the full enjoyment of the HRtW (Knox, 2015). In other words, a hotel's respect for the HRtW is a precondition to a healthy environment and access to safe and sufficient water. Additionally, the obligation to respect the HRtW within environmental regulations can only be advocated under the broader term of environmental rights, which also covers the right to water (Knox, 2015). Underpinning this argument is the inextricable link between the right to water and the right to the highest attainable standard of health, enshrined in Article 12(1) of the 1966 Covenant on Civil and Political Rights (McIntyre, 2019). Furthermore, Gleick (1998) posited that access to water could easily be inferred as a derivative right necessary to comply with both explicit health rights and an adequate standard of living. Organizations such as the Institute for Sustainable Tourism have been advocating for an integrated assessment where human rights (including the HRtW) are embedded within the scope of health impact assessments (Dietrich et al., 2017). This clearly indicates that the tourism sector is increasingly aware of the interconnections between HRtW and the right to a healthy environment.

Right of the Indigenous People

Internationally, indigenous peoples are known as the "guardians of water" and have fought to protect it from overexploitation and pollution (United Nations Declaration on the Rights of Indigenous Peoples/UNDRIP). For them, water is not only sacred but also the lifeblood of their cultures, rituals, lives, and beliefs (Chief, 2020). Their attachment to water is deep. Article 25 of UNDRIP states that "Indigenous peoples have the right to maintain and strengthen their distinctive spiritual relationship with their traditionally owned or otherwise occupied and used lands, territories, waters, and coastal seas and other resources and to uphold their responsibilities to future generations in this regard." For indigenous peoples, the origin, occurrence, morphology, and quality of water often define their identities, both individually and communally, making it impossible to distinguish between people and water (Chief, 2020).

Indigenous communities around the world depend on freshwater systems for their way of life, culture, and traditions. Unfortunately, many of these systems are threatened or negatively impacted by economic development, including tourism. This has resulted in indigenous people losing their spiritual and cultural connection to their ancestral land, as well as valuable local knowledge that has been passed down through generations. For instance, in Bali, Indonesia, around 1000 hectares of rice terraces have been destroyed, putting the iconic rice paddies and the indigenous water management system at risk of irreversible changes caused by uncontrolled tourism expansion (Cole, 2014). Another example of indigenous water conflict with tourism is the case of the Mapuche people in Chile. The Mapuche people have long-standing claims to their ancestral land, including water rights, which have been threatened by the development of the tourist industry in the region (Dell'Orto, 2022). In particular, the expansion of ski resorts and other tourism activities in the Andean Mountain region has put significant pressure on water resources, leading to conflicts with indigenous communities over access and use of water (Barros et al., 2015).

Water Worries for Women and Children

Water scarcity has a greater impact on women and children, particularly in rural and low-income households. The burden of domestic activities that require water, such as cooking, cleaning, washing, childcare, and small-scale agriculture, falls mainly on women (Sorenson et al., 2011). Moreover, women bear the primary responsibility for water acquisition and are more vulnerable to the negative consequences of water scarcity, including physical strain, miscarriage, and attacks by animals or people (Tallman et al., 2023). Women are also more likely to be blamed for their inability to maintain cleanliness in their homes and for their families, even when water shortages are beyond their control (Karim et al., 2012). Studies have even revealed instances of gender-based violence related to water insecurity (Choudhary et al., 2020; Logie et al., 2021).

Furthermore, the development of tourism zones has gradually depleted local water supplies and enclosed coastal or forest resources, with particularly adverse effects on women's livelihoods (Neef, 2019). In Labuan Bajo, Indonesia, Cole (2017) found that the rapid growth of tourism has made women the victims and bearers of the greatest burden due to the strain of managing increasingly complex water needs resulting from increased demand for water in the tourism sector. For the younger generation, the increasing water burden is contributing to their struggle to work (Cole, 2017). Meanwhile, in Colombia, the privatization of water resources linked with the growth of tourism has predominantly impacted women residing in rural areas (Ojeda, 2016; Ojeda et al., 2015). Ultimately, when tourism takes priority over communities, multifaceted violations of HRtW occur, and the potential for tourism to contribute to sustainable development is undermined. In the following section, we will explore the connections between HRtW and three of the Sustainable Development Goals.

Tourism and Water

Linkage With the SDGs

In 2016, the United Nations Sustainable Development Goals (SDGs) were officially adopted. The SDGs contain 17 goals, along with 169 affiliated targets, and 232 accompanying indicators by which progress is measured. The SDGs were created due to uneven progress on the previous Millennium Development Goals. The UN set out a 15-year plan to achieve the goals, recognizing the urgency to address ongoing economic, environmental, and sociocultural issues, especially in less economically developed countries (Salvia et al., 2019).

According to the UN, the 17 SDGs and their targets are aimed at achieving human rights for everyone (United Nations, 2015). They are based on international human rights agreements, including the Universal Declaration of Human Rights, and emphasize the responsibility of states to protect, respect, and promote human rights and fundamental freedoms for everyone, without any form of discrimination. Many of the SDGs and targets correspond to crucial aspects of states' human rights commitments, which are outlined in various international human rights agreements, such as International Covenant on Civil and Political Rights (ICCPR), the International Covenant on Economic, Social and Cultural Rights (ICESCR), the Convention on the Elimination of All Forms of Discrimination Against Women (CEDAW) and the Convention on the Rights of the Child (CRC), and other human rights-related documents at international and regional levels. Moreover, the Danish Institute for Human Rights has created a guide that connects the SDGs and targets with the obligations of states under human rights, labor, and environmental international and regional instruments, as well as voluntary commitments. In the following section, we examine the links between SDG 5, 6 and 10 and the HRtW.

Sustainable Development Goal 5

Sustainable Development Goal (SDG) 5 focuses on achieving gender equality and empowering women and girls. Although the SDG 5 does not explicitly mention the human right to water, it is particularly relevant because women and girls are disproportionately affected by the lack of access to clean water. Women and girls are often responsible for collecting water for their families, which can take up a significant amount of their time and energy. This can prevent them from attending school or engaging in other productive activities. Additionally, women and girls may face discrimination in accessing water sources, particularly in communities where traditional gender roles are deeply ingrained. One of the targets of SDG 5 is to ensure universal access to sexual and reproductive health and reproductive rights both are threatened by a lack of clean water. By ensuring universal access to clean water, SDG 5 can help to promote gender equality and empower women and

21

girls. When women and girls have access to clean water, they can spend more time on education and economic activities, leading to improved health and economic outcomes (Andersen & Dowdell, 2019; Arku, 2010). Furthermore, providing access to clean water can reduce the burden of water collection on women and girls, which promotes gender equality and reduces gender-based violence (Tallman et al., 2023). Since tourism has a significant impact on SDG 5, achieving gender equality in tourism requires addressing the challenges women face, such as gender-based discrimination, violence, and unequal access to resources.

Sustainable Development Goal 6

There is a strong connection between the HRtW and the Sustainable Development Goal 6 (SDG 6) of ensuring access to water and sanitation for all. SDG 6 recognizes that access to safe water, sanitation, and hygiene is a fundamental human need for health and well-being. Its aim is to ensure the availability and sustainable management of water and sanitation for everyone. This goal acknowledges that access to clean water and sanitation is a basic human right enshrined in the Universal Declaration of Human Rights and other international human rights instruments. The realization of this right is crucial for the enjoyment of other human rights, such as the rights to life, health, and a decent standard of living.

There are several specific targets under SDG 6 that are directly linked to human rights to water. For example, Target 6.1 aims to achieve universal and equitable access to safe and affordable drinking water for all. This target recognizes that everyone has the right to access clean and safe drinking water, regardless of their location, ethnicity, or socio-economic status. Similarly, Target 6.2 seeks to provide access to adequate and equitable sanitation and hygiene for all, including ending open defecation and ensuring access to safe and hygienic toilet facilities.

The links between SDG 6 and human rights to water are further reinforced by the fact that achieving this goal requires addressing issues related to inequality, discrimination, and marginalized groups. For instance, ensuring access to water and sanitation in remote and underserved areas, or for marginalized groups, such as women and girls, indigenous peoples, and people with disabilities, requires identifying and addressing underlying factors and root causes of discrimination and inequality, such as poverty, gender discrimination, and exclusion from decision-making processes.

Prioritizing human rights to water and sanitation can promote social inclusion, reduce inequalities, and ensure that sustainable development benefits everyone. Because tourism is a water-intensive industry, its operations can significantly impact local water resources. Therefore, achieving SDG 6's goal of ensuring access to clean water and sanitation for all is critical if tourism development is to be sustainable.

Tourism and Water

Sustainable Development Goal 10

Sustainable Development Goal (SDG) 10 focuses on reducing inequality within and among countries. One of the targets of SDG 10 is to ensure equal opportunities and reduce inequalities of outcome, including by eliminating discriminatory laws, policies, and practices and promoting appropriate legislation, policies, and action. Although SDG 10 does not explicitly mention the human right to water it recognizes that inequalities exist in access to basic services, including water and sanitation, and aims to reduce these inequalities. In many countries, marginalized groups, such as indigenous peoples, ethnic minorities, and people living in poverty, are disproportionately affected by the lack of access to clean water (Jackson, 2016; Spicer et al., 2020). Inequalities in access to clean water can exacerbate social and economic inequalities. Furthermore, discriminatory laws, policies, and practices may prevent these groups from accessing water sources, leading to further marginalization and inequality. By working towards SDG 10, governments and other stakeholders can address the barriers that prevent marginalized groups from accessing clean water.

Achieving SDG 10 includes measures to eliminate discrimination, such as providing legal recognition and protection for the human right to water and implementing policies and programs that prioritize marginalized communities' needs. Moreover, other aspects that need to be included are participation and accountability. The human right to water includes the right to participate in decision-making processes that affect access to water. SDG 10 aims to promote the participation of all people in decision-making processes, including marginalized groups, ensuring that their perspectives and needs are considered when decisions are made about water management. Meanwhile, in terms of accountability, the human right to water includes the right to hold governments and other actors accountable for ensuring access to clean water. SDG 10 aims to promote accountability for ensuring access to basic services, including water and sanitation, by strengthening institutions and promoting transparency and accountability. Ultimately, tourism plays a crucial role in achieving SDG 10 particularly by addressing all forms of discrimination, promoting participation, and strengthening accountability.

What Can Be Done?

Human Rights to Water Impact Assessment

Elsewhere we have discussed the challenges of utilizing a human rights approach to enhance the water usage and sustainability of hotels (Sandang & Cole, 2022). We contend that it is improbable for hotels to willingly comply with the Human Right to Water (HRtW) without robust controls and balances between public law and civil society governance to guide and pressure them. Voluntary adoption of the GPs in relation to the HRtW is inadequate for several reasons: a lack of awareness, limited substantive voluntary initiatives, the groundwater tariff, inadequate data collection and management, prioritization of profit, return on investment, and public image over environmental considerations, as well as insufficient regulations and enforcement. To attain sustainable water usage in tourist destinations, government, tourism businesses, and communities need to collaborate and fulfill their respective responsibilities in a coordinated manner.

The integration of human rights to water impact assessments (HRtWIA) into the existing environmental impact assessment (EIA) framework is a potential remedy for the impact of water use by tourism businesses (Sandang & Cole, 2022). The similarities between EIA and HRtWIA offer an opportunity to link environmental stewardship and human rights language. Moreover, HRtWIA emphasizes community participation, and the principle of inclusive participation extends beyond consultation, where people have the right to participate in decisions that affect them. Collaboration between tourism businesses and local stakeholders is crucial in analyzing water consumption and adopting a participatory and contextual approach to water management that upholds the HRtW. There are five areas for consideration so a HRtW impact assessment fosters collaboration with local communities and manages water sustainably (Table 1). This would involve preparing for and addressing any issues through legitimate processes to respect the human right to water, as outlined in Principle 22 of the GPs.

Table 1. Critical areas of understanding of HRtWIA for hotels

Areas of Understanding	● The impact of water use, both on quality and quantity, on available water supplies ● Other users being affected. ● The present availability of water access including seasonality. ● The cumulative impact and future water supply (including, for example, deforestation, major planned development, and climate change) ● Community structures and socio-cultural dynamics that affect water availability (including ethnicity, gender, minorities, vulnerable groups, and their intersectionality)

Source: Sandang and Cole (2022)

Socio-Political Action

Claiming the Human Right to Water (HRtW) is inherently political and requires community agencies and advocacy. In turn, this requires increased awareness, negotiating skills, and advocacy capacity. Research has indicated that to prevent tourism from becoming merely another extractive industry, local communities need to be able to participate in and have a sense of ownership in decision-making processes related to tourism. (Cole, 2006; Boley & McGehee, 2014; Scheyvens & Biddulph, 2018; Moayerian et al., 2022). When communities assert their HRtW, they are viewed as a political entity that serves as a foundation for representation, group decision-making, mobilization, and action (Chaskin, 2012).

In Costa Rica, Cole and Ferguson (2015) noted that women were the driving force behind the effort to address unequal power relations between the tourism industry and local communities regarding water allocation. Meanwhile, in Yogyakarta, the water conflict between hotels and the community has been a catalyst for citizens to engage in social and political action (Sandang, 2022). Furthermore, in Bali, a charity (IDEP) took further action to install rainwater catchment and water pipes to the driest Northeast region and produced a film about water conservation which was screened at an international film festival (Equality in Tourism, 2015). Under the banner of the Bali Water Protection (BWP) initiative, IDEP collaborates with various stakeholders' including hotels, government, academia, and community groups. The BWP program includes public education, public awareness, and aquifer rehabilitation. It also reaches out to hotel environmental and engineering managers in collaboration with the Bali Hotel Association (Bali Water Project, 2017).

Engaging With the SDGs

In order to promote respect for human rights in the tourism industry, it is important to engage tourism stakeholders, particularly businesses, and to use the Sustainable Development Goals (SDGs) as a framework for aligning their operations with sustainable development objectives. This framework highlights the need for partnerships among governments, the private sector, civil society, and other stakeholders to achieve the SDGs. Such partnerships can facilitate the sharing of knowledge and resources, the development of innovative solutions, and the coordination of efforts to address complex challenges. Scheyvens & Cheer (2021) provides examples of successful partnerships that have contributed to progress towards the SDGs in the tourism industry, including the Global Sustainable Tourism Council, the Tourism for SDGs Platform, and the Tourism Partnerships for Development. These partnerships have helped to promote sustainable tourism practices, support local communities, protect biodiversity, and improve working conditions for tourism workers.

The Global Sustainable Tourism Council (GSTC) is notable for providing hotels with sustainable criteria that align with the human rights agenda, serving as a framework for a sustainable management system (Global Sustainable Tourism Council, 2016). To address water sustainability and SDG 6, the criteria include:

ensuring water use is legally valid, respecting local communal and indigenous rights, avoiding harm to neighboring communities' access to basic water services, monitoring the impact of water use, providing communication, feedback, and grievance mechanisms, conducting water risk assessments, and measuring water use periodically. In addition, the GSTC criteria for hotels correspond to SDG 5 and 10 and include indicators such as: implementing a policy against exploitation or harassment, especially of vulnerable groups like children, adolescents, women, minorities, and others; ensuring equal employment opportunities, including in management positions, without discrimination based on gender, race, religion, disability, or other factors; providing appropriate access and information for persons with special needs; and offering equal opportunities for local residents to advance in employment, including management positions.

Research has shown that progress in one area can contribute to progress in another (Fonseca et al., 2020; Salvia et al., 2019). SDG 5 seeks to achieve gender equality and empower women and girls, which is closely related to SDG 6's goal of ensuring access to water and sanitation for all and SDG 10's aim of reducing inequality (Alarcón & Cole, 2019). Gender equality is crucial to sustainable development and requires addressing discrimination, violence, and unequal access to resources. In tourism, gender equality is vital for sustainable development and requires addressing the challenges faced by women in the industry. SDG 6's success is also linked to gender equality because women and girls are disproportionately affected by the lack of access to clean water and sanitation. SDG 10 targets reducing inequalities within and among countries, necessitating the elimination of gender-based discrimination and women's unequal participation in decision-making.

In light of the challenges facing the achievement of Sustainable Development Goals 5 and 6, tourism is identified as a promising contributor towards advancing a gender-sensitive water agenda. Tourism has been noted to have a positive impact on infrastructure, particularly in relation to the provision of improved water and sanitation facilities (Wall & Mathieson, 2006). However, as pointed out by Alarcón and Cole (2019), to ensure that tourism maximizes its potential to contribute to these goals, several critical actions need to be taken. First, it is necessary to recognize the value of unpaid and domestic work, including the opportunity costs of women's water work. This is crucial for promoting gender equality and empowering women in the tourism industry. Second, affirmative action is required to address gender imbalances in water governance, particularly in relation to water allocation and distribution. Such actions would involve empowering women to have a voice in accessing and controlling water supplies, managing water use and pricing, and participating in water management and decision-making without increasing their workload. Finally, research suggests that taking a human rights-based approach

Tourism and Water

to destination management can improve leadership and foster more inclusive and sustainable tourism practices (Cole, 2014).

CONCLUSION

In this chapter we have shown that acknowledging water as a human right affects government, business, and local communities in tourism. Tourism businesses bear the responsibility of respecting and protecting the right to water, which aligns with the SDGs. When the HRtW is not protected and respected, multifaceted violations occur and the potential for tourism to contribute to sustainable development will be undermined. We also have demonstrated that SDGs 5, 6, and 10 are interconnected, and linked to tourism. In conclusion, the human right to water is a critical principle that has important implications for the tourism industry. Moreover, to achieve the SDGs and uphold the right to water, it is necessary to identify and implement effective remedies and ways forward for improving tourism water management and preventing further abuse of human rights. By adopting responsible water management practices and engaging in partnerships with local communities, the tourism industry can help to promote the realization of the human right to water while also contributing to sustainable tourism.

We propose several potential research directions for future studies. Firstly, an evaluation of the effectiveness of the solutions proposed to enhance water management in tourism and prevent human rights abuses. This may entail assessing the practicality and feasibility of implementing these measures in diverse tourism settings. Secondly, an investigation into how recognizing water as a human right affects the conduct and behavior of tourism businesses. This could include exploring whether such recognition results in significant changes in businesses' adherence to their responsibilities to protect and respect water rights. Thirdly, an analysis of the interlinkages between Sustainable Development Goals relating to water and tourism. This study could examine possible conflicts and synergies between these goals and identify ways to address them through integrated approaches to sustainable tourism. Lastly, a comparative analysis of the different approaches taken by countries and regions in acknowledging and upholding the right to water in the context of tourism. This might involve examining legal and policy frameworks, institutional arrangements, and practices related to water and tourism across diverse contexts. Overall, investigating these areas could provide valuable insights into effective strategies for promoting sustainable and equitable tourism practices and deepen our understanding of the linkages between water, human rights, and sustainable tourism.

REFERENCES

Alarcón, D. M., & Cole, S. (2019). No sustainability for tourism without gender equality. *Journal of Sustainable Tourism*, *27*(7), 903–919. doi:10.1080/09669582.2019.1588283

Andersen, L., & Dowdell, E. B. (2019). Access to clean water and urinary tract infections in Haitian women. *Public Health Nursing (Boston, Mass.)*, *36*(6), 800–805. doi:10.1111/phn.12660 PMID:31465129

Andreen, W. L. (2011). Water resources planning and management Water law and the search for sustainability: a comparative analysis. In R. Q. Grafton & K. Hussey (Eds.), *Water Resources Planning and Management* (1st ed., pp. 115–174). Cambridge University Press. doi:10.1017/CBO9780511974304.011

Apriando, T. (2015). *Izin Lingkungan Banyak Kejanggalan, Warga Karangwuni Gugat Apartemen Uttara*. Mongabay. https://www.mongabay.co.id/2015/12/23/izin-lingkungan-banyak-kejanggalan-warga-karangwuni-gugat-apartemen-uttara/

Arku, F. S. (2010). Time savings from easy access to clean water. *Progress in Development Studies*, *10*(3), 233–246. doi:10.1177/146499340901000303

Baillat, A. (2013). *Corruption and the human right to water and sanitation: Human right-based approach to tackling corruption in the water sector*. Water Integrity Network, Berlin and WaterLex. https://www.waterlex.org/new/wp-content/uploads/2013/12/2013-WaterLex-WIN_Corruption-and-the-HRWS-.pdf

Baldacchino, G. (2006). Warm versus cold water island tourism: A review of policy implications. *Island Studies Journal*, *1*(2), 183–200. doi:10.24043/isj.193

Bali Water Project. (2017). *IDEP was invited by the bali hotel association to present the bali water protection program to a pool of hotel environmental and engineering-managers*. https://baliwaterprotection.net/idep-was-invited-by-the-bali-hotel-association-to-present-the-bali-water-protection-program-to-a-pool-of-hotel-environmental-and-engineering-managers/

Barros, A., Monz, C., & Pickering, C. (2015). Is tourism damaging ecosystems in the Andes? Current knowledge and an agenda for future research. *Ambio*, *44*(2), 82–98. doi:10.100713280-014-0550-7 PMID:25201299

Becken, S. (2014). Water equity–Contrasting tourism water use with that of the local community. *Water Resources and Industry*, *7*, 9–22. doi:10.1016/j.wri.2014.09.002

Bohoslavsky, J. P., Martín, L., & Justo, J. (2015). The state duty to protect from business-related human rights violations in water and sanitation services: Regulatory and BITS implications. *International Law. Revista Colombiana de Derecho Internacional*, 26, 63–116. doi:10.11144/Javeriana.il15-26.sdpb

Bolaños, C. (2019). Conflictos socioambientales por la gestión del agua: el caso de la comunidad de Playa Potrero, Guanacaste. In F. Alpízar (Ed.), Agua y poder en Costa Rica 1980-2017 (pp. 193–238). Centro de Investigación y Estudios Políticos (CIEP), Universidad de Costa Rica.

Brooks, D. B. (2007). Human rights to water in North Africa and the Middle East: What is new and what is not; what is important and what is not. *International Journal of Water Resources Development*, 23(2), 227–241. doi:10.1080/07900620601097075

Campón-Cerro, A. M., Di-Clemente, E., Hernández-Mogollón, J. M., & Folgado-Fernández, J. A. (2020). Healthy water-based tourism experiences: Their contribution to quality of life, satisfaction and loyalty. *International Journal of Environmental Research and Public Health*, 17(6), 1961. doi:10.3390/ijerph17061961 PMID:32192098

Cañada, E. (2019). Conflictos por el agua en Guanacaste, Costa Rica: Respuestas al desarrollo turístico. *Anuario de Estudios Centroamericanos*, 45, 323–344. doi:10.15517/aeca.v45i0.37666

Cazcarro, I., Hoekstra, A. Y., & Chóliz, J. S. (2014). The water footprint of tourism in Spain. *Tourism Management*, 40, 90–101. doi:10.1016/j.tourman.2013.05.010

Chief, K. (2020). Water in the Native World. *Journal of Contemporary Water Research & Education*, 169(1), 1–7. doi:10.1111/j.1936-704X.2020.03328.x

Choudhary, N., Brewis, A., Wutich, A., & Udas, P. B. (2020). Sub-optimal household water access is associated with greater risk of intimate partner violence against women: Evidence from Nepal. *Journal of Water and Health*, 18(4), 579–594. doi:10.2166/wh.2020.024 PMID:32833684

Cole, S. (2012). A political ecology of water equity and tourism. A Case Study from Bali. *Annals of Tourism Research*, 39(2), 1221–1241. doi:10.1016/j.annals.2012.01.003

Cole, S. (2012). A political ecology of water equity and tourism: A case study from Bali. *Annals of Tourism Research*, 39(2), 1221–1241. doi:10.1016/j.annals.2012.01.003

Cole, S. (2014). Tourism and water: From stakeholders to rights holders, and what tourism businesses need to do. *Journal of Sustainable Tourism*, *22*(1), 89–106. doi:10.1080/09669582.2013.776062

Cole, S. (2017). Water worries: An intersectional feminist political ecology of tourism and water in Labuan Bajo, Indonesia. *Annals of Tourism Research*, *67*, 14–24. doi:10.1016/j.annals.2017.07.018

Cole, S., & Browne, M. (2015). Tourism and Water Inequity in Bali: A Social-Ecological Systems Analysis. *Human Ecology: an Interdisciplinary Journal*, *43*(3), 439–450. doi:10.100710745-015-9739-z

Cole, S., & Ferguson, L. (2015). Towards a gendered political economy of water and tourism. *Tourism Geographies*, *17*(4), 511–528. doi:10.1080/14616688.2015.1065509

Cole, S., Wardana, A., & Dharmiasih, W. (2021). Making an impact on Bali's water crisis: Research to mobilize NGOs, the tourism industry and policy makers. *Annals of Tourism Research*, *87*, 103119. doi:10.1016/j.annals.2020.103119

Cole, S. K. G., Mullor, E. C., Ma, Y., & Sandang, Y. (2020). "Tourism, water, and gender"—An international review of an unexplored nexus. *WIREs. Water*, *7*(4), 1–16. doi:10.1002/wat2.1442

Dell'Orto, G. (2022, August 20). *On Chile rivers, Native spirituality and development clash | AP News.* https://apnews.com/article/sacred-rivers-religion-chile-7112a8bf f283516c44799840c7b47df3

Deva, S. (2020). From business or human rights to business and human rights: What next? *Research Handbook on Human Rights and Business*, *2015*, 1–21. doi:10.4337/9781786436405.00005

Dietrich, L., Koalick, M., & Leisinger, M. (2017). *Human Rights Assessments in the Tourism Sector: A data collection guide for practitioners.* Institut für nachhaltigen Tourismus GmbH (Inatour). https://www.humanrights-in-tourism.net/file/1153/download?token=DTQXcBXi

Donnelly, J. (2013). *Universal Human Rights in Theory and Practice.* Cornell University Press. doi:10.7591/9780801467493

Eliakimu, E. S., & Mans, L. (2022). Addressing Inequalities Toward Inclusive Governance for Achieving One Health: A Rapid Review. *Frontiers in Public Health*, *9*, 755285. Advance online publication. doi:10.3389/fpubh.2021.755285 PMID:35127612

Epler-Wood, M. (2017). *Sustainable Tourism on a Finite Planet* (1st ed.). Routledge., doi:10.4324/9781315439808

Equality in Tourism. (2015). *Stroma Cole's Bali presentation on tourism-related water shortages.* http://equalityintourism.org/stroma-coles-bali-presentation-on-tourism-related-water-shortages-in-bali/

Eriksson, J., Noble, R., Pattullo, P., Barnett, T., Eriksson, J., Noble, R., Pattullo, P., & Barnett, T. (2009). *Putting Tourism to Rights.* https://www.tourismconcern.org.uk/wp-content/uploads/2014/10/LowRes_Putting-Tourism-to-Rights_A-report-by-TourismConcern2.pdf

Fantini, E. (2019). An introduction to the human right to water: Law, politics, and beyond. *WIREs. Water, 7*(November), 1–8. doi:10.1002/wat2.1405

Fonseca, L. M., Domingues, J. P., & Dima, A. M. (2020). Mapping the Sustainable Development Goals Relationships. *Sustainability (Basel), 12*(8), 3359. doi:10.3390u12083359

Gleick, P. (1998). The human right to water. *Water Policy, 1*(5), 487–503. doi:10.1016/S1366-7017(99)00008-2

Global Sustainable Tourism Council. (2016). *GSTC Hotel Criteria.* https://www.gstcouncil.org/wp-content/uploads/2015/11/GSTC-Hotel_Industry_Criteria_with_hotel_indicators_21-Dec-2016_Final.pdf

Gössling, S. (2006). Tourism and water. In *Tourism and global environmental change* (pp. 180–194). Routledge. doi:10.4324/9780203011911-12

Gössling, S., Hall, C. M., & Scott, D. (2015). *Tourism and water* (Vol. 2). Channel View Publications. doi:10.21832/9781845415006

Götzmann, N. (2017). Human Rights Impact Assessment of Business Activities: Key Criteria for Establishing a Meaningful Practice. *Business and Human Rights Journal, 2*(1), 87–108. doi:10.1017/bhj.2016.24

Hadjikakou, M., Chenoweth, J., & Miller, G. (2012). Water and tourism. In A. Holden & D. Fennell (Eds.), *The Routledge handbook of tourism and the environment* (1st ed., pp. 457–468). Routledge. https://www.taylorfrancis.com/books/e/9780203121108/chapters/10.4324/9780203121108-52

Harris, L. M., McKenzie, S., Rodina, L., Shah, S., & Wilson, N. (2017). Water Justice: Concepts, debates and research agendas. In R. Holifield, J. Chakraborty, & G. Walker (Eds.), *Handbook of Environmental Justice* (1st ed.). Routledge.

Hernández Peñaloza, N., Zizumbo Villarreal, L., & Torregrosa Martí, T. (2017). Agua y turismo como instrumentos de acumulación de capital, el caso de Benidorm, España. *Teoría y Praxis*, *13*(21), 31–53. doi:10.22403/UQROOMX/TYP21/02

Hof, A., & Blázquez-Salom, M. (2015). Changing tourism patterns, capital accumulation, and urban water consumption in Mallorca, Spain: A sustainability fix? *Journal of Sustainable Tourism*, *23*(5), 770–796. doi:10.1080/09669582.2014.991397

Human Rights Council. (2010). *Human rights and access to safe drinking water and sanitation*. Pub. L. No. A/HRC/RES/15/9 (2010). https://ap.ohchr.org/documents/dpage_e.aspx?si=A/HRC/RES/15/9

Institute for Human Rights and Business. (2011). *More than resources: Water, Business and Human Rights*. https://www.ihrb.org/pdf/More_than_a_resource_Water_business_and_human_rights.pdf

Jackson, S. (2016). *Indigenous Peoples and Water Justice in a Globalizing World* (K. Conca & E. Weinthal, Eds., Vol. 1). Oxford University Press. doi:10.1093/oxfordhb/9780199335084.013.5

Jennings, G. (2007). *Water-based tourism, sport, leisure, and recreation experiences*. Routledge. doi:10.4324/9780080468310

Karim, K. M. R., Emmelin, M., Resurreccion, B. P., & Wamala, S. (2012). Water Development Projects and Marital Violence: Experiences from Rural Bangladesh. *Health Care for Women International*, *33*(3), 200–216. doi:10.1080/07399332.2011.603861 PMID:22325022

Kiper, V. O., Saraç, Ö., & Batman, O. (2022). Drought Tourism: Adopting Tourism for Water Scarcity. In E. Christou & A. Fotiadis (Eds.), *Restarting tourism, travel and hospitality* (1st ed., pp. 248–257). School of Economics and Business, International Hellenic University.

Knox, J. H. (2015). Human Rights, Environmental Protection, and the Sustainable Development Goals. *Washington International Law Journal*, *24*(3), 517–536.

Logie, C. H., Okumu, M., Latif, M., Musoke, D. K., Odong Lukone, S., Mwima, S., & Kyambadde, P. (2021). Exploring resource scarcity and contextual influences on wellbeing among young refugees in Bidi Bidi refugee settlement, Uganda: Findings from a qualitative study. *Conflict and Health*, *15*(1), 3. doi:10.118613031-020-00336-3 PMID:33413546

McIntyre, O. (2019). The Emergence of Standards Regarding the Right of Access to Water and Sanitation. In S. J. Turner, D. L. Shelton, J. Razzaque, O. McIntyre, & J. R. May (Eds.), *Environmental Rights: The Oxford Handbook of International Environmental Law* (1st ed., pp. 147–173). Cambridge University Press. doi:10.1017/9781108612500.007

Mckay, T. J. (2014). White water adventure tourism on the Ash River, South Africa. *African Journal for Physical, Health Education, Recreation & Dance, 20*(1), 1–15.

Moayerian, N., McGehee, N. G., & Stephenson, M. O. Jr. (2022). Community cultural development: Exploring the connections between collective art making, capacity building and sustainable community-based tourism. *Annals of Tourism Research, 93*, 103355. doi:10.1016/j.annals.2022.103355

Morinville, C., & Rodina, L. (2013). Rethinking the Human Right to Water: Water access and dispossession in Botswana's Central Kalahari game reserve. *Geoforum, 49*, 150–159. doi:10.1016/j.geoforum.2013.06.012

Neef, A. (2019). *Tourism, Land Grabs and Displacement: A Study with Particular Focus on the Global South.* Academic Press.

Noble, R., Smith, P., Pattullo, P., Brown, M., Cole, S., Slade, L., Latchford, R., Niang, D., & Gama, A. de. (2012). *Water equity in tourism: a human right, a global responsibility.* Tourism Concern research report.

Ojeda, D. (2016). Los paisajes del despojo: Propuestas para un análisis desde las reconfiguraciones socioespaciales. *Revista Colombiana de Antropología, 52*(2), 19–43. doi:10.22380/2539472X38

Ojeda, D., Petzl, J., Quiroga, C., Ana Catalina, R., & Juan Guillermo, R. (2015). Paisajes del despojo cotidiano: Acaparamiento de tierra y agua en Montes de María, Colombia. *Revista de Estudios Sociales, 54*(54), 107–119. doi:10.7440/res54.2015.08

Pitts, C. (2016). The United Nations' Protect, Respect, Remedy' Framework and Guiding Principles. In D. Baumann-Pauly & J. Nolan (Eds.), *Business and Human Rights from Principles to Practice* (1st ed., pp. 51–63). Routledge.

Ruggie, J. G. (2008). Protect, Respect and Remedy: A Framework for Business and Human Rights. *Innovations: Technology, Governance, Globalization, 3*(2), 189–212. doi:10.1162/itgg.2008.3.2.189

Salvia, A. L., Leal Filho, W., Brandli, L. L., & Griebeler, J. S. (2019). Assessing research trends related to Sustainable Development Goals: Local and global issues. *Journal of Cleaner Production, 208*, 841–849. doi:10.1016/j.jclepro.2018.09.242

Sandang, Y. (2022). *Hotels and the human right to water: prospect and challenges in Yogyakarta, Indonesia* [Doctoral dissertation]. Faculty of Environment and Technology, University of the West of England.

Sandang, Y., & Cole, S. (2022). Using a human rights approach to improve hotels' water use and sustainability. *Journal of Sustainable Tourism*, 1–19. doi:10.1080/09669582.2022.2108041

Santoro, M. A. (2015). Business and Human Rights in Historical Perspective. *Journal of Human Rights*, *14*(2), 155–161. doi:10.1080/14754835.2015.1025945

Scheyvens, R., & Cheer, J. M. (2021). Tourism, the SDGs and partnerships. *Journal of Sustainable Tourism*, *0*(0), 1–11. doi:10.1080/09669582.2021.1982953

Sorenson, S. B., Morssink, C., & Campos, P. A. (2011). Safe access to safe water in low-income countries: Water fetching in current times. *Social Science & Medicine*, *72*(9), 1522–1526. doi:10.1016/j.socscimed.2011.03.010 PMID:21481508

Spicer, N., Parlee, B., Chisaakay, M., & Lamalice, D. (2020). Drinking Water Consumption Patterns: An Exploration of Risk Perception and Governance in Two First Nations Communities. *Sustainability (Basel)*, *12*(17), 6851. doi:10.3390u12176851

Staddon, C., Appleby, T., & Grant, E. (2012). A Right to Water? Geographico-legal perspectives. In F. Sultana & A. Loftus (Eds.), The Right to Water: Politics, governance and social struggles (pp. 61–77). Earthscan, Taylor & Francis.

Strauß, S. (2011). Water Conflicts among Different User Groups in South Bali, Indonesia. *Human Ecology: an Interdisciplinary Journal*, *39*(1), 69–79. doi:10.100710745-011-9381-3

Tallman, P. S., Collins, S., Salmon-Mulanovich, G., Rusyidi, B., Kothadia, A., & Cole, S. (2023). Water insecurity and gender-based violence: A global review of the evidence. *WIREs. Water*, *10*(1). Advance online publication. doi:10.1002/wat2.1619

Tirado Bennasar, D. (2014). Water consumption, tourism. In J. Jafari & H. Xiao (Eds.), *Encyclopedia of Tourism*. Springer. doi:10.1007/978-3-319-01669-6_313-1

UN-Water Decade Programme on Advocacy and Communication and Water Supply and Sanitation Collaborative Council. (n.d.). *The Human Right to Water and Sanitation Media Brief*.

United Nations. (2015). *The 17 Goals | Sustainable Development*. https://sdgs.un.org/goals

Warren, C., & Becken, S. (2017). Saving energy and water in tourist accommodation: A systematic literature review (1987–2015). *International Journal of Tourism Research, 19*(3), 289–303. doi:10.1002/jtr.2112

Winkler, I. (2014). *The human right to water: significance, legal status and implications for water allocation*. Hart Publishing.

KEY TERMS AND DEFINITIONS

Human Rights: Should be defined as a set of moral principles created to protect and regulate human relations.

Sustainability: Is a social goal marked by the ability of persons to protect the non-renewable resources for the next generations.

Tourism: Is a subservice sector, commercial activity or industry dedicated to organize tours and travels following pleasure for travels.

Water Access: Is a basic right endorsed to all citizens without distinction of class, ethnicity, or nationality.

Water Justice: Is seen as a set of actions, laws and regulations orchestrated to ensure the equal access to water for all citizens.

Chapter 3

Expanding and Updating Human Rights:
Tourism as a Social Right in Contemporary Societies

Thiago Duarte Pimentel
Federal University of Juiz de Fora, Brazil

Mariana Pereira Chaves Pimentel
Federal University of Juiz de Fora, Brazil

Marcela Costa Bifano de Oliveira
Federal University of Juiz de Fora, Brazil

João Paulo Louzada Vieira
Federal University of Juiz de Fora, Brazil

Paulo Rodrigues Cerqueira
Federal University of Juiz de Fora, Brazil

ABSTRACT

This chapter argues that tourism should be included as a social right because it synthesizes and represents the zeitgeist of contemporaneity. This idea is supported by three main arguments: (1) That there is a shift from a work-oriented society to a new consumption-oriented one, implying the revision of the meaning of current practices. (2) As a social force, tourism is a privileged category to represent, understand, and explain contemporary societies because it goes beyond the market and can heuristically express a complex and multifaceted human practice. (3) The

DOI: 10.4018/978-1-6684-8726-6.ch003

Copyright © 2023, IGI Global. Copying or distributing in print or electronic forms without written permission of IGI Global is prohibited.

Expanding and Updating Human Rights

references based on the previous societies' ideals, such as the right to work, must be revised and expanded to include tourism as a fundamental right, because (a) it can internationally represent a new kind of global citizenship, (b) basic material and economic human needs must be met for tourism to happen, and (c) it contributes to personal development, cultural exchange, and systemically update societies' development.

INTRODUCTION: THE MEANING OF TOURISM IN A CONTEMPORARY WORLD

Tourism – at least as it is known currently – is a recent social practice and economic sector (industry). As a transversal and an interdisciplinary object, tourism history oscillates between a broader, more historical, social and no-economic orientated interpretation, and a narrow one, focused on the economic aspect of activity, its financial effects and its circumscription to the capitalist economic system as a commodity to be sold (exchanged) into the market (César, 2015; César Arnaiz & César, 2017). While the former view is a sort of continuing interpretation of the evolution of – a mix of – social practices through the human history since the old times (nevertheless, the common trace of its object [either leisure, hospitality, or displacement] has not necessarily the same); the former is a kind of conception emerged in the modern era, which is sustained by the embrace of the re-arrangement of the mode of production (from a feudal to a capitalist one) and the political power (from absolute monarchies to a national state).

In its current form, tourism is embedded in capitalist modern societies systems. Recently, it has become one of the most important industries in the world. In 2019, International tourism was the world's third largest export category, worth $1,742 billion. In first place was fuels with $2,310 billion, followed by chemicals with $2,194 billion (UNWTO, 2020). Moreover, in the same year, the tourism sector generated 333 million jobs worldwide (WTTC, 2022), i.e., 1 in 10 jobs belonged to this sector. In addition, it contributed 10.3% of global GDP (WTTC, 2022).

Despite its growing, in terms of the volume of travels and moved (?), and the huge economic impact on the world economies, tourism is not yet a well distributed activity among the different societies in the world. It is not accessible to the biggest part of the populations in most of the countries, nor even internally at the same country.

Figure 1. International tourist arrivals by region
Source: Roser and Herre (2017)

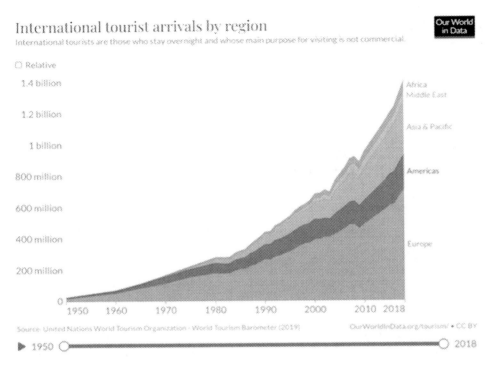

Ouriques' research (2012) reveals the inequalities in its distribution of wealth as it shows that higher income countries accounted for 72.44% of tourism revenues in 2009, while Latin America and the Caribbean accounted for 6.05% in the same year, demonstrating the unequal participation of regions/countries in the distribution of global revenues. The data show the unequal distribution of tourism revenues worldwide and show that the central economies have the most developed tourism systems (sistur), capable of attracting and receiving thousands of tourists (tourist flow), that is, the most visited by tourists and where they spend the greatest amounts of money. So, ingeneral, there is a direct positive correlation between a country's level of development (HDI) and the level of development of its tourism system (Biagi, Ladu & Royuela, 2017; Croes, Ridderstaat & Shapoval, 2020), being especially valid for developed countries (Cárdenas-García, Sánchez-Rivero & Pulido-Fernández, 2015; Pulido-Fernández & Cárdenas-García, 2021)2, with the capacity to receive large tourist flows.

Figure 2. GDP from tourism as a share of total GPD, 2020
Source: Roser and Herre (2017)

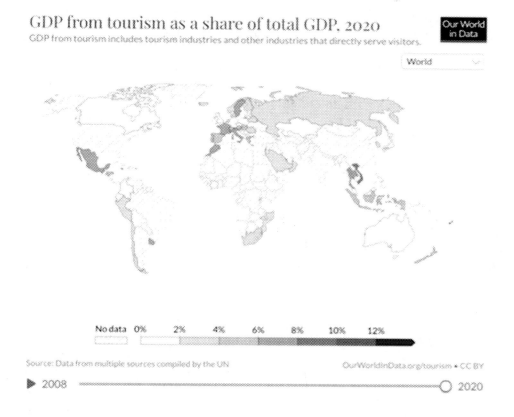

Europe represents almost 1 out of every 2 trips in the world, representing 48% of outbound tourism in the world (WTO, 2020). China is the country with the highest international tourism spending, followed by the United States, Germany, the United Kingdom, and France (WTO, 2020). Evidencing that those who have access to tourism are also people from the central economic countries. In this way, tourism represents a certain level of development, both of the receiving communities by having a tourism system capable of receiving large tourist flows, and also of the tourists, those with the capacity/access to travel.

Considering this scenario, this paper argues that tourism should be considered and included as a social right in the contemporary world, because reflects a level of development since it synthesizes and represents the *ethos* of contemporaneity from at least 3 fundamental dimensions: a) mobility and global citizenship, b) minimum level of economic-material income and capacity of consumption, and c) individual and collective human enrichment and fulfillment.

The transition of a society oriented by a stable and predictable productive system, anchored in the work as one of its central categories, to a society oriented by consumption as its main social category has largely promoted tourism. As a kind of conspicuous consumption (Veblen, 1979[1899]), tourism represents a special indicator of consumption since it can be reach only if the basic needs are previously fulfilled. Also, the mobility generated by tourism is an enabling factor of the citizenship and democracy, because people can voluntarily choose and express their will and in doing so, it expresses the more basic human rights achievement. Especially at the international level, tourism mobility can express a new kind of "social contract" (Sousa Santos, 2006) where people can achieve a global citizenship. Finally, tourism can be seen as a factor of progress, leading to individual and collective human enrichment and fulfillment (Telfer & Sharpley, 2008; Biagi, Ladu & Royuela, 2017; Croes, Ridderstaat & Shapoval, 2020).

2. HUMAN RIGHTS: THEIR HISTORICAL EVOLUTION AND MEANING AS A SIGNAL OF ONE ERA

Historically, the elaboration process of what is conventionally called human rights has gone through several phases of building up and reformulation. One of the first documents that seeks to stipulate basic rights is the Code of Hammurabi. Prepared by the sixth king of Babylon, this document has 282 articles that address the need to regulate the social relations, that means the people's rights and responsibilities which addressed the basic issues to live in society at the time (Altavila, 1989).

In 1879 it was discovered what would be considered one of the oldest documents in the world – the Cylinder of Cyrus (539 BC) – which dealt with issues that later came to be incorporated into human rights. It contained elements that were totally innovative, since it defended religious freedom and the abolition of slavery. Its *avant-gard* position, according to historians, can be considered the first treaty for human rights (Hunt, 2009; Altavila, 1989), because it wasn't just aimed to regulate social relations, but to extend its basis and achieve a minimum level of "quality" of life. Regarding the context into which it was inserted, the document is emblematic and therefore was translated into all official languages by the United Nations Organization in 1971 (Altavila, 1989).

The Greco-Roman civilization also contributed to the foundation and structuring of human rights. The surpass of the ancient regime incited some debates on equality, delegitimization of wars and disputes over principles and rights (Coulanges, 2005). However, it was in the Middle Ages that the first document of a constitutional nature was developed to guarantee the rights of the population. This document became known as the *English Magna Carta*. It was written in Latin and signed by King John of England (João Sem Terra) in 1215, and established that no man is above the law, including the king himself (Hunt, 2009; Altavila, 1989).

The modern age was a period of transition, marked by struggles and wars in the context that absolutism became surpassed by the liberal state in European countries. Among the documents that represent these changes an important one is the *Bill of Rights*, which is considered to be the starting point of the english liberalism of the 18th century. Although it wasn't arisen from the will of the people, the *Bill of Rights* sought to protect people from the abuses of the crown, and postulates freedom of speech and the right to private property (Altavila, 1989; Hobsbawn, 1995). In the second half of this century, in the United States of America, the Virginia Declaration of Rights was the first legal document that made it possible for human rights to become law appeared. This document, drafted by George Mason in 1776, influenced Thomas Jefferson to write the Declaration of Independence of the United States of America. It already preconized and advocated for the guarantee of freedom, equality, and happiness among men (Hunt, 2009).

After the events of the fall of the Bastille and the advent of the French Revolution in 1789 (Hobsbawn, 1991), the *Lafayete's Marquis* (a Thomas Jefferson's friend and who directly opened for his suggestions) drafted a declaration containing 24 articles on the matter and sent it to the French National Assembly for voting. After an intense debate among 40 French deputies, seventeen articles were approved and became to characterize the *Declaration of the Rights of Man*. The Document was acclaimed for its simplicity, as it avoided to mention political and religious issues and institutions and sought to strengthen the power of the nation and equality of men before birth, having great implications on discussions on the theme on a worldwide scale, both positive and negative (Hunt, 2009). Although not having as a fundamental premise the debate on human rights, the Communist Party Manifesto written by Marx and Engels is a symbolic document of the 19th century, as it exposed the subhuman conditions of people and industrial workers in the productive system of that moment of capitalism, proposing ways to overcome its essential conflicts and contradictions.

In the 20th century, due to the atrocities of the World Wars (Hobsbawn, 1995), an international committee of the United Nations was formed with the purpose of establishing a set of norms and guidelines to ensure human integrity and the necessary conditions for life in society. From this committee arose the *Universal Declaration of Human Rights (UDHR)*. Despite of not having a direct legal validity to all societies, the UDHR is widely accepted as an international norm and is adopted by the United Nations (UN) (Bobbio, 1992).

The phenomena of social change in modern society brought important changes to various segments of collective life and social institutions. In this context, the rapid changes in the political, cultural, and economic system, impacted the social order as a whole and intensified a need for the regulation of essential rights in a world stage

(Giddens, 2008). Hence, it is evident that in the course of history, the socio-cultural moment directly impacts the conceptions and desires of a people and, in turn, may reverberate in future postulations. In view of this, appropriating the perspective of Alves (1997), one can conceive that the three main pillars of the international order of protection of human rights are: *The 1948 Universal Declaration of Human Rights*, the *International Covenant on Civil and Political Rights*, and the *International Covenant on Economic, Social and Cultural Rights*. The first became the initial milestone in the protection of human and women's rights, while the covenants came to complement and bring more normative and legal strength to it. Thus, the union of these three documents became known historically as the *Bill of Human Rights*, which has been considered as a remarkable achievement of human societies on the grounds of 20th century (Gurvitch, 1946).

3 TOURISM AND THE HUMAN RIGHTS: SOME PREVIOUS ARGUMENTS

In opposition to the dominant views on tourism, and to understand it more completely and profoundly, critical studies have been discussing its role in societies and proposing a new look at this phenomenon. In a seminal paper on the topic, Higgins-Desbiolles (2006) argues that tourism is an activity that can serve human needs as a public good and can act as a powerful "social force" that plays a broader role in global societies and local communities, especially when it is detached from the neoliberal market. In this sense, her argument is that travel and tourism can be understood as a human right, but this purpose has been systematically forgotten and substituted by the logic of economic development that is naturalized as the only valid premise. Despite the incorporation of the idea of the "right to travel" in various international documents, tourism is still not declared as a human right. Many are the reasons mobilized to defend that inclusion: for example, that here are direct effects on the social, cultural, educational and economic sectors of national societies and their international relations (Higgins-Desbiolles, 2006). Also, there are other benefits that go beyond the economic ones (foreign exchange, jobs, world's largest exporter, alternative to extractive industries): improved individual well-being, preservation of cultures, intercultural understanding, facilitation of learning, contribution to social protection, contribution to development, restoration and conservation of the environment, promotion of peace and understanding among peoples (Higgins-Desbiolles, 2006). In short, the existing evidence indicates the benefits of tourism as a leisure practice and, therefore, its relation to subjective well-being, which leads to the debate about the role of tourism in societies, their economic and social development and international relations (McCabe & Qiao, 2020).

Expanding and Updating Human Rights

The tourism is directly associated with the social and economic development of nations as a mean to access rest and creative vacations in addition to freedom to travel (Higgins-Desbiolles, 2006).

Moreover, taking into account that tourism is not yet a well-distributed activity due to the context of structural inequalities and therefore barriers that could affect people's access to travel opportunities - economic resources, gender, age, lack of knowledge, health, environmental aspects (physical infrastructure), interactive issues such as communication, time and availability - the notion of tourism as a human right makes sense, due to its direct effects on the social, cultural, educational and economic sectors of national societies and their international relations (Higgins-Desbiolles, 2006). So much so, that some authors have been discussing the role of tourism in addressing social exclusion (McCabe and Qiao, 2020).

In this movement, social tourism emerges as an alternative model of welfare based on principles of citizenship rights and social rights, which considers the inclusion of disadvantaged or excluded groups (McCabe & Qiao, 2020) and seeks to give access to travel and leisure opportunities for all (Higgins-Desbiolles, 2006). However, confronting the dominant neoliberal paradigm has not been an easy task, as shown in the literature (Higgins-Desbiolles, 2006). Tourism seen as a human right needs the involvement of communities and governments so that its benefits are fairly distributed, confronting the invisible hand of the market and the neoliberal model (Higgins-Desbiolles, 2006). Furthermore, there is still a long way to materialize the promise of "tourism for all", especially is because many governments in developing countries cannot even reproduce the most basic needs of the population, much less will fulfill the right to travel (Higgins-Desbiolles, 2006).

Tourism then expresses a fundamental 'mobility paradox'. It is a progressive social force articulating closely with the values and principles underpinning the freedom of movement while at the same time constituting a predominant source of corporate profit-making and capital accumulation, processes serving to undermine development rights and prosperity for all, particularly, but not exclusively, within destinations (Bianchi & Stephenson, 2013: 8).

In this scenario, we can identify two models of tourism in dispute, as it is systematized in Figure 3.

This discussion is drawn upon a critical reflection on tourism, which tries to take a broader perspective that shifts the current economic-managerial orientation to a deeper one that qualifies the activity also in its subjective and not-utilitarian aspects as a social force. Naming it this way (Bourdieu, 1989) is already a step forward into the movement of going beyond the limitations of current mainstream perspective. These seminal studies in the critical tourism field have the merit to excavate these

43

deeper layers of the activities phenomena and make them visible and available for discussion. Despite these merits, what is left aside is a deeper assessment of tourism meaning in the context of a changing society.

Figure 3. Perspectives on the purpose of tourism: Tourism as an industry and Tourism as a social force (NB: specific ventures may demonstrate characteristics of both phenomena)
Source: Reproduced from Higgins-Desbiolles (2006, p. 1198)

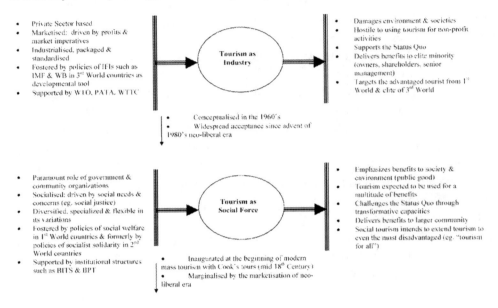

In this sense, three are the main cornerstones underlying the declaration of human rights from 1948. Against the forms of oppression and social exclusion, these rights are directed to the establishment of a minimum pattern of life in terms of dignity, autonomy and protection. The first one is the right to be part of a social system – a national state – and to be included, protected, and receive an egalitarian treatment independently of someone's status (economic, political, social, military, religious, etc.) someone in this particular society, i.e. - by being part of a National Stat and having a citizenship; and as a member, being equivalent to anybody else, being treated in the same level of dignity. The second one is the liberty, which is inspired by a just-naturalism perspective and is directed to the reproduction of biological body itself, extended to the material environment surroundings of the individual (e.g., this belongings, things, space and properties), as well as the immaterial ones (psychological sources of the self, his ideas, beliefs, etc.). Finally, the third

Expanding and Updating Human Rights

one involves the inclusion in the productive system. In order to contribute to this discussion, this paper examines theses main contextual transformations occurred in the 20th century, taking into account their implications on tourism ground, finally debating how and why tourism could be incorporated as a human right.

4. THE CHANGES AND TRENDS IN OUR CONTEMPORARY WORLD AND THEIR IMPLICATIONS TO TOURISM AGENDA

If we could systematize the world of the 20th century, it could be seen as socially stable (Parsons, 1974), economically massive and industrial (Harvey, 2008[1989]), culturally homogeneous (Jameson, 1984; 1991) and politically oriented by the binary logic of capitalism *versus* socialism. Now, in the 21st century, we face a different landscape marked by a post post-modern (Nealon, 2012), immaterial (Touraine, 1971), ephemeral and more diversified (Bauman, 2008) society that has emerged mainly driven by the social forces of acceleration processes (Rosa, 2019) that occur in different systems and subsystems. A new world has then emerged, but it is not radically different from the previous one in terms of its core and essential structures and logics, but it is much more diverse and extended in its range of options, demanding additional efforts in terms of integration and cohesion.

In this sense, we argue that this "new" world is an extension, intensification and acceleration of the processes running on the previous one in a way we are witnessing a movement of, what Giddens (1991) called, the *disembedding* of the social systems. Our defense is that there are in course three main *disembedding* processes: a) the displacement of a world oriented to work to a world oriented to consumption; b) the revision of the social contracts (and social ties) based on the centrality of the consumption; and c) the mobility is treated as a (core) value – and a *modus operandi* (symbolic token) – which would lead to the characteristics of the global tourist-consumer-citizenship.

Considering *the displacement of a world oriented to work to a world oriented to consumption*, it is important to stat that the 20th century witnessed the emergence, development and consolidation of reasonably stable, predictable and mass modern societies, in terms of the orientation of their productive economic system. Such societies arose in the wake of long-lasting (*longué duree*) economic and social macro-processes, such as the processes of rationalization (as emblematically characterized and described by Max Weber), of industrialization (as amply described and explained by Raymond Aron), and urbanization and social change (Brenner & Schmidt, 2016; Brenner, 2018) (although other themes can be explored for a characterization of social theory throughout the 20th century [cf. Nisbet, 1969]).

Expanding and Updating Human Rights

More specifically, we are witnessing an evolution of internal transformations in the capitalist mode of production throughout the 20th century, which could be identified and characterized in three major stages: a) Taylorism-Fordism production system, b) post-Fordism or lean production system and c) Cyber-Fordism (or contemporary) production system or of the technological informational and symbolic economy mode of production.

Table 1. Comparison: Fordism, post-Fordism, and cyber Fordism

Comparison: Fordism, Post-Fordism, and Cyber Fordism

	Fordism	**Post-Fordism**	**Cyber Fordism**
Mechanistic level	Man-Machine	Man-Machines	Machine-Machine
	Rigidity	Flexibility	Systemic integration
Labor level	Overspecialization of the workforce	Specialization of the workforce	Automação da mão de obra
Relationship between employees and managers	Separation between manual and intellectual work	Connection between manual/automated and intellectual work	Connection between automated work and artificial intelligence
Capital-work relation	Regulation of work	Deregulation of work	Post-work
Industrial paradigm	Industry 1.0 and 2.0	Industry 3.0	Industry 4.0
Economic paradigm	Keynesianism	Neoliberalism	Ultra-neoliberalism
	Welfare state	Minimum state	State as guardian of the market

Source: Reproduced from Paes de Paula and Paes (2021, p. 1055)

On *the revision of the social contract (and social ties) and the new forms of inclusion,* the shift of a society oriented for work to one oriented for consumption has consequences in the other societal spheres besides the economic one, impacting in different forms of concluding the social contract. According to Sousa Santos (2006: 7), "The social contract is the meta-narrative on which modern political obligation is based modern political obligation. [...] established between free men and for the purpose of maximizing ... [...] freedom. The social contract thus contains a dialectical tension between social regulation and social emancipation [...].". The contract, in turn, links individuals to society by means of borders (forms of inclusion/exclusion), of a territorially founded citizenship and of the public trade of interests.

According to Barcellos-Mathiasi & Duarte-Pimentel (2021: 2), "understanding the historical formation and development of *citizenship* - as well as of the categories of identity and the public sphere - is a key to of the categories identity and public sphere - that is, the formation of this political category as a look at the formation of this political category as a glimpse into the unfolding of civil, political and social rights, is important for interpreting how states, governments and peoples feel, live and struggle for the maintenance and conquest of their rights".

Expanding and Updating Human Rights

However, if in the last century the right to work and social inclusion was given mainly by the inclusion of people through the economic and productive system – in a productive and positive way –, in the current century there is no promise of work for all. Work –in its legal form, under formal and regular contracts, and least properly paid – is increasingly a distant "dream". On the contrary, we are witnessing the institutionalization of precarious work (Antunes, 2000; Barcellos-Mathiasi & Duarte-Pimentel, 2019; 2020, Barcellos-Mathiasi, 2021). Thus, if in the past productive work was a central category for the constitution of identity and social integration, now this category has progressively lost its importance, which has been replaced by consumption. As Baumann (2008) points out, the person who does not consume is dysfunctional to the current form of capitalism. Therefore, according to him, the main key to social integration – whether in relation to the state or to social relations – is through consumption. This rapid transformation that moves from a solid modernity to a liquid modernity also elucidates the increase in human consumption patterns, which becomes a routine activity without any advance planning. In the course of history, consumption was salutary for the physiological processes of all terrestrial biodiversity and the maintenance of life, since food is a source of vital energy for living beings (Bauman, 2008). Todays exacerbated consumerism is not limited to the food (?) system. It involves different aspects of human life and promotes changes even in economic systems that are not directly related to the moment of production. This transformation occurred mainly after the implementation of the Fordism production model and the modification of work, starting in the 1970s (Gidddens, 2008). In this scenario, the social change caused mainly by immediacy and acceleration, as pointed out by Rosa (2019), consumption needs start to incorporate even other sectors that were not part of consumerism before, such as tourism.

Additionally, the argument pointed out by Sousa Santos (2006) in the course of the 21th century has gotten even stronger due to the impacts of the pandemics. The SARS-COV 19 has suddenly and dramatically changed the human landscape in the last 3 years (Košcˇak & O'Rourke, 2021; Korstanje & George, 2022; Korstanje, Gowreesunkar & Maingi, 2023). If, in one hand, some countries we have seen the proactive behavior of the National States taking decisions and implementing mechanisms to mitigate the pandemics, in the other hand, we are witnessing omissions in the relation to peripherical poor countries (Vidal, 2022). This has also implications to the social contract, as its prerogative is to protect the people and secure their lives, especially when we see the State exempting itself from its responsibilities. In this case, what is left after all? Thus, the *ethos* of the social integration lays on the market and consumer relations, and the projection of desires in objects, services and situations (Bauman, 2008).

On mobility and global citizenship, according to Giddens (2008), the phenomenon of globalization, which has intensified the strengthening of relationships on a global level, is a very recent event in the history of humanity. In the last 30 or 40 years, large-scale changes have occurred in the means of communication, technology, and transportation transforming significantly the way of life of individuals, causing mainly an increase in interdependence and consumption relations. The connection that has been established between the local and the global has fostered a rise in the capitalist production mode. As an example, a simple walk to the supermarket is possible to find products from various places in the world.

Moreover, tourism-related mobility is linked to the diffusion of a culture that values travel-related consumption (Hall, 2005), associated with a global citizenship that expands from the nation to the globe (Butcher, 2017) in a movement in which individuals increasingly belong to diverse groups (Coles, 2008). Thus, in the world of globalization, the national state territory is no longer the unique space for citizenship to act (Schonardie & Winkelmann, 2022), and the definition of citizenship is extended beyond the boundaries of the nation-state (Bianchi & Stephenson, 2013).

In this context of expanding borders, change and recognition of the pluralities of cultural identities, debates about the notions of global or world citizenship emerge, and tourism acts as a vector through which notions of citizenship are being expanded, redefined and contested. Tourism increasingly presents itself as a human and universal right not only "to freedom of movement and leisure, but also to the right to consume other cultures and other territories" (Bianchi & Stephenson, 2013: 10).

5. FINAL REMARKS: THE MEANING OF TOURISM TO THE HUMAN RIGHTS IN THE LIGHT OF 21ST CENTURY AND VICE-VERSA (*OR WHY SHOULD TOURISM BE INCORPORATED AS AN HUMAN RIGHT*)?

At this point we would like to develop three main and intertwined arguments in favor of the possible inclusion of tourism as a human right: (1) that consumption is a new form of dominant social practices in the current societies and, in doing so, it assumes a new centrality as privileged social category to describe, understand and explain the contemporaneity; (2) there is a displacement form the work oriented social form of inclusion in the social system to a new one based on consumption; (3) inside the consumption system, tourism is one of the most privileged social categories to represent, understand, and explain contemporary societies because tourism represents a social force that goes beyond the market itself and can heuristically express a complex and multifaceted social practice, the *zeitgeist* of contemporaneity (Giddens, 2008).

Expanding and Updating Human Rights

Mobility is a new form of capital in the contemporaneity. Also, the revision of the revision of the social contract, which tends to reframe the boarders of the inclusion and exclusion in the social contract, because the tourist consumption generates a new class of people who achieve a kind of global citizenship, since they can reach other spaces and social spheres, beyond the regular activities. Hence, mobility allied to the porosity of global social boundaries enables the tourist (specially the international one) in a kind of global citizen, who has the right to come and go in the "global society", not only formal, but factually. Thus, it represents a factually embodies global citizenship.

The main category then, in the 20th century, so many people have a positive identity, for them to be recognized and have a citizenship by the state and have a productive social inclusion, income, etc. In the 21st century, this category is losing strength because we have gone through a series of transformations so productive human labor is no longer of predominant importance. The nature of work has changed, being displaced by consumption because everyone consumes, even though not work. And the idea that is being defended is that tourism is a type of consumption that is special or that says a lot sociologically, as Giddens says, a lot about the current Society. This is so because it envelops, presupposes and needs a series of other previous achievements. Thus, it could be seen as an index (which presupposes a set of indicators) which is very representative (in a heuristic or methodological way) of a certain degree of social development of one society. So, the argument is that tourism consumption is important perhaps more than others because it is presupposing a series of previous basic achievements so that it can occur like this the person has to have a minimum income that needs to eat before traveling right so it needs to satisfy in the city basic economic material first second is not from the social point of view from the point of view of collective integration is not only identity the integration of the system is not only the tourist consumption the person that has this kind of action.

In short, the income level, as well as the volume of capital circulation, and the access to consumption are the factors experienced in tourism, which allows to the tourists having access to tourism itself and the tourist consumption. It represents (it is implied) a minimum income level, since the most elementary elements in the human scale of the hierarchy of needs must be satisfied on a permanent basis, and having access to tourism means that, in some way, those elements have been, at least partially, achieved. In this sense, when it occurs, tourism consumption express – directly or, most frequently, indirectly – a level of consumption which presupposes a minimum level a material needs satisfied previously. In doing so, this kind of conspicuous consumption (Veblen, 1899[1979]) express a certain kind of quality of life or human development achieved by a person or a society.

The person while in travel can integrate different social systems and can achieve a new kind of citizenship, accessing social spheres that others do not have, an extended citizenship, and this is very clearly visible when we talk about a tourist flow International tourism is not where mobility is not and this access to other nation states makes us have population segments that have a kind of global citizenship the person can circulate and frequent any spaces while others do not have.

So, from a social sociological point of view, we can say a new revision of the social contract of nations. The social barriers that include and exclude both when we revise the contract and update this social contract for the 21st century when we are talking about people who have this kind of access to capital, in terms of mobility, they can also expand their area of citizenship, they become global citizens. In doing so, he is accessing a kind of nation state that is not yet a UN state but he is accessing a kind of supra citizenship from that to national citizenship he is going to the international space being a global citizen while most are not, so what does this mean? human dignity which is what human rights defend ultimately right has a minimum standard of living with quality dignity for everyone so let's say the person who can do this has managed to meet other basic requirements and has reached this minimum level is not actually even higher than the others quality of life so it's another point is not it and a third argument that is the argument that from the point of view is both say individual and social as well as collective right the realization of this type of exchange there will not get more culture.

The third argument is that from the point of view of the individual as well as the social and collective point of view, the realization of this type of exchange is not only a cultural exchange with others, but it also allows an oxygenation and enrichment of the social system. As Roy Bhaskar (1980) points out, that is human flourishing, so other authors, not the ones who write them, are going to talk about human enrichment or human development. Thus, this personal achievement (development), also appears at the collective level as a form of cultural exchange, and yet at the societies' level as a systemic updating of the social systems. In this sense, social tourism can bring some contributions to for human flourishing by reactivate the ethical dimension inherent in human praxis, which is associated with the ineliminable processes of freedom development and transcendence.

For this process to occur, Bhaskar (1993) argues that transformations are necessary in the ontological and epistemic scopes to: (a) deny and overcome all sorts of constraints that are generalized in structures of domination, exploitation and control over throughout the social tissue, that are activated by moralized power relations and discourses that reify, fetishize and commodify social relations and establish a rhythm of life reproduction that impede the development of the political skill and practical wisdom necessary for an intentional, a holistic and a practical change to a way of life in which each human being manages to develop individually

Expanding and Updating Human Rights

freely, without blurring the links with nature and the social substantiality, that is, the collectivity and universality of gender; (b) moreover, deny the institutionalized forms of ideological legitimation and epistemic surveillance that block critical and transitional modes of theorizing and communication, in order to overcome unrealistic (non-transcendental) and deontological worldviews which reduce reality to epistemic and conservative assessments of the bourgeois world, and enable a hermeneutics based on the logic of transformative praxis, alectic truth and universalizability. In this sense, flourishing refers to the movement of change from restrictive causalities, the rhythmic process and the justifications that mediate the extremely alienating and unequal reproduction of people in everyday life, towards a society founded on universal human autonomy, with a libertarian, dialectical and universal axiology, whose logic will be "totalizing and oriented towards the real needs and interests of the concrete uniqueness of each individual", so that people can expand their rights (also have them recognized) and participate in society equally and with due resources (BHASKAR, 1993, p. 160).

Corroborating Bhaskar's ideas, Archer (2017) exposes contemporary society as being marketed by the predominance of morphogenetic processes that exponent the contradictions between what is 'new' and what is 'good'. That is, between processes that, on the one hand, enable and contribute to the incessant generation of new information, expansion of the creation of goods and the realization of services, thus contributing to the development and more complete use of capabilities of people, which, on the other hand, disconnect them from the community, imprison them in their particular universe, downgrade the forms of incentives to cooperation or redistributive measures and, not least, establish and generalize a normative crisis in the different dimensions of life. Because of this, Archer (2017) argues for the transformation of current society into a 'good society', so that it is guided by the creation of common and 'real relational' goods, that is, that have as a presupposition, and purpose, the concern, trust and reciprocity in relationships with others.

REFERENCES

Altavila, J. (1989). *Origem dos direitos dos povos* [Origin of the rights of peoples]. Ícone.

Alves, J. A. L. (1997). *A Arquitetura Internacional dos Direitos Humanos* [The International Architecture of Human Rights]. Ed. FTD.

Antunes, R. (2000). Trabalho e precarização numa ordem neoliberal. In *La Ciudadania Negada. Políticas de Exclusión en la Educación y el Trabajo*. CLACSO, Consejo Latinoamericano de Ciencias Sociales. Available at: https://bibliotecavirtual.clacso.org.ar/clacso/gt/20101010021549/3antunes.pdf

Archer, M. S. (2017). Introduction: has a morphogenic society arrived? In M. Archer (Ed.), *Morphogenesis and human flourishing* (pp. 29–43). Springer.

Barcellos-Mathiasi, F. (2021). *La Reforma Laboral generan precarización del trabajo?? Un estudio comparado entre las leyes de Reforma Laboral en Brasil y México* [Unpublished Doctoral Thesis]. Universidad Autónoma de Sinaloa y Universidad Federal de Juiz de Fora. Culiacán, Sinaloa, México y Juiz de Fora, Minas Gerais, Brasil.

Barcellos-Mathiasi, F. B., & Duarte-Pimentel, T. D. (2019). El Neoliberalismo en el Mundo y la Precarización del Trabajo: un estudio histórico comparado en Alemania, España, Reino Unido, Italia, Brasil y México. Teoria Jurídica Contemporânea, v. Esp, p. 62-88.

Barcellos-Mathiasi, F. B., & Duarte-Pimentel, T. D. (2020). Trabajo decente versus precariedad laboral: La acción sindical como elemento para el desarrollo de los derechos humanos laborales. *Revista Interdisciplinar De Direitos Humanos*, *8*, 1–292.

Barcellos-Mathiasi, F., & Duarte-Pimentel, T. (2021). Estado nacional, ciudadanía y calidad laboral. *Revista Espiga*, *20*(42), 1–22. doi:10.22458/re.v20i42.3631

Bhaskar, R. R. (1980). Scientific Explanation and Human Emancipation. *Radical Philosophy*, *26*, 1980.

Bhaskar, R. (1993). *Dialectic: The pulse of freedom*. Verso.

Bauman, Z. (2008). *Vida para consumo*. Zahar.

Biagi, B., Ladu, M. G., & Royuela, V. (2017). Human development and tourism specialization. Evidence from a panel of developed and developing countries. *International Journal of Tourism Research*, *19*(2), 160–178. doi:10.1002/jtr.2094

Bianchi, R. V., & Stephenson, M. L. (2013). Deciphering Tourism and Citizenship in a Globalized World. *Tourism Management*, *39*, 10–20.

Bobbio, N. (1992). *A era dos direitos* [The Age of Rights]. Campus.

Bourdieu, P. Social Space and Symbolic Power. Sociological Theory, vol. 7, n°. 1, (Spring, 1989), pp. 14-25, [Published by: American Sociological Association. Stable URL: <http://www.jstor.org/stable/202060>]. Acess: 15 jan. 2012.

Expanding and Updating Human Rights

Brenner, N. (2018). *Espaços da urbanização: o urbano a partir da teoria crítica.* Observatório das Metrópoles.

Brenner, N., & Shimid, C. (2016). La "era urbana" en debate. *EURE (Santiago), 42*(127), 307–339. doi:10.4067/S0250-71612016000300013

Butcher, J. (2017). Citizenship, Global Citizenship and Volunteer Tourism: A Critical Analysis. *Tourism Recreation Research, 42*(2), 129–138. doi:10.1080/025 08281.2017.1295172

Cárdenas-García, P. J., Sánchez-Rivero, M., & Pulido-Fernández, J. I. (2015). Does tourism growth influence economic development? *Journal of Travel Research, 54*(2), 206–221. doi:10.1177/0047287513514297

César, A. A. D. (2015). El turismo: ¿un modelo funcional al capitalismo? *RLAT, 1*(1), 16–26.

César, A. A. D., Arnaiz, S. M. B., & César, F. C. (2017). *Capitalismo, Sociedad y Turismo.* Universidad de Guadalajara.

Coles, T. (2008). Citizenship and the state: hidden features in the internationalisation of tourism. In T. Coles & C. M. Hall (Eds.), *International Business and Tourism.* Routledge.

Coulanges, F. d. (2005). *A Cidade Antiga* [The Ancient City] (H. d. Burati, Trans.). Rideel.

Croes, R., Ridderstaat, J., & Shapoval, V. (2020). Extending tourism competitiveness to human development. *Annals of Tourism Research, 80*, 102825. doi:10.1016/j. annals.2019.102825

Giddens, A. (1991). *As conseqüências da modernidade.* Editora UNESP.

Giddens, A. (2008). *Sociologia* [Sociology.] (6th ed., A. Figueiredo & A. P. D. Baltazar, Trans.). Fundação Calouste Gulbenkian.

Gurvitch, G. (1946). *The Bill of Social Rights.* International Universities Press.

Hall, C. M. (2005). *Tourism: Rethinking the Social Science of Mobility.* Sintesis.

Harvey, D. (2008). *A Condição Pós-Moderna* (17th ed.). Edições Loyola. (Original work published 1989)

Higgins-Desbiolles, F. (2006). More than an "industry": The forgotten power of tourism as a social force. *Tourism Management, 27*, 1192–1208.

Hobsbawn, E. J. (1991). *A Era das Revoluções: Europa 1789 -1848* [The Age of Revolutions: Europe 1789 -1848.] (M. T. L. Teixeira & M. Penchel, Trans.). Paz e Terra.

Hobsbawn, E. J. (1995). *A Era dos Extremos: o breve século XX (1914-1991)* [The Age of Extremes: the brief twentieth century (1914-1991)] (M. Santarrita, Trans.). Companhia das Letras.

Hunt, L. (2009). *A invenção dos Direitos Humanos: Uma História* [The Invention of Human Rights: A History] (R. Eichenberg, Trans.). Companhia das Letras.

International Labor Organization (ILO) (2021). Serie Panorama Laboral en América Latina y el Caribe 2021. Nota técnica: Hacia una recuperación sostenible del empleo en el sector del turismo en América Latina y el Caribe.

Jameson, F. (1984). Posmodernism, or, The cultural Logic of Late Capitalism. *New Left Review*, 146.

Jameson, F. (1991). *Ensayos sobre el posmodernismo*. Ediciones Imago Mundi.

Korstanje, M. E., & George, B. (2022). *The Nature and Future of Tourism: a Post-COVID-19 Context*. Apple Academic Press, Inc. doi:10.1201/9781003277507

Korstanje, M. E., Gowreesunkar, V. G. B., & Maingi, S. W. (2023). *Tourism in Crisis*. Nova Science Publishers, Inc. doi:10.52305/JQWY2999

Koščˇak, M., & O'Rourke, T. (2021). Post-Pandemic Sustainable Tourism Management: The new reality of managing ethical and responsible tourism. Taylor & Francis Group/Routledge Focus.

McCabe, S., & Qiao, G. (2020). A review of research into social tourism: Launching the Annals of Tourism Research Curated Collection on Social Tourism. *Annals of Tourism Research*, *85*, 1–19. doi:10.1016/j.annals.2020.103103

Nealon, J. T. (2012). *Post-Postmodernism or, The Cultural Logic of Just-in-Time Capitalism*. Stanford University Press. doi:10.1515/9780804783217

Nisbet, R. (n.d.). *La formación del pensamiento sociológico*. Buenos Aires: Amorrotu Editores.

Ouriques, H. R. (2012). O turismo internacional na economia-mundo capitalista: Elementos para uma crítica. *Acta Scientiarum, Human and Social Sciences*, *34*(2), 147–157.

Paes De Paula, A. P., & Paes, K. D. (2021). *Fordismo, pós-fordismo e ciberfordismo: os (des)caminhos da Indústria 4.0. Cadernos EBAPE.BR* (4th ed., Vol. 19). Oct-Dec.

Parsons, T. (1974). *O Sistema das Sociedades Modernas*. Pioneira.

Pulido-Fernández, J. I., & Cárdenas-García, P. J. (2021). Analyzing the Bidirectional Relationship between Tourism Growth and Economic Development. *Journal of Travel Research*, *60*(3), 583–602. doi:10.1177/0047287520922316

Rosa, H. (2019). *Aceleração: a transformação das estruturas temporais na Modernidade* (R. Silveira, Trans.). UNESP.

Roser, M., & Herre, B. (2017) – "Tourism". Published online at OurWorldInData. org. https://ourworldindata.org/tourism

Sousa Santos, B. (2006). *Reinventar la Democracia. Reinventar el estado*. Consejo Latinoamericano de Ciencias Sociales / CLACSO.

Telfer, D. J., & Sharpley, R. (2008). *Tourism and Development in the Developing World*. Routledge.

Touraine, A. (1971). *The Post-Industrial Society: Tomorrow's Social History: Classes, Conflicts and Culture in the Programmed Society*. Random House.

Veblen, T. (1979). *The Theory of the Leisure Class*. Penguin Books. (Original work published 1899)

World Travel and Tourism Concil (WTTC). (2022a). France's Travel & Tourism could surpass pre-pandemic levels in 2023. Disponible en: https://wttc.org/News-Article/Frances-Travel-and-Tourism-could-surpass-pre-pandemic-levels-in-2023#:~:text=Before%20the%20pandemic%2C%20France's%20Travel,representing%20a%20staggering%2045.8%25%20loss. Acceso en: 20 ago. 2022.

World Travel and Tourism Concil (WTTC). (2022b). United States: Annual Research: Key Highlights. Disponible en: https://wttc.org/Research/Economic-Impact Acceso en: 20 ago. 2022.

ADDITIONAL READING

Boukhris, L.; Chapuis, A. (2016). Circulations, espace et pouvoir - Penser le tourisme pour penser le politique. *Géographies politiques du tourisme, 28*(1), 1-21.

César, A. A. D. (2015). El turismo: ¿un modelo funcional al capitalismo? *Rev. Latino-Am. Turismologia / RELAT*, 1(1), p.16-26.

César, A. A. D., Arnaiz, S. M. B., & César, F. C. (2017). *Capitalismo, Sociedad y Turismo*. Universidad de Guadalajara.

Corbari, S. D. (2021). Turismo e capitaloceno: uma primeira aproximação. *Rev. Latino-Am. Turismologia*, *7*, 1 – 9.

Drath, R., & Horch, A. (2014). Industrie 4.0: Hit or hype? *IEEE Industrial Electronics Magazine*, *8*(2), 56–58. doi:10.1109/MIE.2014.2312079

Harvey, D. (2008b). El Neoliberalismo como Destrucción Creativa. *Revista Apuntes del CENES*, *27*(45), 1–25.

Harvey, D. (2013b). *Os Limites do Capital*. Boitempo.

Harvey, D. (2014). *Diecisiete contradicciones del capital y el fin del neoliberalismo*. Traficantes de Sueños.

Hiernaux-Nicolás, D. (2006). Geografía del Turismo. In Tratado de Geografía Humana. Mexico: UAM.

Higgins-Desbiolles, F. (2006). More than an "industry": The forgotten power of tourism as a social force. *Tourism Management*, *27*(6), 1192–1208. doi:10.1016/j.tourman.2005.05.020

Higgins-Desbiolles, F. (2008). Justice Tourism and Alternative Globalisation. *Journal of Sustainable Tourism*, *16*(3), 345–364. doi:10.1080/09669580802154132

Higgins-Desbiolles, F. (2009). International Solidarity Movement: A case study in volunteer tourism for justice. *Annals of Leisure Research*, *12*(3-4), 3–4, 333–349. doi:10.1080/11745398.2009.9686828

Higgins-Desbiolles, F. (2018). The potential for justice through tourism. *Via*, *13*(13), 110. doi:10.4000/viatourism.2469

Jeannite, S.; Lapointe, D. (2016). La production de l'espace touristique de l'Île-à-Vache (Haïti): illustration du processus de développement géographique inégal. *Études caribéennes*, *33*, 34, p.1-12.

Jurdao, F. A. (1990). *España en Venta*. Endymion.

Jurdao, F. A. (1992). *Los Mitos del turismo*. Endymion.

Mantecón, A. (2020). La crisis sistémica del turismo: una perspectiva global en tiempos de pandemia. In *Turismo pos-COVID-19 Reflexiones, retos y oportunidades*. Universidad de La Laguna.

Expanding and Updating Human Rights

Piccarozzi, M., Aquilani, B., & Gatti, C. (2018). Industry 4.0 in Management Studies: A Systematic Literature Review. *Sustainability (Basel)*, *10*(10), 1–24. doi:10.3390u10103821

Raga, M. (2019). *Tourism: the false fix – concentration of profits and social debt.* Barcelona: Observatory of the Debt in Globalization (ODG).

Ramos, A. G. (1981). *A nova ciência das organizações: uma reconceituação da riqueza das nações*. Editora FGV.

Smith, N. (2020). *Desarrollo desigual. Naturaleza, capital y la producción del espacio*. Traficantes de Sueños.

Tomassini, L., & Lamond, I. (2022). Rethinking the space of tourism, its power-geometries, and spatial justice. *Journal of Sustainable Tourism*, 1–14. Advance online publication. doi:10.1080/09669582.2022.2091141

Turner, L., & Ash, J. (1991). *La Horda Dorada. El turismo internacional y la periferia del placer*. Endymión.

Wynberg, R., & Hauck, M. (2014). People, power, and the coast: A conceptual framework for understanding and implementing benefit sharing. *Ecology and Society*, *19*(1), 27. doi:10.5751/ES-06250-190127

KEY TERMS AND DEFINITIONS

4.0 Industry: Industry 4.0 has emerged from the overlap between the financialization of the economy and an exacerbated neoliberalism, intensifying the use of digital technologies in production systems and the replacement of human labor (Antunes, 2019).

Conspicuous Consumption: Conspicuous consumption has typically analyzed how people spend money on products that signal status (Bellezza et al., 2017).

Cyber Fordism: Cyber Fordism is a production model that preserves flexibility and the search for quality as well as cost reduction, like classic Fordism, but requires new interfaces between man and machine and between machines, marked by reduced human labor and increased automation (Paes-De-Paula, Paes, 2021).

Global Citizenship: The term global citizenship denotes the commitment to avoid the increase of world poverty and the destruction of ancient cultures and the natural environment, and also the complexity of individual connections with international law and overlapping political institutions in a globalized world (Carter, 2001).

Social Rights: Social rights are rights of citizens to receive services such as food, health care, housing, and social security (Landau, 2012, p. 190).

ENDNOTES

[1] For example, in Antigua and Barbuda tourism contributed 42.7% of GDP; in Saint Lucia with 40.7%; the Bahamas with 43.3%; Belize with 37.2%; Uruguay with 16.4% and Mexico with 15.5% (ILO, 2021), just to mention a few. On the other hand, France (a country that receives the most tourists in the world and is the third country in the world that receives the most tourism revenues [UNWTO, 2020]) had a contribution of tourism in GDP of 8.4% in 2019 (WTTC, 2022a). The United States (the third most tourist-receiving country in the world and the first country in the world with the highest tourism receipts [UNWTO, 2020]), had a tourism contribution to GDP of 8.8% (WTTC, 2022b).

[2] On the other hand, undeveloped or developing countries that tend to have partially or completely developed tourism structures and systems selectively exploit some key elements of certain segments and give access to the domestic market only to a negligible portion of their societies, thus tending to generate a negative balance of payments balance between inflow of foreign tourists and outflow of domestic tourists abroad. Exceptions occur in the case of countries whose economy is highly specialized and dependent on the tourism sector, generally small countries like Fiji or Jamaica), or even in larger countries like Mexico, but due to the proximity of the issuing markets, the United States and Canada, whose share of the Mexican tourism market reaches almost 90%.

Chapter 4

Dark Tourism and Human Rights:
A Philosophical Quandary?

Maximiliano Emanuel Korstanje
iD https://orcid.org/0000-0002-5149-1669
University of Palermo, Argentina

ABSTRACT

Over the recent years, scholars have focused their attention on dark tourism as a newly emerging and global trend. Without any doubt, dark tourism remains a more-than-interesting object of study for social scientists and academia. At first glimpse, dark tourism exhibits a new morbid taste generated in post-disaster contexts, as well as environments of mass death and suffering. Paradoxically, dark consumption opens a much deeper question revolving around human rights. This chapter interrogates the intersection of dark consumption (as a type of commoditizing process) and human rights. As Zygmunt Bauman puts it, one of the paradoxes of memorizing the tragedy is that its roots are ultimately forgotten. In consonance with this, the authors hold the thesis that dark tourism enhances resiliency and local community, but at the same time, it generates a biased story of what should be memorized.

INTRODUCTION

Not surprisingly, the dilemma of human rights has impregnated all levels of social sciences and beyond. Since the end of WWII, scholars interrogated furtherly the violence perpetrated against ethnic minorities as well as the urgency to make the necessary institution not to repeat "this holocaust" in the future (Keet 2012). Human

DOI: 10.4018/978-1-6684-8726-6.ch004

Copyright © 2023, IGI Global. Copying or distributing in print or electronic forms without written permission of IGI Global is prohibited.

rights have been thought to protect the lay-citizens from the abuse or crimes of the proper state. At a closer look, human rights, have been contemplated as a necessary step to protect not only the basic rights but also the privacy of lay citizens. The paradox seems to be given by the fact the same state which serves as the WatchGuard of human rights violates them under some conditions (Levy & Sznaider 2006). Of course, this debate is not new and remains open in the fields of humanism and the core of academic debate (Ignatieff 2011; Frezzo 2014). In consonance with this, human rights have certainly entered the core of tourism research as a result of different combined factors. At first glimpse, the lack of legal follow-up of governments to monitor clandestine and criminal activities such as human trafficking or child prostitution. It is very difficult for authorities to implement efficient policies that scrutinize closely and globally the demands of these activities. Eli Roth´s film *Hostel* amply narrates the sad story of three young tourists who are kidnapped, tortured and killed by millionaire tourists taking part in a dark and criminal network in Eastern Europe. Tourists not only are vulnerable to criminal activities but also in some cases, they are active players in atrocious acts; what is more important, leisure activities go a much deep sinister direction where the "Other´s pain" is the main commodity to exchange (Korstanje & Olsen 2011; Korstanje & Tarlow 2012). Having said this, human rights encompass not only the security of tourists but also locals. Over the recent years, some studies have alerted on the importance to instrumentalize "dark tourism" as an efficient form of recovery just after a disaster takes a hit. Dark, Thana or post-disaster tourism revitalizes obliterated zones while accelerating the recovery timeframe without mentioning the reciprocity between victims and outsiders (Miller, Gonzalez & Hutter, 2017; Martini & Buda 2020). Soulard et al (2022) argue convincingly that one of the main lessons given by dark tourism rests on activating a memorizing process for the traumatic event not to be repeated in the future. This process is very well applied to the Holocaust and other manslaughters. Dark tourism enhances efficiently social cohesion (among survivors) as well as solidarity equating all persons before the tragedy. In this vein, dark tourism shows potential for emotional mobilization in the context of genocide, ethnic cleansing and extreme violence. To some extent, dark tourism proffers a pedagogic nature educating visitors through dark experiences. In Phillip Stone´s terms, dark tourism exhibits a necessary attempt to understand the own finitude through the significant "Other death" (Stone 2012; Raine 2013). This begs a more than interesting question: is dark tourism seen as a mechanism to reaffirm the importance of human rights or simply an ideological driver that ultimately tergiversates the roots of events to protect status-quo?

The present book chapter centers on the dilemma of dark tourism and human rights, in the context of post-disaster, violence and genocide. This moot point remains overlooked by Academia as well as the specialized literature. The goals of this contribution are twofold. On one hand, we focused on the literature and emerging definitions of dark tourism. On another, we put a critical debate on how human rights and social memory can be molded to the economic interests of international demand.

DARK TOURISM, DARK CONSUMPTION

It is important to note that dark tourism circumscribes as a new emerging segment or nice of consumption mainly moved by persons who visit spaces of mass death, genocide, extermination or suffering. The broad specter of dark tourism leads to some generalizations and problems to operationalize variables and definitions. The burgeoning interest of academics, scholars and fieldworkers in dark consumption has ushered the discipline into a knowledge dispersion where terms are not correctly defined. The opposite is equally true, dark tourism condenses a set of different or similar activities such as war tourism, mourning tourism, thana tourism, and prison tourism only to name a few (Hooper & Lennon 2016). Dark tourism occupies a central position in the academic discourse as a key driver towards economic revitalization in post-disaster or post-conflict zones (Korstanje & Ivanov, 2012; Isaac, Cakmak & Butler, 2019). Dark tourism is classically defined as a new niche psychologically motivated to visit (if not experience) spaces of mass death, suffering or destruction. Dark consumption includes sites of macabre experiences or torture, or post-disaster spaces, without mentioning haunted houses, or prisons (Light 2017). The specialized publications can be grouped into three clear-cut families: a) the anthropological wave, b) heritage management, and c) the critical turn.

Anthropological Wave

At a closer look, some voices have applauded the idea that dark consumption derives from the anthropological attempt to domesticate death in secularized society, which means to give sense to death in a world where spiritual transcendence is withered away. As a way of understanding the own finitude through the Other´s death, dark tourism engages directly with one of the mysteries of this world, *the afterlife* (Stone & Sharpley, 2008; Stone et al 2018; Powell & Kennell 2016). To these studies, humankind has developed a strange fascination for death, because it is the only drive which cannot be controlled. In view of this, human fascination for death is nothing new. Anyway, dark tourism contains an important element this school dubbed as Thanatosis which means the reflexive interpretation of life through the "Other´s death". Likewise, visitors look not only to understand their own lives but also to give legitimacy to their institutions and environments. For the anthropological wave, dark tourism is a postmodern phenomenon derived from the secularizing process which altered how the afterlife is ultimately imagined (Seaton 1996; Miles 2014; Sharpley 2006).

Heritage Management

For this school, dark tourism should be interpreted as a rite resulting from dark heritage consumption. These works emphasize not only that disasters take place in a specific territory but also eloquently move collective emotions towards the construction of a shared heritage which is memorized and venerated so that the affected community avoids a similar traumatic event in future. Heritage management alludes to dark tourism as a rite of passage, a type of pilgrimage that opens the doors between here-now and there-tomorrow (Collins-Kreiner 2016). Visitors simply are in quest of outstanding experiences based on tragedies, disasters and traumatic events. Beyond their motivation, dark tourists show a manifest interest in historical facts or history. In this way, consumption combines the subject experiences proper of visitors with the intrinsic and symbolic meaning assigned to the site. Having said this, the dark experience is mainly based on the need of learning as well as a deep empathy marked by the desire to see to believe (Biran, Poria & Oren 2011). In Tarlow´s terms, a type of nostalgia for disasters and the past time (Tarlow 2007). Last but not least, there is a clear dissociation between those sites where the real tragic events took place, and those replicated to rememorizing a certain tragedy. This happens simply because in nature dark tourism follows an educational nature (Cohen 2011).

The Radical Turn

The radical turn should be seen as an academic wave mainly formed by critical studies which see dark tourism as a new mechanism of hegemony and control over the periphery. To some extent, the political power intervenes in the heritage formation (just after a disaster) to tergiversate the real reasons behind the event (Sather-Wagstaff, 2016a; 2016b). What are more important, dark tourists who come from developed nations have little knowledge of the crime perpetrated by their nations in the colonial period. By this token, dark tourism cements the center-periphery dependency forged during the colonial era (Tzanelli 2016). Other works focus on dark tourism as a sadist play where visitors look to reaffirm their institutions and beliefs exorcising death to the non-Western "Other" which is packaged as inferior and vulnerable (Korstanje 2016). The critical turn holds the polemic thesis that dark tourism acts as an ideological instrument that commoditizes the "Other´s death" in form of a palpable and profitable spectacle. One of the contributions of this wave consists in putting a dilemma around dark tourism. If disasters become the main commodity to exchange there is no clear basis to what extent dark tourism helps the community or simply prepares it for the next disaster. At the time the reasons behind the event have been forgotten the possibility of a new calamity turning higher. In num, in dark tourism lies a sadist drive oriented to understand death as a sign of inferiority as well as a spiritual weakness (Bowman & Pezzulo, 2009; Korstanje 2020; Tzanelli & Korstanje 2019).

GENOCIDES AND SOCIAL MEMORY

Beyond any discrepancy, heritage, social memory and disasters are inevitably entwined. Maria Tumarkin coins the term *traumaescape* to denote the individual or collective adscription to mourning-related sites. Per her viewpoint, disasters and catastrophes are sudden events that shock cultures while accelerating radical shifts in social institutions, but at a closer look, they had the power to re-condition human existence. She narrates and describes how different tragedies attract thousands of tourists weeks later creating a vast memorial mainly marked by psychological trauma. This happens because disasters often transform places inscribing an uncanny sense of belonging where visitors engage during their stay. This sentiment of engagement is based on the human solidarity activated just after a disaster takes room. Social memory sublimates collective suffering through the creation of limonoid spaces where events are memorized and forgotten at the same time. As she puts it, a traumatic experience, a word which derives from psychiatry, speaks to us of a person who is overwhelmed by a traumatic event. Hand-tied with keeping a fresh reminder or looking back to the past, the person experiences the world in a type of zigzag. Traumatized people are far from understanding their worlds, unless by calling for a partial reliving of an unaccepted past. Having said this, traumatized persons are pressed to live with a past which interrogates them, as an intruder not as welcome guests. The trauma is ultimately contained not in the event as it has historically occurred, but in how it is tergiversated and rememorized. Over time, these experiences would be replicated by the construction of dark memorials Tumarkin dubbed "traumascapes" (Tumarkin, 2001, 2005, 2019). It is important to clarify this concept of trauma is not associated with a psychological state, but with a collective mobilization sometimes manipulated by authorities or following political ends. From the same point departs Joy Sather-Wagstaff who argues convincingly that death makes equal all human beings but the intervention of politics is framed by legitimating specific practices. To wit, she mentions the example of 9/11, a traumatic event that woke up the solidarity of all nations in the US. At the time, this solidarity sets the pace for apathy and discontent when Bush`s administration disposed of two unilateral invasions. As Sather-Wagstaff eloquently observes, unlike memory which is articulated through the knowledge incorporated in the experience, heritage is socially constructed engaging with landscapes, individual performance and narratives. Heritage is far from describing historical facts [as they happened] but gathering selected piecemeal fragments to cement a collective memory. In view of this, heritage is political and an arbitrary driver towards an ideologized past. Death opens the doors to a collective sense of loss which is filled by different sublimations. Dark tourism acts as a catalyst between a sad present and the future. What disasters precisely remind us is the irreversibility of death and that we need a reason to live. In this respect, dark tourists engage with the "Other`s pain" but once the sentiment is packaged and commoditized, visitors go far from hearing the truth. Dark tourism also sells fabricated stories revolving around mass death and mourning while legitimating the interests of status-quo. The figure of heritage domesticates unilaterally the trauma moving resources towards a unified narrative. The monopoly of meaning, which is often disputed by various groups, is homogenized in the hands of the ruling elite. Anyway, dark tourists struggle with governments to negotiate their meanings and experiences at the dark sites (Sather-Wagstaff, 2015, 2016a, 2016b). In consonance with this, Rodanthi Tzanelli (2016) holds a more than interesting argument which needs to be discussed. The ethical dilemma of dark tourism is given by what she names "the cinematic representation of risk". This representation mediates (as a parallel reality) between sightseers and natives. The media coverage as well as the interest of the cinema in disasters creates the conditions towards a pseudo-reality where workers are immobilized. Stuck by the screen, citizens are unable to discern the reasons behind disasters though they enjoy the effects. Likewise, capitalism recycles itself through the imposition of a destructive creation (citing Schumpeter). Tzanelli discusses to what extent dark tourism flourishes recently in devastated areas or poor (slum) life conditions, most of them provoked by colonial exploitation in former centuries. These dark zones which are characterized by extreme poverty resulted from decades of exploitation and violence perpetrated by European powers. Nowadays, European citizens enjoy visiting these dark sites ignoring (or at least pretending) the role played by their states in the bloody past. The inflation of some global risks works as the locus of a polyphonic hermeneutics based on a multiple sense of places where death is the protagonist. To put the same simply, dark tourism offers a fertile ground for global capitalism to trade with the "Other`s pain" reaffirming the asymmetries of the colonial order. These inequalities (between North and South) are certainly legitimized through the creation of dark narratives, as Tzanelli brilliantly concludes (Tzanelli, 2015, 2016, 2021). This point poses a more than pungent dilemma around the figure of human rights. The question of whether dark memorials are orchestrated to remind us how important human rights are, says little about what we dub *"the banality of dark tourism"*. In his seminal book *Liquid Fear* Zygmunt Bauman explains that one of

Dark Tourism and Human Rights

the dangers of commoditizing disasters lies in the fact society tends to forget the origins or the preconditions that led to the state of disaster. This invariably means that the probability to experience a similar event make higher (Bauman, 2013). For the sake of clarity, the matter will be discussed with accuracy in the next section.

DARK TOURISM AND HUMAN RIGHTS

Although the specialized publications in the field of dark tourism have notably triplicated in recent years, less attention was certainly given to the intersection of dark tourism and human rights. As Sarah Lischer (2019) noted, dark tourism acts as a double-edged sword in the formation of genocide memorials as well as the application of human rights conventions. On one hand, tourists interact with a troublesome past that ultimately interrogates their finitude. On another, these narratives are unilaterally monopolized by governments dehumanizing victims and discouraging an adequate context for uninformed tourists. To some extent, genocide memorials help survivors to deal with the deepness of trauma. The power of speaking or sharing an experience leads invariably to the gift of being heard. In that way, dark tourism offers an environment to recover a ravaged society by restoring sanitized political power. However, at a closer look, the spectacle of genocide, as the author puts it, mainly developed by Western visitors affirms an unspoken dehumanizing aspect of modern tourism giving priority to an exclusionary version of the facts. The reversal is equally true, some international donors keep some pressure to impose specific narratives that display a part of the story. With the benefits of hindsight, the author goes on to write:

The dark tourists in search of an authentic, unmediated encounter with past suffering will remain unfulfilled, however. Ironically, many visitors do not realise that the 'real killing fields, for example, have been carefully curated and publicised to promote the chosen government narrative. The authenticity of human bones is not in dispute. Foreigners may find it difficult to honour the authenticity of piles of human bones while simultaneously questioning the authenticity of the surrounding narrative. (Lischer, 2019, p. 9)

Some critical studies have turned attention to the employment of marketing to make a disaster a simple spectacle. Per these voices, this not only represents an over-simplification of the genocide [as well as its origins] but also an objectivation of human suffering. The fascination for these sites overlooks often the role of the state in the right violations. In the case of South Africa, Argentina, and Cambodia, the state has systematically inflicted considerable harm on their citizens. Rather, local residents make the decision to emphasize the daily lives or the economic benefits of tourism to revitalize a beaten society. In so doing, the show rests on the need of replaying the atrocity once and once again. Having said this, visitors accept or negotiate their version of the tragedy which is previously determined by their biographies, their experiences and their attachment to social institutions. The paradox precisely lies in the fact dark tourism may very well legitimate an authoritarian regime that offers a dark spectacle based on its own crimes (Lischer, 2019; Soulard et al., 2022; Korstanje & Baker, 2018). For some reason, the politics of dark tourism remains unexplored in the literature. Last but not least, starting from the premise that (genocide) memorials pave the pathways for the rise of a shared and unified narrative that heal a bloody past, no less true seems to be that the theatricalization of these types of sites leads to gridlock. At first glimpse, memorials help society to understand a much deeper traumatic past to face a new promising future. But when the causes of the genocide are covered or biased, the event is packaged and commercialized as a fascinating story. This would improve the local economy if some conditions are granted, but in the long run, so to say it transforms the disaster into a commodity. The commoditization of disasters is not organized to prevent the next disaster, but to replicate it adapting society to suffering. Hence, when this happens, not only the lesson is corrupted, but also the disaster will repeat again. The commodity situates as the main exchange in a society oriented to consume the "Other`s death" cyclically (Korstanje 2016).

CONCLUSION

At the time, I am finishing this book chapter I received a new review invitation to inspect a dark tourism article. In 2022, I have certainly reviewed almost more than 120 papers for tourism-related journals as well as sociological journals. This reflects not only the interests of social sciences in dark tourism consumption but also the divergence of viewpoints around the same issue. This book chapter has been innovative in entering into a new discussion. I have focused on the connection of dark tourism with human rights conventions. As stated, scholars have focused their attention on dark tourism as a newly emerging and global trend. Without any doubt, dark tourism remains a more than interesting object of study for social scientists and Academia. At first glimpse, dark tourism exhibits a new morbid taste generated in post-disaster contexts, as well as environments of mass death and suffering. Paradoxically, dark consumption opens a much deep question revolving around human rights. This book chapter interrogates furtherly the intersection of dark consumption (as a type of commoditizing process) and human rights. As Zygmunt Bauman puts it, one of the paradoxes of memorizing the tragedy is that its roots are ultimately forgotten.

Dark Tourism and Human Rights

In consonance with this, we hold the thesis dark tourism enhances resiliency and local community but at the same time, it generates a biased story of what should be memorized.

REFERENCES

Bauman, Z. (2013). *Liquid fear*. John Wiley & Sons.

Bowman, M. S., & Pezzullo, P. C. (2009). What's so 'dark about 'dark tourism'?: Death, tours, and performance. *Tourist Studies*, *9*(3), 187–202. doi:10.1177/1468797610382699

Cohen, E. H. (2011). Educational dark tourism at an populo site: The Holocaust Museum in Jerusalem. *Annals of Tourism Research*, *38*(1), 193–209. doi:10.1016/j.annals.2010.08.003

Collins-Kreiner, N. (2016). Dark tourism as/is pilgrimage. *Current Issues in Tourism*, *19*(12), 1185–1189. doi:10.1080/13683500.2015.1078299

Frezzo, M. (2014). *The sociology of human rights*. John Wiley & Sons.

Hooper, G., & Lennon, J. (2016). *Dark tourism*. Taylor & Francis. doi:10.4324/9781315575865

Ignatieff, M. (2011). Human rights as idolatry. In *Human rights as politics and idolatry* (pp. 53–98). Princeton University Press.

Isaac, R. K., Çakmak, E., & Butler, R. (Eds.). (2019). *Tourism and hospitality in conflict-ridden destinations*. Routledge. doi:10.4324/9780429463235

Keet, A. (2012). Discourse, betrayal, critique: The renewal of human rights education. In *Safe spaces* (pp. 5–27). Brill. doi:10.1007/978-94-6091-936-7_2

Korstanje, M. E. (2016). *The rise of thana-capitalism and tourism*. Routledge. doi:10.4324/9781315457482

Korstanje, M. E. (2020). *The dark tourist: Consuming dark spaces in the periphery. In Tourism, terrorism and security*. Emerald. doi:10.1108/9781838679057

Korstanje, M. E., & Baker, D. (2018). Politics of dark tourism: The case of Cromanon and ESMA, Buenos Aires, Argentina. In *The Palgrave Handbook of Dark Tourism Studies* (pp. 533–552). Palgrave Macmillan. doi:10.1057/978-1-137-47566-4_22

Korstanje, M. E., & Ivanov, S. H. (2012). Tourism as a form of new psychological resilience: The inception of dark tourism. *SSRN*, *6*(4), 56–71. doi:10.2139srn.2168400

Korstanje, M. E., & Olsen, D. H. (2011). The discourse of risk in horror movies posts 9/11: Hospitality and hostility in perspective. *International Journal of Tourism Anthropology*, *1*(3), 304–317. doi:10.1504/IJTA.2011.043712

Korstanje, M. E., & Tarlow, P. (2012). Being lost: Tourism, risk and vulnerability in the post-'9/11'entertainment industry. *Journal of Tourism and Cultural Change*, *10*(1), 22–33. doi:10.1080/14766825.2011.639455

Levy, D., & Sznaider, N. (2006). Sovereignty transformed: Sociology of human rights 1. *The British Journal of Sociology*, *57*(4), 657–676. doi:10.1111/j.1468-4446.2006.00130.x PMID:17168943

Light, D. (2017). Progress in dark tourism and thanatourism research: An uneasy relationship with heritage tourism. *Tourism Management*, *61*, 275–301. doi:10.1016/j.tourman.2017.01.011

Lischer, S. K. (2019). Narrating atrocity: Genocide memorials, dark tourism, and the politics of memory. *Review of International Studies*, *45*(5), 805–827. doi:10.1017/S0260210519000226

Martini, A., & Buda, D. M. (2020). Dark tourism and affect: Framing places of death and disaster. *Current Issues in Tourism*, *23*(6), 679–692. doi:10.1080/13683500.2018.1518972

Miles, S. (2014). Battlefield sites as dark tourism attractions: An analysis of experience. *Journal of Heritage Tourism*, *9*(2), 134–147. doi:10.1080/1743873X.2013.871017

Miller, D. S., Gonzalez, C., & Hutter, M. (2017). Phoenix tourism within dark tourism: Rebirth, rebuilding and rebranding of tourist destinations following disasters. *Worldwide Hospitality and Tourism Themes*, *9*(2), 196–215. doi:10.1108/WHATT-08-2016-0040

Powell, R., & Kennell, J. (2016). Dark cities? Developing a methodology for researching dark tourism in European cities. In *Tourism and culture in the age of innovation* (pp. 303–319). Springer. doi:10.1007/978-3-319-27528-4_21

Raine, R. (2013). A dark tourist spectrum. *International Journal of Culture, Tourism and Hospitality Research*, *7*(3), 242–256. doi:10.1108/IJCTHR-05-2012-0037

Sather-Wagstaff, J. (2015). Heritage and memory. In *The Palgrave handbook of contemporary heritage research* (pp. 191–204). Palgrave Macmillan. doi:10.1057/9781137293565_12

Sather-Wagstaff, J. (2016a). *Heritage that hurts: Tourists in the memoryscapes of September 11*. Routledge. doi:10.4324/9781315427539

Sather-Wagstaff, J. (2016b). Making polysense of the world: Affect, memory, heritage. In *Heritage, affect and emotion* (pp. 30–48). Routledge.

Seaton, A. V. (1996). Guided by the dark: From thanatopsis to thanatourism. *International Journal of Heritage Studies*, *2*(4), 234–244. doi:10.1080/13527259608722178

Sharpley, R. (2006). Travels to the edge of darkness: Towards a typology of "dark tourism". In *Taking tourism to the limits* (pp. 239–250). Routledge.

Soulard, J., Stewart, W., Larson, M., & Samson, E. (2022). Dark Tourism and Social Mobilization: Transforming Travelers After Visiting a Holocaust Museum. *Journal of Travel Research*.

Stone, P., & Sharpley, R. (2008). Consuming dark tourism: A thanatological perspective. *Annals of Tourism Research*, *35*(2), 574–595. doi:10.1016/j.annals.2008.02.003

Stone, P. R. (2012). Dark tourism and significant other death: Towards a model of mortality mediation. *Annals of Tourism Research*, *39*(3), 1565–1587. doi:10.1016/j.annals.2012.04.007

Stone, P. R., Hartmann, R., Seaton, A. V., Sharpley, R., & White, L. (Eds.). (2018). *The Palgrave handbook of dark tourism studies* (pp. 335–354). Palgrave Macmillan. doi:10.1057/978-1-137-47566-4

Tarlow, P. (2007). Dark tourism–the appealing 'dark' side of tourism and more. In *Niche tourism* (pp. 61–72). Routledge.

Tumarkin, M. (2001). 'Wishing you weren't here...': Thinking about trauma, place and the port Arthur massacre. *Journal of Australian Studies*, *25*(67), 196–205. doi:10.1080/14443050109387653

Tumarkin, M. (2019). Twenty years of thinking about traumascapes. *Fabrications*, *29*(1), 4–20. doi:10.1080/10331867.2018.1540077

Tumarkin, M. M. (2005). *Traumascapes: The power and fate of places transformed by tragedy*. Melbourne Univ. Publishing.

Tzanelli, R. (2015). On avatar's (2009) semiotechnologies: From cinematic utopias to chinese heritage tourism. *Tourism Analysis*, *20*(3), 269–282. doi:10.3727/108354215X14356694891771

Tzanelli, R. (2016). *Thanatourism and cinematic representations of risk: Screening the end of tourism*. Routledge. doi:10.4324/9781315624105

Tzanelli, R. (2021). Post-viral tourism's antagonistic tourist imaginaries. *Journal of Tourism Futures*, *7*(3), 377–389. doi:10.1108/JTF-07-2020-0105

Tzanelli, R., & Korstanje, M. E. (2019). On killing the 'toured object': Anti-terrorist fantasy, touristic edgework and morbid consumption in the illegal settlements in West Bank, Palestine. In *Tourism and hospitality in conflict-ridden destinations* (pp. 71–83). Routledge.

ADDITIONAL READING

Bec, A., McLennan, C. L., & Moyle, B. D. (2016). Community resilience to long-term tourism decline and rejuvenation: A literature review and conceptual model. *Current Issues in Tourism*, *19*(5), 431–457. doi:10.1080/13683500.2015.1083538

Brouder, P. (2020). Reset redux: Possible evolutionary pathways towards the transformation of tourism in a COVID-19 world. *Tourism Geographies*, *22*(3), 484–490. doi:10.1080/14616688.2020.1760928

Cochrane, J. (2010). The sphere of tourism resilience. *Tourism Recreation Research*, *35*(2), 173–185. doi:10.1080/02508281.2010.11081632

Farmaki, A. (2015). Regional network governance and sustainable tourism. *Tourism Geographies*, *17*(3), 385–407. doi:10.1080/14616688.2015.1036915

Hall, C. M., Prayag, G., & Amore, A. (2017). *Tourism and resilience: Individual, organisational and destination perspectives* (Vol. 5). Channel View Publications.

Korstanje, M., & George, B. (Eds.). (2017). *Virtual traumascapes and exploring the roots of dark tourism*. IGI global.

Korstanje, M. E., & Baker, D. (2018). Politics of dark tourism: the case of Cromañón and ESMA, Buenos Aires, Argentina. The Palgrave handbook of dark tourism studies, 533-552.

Korstanje, M. E., & Bintang, H. (2020). Virtual Dark Tourism: The Role of Sound Branding and Augmented Reality for Death Sites. In *Applying Innovative Technologies in Heritage Science* (pp. 231–249). IGI Global. doi:10.4018/978-1-7998-2871-6. ch011

Korstanje, M. E., & Olsen, D. H. (2020). Negotiating the intersections between dark tourism and pilgrimage. In *Dark tourism and pilgrimage* (pp. 1–15). CABI. doi:10.1079/9781789241877.0001

Lew, A. A. (2014). Scale, change and resilience in community tourism planning. *Tourism Geographies*, *16*(1), 14–22. doi:10.1080/14616688.2013.864325

Magano, J., Fraiz-Brea, J. A., & Leite, Â. (2023). Dark tourism, the holocaust, and well-being: A systematic review. *Heliyon*, *9*(1), 13064. doi:10.1016/j.heliyon.2023. e13064 PMID:36711286

Orchiston, C., Prayag, G., & Brown, C. (2016). Organizational resilience in the tourism sector. *Annals of Tourism Research*, *56*, 145–148. doi:10.1016/j.annals.2015.11.002

Saarinen, J. (2021). Is being responsible sustainable in tourism? Connections and critical differences. *Sustainability (Basel)*, *13*(12), 6599. doi:10.3390u13126599

Seraphin, H., & Korstanje, M. E. (2021). *Dark tourism tribes: social capital as a variable. In Consumer Tribes in Tourism: Contemporary Perspectives on Special-Interest Tourism*. Springer.

Tyrrell, T. J., & Johnston, R. J. (2008). Tourism sustainability, resiliency and dynamics: Towards a more comprehensive perspective. *Tourism and Hospitality Research*, *8*(1), 14–24. doi:10.1057/thr.2008.8

Tzanelli, R., & Korstanje, M. E. (2016). Tourism in the European economic crisis: Mediatised worldmaking and new tourist imaginaries in Greece. *Tourist Studies*, *16*(3), 296–314. doi:10.1177/1468797616648542

KEY TERMS AND DEFINITIONS

Dark Tourism: Is an emerging nice of tourism which consists in the visit to spaces of mass death or suffering.

Heritage: Is a full range of inherited traditions, objects or monuments that belong to our cultural background.

Heritage Management: Should be seen as the application of techniques aimed at conserving cultural resources.

Human Rights: Is a set of rights which belonging to every person has oriented to protect its integrity.

Trauma: Is a pervasive psychological problem derived from an exposure to severe incidents or events emotionally disturbing for the subject.

Chapter 5
Revenge Travel:
A Case of Pandemic Fatigue and Boredom

Charul Agrawal
https://orcid.org/0000-0002-5471-8320
Amity University, India

Taranjeet Duggal
Amity University, India

Parul Gupta
I.T.S. Ghaziabad, India

ABSTRACT

With the onset of the coronavirus pandemic, the people and their lives have been affected. The social distancing norms and the hygiene issues completely broke down the travel and tourism sector and people forgot what holidays and vacations were. Then came the period when the clutches of virus loosened and so did the lockdown, and people got an opportunity to open their windows and step out of their homes. Trapped under boredom and fatigue due to pandemic, people wanted to visit more, spend more on their holidays and trips, and thus emerged the concept of revenge tourism. Not only domestically, this phenomenon was observed globally when people flocked to nearby tourist destinations to ease their psychological stress as and when restrictions on lockdown were lifted. Revenge tourism is a recent phenomenon that is fueled by the monotony and the boredom faced by the people during the lockdowns imposed on them. The desire to participate in such a practice has been accentuated by the strict health rules and prolonged home traps.

DOI: 10.4018/978-1-6684-8726-6.ch005

Copyright © 2023, IGI Global. Copying or distributing in print or electronic forms without written permission of IGI Global is prohibited.

Revenge Travel

INTRODUCTION

With the onset of the Coronavirus pandemic, people and their lives have been affected in multiple ways. Many lives have been lost, families destroyed and crippled, and those who were saved were trapped in their houses in the name of Lockdown. India also had its share from March 2020 when the first case of COVID was reported in the country. The country witnessed deadly waves where millions of people and their lives came to a standstill. It was only due to forced lockdown and other strict measures that the country could come out from the clasps of COVID. All the industries were severely impacted and faced huge losses, and one such sector was Tourism. The flights were cancelled, the hotels were shut down and the ticketing windows were deserted. It would be fair to say that Tourism was by far one sector which felt the maximum heat due to Covid, the social distancing norms and the hygiene issues completely broke down the Travel and Tourism sector and people forgot what holidays and vacations were. This was seen in both global as well as domestic tourism.

As a result of the pandemic, international tourist arrivals worldwide reached around 409,5 million in 2020, the lowest figure recorded since 1989, then went up by nine per cent in 2021. In Europe - the most visited global region by international travellers - inbound arrivals decreased by 68 per cent in the first year of the health crisis, then went up to 303 million in 2021. (https://www.statista.com/statistics/273123/total-international-tourism-receipts)

The crash in international tourism due to the coronavirus pandemic could cause a loss of more than $4 trillion to the global GDP for the years 2020 and 2021, according to a UNCTAD report published on 30 June. (https://www.unwto.org/news/global-economy-could-lose-over-4-trillion-due-to-covid-19-impact-on-tourism)

This resulted in huge economic and social loss placing over 100 million direct tourism jobs at risk, especially in micro, small and medium-sized enterprises, which represent 80% of the sector and employ a high share of women and young people.

The downturn in the tourism sector was primarily due to restricted mobility and health contingencies. This was further worsened by the psychological repercussions of the pandemic. The combined effect of negative emotions increased during the phase of lockdown where the intensity of emotions like "upset," "distressed," "and afraid was highly prevalent" (Gismero-González et al., 2020) and can lead to psychological symptoms (Hull, 2005) However efforts should be made to make the people understand the reason and necessity of such a forced lockdown as deriving people from their liberty is a daunting task and needs to be handled carefully (Brooks et al., n.d.).

Then came the period when the clutches of the virus loosened and so did the Lockdown, and people got an opportunity to open their windows and step out of their homes. Trapped under boredom and fatigue due to the pandemic, people wanted to visit more, spend more on their holidays and trips, and thus emerged the concept of Revenge Tourism. Not only domestically, but this phenomenon was also observed globally when people flocked to nearby tourist destinations to ease out their psychological stress as and when restrictions on lockdown were lifted.

Revenge Tourism is a recent phenomenon which is fueled by the monotony and the boredom faced by the people during the lockdowns imposed on them. The desire to participate in such a practice has been accentuated by strict health rules and prolonged home traps (Ghosh, 2021).

After two years of being cooped up inside, Indians are now travelling with a vengeance - 'revenge travel', as the phenomenon is called. And many, experts say, now prefer to travel within the country instead of flying to more expensive destinations abroad.

The industry is also benefiting from new trends borne of the pandemic such as micro-holidays and workcations. (https://www.bbc.com/news/world-asia-india-62978198)

Figure 1. Illustration of the trend of revenue recovery post-COVID-19 times
Source: https://www.itic.ie/RECOVERY/wp-content/uploads/2021/02/CHART-3-Recovery-Scenarios-Overseas-Tourist-Revenues-to-2025.png

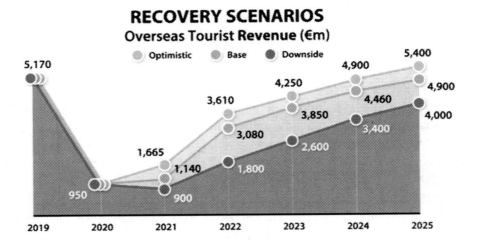

The feeling of being trapped indoors and not being able to move out freely has made people realize that they should make up for the lost time and this could be done by making domestic and international travel plans (Wachyuni & Kusumaningrum, 2020). The Indian tourists will bounce back from the impositions of forced restrictions but still, hygiene and cleanliness will be the major criteria for deciding upon the next destination for their travel. There could be the growth of adventure tourism also (*Post-Pandemic Tourism: The Desired Wave of Recovery in India*, n.d.).

Figure 2. Percentage change in international tourist arrivals worldwide due to COVID-19 from 2020 to 2022 region wise

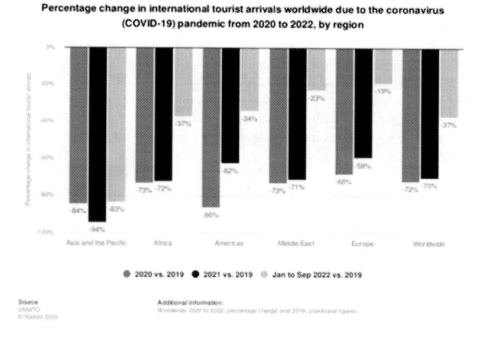

A lot of research has been done on the theoretical proclamations of the effect of covid on sustainable tourism but as such there is a dearth of extensive literature which can substantiate the foundations of these proclaimed theories (*A Bibliometric Review of Research on COVID-19 and Tourism: Reflections for Moving Forward*, n.d.).Revenge tourism has indeed been a dominant tourist behavior globally which gives a strong signal that tourism would once again be revived yet there are no significant studies which can focus on the factors that will fuel the growth of this mechanism (*Sustainable or a Butterfly Effect in Global Tourism? Nexus of Pandemic Fatigue, Covid-19-Branded Destination Safety, Travel Stimulus Incentives, and Post-Pandemic Revenge Travel*, n.d.). The general trend that has been noticed is that many tourist destinations have been revived post pandemic yet it is still to be studies that what would be the major determinants which will impact the demand in the new normal (Duong et al., 2022).

As it is well known that covid has severely affected global tourism the need is to develop a model for sustainable tourism which is based on the foundation of resilience (Sharma et al., 2021). In the case of Cosmopolitan tourists where rationality takes priority, it is seen that fear can cause a setback to international travel. Studies suggest that fear has taken birth owing to COVID-19 (*Cosmopolitan Tourists: The Most Resilient Travellers in the Face of COVID-19*, n.d.).

Studies were conducted and comparisons were drawn between the first and second waves it was observed that the youth perceived the concept of risk difference between the two consecutive waves, for future it is required that more protective measures should be focused especially where group settings are involved (Caldeira et al., 2022). Tourism impacts the development status of every country, and it is seen that covid has impacted tourism-based competitiveness among different counties of the world. There is a requirement to understand that the gaps have increased post covid and the need is to develop a sustainable post-pandemic tourism recovery strategy (Camară, 2022). Given the effect of Covid on tourism and its related domains, it is essential to develop an analytical perspective which can help in the knowledge enhancement of various stakeholders involved in the Tourism sector (Das et al., 2023).

The proposed study intends to bring forward some of the determining factors which have fostered the growth of the Revenge Tourism post-pandemic, though the fear of COVID has still not been surpassed. The free spirit of tourists is deterred by the forced restrictions whether in the form of social distancing norms or compulsory Lockdown.

With the ease in the restrictions, people are bound to travel and feel the freedom once gained.

IMPACT OF COVID-19 ON THE TOURISM INDUSTRY

There is no doubt in stating that the Coronavirus has had a deadly effect on the Tourism industry which broadly comprise of Aviation and Hospitality sector. When the pandemic struck, air transport was completely shut down and at the same time, millions lost their jobs in hotels and resorts. Considering a country like India which has always been a traveller's preference given the fact that it is blessed with a variety of landscapes, the impact of Covid was huge. Though the country was able to

Revenge Travel

survive the first wave the second wave was far more deadly and catastrophic where Tourism completely came to a standstill, with absolutely zero incoming international tourists. Similarly, even domestic tourism was impacted which led to the loss of jobs, depleting household incomes and overall, a huge loss of GDP to the Indian economy. The impact which the pandemic has exerted on all the economies of the world cannot be summed up easily. Whether it was developed nations like USA and France, or countries like Thailand and Maldives which are majorly dependent on Tourism, Covid bought all to a knees, where a major restructuring was required. Resources were to be mobilized, infrastructure was to be revamped, and participation from Government was required as a tourist has become all the more conscious about health and hygiene which have now become a deciding factor once people step out of their homes. In the study done by (Bakar & Rosbi, 2020) the author evaluated the impact of Covid on the supply and demand curve to detect the status of economic changes in the Tourism sector and he concluded that demand has reduced owing to the panic created by Covid.

Numerous studies have been conducted and a great amount of data is available which depicts the widespread impact of this deadly virus.

Export revenues from tourism could fall by $910 billion to $1.2 trillion in 2020. This will have a wider impact and could reduce global GDP by 1.5% to 2.8%.

Women, who make up 54% of the tourism workforce, youth and workers in the informal economy are among the most at-risk categories. (https://www.unwto.org/tourism-and-covid-19-unprecedented-economic-impacts)

In 2020, and with the severe impact of the COVID-19 Pandemic, international tourism went down by 22% in Q1 and by 65% in the first half of 2020 when compared with 2019 figures.

IATA's Director General and CEO stated that "Financially, 2020 will go down as the worst year in the history of aviation. On average, every day of this year will add $230 million to industry losses. In total that's a loss of $84.3 billion". (https://infomineo.com/covid-19-impacted-travel-tourism-industry/)

The effect has been destructive and negative not only on the tourism sector but on the entire economy and it may take more than a year to completely revive from the outbreak(Škare et al., 2021)The decision to quarantine during the outbreak are critical and it directly impacts the trade, tourism and supply chain of any economy, in the study conducted keeping Istanbul as the focal area the authors which is a developing economy mainly dependent on tourism(Altuntas Fatma & SahinGok

Mehmet, 2021). As per the estimates by (Mariolis et al., 2021) there has been a decrease in the international travel receipts on output, employment and trade deficits in the range of 3.5 to 10.5 billion euros concerning the Greek economy.

Figure 3. Global data of international tourists during the first wave of corona virus
Source: https://webunwto.s3.eu-west-1.amazonaws.com/s3fs-public/2020-08/UN-Tourism-Policy-Brief-Visuals.pdf

Post-Pandemic and Tourism: Factors Contributing to Revenge Tourism

The pandemic has had an unprecedented impact globally, countless lives were lost and millions of households were destroyed. So many orphaned, so many lost jobs and the economy of so many countries crippled to the ground The authors have suggested that since the hospitality industry is based and built on the trust and confidence they receive frothier customers hence they should work towards self-protection behavior of the consumers (Foroudi et al., 2021). The study indicates that a crisis like Covid can bring about temporary or even permanent changes in the Consumer decision-making process for hospitality services where the intensity of emotion played a major role (Torres et al., 2021). The study confirms that there exists a direct relationship between the tourist knowledge and their risk perception

Revenge Travel

and this relationship can reduce or increase the anxieties and promote safe tourism during pandemic (Liu et al., 2022).

Due to the perceived severity of Covid pandemic, the consumer's activities were limited, it was seen that this severity increased the willingness of the consumers to purchase and consume more post-pandemic (Deng et al., 2020). Psychological factors play an important role in boosting or suppressing travel demand among general consumers. There exists a direct connection between boredom generated post-pandemic and the travel plans made to compensate for that (Yao et al., 2023). The study has highlighted the role of nostalgia, which is again a psychological phenomenon which has helped consumers to cope with the pandemic distress and motivated them to pick up leisure travel (Feng & Lan, 2021).

A radical change has been observed in the tourism sector post-Covid, where on one side people are flocking to tourist destinations in great numbers, which is a direct result of the earlier restrictions, and on the other side the travel business houses are finding it particularly difficult to cope up as the norms of social distancing are making the things all the more difficult to cope up with the increasing demand. To date, not all economies have opened up completely for international arrivals. As the consumers are under forced travel restrictions, they are in fear of health and safety measures, and in some countries, the health and safety measures are still not in an adequate position. Covid has brought a revolutionary change in the landscape of travel and tourism, the smell of sanitisers, the put-on mask signs, the request to maintain social distance and their corresponding markings on the ground, the change in cabin crew announcements, the inclusion of extended window screens and thermal scanners are some of the things that we have now become used to as no one can be ever sure that when a new variant of the pandemic can return and cause havoc. The recovery phase of different tourist destinations is bound to be different. Studies conducted have shown that in many cases the recovery of rural tourism and nature-based destinations has been fast the same does not hold for all metros.

A few distinct factors which have led to the growth of Revenge Tourism can be listed under.

Psychological Stress and Boredom

The COVID-19 pandemic generated feelings of being 'alone' and 'trapped' with an 'uncertain' future among people across the globe. Irrespective of geography, age, gender and occupation, people felt trapped and restricted. This not only increased the mental fatigue and boredom but also strengthened the desire to be 'free' again; to be able to go to desired places and enjoy life 'normally'. Psychological factors emerged as one of the strongest motivators for people to travel once the opportunity presented itself. The vacations however small in duration and near in distance appeared lucrative and were preferred by millions across the continents. Given the perceived severity of Covid pandemic, the consumer's activities were limited, and it was seen that this severity increased the willingness of the consumers to purchase and consume more post-pandemic. Psychological factors play an important role in boosting or suppressing travel demand among general consumers. There exists a direct connection between boredom which is generated post-pandemic and travel plans have been made to compensate for that. The researchers have highlighted the role of nostalgia, which is again a psychological phenomenon which has helped the consumers to cope with the pandemic distress and motivated them to pick up leisure travel.

THE EMERGENCE OF STAYCATIONS

The concept of Staycation has become all the more relevant in the post covid phase. Due to forced restrictions when people were unable to enjoy their vacations, especially to an international destination, Staycation brought respite. The basic difference between vacation and staycation is basically when one is on a staycation, they choose a destination closer to their home town, which involves lower cost, zero visas and insurance fees.

Between 2019 and 2021, work from home tripled from 5.7% to 17.9%, according to new data released by the U.S. Census Bureau, and in the UK, remote workers skyrocketed in the past two years. As of the second quarter of 2022, Airbnb saw long-term stays (28 days or more) increase by nearly 25 per cent from 2021 and nearly 90 per cent from 2019. (https://www.traveldailymedia.com/7-significant-travel-trends-to-expect-in-2023/)

For example, an enthusiast living in Sydney could go Camping in the Blue Mountains which is just an hour's drive from Sydney. A developing economy like India has however extended this concept and added work to it. One of the biggest gifts of Covid to the working population is the concept of "Work from Home "which was later changed to "Work from anywhere". Because of the pandemic where people were forced to work indoors, the travel companies saw a profitable opportunity and gave the concept of staycations where the techies can carry their laptops and work remotely.

In India, from the hills of Leh and Ladakh to the mesmerizing views of Rishikesh multiple avenues opened up where people rushed to set up their workstations. During the Covid phase when more than half the population was working from home, what better opportunity than a staycation, where hotels and resorts gave away

Revenge Travel

unlimited internet and home-cooked meals, this trend has picked up and it is here to stay. Multiple destinations emerged as popular hotspots where people could enjoy extended vacations and at the same time meet deadlines at Workfront.

Increased Digitization

Covid has made people more and more tech-savvy. As the population was forced indoors more and more people found respite online. The online presence increased be it binge-watching on Netflix, online payment of utility bills or celebrating birthdays and anniversaries on Zoom. Given the fact the number of netizens has increased and so are their activities, this trend of digitization has brought a complete transformation. As far as travel and other allied activities are concerned, more and more activities are being performed digitally. From booking tickets to compulsory web check-in, from keyless hotel rooms to virtual queues in an amusement park, and from virtual tours to the usage of Robots and chatbots the travel industry is all set on the path to digitization.

With the increased usage of smart devices such as smartphones and tablets, consumers have all the information at their fingertips; moreover, today's traveller is very conscious of getting his money's worth. Such easy access to information that too at nominal prices force the business to keep innovating and make sure that they are not left behind in the race of competition. All the added features of enhanced technology help in boosting customer confidence, which has become very vulnerable.

The Increased Role of Social Media

Social media, the favorite kind of digitization has also impacted the tourism scenario. Social media which was once a means to increase social connectivity has now become a platform to showcase pictures of vacations. People post anything and everything from their holidays. From the check-in done on the Facebook page which is nothing but announcing their holiday to making reels for Instagram, these social media platforms keep them busy during their entire holidays rather it leads to oversharing.

In some cases, the behavior becomes very questionable when they post to simply show off their luxury vacation plans. Most the people take help of social media before choosing their holiday destination. Once they see their known ones posting their pics, a desire to visit the same place is born. Some Insta crazy people even think about how and what effect posing pics will have on their social profile when they will visit the same destination. Consider a case when a lot of people post pics and blogs about one particular tourist destination, say for example destinations like Thailand, Switzerland and Maldives.

This could even lead to Over tourism a case where a lot of people go under the so-called influence of Facebook and disturb the ecological balance of that place. The opposite can also hold good, a place which is less posted and popularized may be in the category of under-tourism. To sum it up, Facebook or Instagram posts and pics shared on these media do entice people to go ahead and book their next vacation.

RISE OF SOLO TRAVEL

The need of understanding oneself and the quest for new experiences is what led to the growth of Solo travel, particularly post Covid when people were under lockdown and isolation, this trend became all the more pertinent.

According to a 2021 survey, the main motivation of travellers from the United States, Canada, United Kingdom, and Australia to travel solo was the willingness to see the world and not to wait for others. Furthermore, almost half of the respondents mentioned being motivated by the feeling of freedom and independence, while over 40 per cent were motivated by meeting new people. (https://www.statista.com/statistics/1303489/solo-travelers-motivations)

A solo traveller need not plan according to someone else schedule and neither can spend and indulge in any activity as per one's desire. Another promising trend noticed by many studies and surveys conducted is that females have a higher ratio in the category of solo travellers. Gone are the days when females were subjected to the patriarchy where their decisions were taken by the males of the house, and they had practically no say. Today women have become more confident of course with higher education and earning capacity. A female can boost her self-image and learn a lot more when she travels alone.

The global leisure travel market was valued at $1,006.5 billion in 2019, and researchers project it to reach $1,737.3 billion by 2027, creating a Compound Annual Growth Rate (CAGR) of 22.6% from 2021 to 2027. This market is split into two segments: solo travellers and group travellers. Group travellers hold a major share of the market, but solo travellers are expected to see growth at the highest CAGR during the next forecast period. (https://travel.radicalstorage.com/solo-travel-statistics)

Revenge Travel

The Reason Why People Travel Has Changed

Earlier when people planned for their vacations, the most obvious reason was taking a respite from the usual office work, but after the pandemic, the meaning of life has changed for people. The value of life has taken a different meaning altogether, the people now realize the importance of relationships. Covid has taught multiple lessons. Now they have varied reasons for taking up vacations, it could be a short weekend trip with their loved ones, or a wellness break given the fact that now people realize the importance of a healthy mind in a healthy body, or maybe a soul-searching sojourn. What people are now looking for is attaching meaning to their trips keeping in mind the impact that holiday will have on them and the planet. More and more people are becoming conscious of their contribution to the land in terms of give and take. Travelling slower and greener are becoming the priority, with more and more travellers turning vegan and reducing their carbon footprint.

CHALLENGES POST COVID-19

There is no second opinion to the fact that Corona has left some hard prints on mind and body, where people have come close to the reality that anything can happen to their lives, so they must utilize whatever time they have and utilize it well with their loved ones. The post-Covid phase has been equally difficult for all, where one is always under the constant fear that anytime a new variant may arise as the virus mitigates. Though the deadly waves have passed, people have become all the more cautious to observe all the norms so that they can avoid any possible threat from the virus.

The tourists who are travelling in the post covid phase are observed to be more respectable and supportive during their travel and prefer to travel with their relatives more often (Orden-Mejía et al., 2022).

Increased Focus on Public Health and Hygiene

The Corona phase has drained every economy's resources, and most importantly the loss of human resources. The Governments of almost all countries need to divert their resources to building up adequate infrastructure in terms of public health and hygiene.

Given the fact that the world is still struggling to come out of the grip of Corona Virus, the need of the hour is to redesign the tourism strategies completely so that all the stakeholders comprising the destination managers and practitioners can hope to revive the industry altogether in European destinations. Some specifically designed strategies could be in the areas of managing tourist expectations in terms of post covid hygiene issues and collaboration and also managing sustainability issues. This becomes all the more important as herd immunity has still not developed to the expected level (Seyitoğlu & Costa, 2022).

The study confirms that post-pandemic travellers prefer a destination which has taken robust initiatives in terms of health and hygiene, a destination which poses a risk to their health safety will not be preferred by them (Abhishek et al., 2022). By taking Maldives as an example the author has conducted the study on small islands developing states which are all the more dependent on Tourism for their development. Four different techniques were tested to examine the changed tourist perception toward the tourist destination, and it was found that the Bubble Strategy was the most effective, which implies maintaining limited interaction with people outside the bubble (Gu et al., 2022).

The Increased Role of Various Stakeholders

No industry can thrive without the adequate support of society and the Government. With all industries, various stakeholders gain prominence. In the case of Travel and Tourism also distinct stakeholder management is of immense importance. From the local travel guides to the Aviation and Tourism ministry of every country, the biggest challenge would be to integrate them on a single platform.

The authors have recognized that the landscape has changed owing to the pandemic set in 2020, where previously the areas of concern were limited to environmental conservation and involvement of local community challenges, post-pandemic the situation has become more demanding and safety has emerged as the biggest concern, the authors highlight how increased participation from the stakeholders in the entire value chain can bring the required changes (Rivera et al., 2022). The study done by Sigala (2020) has recognized three major tourism stakeholders which are tourism demand, supply and destination management and policymakers which play a crucial role in recovery and response from COVID-19.

The authors highlight the role of stakeholder management, where a strong value chain strategy is recommended rather than a destination strategy, where all the members of the chain be it the local vendors or the local guide play a significant role as they play a crucial part in regaining the tourist confidence (Roxas et al., 2022).

Revenge Travel

REGAIN TOURISM CONFIDENCE

The world has witnessed pandemics before, from the Spanish flu in 1918 to Asian Flu in 1957, and the outbreak of two major World wars. Such events can reform and transform the world economy. The outbreak of the Corona was one such event which has brought catastrophic changes everywhere on Earth, no country and no family were spared. What is left now are the lessons that Covid has taught us to survive and become resilient.

Now that the pandemic is coming to an end and the doors are opening for tourist, it is required that the Travel Companies gear up and prepare themselves for the new post covid phase where the tourist is more prepared and cautious. It would be a daunting task for every tour manager and every country to win back the confidence of the consumer which is shaken due to uncertainty and the spending on tourist activities has also gone down significantly. Now that the tourist is free from the shackles of forced lockdown he will hit the sea, sky and road to explore more than ever before. Some exemplary initiatives have been adopted for Tourism and the market can now witness some exceptionally outstanding trends which have the power to revamp the sector altogether. Giving him updated and clear information will a long way to reduce ambiguity and make him feel more secure before he books a ticket.

Government's Initiatives

The onus of providing a safe and secure holiday lies mainly on the Government of the country. All the efforts should be directed towards building a sustainable and resilient tourism policy. At this juncture, every country must understand the long-term implications of the pandemic and the steps it should undertake to mitigate the threat as much as possible. Well-coordinated management of the private and public parties directly or indirectly involved in boosting tourism in the country should be the priority.

Since international tourism will take more time to revive completely due to enhanced restrictions, the Government should boost domestic tourism to cover the gaps.

According to the Swiss Economic Institute (KOF), the number of overnight stays is predicted to fall by 34% in 2020. The slump in domestic demand is forecast to be relatively small (down by 14%), with the loss in international business significant (down by 55%). Domestic and European demand is expected to recover steadily, but demand from overseas markets is not expected to recover until 2023. Except for a few hotspots, hotel prices are also expected to fall and recover in 2022. Fares on mountain railways could rise significantly if passenger numbers are drastically reduced. (https://www.oecd.org/coronavirus/policy-responses/rebuilding-tourism-for-the-future-covid-19-policy-responses-and-recovery-bced9859/)

It is time that policymakers take advantage of the increased digitization and accordingly frame sustainable policies so that robust risk assessment measures can be implemented. A well-planned crisis response plan will go a long way in improving the vulnerability of the tourism business. As per the study (Yeh, 2021) the author has suggested that Government sponsored Loans and open communication can be key to gaining back the crippling tourism industry.

The Government needs to chalk out a collaborative plan across borders to revive tourist confidence and generate demand once again. Multi-country forums and associations can always work toward a common policy which can facilitate larger regional cooperation.

CONCLUSION

When the virus was first detected in Wuhan, China in 2019 little did the world know what was ahead. The next two years were spent in grief and uncertainty, with millions of deaths with no count of unreported deaths, the loss of jobs by so many employed, the factories shut down and only the hospitals saw the crowd. The virus expanded and mutated and in three months the entire globe was in its clutches. No country was spared on Earth. With all the negatives Covid has taught some important lessons too, the economies are now better prepared to face such pandemic situations, people switched to alternate employment and some switched their homes to offices, what was done offline was now done online. Overall Covid transformed our lives and economies.

When the impact is so strong, the recovery also happens gradually, and the same happened with Travel and Tourism. With the countries shut down completely and extended lockdowns, there were zero tourist activities happening anywhere on the planet. This dark phase saw a faint beam of light when the social distancing norms were relaxed and lockdowns lifted. The people took to travel frantically and it was felt as if the sudden splurge was revenge against the disease. Human nature is in constant need of new experiences, which it could not enjoy because of the pandemic and the fear of losing one's life because of the virus. The pandemic gave people boredom and fatigue which resulted in the loss of any activity. This absolute foundation gave them all the more reason to move and explore more new destinations. The same understanding was developed by the supply side also. From the airlines, hotels, resorts, and travel planners to the local guide all have built on the same and welcomed the tourist in the post-pandemic phase.

Revenge Travel

The concept of Revenge travel might seem to have negative connotations associated with it, but the impact is surely positive. The people are looking for compensating for the lost time and trips which they could not because of covid, not only they want to travel more but they want to travel so that it counts. For some revenge might mean going big such as some international fancy trip and for some it could be a wellness retreat which could be soul searching and transforming them from within and still for some, it was just a reunion. The realization that each day is valuable and each moment spent happily is worthwhile because one never knows in what form can covid return.

If covid was challenging, then post covid is no less. The airlines, hotels, and tour planners struggling with the after-effects such as increased demand and oil prices, weak confidence of the consumers, infrastructural challenges and staff shortage to name a few. The forced lockdown and constant fear of health and safety are not a cakewalk. The burden to give better services and experiences to a tourist has become all the more difficult. Revenge Tourism may get the bags packed but it makes the shoulders surely heavy.

REFERENCES

Abhishek, B., Zohre, M., Manisha, A., Zilmiyah, K., & Gerardine, D.-T. (2022). Post COVID-19: Cautious or courageous travel behaviour? *Asia Pacific Journal of Tourism Research*, 581–600.

Bakar, N. A., & Rosbi, S. (2020). Effect of Coronavirus disease (COVID-19) to tourism industry. *International Journal of Advanced Engineering Research and Science*, 7(4), 189–193. doi:10.22161/ijaers.74.23

A bibliometric review of research on COVID-19 and tourism: Reflections for moving forward. (n.d.). Academic Press.

Brooks, R. K., Webster, R. K., Smith, L. E., Woodland, L., Wessely, S., Greenberg, N., & Rubin, G. J. (2020, March). The psychological impact of quarantine and how to reduce it: Rapid review of the evidence. *Lancet*, 395(10227), 912–920. doi:10.1016/S0140-6736(20)30460-8 PMID:32112714

Caldeira, A. M., Seabra, C., & AlAshry, M. S. (2022). Contrasting the COVID-19 Effects on Tourism Safety Perceptions and Coping Behavior among Young People during Two Pandemic Waves: Evidence from Egypt. *Sustainability*. https://doi.org/ https://doi.org/10.3390/su14127492

Camară, G. (2022). The COVID-19 Pandemic and the Enhanced Marginalisation of Marginal Tourist Destinations. *COVID-19 and Marginalisation of People and Places*, 117–129. https://doi.org/https://doi.org/10.1007/978-3-031-11139-6_9

Cosmopolitan tourists: the most resilient travellers in the face of COVID-19. (n.d.). Academic Press.

Das, Nayak, & Naik. (2023). An impact study on COVID-19 and tourism sustainability: intelligent solutions, issues and future challenges. *World Review of Science, Technology and Sustainable Development, 19*, 92–119. doi:10.1504/WRSTSD.2021.10038456

Deng, S., Wang, W., Xie, P., Chao, Y., & Zhu, J. (2020). Perceived severity of COVID-19 and post-pandemic consumption willingness: The roles of boredom and sensation-seeking. *Frontiers in Psychology, 11*, 11. doi:10.3389/fpsyg.2020.567784 PMID:33041933

Duong, L. H., Phan, Q. D., Nguyen, T. T., Huynh, D. V., Truong, T. T., & Duong, K. Q. (2022). Understanding Tourists' Behavioral Intention and Destination Support in Post-pandemic Recovery: The Case of the Vietnamese Domestic Market. *Sustainability (Basel), 14*(16), 9969. doi:10.3390u14169969

Faruk, S., & Carlos, C. (2022). A scenario planning framework for (post-)pandemic tourism in European destinations. *European Planning Studies, 30*(12).

Fatma, & Mehmet. (2021). The effect of COVID-19 pandemic on domestic tourism: A DEMATEL method analysis on quarantine decisions. *International Journal of Hospitality Management*, 92. PMID:33519015

Feng, W. J., & Lan, X. (2021). Revenge travel: Nostalgia and desire for leisure travel post COVID-19. *Journal of Travel & Tourism Marketing*, 935–955.

Foroudi, P. H., Tabaghdehi, S. A., & Marvi, R. (2021). The gloom of the COVID-19 shock in the hospitality industry: A study of consumer risk perception and adaptive belief in the dark cloud of a pandemic. *International Journal of Hospitality Management, 92*, 102717. doi:10.1016/j.ijhm.2020.102717 PMID:36919037

Ghosh, R. (n.d.). What Is Revenge Travel? India Today.

Gismero-González, E., Bermejo-Toro, L., Cagigal, V., Roldán, A., Martínez-Beltrán, M. J., & Halty, L. (2020). Emotional Impact of COVID-19 Lockdown Among the Spanish Population. *Frontiers in Psychology, 11*, 11. doi:10.3389/fpsyg.2020.616978 PMID:33391136

Gu, Y., Onggo, B. S., Kunc, M. H., & Bayer, S. (2022). Small Island Developing States (SIDS) COVID-19 post-pandemic tourism recovery: A system dynamics approach. *Current Issues in Tourism*, 25(9), 1481–1508. doi:10.1080/13683500.2 021.1924636

Hull, H. F. (2005). SARS control and psychological effects of quarantine, Toronto, Canada. *Emerging Infectious Diseases*, 11(2), 354–355. doi:10.3201/eid1102.040760 PMID:15759346

Liu, C. L., Jeon, C. Y., Song, W. G., & Yang, H. W. (2022). The COVID-19 Pandemic and Its Impact on Tourism: The Effect of Tourism Knowledge on Risk Perception, Attitude, and Intention. *Journal of Quality Assurance in Hospitality & Tourism*, 1–17. doi:10.1080/1528008X.2022.2077887

Mariolis, T., Rodousakis, N., & Soklis, G. (2021). The COVID-19 multiplier effects of tourism on the Greek economy. *Tourism Economics*, 27(8), 1848–1855. doi:10.1177/1354816620946547

Orden-Mejía, M., Carvache-Franco, M., Huertas, A., Carvache-Franco, W., Landeta-Bejarano, N., & Carvache-Franco. (2022). Post-COVID-19 Tourists' Preferences, Attitudes and Travel Expectations: A Study in Guayaquil, Ecuador. *International Journal of Environmental Research and Public Health.*

Post-pandemic tourism: The desired wave of recovery in India. (n.d.). Academic Press.

Rivera, Gutierrez, & Roxas. (2022). Re-thinking Governance in Tourism: Harnessing Tourism's post-COVID-19 Economic Potential. *Journal of Quality Assurance in Hospitality & Tourism.*

Roxas, J. P. R., & Gutierrez, E. L. M. (2022). Bootstrapping tourism post-COVID-19: A systems thinking approach. *Tourism and Hospitality Research*, 22(1), 86–101. doi:10.1177/14673584211038859

Sharma, G. D., Thomas, A., & Paul, J. (2021). Reviving tourism industry post-COVID-19: A resilience-based framework. *Tourism Management Perspectives*, 37, 100786. doi:10.1016/j.tmp.2020.100786 PMID:33391988

Sigala, M. (2020). Tourism and COVID-19: Impacts and implications for advancing and resetting industry and research. *Journal of Business Research*, 117, 312–321. doi:10.1016/j.jbusres.2020.06.015 PMID:32546875

Škare, M., Soriano, D. R., & Porada-Rochoń, M. (2021). Impact of COVID-19 on the travel and tourism industry. *Technological Forecasting and Social Change*, 163, 120469. doi:10.1016/j.techfore.2020.120469 PMID:35721368

Sustainable or a butterfly effect in global tourism? Nexus of pandemic fatigue, covid-19-branded destination safety, travel stimulus incentives, and post-pandemic revenge travel. (n.d.). Academic Press.

Torres, E. N., Ridderstaat, J., & Wei, W. (2021). Negative affectivity and people's return intentions to hospitality and tourism activities: The early stages of COVID-19. *Journal of Hospitality and Tourism Management, 49,* 89–100. doi:10.1016/j.jhtm.2021.08.021

Wachyuni, S. S., & Kusumaningrum, D. A. (2020). The Effect of COVID-19 Pandemic: How are the Future Tourist Behavior? *J. Educ. Soc. Behav. Sci., 33,* 67–76. doi:10.9734/jesbs/2020/v33i430219

Yao, Y., Zhao, X., Ren, L., & Jia, G. (2023). Compensatory travel in the post COVID-19 pandemic era: How does boredom stimulate intentions? *Journal of Hospitality and Tourism Management, 54,* 56–64. doi:10.1016/j.jhtm.2022.12.003

Yeh, S. S. (2021). Tourism recovery strategy against COVID-19 pandemic. *Tourism Recreation Research, 46*(2), 188–194. doi:10.1080/02508281.2020.1805933

ADDITIONAL READING

Baum, T., & Hai, N. T. T. (2020). Hospitality, tourism, human rights and the impact of COVID-19. *International Journal of Contemporary Hospitality Management, 32*(7), 2397–2407. doi:10.1108/IJCHM-03-2020-0242

Korstanje, M. E., & George, B. (2021). *Mobility and globalization in the aftermath of COVID-19: Emerging new geographies in a locked world.* Palgrave Macmillan. doi:10.1007/978-3-030-78845-2

Li, Z., Zhang, S., Liu, X., Kozak, M., & Wen, J. (2020). Seeing the invisible hand: Underlying effects of COVID-19 on tourists' behavioral patterns. *Journal of Destination Marketing & Management, 18,* 100502. doi:10.1016/j.jdmm.2020.100502

Lin, V. S., Qin, Y., Li, G., & Jiang, F. (2022). Multiple effects of "distance" on domestic tourism demand: A comparison before and after the emergence of COVID-19. *Annals of Tourism Research, 95,* 103440. doi:10.1016/j.annals.2022.103440

Madani, A., Boutebal, S. E., Benhamida, H., & Bryant, C. R. (2020). The impact of Covid-19 outbreak on the tourism needs of the Algerian population. *Sustainability (Basel), 12*(21), 8856. doi:10.3390u12218856

Pillai, S. K. B., Kulshreshtha, S. K., & Korstanje, M. E. (2021). *The Real Implications and Effects of Covid19 in the Tourism Industry: what is the future of tourism in a world without tourists?* Anais Brasileiros de Estudos Turísticos.

Polyzos, S., Samitas, A., & Spyridou, A. E. (2021). Tourism demand and the COVID-19 pandemic: An LSTM approach. *Tourism Recreation Research*, *46*(2), 175–187. doi:10.1080/02508281.2020.1777053

Seyfi, S., Hall, C. M., & Shabani, B. (2020). COVID-19 and international travel restrictions: The geopolitics of health and tourism. *Tourism Geographies*, 1–17.

Yang, T. T., Ruan, W. Q., Zhang, S. N., & Li, Y. Q. (2021). The influence of the COVID-19 pandemic on tourism demand for destinations: An analysis of spatial heterogeneity from a multi-scale perspective. *Asia Pacific Journal of Tourism Research*, *26*(7), 793–810. doi:10.1080/10941665.2021.1919160

Zhang, S. N., Li, Y. Q., Ruan, W. Q., & Liu, C. H. (2022). Would you enjoy virtual travel? The characteristics and causes of virtual tourists' sentiment under the influence of the COVID-19 pandemic. *Tourism Management*, *88*, 104429. doi:10.1016/j.tourman.2021.104429

KEY TERMS AND DEFINITIONS

Boredom: Is a mental state of restlessness due to lack of interest in an activity. It could also be caused by doing repeated work.

COVID-19: Is a pandemic which was caused by Corona virus first detected in the Wuhan province of China in the early phase of 2020.

Fatigue: Is a feeling of continued tiredness, could be mental or physical or both generally experienced by human beings due to extreme physical activity or mental stress.

Revenge Travel: Is a phenomenon where people seek to travel post the period of forced lockdown and travel restrictions which were caused due to pandemic from 2020 to 2022.

Sustainability: Is a practice of ensuring ecological balance along with social being so that the future generations do not suffer.

Tourism: Is a phenomenon/activity where people move from their home locations to other countries or places primarily for leisure, exploration, or professional reasons.

Chapter 6

The Migrantour Experience at Porta Palazzo and Barriera di Milano:
Tourism Consumption in Intercultural Neighborhoods

Adriana Maria Offredi Rodriguez
Universitat Autónoma de Barcelona, Spain

ABSTRACT

Migrantour contributes to spreading a culture of respect for the human rights of migrant communities in European cities by encouraging interactions of mutual respect between people with different origins. Since 2009, it has involved over 11,000 participants in the intercultural itineraries and more than 300 people as intercultural companions. Currently, new projects are under implementation to promote its methodology in rural areas and new cities. Thus, as it will be explained in the chapter, it can represent a successful study case where tourism contributes positively to human rights within the frame of interculturalism. The contribution is a part of a broader study examining the experience of Migrantour in Porta Palazzo and Barriera di Milano, two neighborhoods of the Italian town of Turin, under different grounds. The aim is to further contribute to the debate about the implications of the transformation of intercultural neighbourhoods into places of leisure and consumption for migrant communities.

DOI: 10.4018/978-1-6684-8726-6.ch006

Copyright © 2023, IGI Global. Copying or distributing in print or electronic forms without written permission of IGI Global is prohibited.

INTRODUCTION

The Migrantour Experience at Porta Palazzo and Barriera di Milano

This chapter is part of a broader study conducted in 2021. It examines, under different grounds, the experience of Migrantour in Porta Palazzo and Barriera di Milano, two neighborhoods of the Italian town of Turin. The aim is to further contribute to the debate about the relationship between tourism consumption, human rights, and urban space. It also represents an excellent opportunity to reflect on the implications of urban tourism for the human rights of migrants living in intercultural neighborhoods.

Migrantour is a European network of responsible tourism that works in the frame of interculturalism. It operates in more than 20 European cities and rural areas and has involved 11.000 participants in the intercultural itineraries and more than 300 people as intercultural companions. It was first created in 2009 when Turin, as other European cities, was in the middle of a process of de-industrialization which led to the development of alternative forms of economic production. Since the 2000s, indeed, cities with a strong immigration history had started considering tourism as a resource for socioeconomic development. And cultural diversity had become a means to transform intercultural neighbourhoods into places of leisure and consumption. Migrantour, however, has been designed following a different mindset which is more concerned about the implications of "(inter)cultural tourism" on the rights of the migrant communities involved. In this sense, it promotes the respect for cultural diversity and the rights of migrant communities by tackling the official discourse regarding intercultural neighbourhoods. This is done through intercultural itineraries: two-hour walking tours where participants are invited to engage with the territory and its inhabitants thanks to the mediation of intercultural companions. They are "citizens regardless of their land of origin or the one of their parents" who take the floor to self-represent and speak up for their communities of origin. Migrantour.

For these reasons, the author believes it represents a successful study case where tourism contributes positively to human rights within the frame of intercultural neighbourhoods.

BACKGROUND

Tourism and Intercultural Neighborhoods

During the second half of the 19th century, a new form of urban tourism started growing in medium and big cities due to the interest of a part of the upper bourgeoisie to " visit degraded urban areas" and see how their inhabitants lived. These inhabitants were usually migrant groups and the degradation was the result of the combination between socioeconomic problems and institutional abandonment. Nevertheless, cultural diversity became the main attraction, and slowly, the so-called "slumming" led to the transformation of intercultural neighbourhoods into places of leisure and consumption all around the world (Rath, 2007). From the beginning, concerns were raised regarding the effects of this kind of tourism on the communities involved in terms of:

- The *touristification* of their traditions and lifestyle without taking into account the perspective of the people involved. That is the importance of these features to self-represent a common identity and preserve the relationship both with the land of origin and other peers in the hosting country.
- The promotion of processes of gentrification and urban transformation according to a logic of generalized "beautification" of the territory. In fact, economic and social benefits do not necessarily reach the resident communities while may determine the expulsion of (unwanted) inhabitants from the neighborhood (Semi, 2015).

Yet, it is as well worth mentioning those positions that defend the social potential of Slumming because it might also indirectly lead to value the cultural and social features of these areas:

The tours in the areas where 'the other half' of New Yorkers lived inspired philanthropists, intellectuals, and politicians, giving rise to the birth of charitable associations and important reforms in the social welfare field, including the fundamental one on public housing. (Vietti, 2022, pp. 175-176)

Migrantour has been created following this mindset: a more ethical, conscious, and sustainable perspective aimed to enhance relationships of mutual respect between people with different origins. The narrative proposed promotes the respect for cultural diversity and the human rights of migrant communities by tackling the official discourse regarding intercultural neighbourhoods. In this sense, the author believes it represents a successful study case where tourism contributes positively to human rights within the frame of intercultural neighbourhoods and their transformation into places of leisure and consumption (Rath, 2007; Skoll & Korstanje, 2014).

The Concept of Human Rights

This chapter refers to a notion of human rights that appeared for the first time in 1945 in the UN Charter, the founding document of the United Nations, and was officially established by the adoption of the Universal Declaration of Human Rights (UDHR).. In this context, the idea of 'rights' is linked to the notion of what is 'right'. That is something that fulfils a standard of rightness and, in the case of human rights, finds its entitlement in moral or legal rules. Hence, the existence of universal basic standards of protection of the dignity and worth of the human person. "There is a wide gap between the promises of the UDHR and the real world" but abandoning the universal idea of human rights would mean giving up on the good reasons for supporting them (Freeman, 2011, p. 3).

Tourism was not immediately recognized as a sector where the framework of human rights could be applied. Nevertheless, human rights activists and some authors have often perceived conventional tourism as a form of cyclic violation of the rights of tourists, local communities, and employees. George & Varghese, for example, since 2007 have been claiming to ethics and sustainable tourism to advocate for a tourist practice respectful of human values and to positively accommodate the notion of human rights within tourism studies "as a yardstick for practice" (p. 46). This chapter intends to follow these ideas focusing on the consequences of urban tourism for the human rights of migrant communities living in intercultural neighborhoods under transformation into places of leisure and consumption.

Description of the Territory

Turin is a town in the Piedmont Region, in the North-West of Italy. From the beginning of the 20th century, thanks to a period of industrial expansion, it has welcomed the settlement of different industrial complexes: FIAT automotive company was created here in 1899. Progressively, it became an important centre for the industry sector and, slowly, a destination for people searching for jobs and fortune. The first flows of people arrived in early nighties from the surrounding countryside. Then, between the fifties and the sixties, many people attracted by industry-related jobs arrived from the South of Italy. From the eighties, instead, Turin started welcoming people arriving from all around the world, especially from China, East Europe, Northern Africa, and South America.

Since the 2000s, Economic crisis, deindustrialization, and the Winter Olympic Games (2006) triggered a process of "post -Fordist" transformation where manufacturing has been progressively replaced by alternative forms of economic production: the services sector, the cultural productions sector, and tourism, above all (Nofre et al., 2018). Yet, the path to balance is not easy to reach as cultural diversity, and its tangible and intangible heritage, is not yet completely perceived by all. Today, the population is 861.636 inhabitants, who are distributed in 8 districts. Of these, 131.594 are foreigners, representing approximately 15% of the total population. The foreign communities most represented are the Romanian (47.437), the Moroccan (15.501), the Chinese (7.539), and the Peruvian (6.806) (Municipal Statistical Office of the City of Turin, 2021).

Porta Palazzo

Porta Palazzo today is located near the historical centre of Turin. Although it is not classified as a neighbourhood from an administrative point of view (it belongs to the *Aurora* neighbourhood), it is perceived as a unitary popular area in the collective imagination. The name "*Porta*", gate, and "*Palazzo*", palace, depends on its historic location: just outside of one of the old entrance gates. The market, instead, has spontaneously formed here due to an administrative order of 1835 that prohibited running markets in town to prevent the spread of cholera. Today is considered the largest open market in Europe and is the main reason why people reach this part of the town. Some for shopping, some others looking for employment, housing, or just help and company. The "immigrants" of the past have been gradually replaced by individuals coming from the most diverse points of the globe[3] who have spread around 60 between languages and dialects (Semi, 2009). However, economic opportunities and cultural and historical heritage converge with social problems and institutional abandonment. Therefore, in the collective imagination, it is perceived as a marginal, conflictive, and dangerous neighbourhood that hosts the highest number of people with migrant origins (Semi, 2009) and from which "locals" should stay away (Cingolani, 2018).

Barriera di Milano

The neighbourhood was created at the end of the 19th century just outside of the first "*cinta daziaria*", a customs checkpoint established to control the goods entering town from the North. It has been incorporated into the urban fabric during the 20th century because of the industrial development of the area which has shaped its urban fabric and the lifestyle of the inhabitants. With deindustrialization, processes of urban change have been encouraged by "state-led gentrification" which has pushed it into a deep social and structural crisis (Nofre et al., 2018). From a traditional working-class neighbourhood, it became an area with abandoned warehouses, unemployed inhabitants, and one of the highest rates of young NEET, young people Neither in Employment nor Education or Training. The diversity here is the usual means by which relationships develop between people. Each person identifies himself by

The Migrantour Experience at Porta Palazzo and Barriera di Milano

belonging to one specific group sharing certain characteristics, while migrants from yesterday and today are still perceived as invaders of the territory (Cingolani, 2018)[4].

METHODOLOGY

This contribution is part of a broader study case carried out in 2021. It has examined the experience of Migrantour in the neighborhoods of *Porta Palazzo* and *Barriera di Milano* under different grounds. It has mainly applied a qualitative approach due to the usefulness of this methodology for understanding the subjective meaning of the actions of individuals while paying attention to the context in which they take place. However, a small survey has been carried out to reach the opinion of the participants in intercultural itineraries which otherwise could not have been collected. The purpose was to study reality in its natural context, as it happens, trying to explain phenomena according to the meanings they have for the people involved (Coller, 2005).

In this context, the hypothesis guiding the chapter takes into consideration both the tourist and the socio-political dimensions of Migrantour. The first is linked to the ethical principles of responsible tourism and aims to make visible portions of the urban space by enhancing the influence of migratory processes on the development of cultural heritage. The second is developed to offer alternative storytelling about migrations and to spread a culture of respect for the rights of migrant groups in both urban and rural areas. In this sense, the author believes that Migrantour represents a successful study case where tourism contributes positively to human rights within the frame of intercultural urban neighbourhoods and their transformation into places of leisure and consumption. Furthermore, she has a particular relationship with Migrantour: she has been part of the first group of intercultural companions ever trained in Turin and has been the local coordinator of Migrantour in the Italian town of Genoa between 2018-2019. The opportunity to research arrived in 2021 and it seemed an excellent occasion to analyse Migrantour from a distant and different perspective.

Objectives

General

Contributing to the debate about the relationship between tourism consumption, human rights, and urban space by analyzing the implications of urban tourism for the human rights of migrant communities living in intercultural neighborhoods.

Specific

Addressing theoretically the relationship between Migrantour and he processes of transformation undergoing in Porta Palazzo and Barriera di Milano neighborhoods.

Examining the implications of Migrantour for the human rights of migrant communities living in *Porta Palazzo* and *Barriera di Milano* neighbourhoods through the lens of touristification, urban transformation, and spatial segregation.

Reflecting on the sustainability of urban tourism in the frame of interculturalism by exploring its links with processes of discrimination and expulsion of vulnerable groups in the urban space.

Sources of Information

The fieldwork was carried out between May and July 2021 when sanitary restrictions due to Covid-19 were still in force in Turin. This affected both the number of intercultural itineraries that could be implemented in that period and the completion of the fieldwork. Information has been collected, mainly in Italian[5], through:

1. **Semi-Guided Online Interviews of 11 Individuals:** 7 Migrantour members with different roles; 3 members of NGOs and local organizations that collaborate with Migrantour; and 1 member of the International Cooperation and Peace Department of Turin's City Council. An interview guide was used to cover all the sensitizing topics connected with the research. Informed consent and confidentiality were ethical issues particularly relevant to the researcher. Voluntary consent was obtained from all interviewees. Each one also received a virtual copy of the research when it was concluded.

2. **A small-scale survey** was conducted among the participants in the 29 intercultural itineraries carried out between May and July 2021. Questionnaires have been distributed in person with the support of intercultural companions and the local coordinator. Only 48 questionnaires could be collected (45 for *Porta Palazzo* and 3 for *Barriera di Milano*). The author is conscious that these findings are from a small sample and so their generalizability is limited. Nevertheless, 48 people were generous enough to share their opinions about their experience with Migrantour for this study. Thus, their ideas should not be discarded but instead open up new ways of thinking about the relationship between tourism consumption, human rights, and urban space. In this perspective, some of their opinions about *Porta Palazzo* are mentioned throughout the chapter while the information collected about *Barriera di Milano* has been excluded as it was insufficient to be representative.

3. **Other Sources:** The author has consulted (a) the final assessment about the impact of the project "*Le nostre città invisibili: Incontri e nuove narrazioni del mondo in città*"[6] conducted in 2019 by the International Research Centre on Global Citizenship Education (IRC-GloCEd) of the University of Bologna; (b) three of the articles composing the academic debate about Migrantour published in the Italian Journal "*Antropologia Pubblica*" between 2018 and 2019.

Analysis Techniques

The interviews have been have been transcribed to be analysed thematically together with the information collected from the documents consulted. Analytical categories and subcategories have been created and then grouped in analytical families. Table 1 shows the result of this work.

Table 1. Categorization and analytical families

Analytical Families	Categories	Subcategories
(A) ELEMENTS OF URBAN TRANSFORMATION	Relationship with the Territory	1. Direct Relationship 2. Indirect Relationship
	Effects of Touristification	1. Direct Effects 2. Indirect Effects
(B) INFLUENCE ON COLLECTIVE IMAGINATION	Spatial Dimensions of Economic Integration	1. Market Exchange Dimension 2. Redistribution Dimension 3. Reciprocity Dimension
	Urban Fragmentation	
Source: Self-elaboration based on thematical analysis of interviews and documents		

The information collected through the questionnaires has been codified under different dimensions. Two are relevant for this chapter: (a) perception of participants in intercultural itineraries about *Porta Palazzo;* (b) elements of *touristification* and urban transformation. The variables used to analyze the dimensions were age, initial perception of participants in intercultural itineraries about *Porta Palazzo*, and understanding of the neighbourhood.

In addition, the author could use her perspective to observe Migrantour from a double position -a researcher and an intercultural companion- because although she aimed for being objective, the result of her interpretation of reality has the same scientific value as the one developed by any other person involved in that reality (Coller, 2005, p. 64).

Limitations of the Case Study Method

The study case is a valuable method to "register the behaviour of the people involved in the phenomena under study". It also helps to "comprehend the dynamics operating within unique contexts" and for this reason is widely used by social sciences researchers (Martínez, 2006). Nevertheless, it has some limitations that will be briefly addressed, also introducing the "antidots" used by the author to improve the quality of this research (Coller, 2005).

1. Reliability refers to the possibility of replicating the study in another research. Albeit it is difficult to replicate a study case "under the same conditions in which it occurred" (Quintão et al, 2021, p. 278), introducing a triangulation of data may help to support reliability. In this sense, by using multiple data sources the author has intended to cross-examine the information collected. Moreover, the thematic analysis carried out for both interviews and documents allowed us to identify similarities and contradictions and reach the conclusions proposed.
2. Internal validity establishes causal relationships under specific conditions and their variations when conditions change (Martínez, 2006). In this sense, the construction of the causal argument that supports the results has been based on (a) consolidated literature about the phenomena under study; (b) the recognition of some interviewees as key informants regarding specific topics; (c) the analysis of topics about the territory and context in which the study case took place.
3. External validity refers to the capacity of the study to be generalized. Thus, through the ideas raised by the participants in interviews and questionnaires, the research design provided an opportunity to deeper understand the relationship between tourism consumption, human rights, and urban space. It is valuable to consider that, although the specific socio-territorial aspects of each case must be contemplated, a wider reflection concerning many European cities can be established: a lot of them incorporate portions of territory with similar characteristics to *Porta Palazzo* and *Barriera di Milano*, a feature that has been also crucial for the reproduction of Migrantour around Europe.

To conclude, it is worth adding that the research did not aim to be representative or an extensive sample. Still, analytical representativity can be recognized to some extent if one assumes that the conclusions reached cannot be related to a whole universe but to "the set of theories to which it addresses" (Coller, 2005, p. 56).

The Migrantour Experience at Porta Palazzo and Barriera di Milano

DESCRIPTION OF THE PROJECT

Italy, 2009. While Turin is in the middle of its own "post-Fordist" transformation period, the anthropologist and professor Francesco Vietti start a collaboration with *Viaggi Solidali*, a tour operator active in the field of responsible tourism. They have a common idea: organising intercultural itineraries to allow adults, youth, kids, locals or tourists, to discover the intercultural richness hidden in *Porta Palazzo*. These itineraries are two-hour walks where participants can meet and interact with people of different origins thanks to the "mediation" and guide of intercultural companions. A group of locals -locals irrespective of their region of origin or one of their parents- encourage the participants to interact with the neighbourhoods and understand their social background. The starting point is the reflection that worldwide many intercultural neighbourhoods have been transformed into places of leisure and consumption, but a more ethical and sustainable formula is needed. That is responsible tourism because thanks to its characteristics it can help to (a) promote dynamics of social cohesion that could limit social segregation and spatial discrimination; (b) enhance contacts between inhabitants belonging to different social groups; (c) spread a culture of respect for their rights within the bigger community.

The experience of Migrantour in *Porta Palazzo* (where it is now active for more than 10 years) rapidly attracts the interest of other areas. It starts to be replicated in other neighbourhoods of Turin (like *Barriera di Milano, Mirafiori, San Salvario* for example), in other Italian cities, and finally abroad. With the creation of the European Network in 2013, Migrantour has been growing. Nowadays comprehends over 20 cities (including the ones still under training) and some rural areas. Please refer to figure 1 to better understand its evolution between 2009 and today.

It is worth adding that, even if Migrantour is recognized as a network of cities, it remains closely linked to the local dimension. The main working level is portions of territory, urban or rural, neighbourhoods or parts of them, sharing a common characteristic:

Being in the balance between public representation that stigmatizes them and is connected to the idea that migrations block the valorisation of cultural local heritage, tangible and intangible, and the attempt to propose a new narrative that recognizes cultural plurality as an attractive qualification element of these territories. (F., Migrantour team)

Moreover, only the initiative of a local organization sharing Migrantour objectives and interest in creating intercultural itineraries can lead to the creation of Migrantour in a certain area. The implementation process should relate to the following stages:

The Migrantour Experience at Porta Palazzo and Barriera di Milano

Figure 1. Migrantour evolution from 2009 to today
Source: Self-elaboration on VenngageEditor
*Project "MygranTour: a European network of migrant driven intercultural routes to understanding cultural diversity" funded by the EU Commission.
**EU Project "New Roots. Migrantour intercultural walks building bridges for newcomers' active participation"; AICS Project "Le nostre città invisibili. Incontri e nuove narrazioni del mondo in città".
***EU Project "Rural Migrantour. Paths of Recovery"; EU Project "Migrantour Sustainable Routes".

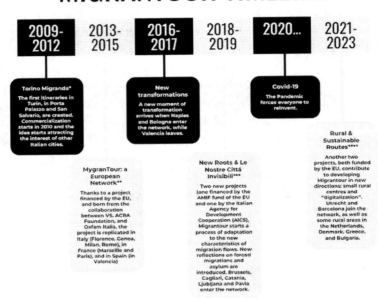

1. The organization in charge of Migrantour must identify at least one neighbourhood where intercultural itineraries can be implemented. Feasibility studies are conducted to identify elements of the cultural and architectonical heritage that can be observed from an intercultural perspective. Also, an analysis of local migration history and its influence on the transformation of the territory is carried out. At this stage, it is important to establish close collaborations with local entities and associations that somehow represent the migrant communities living in town and are willing to host the participants during the itinerary. Whenever possible, stigmatized are should be preferred to "use" Migrantour as a tool for promoting an alternative narrative.

2. Training courses for intercultural companions are designed and a selection process is opened to find the candidates to create the group of intercultural companions[7]. People interested in participating are usually very different in

terms of life stories, educational and professional backgrounds, skills, etc. However, they must share a few relevant characteristics. For instance, knowing the language of the hosting country and being highly curious about the area where the intercultural itineraries will be carried out. Moreover, be willing to share some information about their migration process (or the one of their family), as well as to get involved in the social, cultural, and economic life of the city. Finally, being interested in learning a new form of storytelling that promotes intercultural dialogue and respect for human rights.

3. Training courses have both a theoretical and a practical part. The first is supported by anthropologists, sociologists, geographers, historians, and other experts who are involved to provide participants with resources on different subjects[8]. The group of future intercultural companions must be actively involved in the field research to create each itinerary, which, in the end, should be designed thanks to their collective and participative work. Please now check the following maps to better understand what an intercultural itinerary is. Figure 2 represents the itinerary currently active in *Porta Palazzo*.

While the one currently active in *Barriera di Milano* is displayed in Figure 3a (standard option):

And Figure 3b (extended option):

STUDY CASE

Elements of Urban Transformation

The first analytical family takes into consideration the tourist dimension of Migrantour to understand its relationship with the processes of urban transformation and commodification of *Porta Palazzo* and *Barriera di Milano*. Table 2 summarizes it.

Table 2. Categorization of the analytical family "elements of urban transformation"

Analytical Families	Categories	Subcategories
(A) ELEMENTS OF URBAN TRANSFORMATION	Relationship with the Territory	1. Direct Relationship 2. Indirect Relationship
	Effects of Touristification	1. Direct Effects 2. Indirect Effects
Source: Self-elaboration based on thematical analysis of interviews		

Figure 2. Map of the intercultural itinerary of Porta Palazzo
Source: Self-elaboration on Google Maps

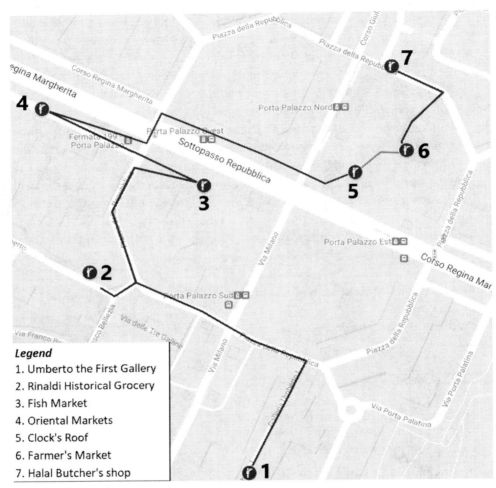

Legend
1. Umberto the First Gallery
2. Rinaldi Historical Grocery
3. Fish Market
4. Oriental Markets
5. Clock's Roof
6. Farmer's Market
7. Halal Butcher's shop

Relationship With Processes of Urban Transformation

Migrantour is implemented in close relationship with the territories where intercultural itineraries are carried out. For this reason, it seems relevant to understand to what extent it can contribute, directly or indirectly, to urban transformation processes and how these influence the communities living in *Porta Palazzo* and *Barriera di Milano*.

Figure 3a. Map of the standard intercultural itinerary of Barriera di Milano
Source: Self-elaboration on Google Maps

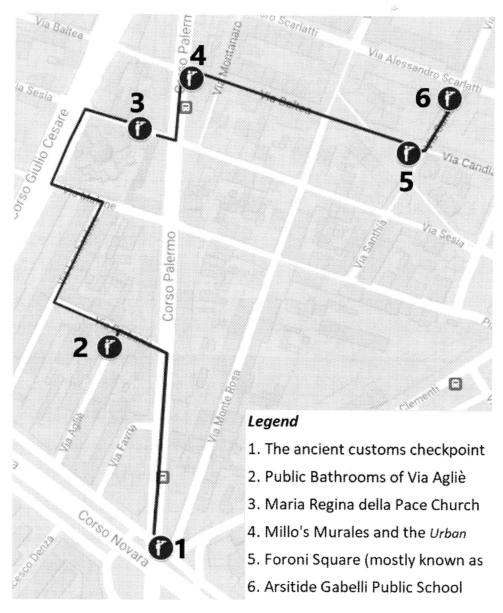

Legend
1. The ancient customs checkpoint
2. Public Bathrooms of Via Agliè
3. Maria Regina della Pace Church
4. Millo's Murales and the *Urban*
5. Foroni Square (mostly known as
6. Arsitide Gabelli Public School

Figure 3b. Map of the extended intercultural itinerary of Barriera di Milano
Source: Self-elaboration on Google Maps

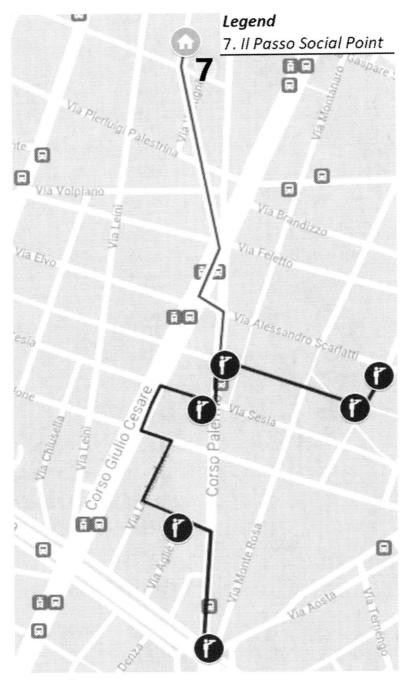

The Migrantour Experience at Porta Palazzo and Barriera di Milano

Intercultural neighborhoods are areas where the combination of (desired and undesired) migrations has created a sense of multiculturalism progressively identified by local authorities as a resource for urban socioeconomic development (Skoll & Korstanje, 2014). And tourism, a relatively new form of economic production that emerged because of deindustrialization, has become the main instrument to transform them into places of leisure and consumption (Rath, 2007). Hence, while at first glance "multicultural tourism" seems just another way to guarantee the socioeconomic inclusion of migrant communities, its effects may go in a different direction. They could establish a certain culture of exploitation of migrant communities, amplifying their segregation and the violation of their human rights (Rath, 2007).

The concept of cultural patrimony is based on selective characteristics of history. It highlights only part of desirable migration. Other ethnicities are often silenced or disciplined by coactive policies. (Skoll & Korstanje, 2014, p. 5)

The work of Sharon Zukin (1991) on this topic helps to develop further considerations. She affirms that transforming intercultural neighborhoods into "tourist destinations" is not a spontaneous process because takes place under the logic of "touristification". In this sense, only a neighborhood with shops, organizations, places of worship, etc. that provide an "ethnic flavor" to the area could be considered. Moreover, part of the community should be interested in transforming the neighborhood into a tourist attraction and seek for the support of the "critical infrastructure"[9] and public policies (Rath, 2007). Consequently, the preferences of the collective opinion would be influenced by the categories and conceptualizations widespread by the critical infrastructure and may end up granting opportunities on some groups while making others invisible. Whereas public policies supporting the transformation of the neighborhood may push to modify stereotypes already existing and "move" them to other areas of the city (Rath, 2007). Through this process, and with an official narrative of the site built, the neighborhood may become a tourist destination. Its attractiveness, in turn, might captivate new investments and ideas of urban refurbishment and heritagization (Skoll & Korstanje, 2014). In this context, "touristification" become one of the main elements of gentrification processes in intercultural neighborhoods (Semi, 2015).

In this sense, the outcomes of these processes for local communities should be examined under the framework of article 25 of UDHR which establishes the right to an adequate standard of living. According to the contribution of the Office of the High Commissioner for Human Rights to the 2014 United Nations ECOSOC Integration Segment[10], any process of urban transformation has a role in the enjoyment of human rights. Hence, any refurbishment project should consider its implications for the housing conditions of the people involved. Not only in terms of (concrete) housing, but also regarding any consequence on the security of tenure, affordability, cultural adequacy, and access to services. On the contrary, focusing only on market development, private investment, or excessive privatization may violate article 25 as it could create inadequate housing conditions and promote forms of discrimination and exclusion.

In this context, the fight against gentrification processes, corruption, and speculation over housing and land is of particular importance. (OHCHR, 2014, p. 2)

In the case of Turin, for instance, most of the urban transformation projects would have been carried out following "top-down multiculturalism" (Schmoll & Semi, 2013 as cited in De Martini Ugolotti, 2018, p. 164). In other words, to promote a specific concept of diversity that does not encourage the social inclusion and mobility of (post)migrant communities in the urban space. According to most of the people interviewed, also *Porta Palazzo* and *Barriera di Milano* have undergone urban transformation processes in recent years. As illustrated by M., a member of Migrantour, it seems that they have not been truly respectful of the rights of the inhabitants because the actors involved had economic and commercial interests in the neighborhoods: "(In *Porta Palazzo*), a space that should be public was left to private individuals who decided to make things a little more luxurious that are not accessible to the poor. In some way, (this has encouraged) more police controls and has pushed people towards the suburbs".

Focusing on Migrantour, it is now important to understand how it relates to processes of urban transformation in the neighborhoods under analysis. Interviewees agreed that there might be a limited relationship because of the essential characteristics of Migrantour. In other words:

- Its ethical values are linked to the principles of responsible tourism. According to these, local communities are the ones in charge of deciding whether to open to tourism or not and under which terms. Moreover, *Viaggi Solidali*, the cooperative that manages Migrantour in Turin, is a member of the AITR, the Italian Association for Responsible Tourism[11]. For these reasons, it is unlikely that Migrantour collaborates with actors going in opposite directions.
- Following the previous point, Migrantour in Turin would be open to collaborating only with initiatives that promote participatory urban transformation. That is through strategies based on participatory approaches that are crucial to assess the needs of the people.
- Lastly, Migrantour is not considered powerful enough to negotiate with the kind of actors who oversee these processes: "Unfortunately (they) are already being implemented and are poorly mediated. I do not think Migrantour has

The Migrantour Experience at Porta Palazzo and Barriera di Milano

the power to decide what to gentrify, those are political plans, and it is a different dimension" (M., UPM - *Porta Palazzo*).

At the same time, the interviewees spoke about the "insufficient" power and dimension of Migrantour when considering its indirect relationship with gentrification and urban transformation processes. That is the ability to attract "certain gazes or interests" to the neighborhoods for the simple fact of carrying out intercultural itineraries. However, some of them admitted that a risk exists, especially in *Porta Palazzo*:

There is this new market, Mercato Centrale[12], where there are small fast foods and restaurants and we can ask ourselves what kind of changes they are bringing to the communities. (L., Migrantour team)

This risk could anyway be reduced by not including these places within the stops of the itineraries:

We have somehow chosen to stay away from places that appeared as products of gentrification. . . . We have decided together to not go there because it is true that stopping by may advertise them, and this did not seem logical to us. (M., Migrantour team)

Finally, it is worth mentioning that for some interviewees the relationship of trust existing between Migrantour and both neighborhoods could be a positive tool to mediate urban transformation processes. In this sense, Migrantour could represent "a joining link so the actors who oversee these processes understand what this neighborhood needs before doing anything. . . . And maybe it could help the administration as well to understand who the inhabitants are" (A., Migrantour team). Especially because Migrantour could transfer the message "that it is not by making everything the same that something is embellished" (M., UPM - *Porta Palazzo*).

Effects of Touristification

Provided that Migrantour works in intercultural neighborhoods at risk of transformation into places of leisure and consumption, it is important to understand its relationship with commodification dynamics. Especially when these dynamics could violate the rights of the inhabitants of *Porta Palazzo* and *Barriera di Milano*, whether they are directly involved in the intercultural itineraries or not. The reflection can start with the ideas of Córdova (2007) who refer to multiculturalism as a call for *recognition of the right to enunciation and representation of cultural differences*:

This call is often coupled with the expectation of the protection of civil liberties by democratic regimes. Consequently, such a right to the enunciation of cultural difference is, in effect, often a demand for freedom of expression, an individual or collective right to speak. (p. 228)

In this respect, the interest of migrant communities to self-represent their common identity in the urban space could be explained as a fundamental part of the right to representation of cultural diversity. Thus, under the logic of freedom of expression defined by article 19 of UDHR, it may go in the opposite direction to "top-down multiculturalism"[13] (De Martini Ugolotti, 2018). In this sense, under Art. 19, strategies aimed at separating those who may embody the notion of diversity institutionally promoted from the ones who "do not have the right characteristics" to be culturally diverse appear to be unjustified. This is because the first could be seen in their "pleasant and exotic diversity", while the latter may find their freedom of (self)expression inhibited within the urban space (De Martini Ugolotti, 2018, p. 166). Therefore, if it is true that thanks to touristification some groups could have access to new opportunities, for many others it might mean the cyclical reproduction of divisions based on "class, gender, and economic achievement" (Rath, 2007, p. 13). In other words, it a discrimination and a violation of their human rights in terms of employment and distribution of resources[14].

And it is exactly on these aspects where Migrantour tries to work, spreading positive storytelling about *Porta Palazzo, Barriera di Milano,* and the other neighborhoods where intercultural itineraries are carried out. As a result, it appears to be able to promote a culture of respect for the rights of migrant communities, also opposing the prejudicial information widespread by the media.

Surely this is an idea that those who do not know the neighborhood still have, and it is unfortunately highly encouraged, in my opinion, by the press. In 90% of cases, they talk about Aurora and Barriera di Milano only when something negative happens, and mostly when these negative things involve migrants. (M., UPM - Porta Palazzo)

Therefore, Migrantour would represent a protected space where "exotic migrants" take the floor to speak about their stories and experiences as migrants.

It is one of the reasons why we do Migrantour. We want them to know us, so they are less afraid of us, and we have the chance to explain that being a foreigner (a migrant) doesn't necessarily mean being a criminal. (M., Migrantour team)

When we talk during the intercultural itinerary, we invite people to enter the place and get to know that community. It's one of the biggest assets of Migrantour, we speak about facts because it is important to consider who the intercultural companions are: people who represent at least one of the cultures (and communities) met during the itinerary. (L., Migrantour team)

As illustrated by R., a member of Migrantour, this is the reason why all intercultural itineraries are designed collectively by the group of intercultural companions and the local coordinator: women and men who have migratory experiences and know the neighborhoods. Moreover, their ideas are supported by statistical and theoretical reflections learned during training courses and moments of group exchange. The storytelling offered to participants is, indeed, not an external story of migrations in the neighborhood, but the self-representation of intercultural companions and the communities to which they belong. In this sense, as underlined by some of the members of local organizations interviewed, although sometimes "people go to visit as if (they) were a safari" (Er., Bagni Pubblici di Via Aglié - Barriera di Milano), Migrantour disseminates a different perception of intercultural neighborhoods. Essentially through the voice of their inhabitants who become "promoters of themselves" (L., Turin City Council).

The opinion of the respondents to questionnaires in 2021 appears to confirm this statement. As Figure 4a shows, for the respondents the main reasons to recommend Migrantour are the "strong educational value" (of intercultural itineraries) and the "opportunity to interact with people (they) usually do not interact with".

Figure 4a. Representation of answers to Q.5 of questionnaires done in 2021
Source: Self-elaboration from data collected

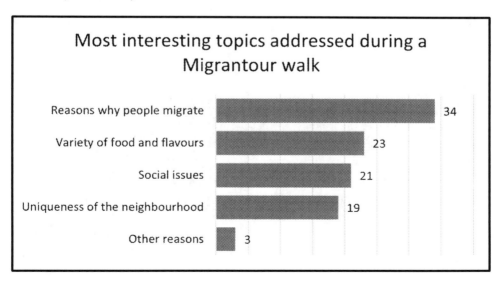

Additionally, as presented in Figure 4b, the "reasons why people migrate", the "variety of foods and flavors", and "social issues" are considered the most interesting topics addressed during the itinerary. Crossing the ideas, Migrantour seems to be able to enhance the interaction between participants and the inhabitants of the neighborhoods where the itineraries are carried out. Besides, choosing to speak about the social concerns and rights of the people, appears to control the use of touristification in the sense previously enunciated.

Figure 4b. Representation of answers to Q.11 of questionnaires done in 2021
Source: Self-elaboration from data collected

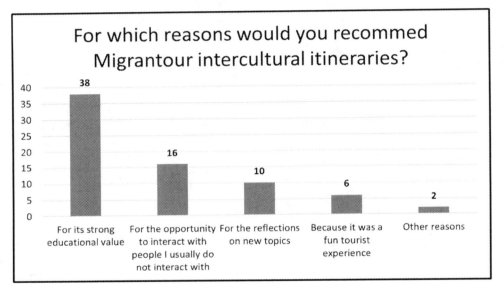

Finally, it is worth pointing out that the positive effect recognized by Migrantour by most of the interviewees tends to fade as the involvement of people within the project decreases. Some of the people interviewed considered this aspect as something to work on to improve the chances of people telling their "neighbors and friends" where "they have been with a Migrantour companion" (H., Migrantour team).

The final assessment about the impact of the project "*Le nostre città invisibili: Incontri e nuove narrazioni del mondo in città*" carried out in 2019 reached similar conclusions. According to this study, those inhabitants directly involved with Migrantour (being stops –*tappe*- of the intercultural itinerary), adhere to the initiative because they aim to spread their perspective about their culture. It is not the same thing for inhabitants who are not directly implicated because it is unlikely that they even note "when intercultural itineraries pass by" (p. 20). Different conclusions can be reached if one analyses this "fading effect" of Migrantour from the perspective of "ethnic commodification." It can be interpreted as another strategy to mitigate the risk of touristification and exploitation of diversity in *Porta Palazzo* and *Barriera di Milano*. As well as a form to limit its effects in terms of violation of the human rights of people "indirectly touched" by intercultural itineraries:

Thus, if the effect of Migrantour is not so evident for the inhabitants of the neighborhood, it means perhaps that it can properly blend with the components of the neighborhood. It is not an alien element acting on the neighborhood. It rather embraces local dynamics, and, for this reason, it is perceived as part of the neighborhood. (R., Migrantour team)

The challenge today, as illustrated by F., a member of Migrantour, is "to include in the storytelling the dimensions of conflict and inequality. Not transforming Migrantour in a form of activism, but fully embracing the idea of including these elements of conflict as they are a good antidote to producing simplified and stereotyped narratives".

Influence on the Collective Imagination

Through using the lens of spatial economic integration and urban fragmentation, the author will examine to what extent *Porta Palazzo* and *Barriera di Milano* can be considered segregated neighborhoods. The analysis will consider also what is the position of Migrantour in this context. Table 3 summarizes this analytical family.

Table 3. Categorization of the analytical family "influence on the collective imagination"

Analytical Families	Categories	Subcategories
(B) INFLUENCE ON COLLECTIVE IMAGINATION	Spatial Dimensions of Economic Integration	1. Market Exchange Dimension 2. Redistribution Dimension 3. Reciprocity Dimension
	Urban Fragmentation	
Source: Self-elaboration based on thematical analysis of interviews		

To begin it is worth briefly going back to the right to an adequate standard of living established by Art. 25 of UDHR in connection with discrimination and spatial segregation. In this regard, according to the Special Rapporteur on the right to adequate housing (2022), spatial segregation is one of the external factors influencing the distribution of social groups in the urban space in an infinite variety of combinations. It is an imposed separation (tangible or intangible) due to factors like "race, caste, ethnicity, language, religion, disability, income or another status" that causes severe inequalities among two or more social groups.

Whether de jure or de facto, spatial segregation is a reflection of multiple, compounded and intersectional forms of discrimination and an incursion on the equal enjoyment of the right to adequate housing. Spatial segregation is also linked to the violation of a wide range of other inter-related human rights. (SRAH, A/HRC/49/48, 2022, p. 3)

Different vulnerable groups are affected by these mechanisms. For this chapter, one will focus on migrant communities:

Systemic housing discrimination is faced by migrants, refugees, and internally displaced persons, in particular in conjunction with multiple other grounds of discrimination, namely, but not limited to, racial, ethnic and gender discrimination. . . . Migrants face discrimination in gaining access to both private and public housing, including increased vulnerability to violence, forced evictions and segregation, and disproportionately experienced inadequate and unhealthy housing conditions. (SRAH, A/76/408, 2021, pp. 13-14)

Spatial Dimensions of Economic Integration

Urban and residential segregation are two of the phenomena influencing the distribution of social groups in the urban space and for this reason, have been studied by different authors. Massey and Denton (1988), for example, have introduced a quantitative method to measure and compare levels of residential segregation by conceiving five dimensions of spatial variation:

We hold that residential segregation is a global construct that subsumes five underlying dimensions of measurement, each corresponding to a different aspect of spatial variation: evenness, exposure, concentration, centralization, and clustering. Each of these distributional characteristics has different social and behavioural implications and each represents a different facet of what researchers have called 'segregation'. (p. 283)

Similarly, Murie and Musterd (2004) introduced important reflections on the relationship between the mechanisms of social exclusion, the models of the economic integration of Karl Polanyi (as cited in Murie & Musterd, 2004), and the socio-

The Migrantour Experience at Porta Palazzo and Barriera di Milano

spatial dimension in which the previous ones take place. According to this theory, it is possible to identify three spatial dimensions of economic integration that are crucial for the distribution of people within the urban space. These are:

- The dimension of market exchange which is influenced by the private sector which might distribute resources to generate profits. It can determine the distribution of people based on their economic position when the quantity and quality of resources, services, and facilities allocated are not equal for the whole city.
- The dimension of redistribution of resources and services which is shaped by Welfare State policies that aim to compensate for market dynamics.
- The dimension of reciprocity implies the existence of bonds and mutual support networks among the inhabitants. It emerges when market dynamics and public policies are felt not favourable for the people and usually depends on the geographical proximity of social groups sharing similar conditions (Murie & Musterd, 2004).

According to interviewees, *Porta Palazzo* and *Barriera di Milano* could be considered places relatively segregated or, in the words of Ciampolini (as cited in Cingolani, 2018, p. 95), *"emiferias"*, places geographically close to the centre of town but represented as marginal and distant in the collective imagination. The reason would be the increasing maldistribution of resources and services, especially considering housing and employment.

(In Barriera di Milano) there is a higher concentration of social housing. There are also apartments at lower prices compared to other parts of town. For this reason, it is a neighborhood inhabited by families who receive assistance from social services because they have many problems and they have even more difficulty getting in touch with the rest of the neighborhood. (E., Mais Ong – Barriera di Milano)

In other words, these neighborhoods would gather (a) "people without work who lack cultural tools, are not qualified, are not graduated and find it difficult to find employment" (Er., Bagni Pubblici di Via Aglié - Barriera di Milano); and (b) people who have recently arrived in Turin and so "go through a period of initial economic difficulty because they have access to less prestigious and less paid jobs compared to the average standard" (F., Migrantour team). As a result, vulnerable groups, especially migrants, usually "choose" to settle here after having a hard time finding an economic place anywhere else in town. Besides, they may be influenced by a perceived sentiment of rejection coming from inhabitants of other neighborhoods. This, in turn, leads them again to prefer areas where there are "people identified as similar and where they feel more protected and less exposed to (negative) comments" (M., Migrantour team).

This process has been explained by the theory of "racism of exclusion" developed by Michel Wieviorka (as cited in Vargas Llovera, 2020). Migrant communities would be often exposed to a generalized rejection linked to the representation of "their culture" which is perceived as very different from the "local". This would be not only because of their language, customs, and appearance but also because their culture is considered an obstacle to the desired progress and modernization. In this sense, the exclusion of migrants could be identified as the "main orientation of racist action" that arise under three dimensions:

- The social dimension is implemented to expel unwanted individuals from social relations.
- The political dimension is mainly connected to limitations of access to citizenship and related rights.
- The cultural dimension is determined by both rejecting multiculturalism and limiting the participation of migrant communities in the dominant culture. This implies the presence of minority groups who are "diverse" because of "their ethnicity, their religion or their memory" and are enclosed "in their specific identity" (Vargas Llovera, 2020, p. 96).

Focusing on *Porta Palazzo* and *Barriera di Milano*, the theory of Wieviorka seems to be applied through the widespread negative reputation of the neighborhoods. This relates to structural factors (the architectural state of buildings, institutional abandonment, etc.) and the stigmatization of the inhabitants.

More than a cultural diversity issue, I think that it is something linked to social and class stigmatization. People living in these neighbourhoods, beyond being variously different, think of themselves mostly as (people) socially and economically in default about what is desired. Neighbourhoods identified as poor are neighbourhoods that risk stigmatization because they could spread their negative characteristics to other areas of the city. (F., Migrantour team)

This issue emerges also analyzing the opinion expressed by the participants in intercultural itineraries surveyed in 2021. As presented in Table 4, 29 people over 45 believe that *Porta Palazzo* has changed over time.

While, as shown in Figure 5, 40% of these considerations that the main reason for the change is the intercultural composition of the population.

Table 4. Summary of answers to Q.4 of the survey done to participants to Migrantour itineraries in 2021

Do You Think Porta Palazzo Has Changed Over Time?	
YES	29
NO	2
Does Not Know	13
Does Not Answer	1
Source: Self-elaboration based on data collected through questionnaires	

Figure 5. Representation of answers to Q.4b of questionnaires done in 2021
Source: Self-elaboration from data collected

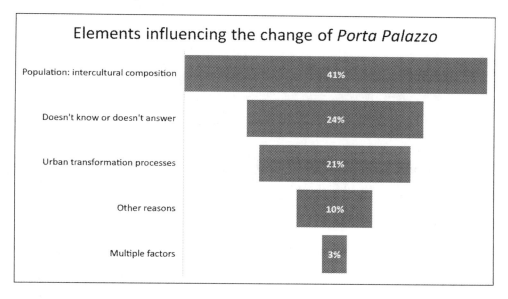

In this context, Migrantour tries to mitigate these dynamics by offering alternative storytelling which is based on a culture of respect for the rights of migrant communities.

I believe that it can indeed be a useful instrument, especially for the members who work in the Communal Council (council of the Turin's City Council) (...) The reality for example of diasporas, understanding it through the citizens of foreign origin in the territory, instead of through the organizations to which they belong, it has been very useful. (L., Turin's City Council)

The Migrantour Experience at Porta Palazzo and Barriera di Milano

This ability to promote positive values is carried out thanks to the dissemination of complete and real information. It does not exaggerate with positive stories nor hides the most difficult and complex aspects of the neighbourhoods, as mentioned by M., a member of Migrantour. And the credit goes to the coordination of intercultural itineraries, suggests L. from the International Cooperation and Peace Department of Turin's City Council:

They involve people that have experience on a local level. They can speak about their story, the context in which they live, and about those who live in the neighborhood in the same conditions as them.

From a broader perspective, it contributes to the development of a more thoughtful look at the relationship between interculturalism and respect for human rights:

In my opinion, I would not have been able to do this job (as a social worker) if I had not had an intercultural experience. Because 80% of the boys we assist come from other cultures. For example, not even knowing on which pillars their religion is based, sometimes we risk making empty interventions that have no results nor lead anywhere. (R., Migrantour team)

Nevertheless, Migrantour cannot be given a bigger role than the one it has. It gives an important contribution to "reduce prejudices or at least to invite a person to wonder a couple of things" (L., Migrantour team). But it is still a two-hour intercultural itinerary that has not to have enough time, resources, or strength to provide an immediate response to all the concerns of the people involved.

Also, by reading through the answers of the participants surveyed in 2021, it appears that participating in an intercultural itinerary may help people to change their perception of _Porta Palazzo_ to some extent. As presented in Figure 6, 95% of the respondents have admitted that the intercultural itinerary had a positive effect on their perception of the neighborhood. The measurement has been done on a scale from 1 to 5, where 1 was "no change of perception" and 5 was "significative change of perception".

Urban Fragmentation

Given the considerations treated in the previous paragraph, it is relevant to also introduce the concept of urban fragmentation.

Figure 6. Representation of answers to Q.6 of questionnaires done in 2021
Source: Self-elaboration from data collected

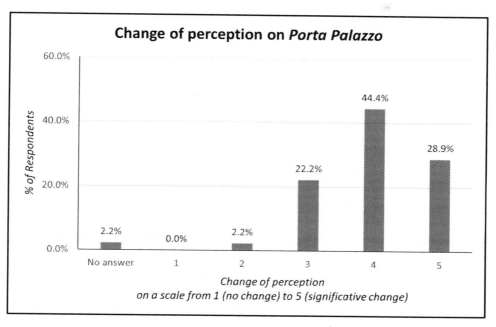

According to Caprón and González Arellano (2006), urban segregation happens when there is an intention to discriminate against a social group that adds to situations of social separation in the urban space. At the same time, urban fragmentation can be defined as a process of "new segregation" resulting from urban policies designed without considering the tendency of cities to divide into separate and unequal portions:

This is important when we accept that segregation relates to the way of occupying the space daily. It is a concept that goes beyond just being in town. Everyday life allows us to identify different aspects: housing, employment, studying, etc. This (indeed) questions those projects based only on the residential space. (p. 74)

In the case of Turin, the reproduction of segregation and spatial discrimination of migrant communities is done by "trapping" them in areas of lower resources. This has led to the construction of symbolic borders, tangible and intangible, between people belonging to different social groups. Thus, the fragmentation perceived is a consequence of the stigmatization and the lack of economic integration of migrant groups that influence the way people live in the space (Murie & Musterd, 2004).

I know many people who came to live here in the last four or five years and are part of the group of 'intellectuals' (of Barriera di Milano) but never really interact with the neighborhood. For instance, they do not register their children in the schools of the neighborhood. They prefer the schools of the city centre. (Er., Bagni Pubblici di Via Aglié - Barriera di Milano).

This idea of urban border is quite evident, and it is one of the ethical and political objectives of Migrantour. (F., Migrantour team)

In this context, Migrantour acts, again, by offering positive storytelling of the neighborhoods through the voice of those inhabitants who are usually discriminated against because of the areas where they live and how their "cultures" are perceived. This may happen because social and cultural diversity are perceived "more as daily life codes and general behaviour rather than as cultural baggage" (Er., Bagni Pubblici di Via Aglié - Barriera di Milano). In this sense, the intercultural dimension would be lived more as a form of multi-society than actual interculturalism.

The work of Migrantour can be read also by analysing the answers of the participants in intercultural itineraries surveyed in 2021. As the graph presented in Figure 7 reveals, the main elements influencing their change of perception about the neighborhoods were meeting intercultural companions and walking around them.

Figure 7. Representation of answers to Q.9 of questionnaires done in 2021
Source: Self-elaboration from data collected

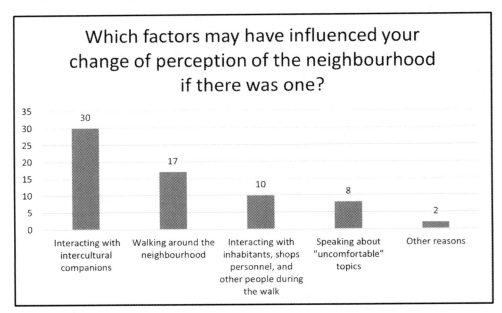

The Migrantour Experience at Porta Palazzo and Barriera di Milano

This could be interpreted as an ability of Migrantour to break the imaginary barriers existing between inhabitants of Turin living in different areas.

Just for the fact of bringing participants to walk the streets of Porta Palazzo and Barriera di Milano which usually create concern and fear and meeting some of the people living there. (E., Mais Ong – Barriera di Milano)

In conclusion, it is worth noting that many interviewees conferred to Migrantour the responsibility to further engage the inhabitants of *Porta Palazzo and Barriera di Milano*. Some suggest involving them as participants in intercultural itineraries to speak about "the area where they live and explain to them that they do not live in the Bronx" (M., UPM - *Porta Palazzo*). While for others, Migrantour should create occasions where people who have lived in these neighbourhoods for many years could tell others about their life there.

CONCLUSION

During her time as a member of Migrantour, the author has witnessed its evolution in terms of social action and respect for cultural diversity. The opportunity of taking distance and examining Migrantour from a different perspective arrived in 2021. In this line, she conducted a study case about the experience of Migrantour in *Porta Palazzo* and *Barriera di Milano*, two neighbourhoods of the Italian town of Turin. The hypothesis guiding the reflection took into consideration both the tourist and socio-political dimensions of Migrantour through the lens of touristification, urban transformation, and spatial segregation. Besides, the author developed the analysis under the framework of the rights 19 (freedom of expression) and 25 (adequate standard of living) of the Universal Declaration of Human Rights. The general objective was contributing to the debate about the relationship between tourism consumption, human rights, and urban space by analyzing the implications of urban tourism for the human rights of migrant communities living in intercultural neighborhoods. The field work was conducted between May and July 2021 through interviews, document consultation, and a small-scale survey.

Firstly, the author analyzed the relationship between Migrantour and processes of gentrification and touristification happening in *Porta Palazzo* and *Barriera di Milano*. The analysis has shown that Migrantour does not seem to be involved in any kind of relationship with these processes. Not only because of the principles of responsible tourism guiding its work, but also thanks to the "limited" power it has when relating with the actors who oversee those processes. Besides, Migrantour appears to be able to build positive and respectful relationships with the people involved in the intercultural itineraries. This ability is perceived as stronger in members, participants, or local dwellers who take part in the itineraries, while it tends to fade as the involvement of people within Migrantour decreases. This is an ingredient that, after all, seems to have prevented it from falling into logics of commodification of diversity and limited its effects in terms of violation of the human rights of migrant communities. In this sense, the central role of intercultural companions cannot be forgotten. They are people with migrant origins who are often inhabitants of the neighborhoods where the intercultural itineraries are carried out. Also, it is thanks to their collective work that intercultural itineraries are designed: the result is a neighborhood that narrates itself while the "exotic migrant" takes the floor to self-represent. Moreover, Migrantour is given an important role: differentiating external actors and avoiding collaborations with the ones that intend to "clean out" vulnerable groups.

In the second part, the author examined to what extent *Porta Palazzo* and *Barriera di Milano* could be considered neighborhoods affected by processes of spatial segregation and urban fragmentation. The analysis also considered what is the position of Migrantour in this context. The fieldwork highlighted that both neighborhoods are characterized by social problems, maldistribution of resources, and institutional abandonment. Moreover, they are represented in the collective imagination as marginal and conflictive areas from which the rest of the population chooses to stay away. This situation seems to influence the way migrant communities live Turin as their choices appear to be expression of economic difficulties and fear of rejection. Migrantour works in this scenario trying to influence positively the collective imagination by offering a more thoughtful look to the relationship between interculturalism and respect for human rights. However, it cannot be given a bigger role than the one it has. It contributes to modify the representation about the neighborhoods, but it cannot provide an immediate response to social concerns. In this context, part of the interviewees suggested Migrantour as a mediator between neighborhoods and public authorities willing to develop common strategies.

In conclusion, Migrantour could be considered a positive example of tourism consumption in intercultural neighbourhoods as it is implemented responsibly, ethically, and with respect for the rights of the migrant communities "touched" by its activities. This is also confirmed if considering the variety of actors interested in these neighbourhoods. In this sense, projects like Migrantour should, not only learn how to deal with these stakeholders, but also start thinking which kind of role they want to assume in this context.

Following these considerations, more comprehensive and in-depth research is needed to further explore the issues raised in this chapter. Such research should look to other cities where Migrantour is implemented and propose a comparative analysis of two or more of them. Indeed, comparing different territories could help to understand how their specificity influence the relationship of Migrantour with the communities involved. Further research is crucial as tourism consumption in the urban space is increasing as well as social concerns linked to it.

REFERENCES

Caprón, G., & González Arellano, S. (2006). Las Escalas de la segregación y de la fragmentación urbana. *Trace (México, DF)*, (49), 65–75. doi:10.22134/trace.49.2006.469

Cingolani, P. (2018). È tutto etnico quel che conta? Conflitto per le risorse e narrazioni della diversità a Barriera di Milano. In Torino, un profilo etnografico (pp. 91-113). Meltemi.

Coller, X. (2005). *Estudio de Casos*. Centro de Investigaciones Sociológicas.

Córdova, N. I. (2008). Between Freedom of Speech and Cultural Diversity of Expression: Bureaucratizing the Multicultural Imagination. In W. Binford & S. Basu (Eds.), *The Role of Freedom of Expression in a Multicultural and Democratic Society* (pp. 215–239). Willamette University.

De Martini Ugolotti, P. (2018). "No sleep 'till Parco Dora": Parkour e i paradossi di una città rigenerata, tra eterotopie e governo della differenza. In Torino, un profilo etnografico (pp. 159-178). Meltemi.

Freeman, M. (2011). *Human Rights: An Interdisciplinary Approach* (4th ed.). Polity Press.

George, B. P., & Varghese, V. (2007). Human Rights in Tourism: Conceptualization and Stakeholder Perspectives. *Electronic Journal of Business Ethics and Organization Studies*, *12*(2), 40–48.

Martínez Carazo, P. C. (2006). El método de estudio de caso: estrategia metodológica de la investigación científica. Pensamiento & Gestión, (20), 65-193.

Massey, D. S., & Denton, N. A. (1988). The Dimensions of Residential Segregation. *Social Forces*, *67*(2), 281–315. doi:10.2307/2579183

Municipal Statistical Office of the City of Turin. (n.d.). *Dati statistici: stranieri per sesso, età, circoscrizione, quartiere, provenienza*. Turin: Municipal Statistical Office. Found on: http://www.comune.torino.it/statistica/dati/

Murie, A., & Musterd, S. (2004). Social Exclusion and Opportunity Structures in European Cities and Neighbourhood Matters. *Urban Studies (Edinburgh, Scotland)*, *41*(8), 1441–1459. doi:10.1080/0042098042000226948

Nofre, J., Giordano, E., Eldridge, A., Martins, J. C., & Sequera, J. (2018). Tourism, nightlife, and planning: Challenges and opportunities for community liveability in La Barceloneta. *Tourism Geographies*, *20*(3), 377–396. doi:10.1080/14616688.20 17.1375972

OHCHR. (2014). *Contribution to the 2014 United Nations Economic and Social Council (ECOSOC) Integration Segment*. United Nations.

Quintão, C., Andrade, P., & Almeida, F. (2021). How to Improve the Validity and Reliability of a Case Study Approach? *Journal of Interdisciplinary Studies in Education*, *9*(2), 264–275.

Rath, J. (2007). *The transformation of ethnic Neighborhoods into Places of Leisure and Consumption*. Working Paper 144. Institute for Migration and Ethic Studies. University of Amsterdam.

Semi, G. (2009). Il mercato come spazio di relazione e di conflittualità interetnica. In Migrazioni (pp. 637-652). Einaudi.

Semi, G. (2015). *Gentrification. Tutte le città come Disneyland*. Il Mulino.

Skoll, G. R., & Korstanje, M. (2014). Urban heritage, gentrification, and tourism in Riverwest and El Abasto. *Journal of Heritage Tourism*, *9*(4), 349–359. doi:10.1 080/1743873X.2014.890624

Special Rapporteur on the right to adequate housing. (2021). *Discrimination in the context of housing - Report A/76/408*. General Assembly, 76th Session.

Special Rapporteur on the right to adequate housing. (2022). *Spatial segregation and the right to adequate housing - Report A/HRC/49/48*. Human Rights Council, 49th Session.

Vargas-Llovera, M. D. (2020). ¿Somos racistas? Caminando a través de los conceptos de racismo, exclusión y segregación urbana y social. In Racismo, etnicidad e identidad en el siglo XXI (pp. 79-99). AnthropiQa 2.0.

Vietti, F. (2022). The Tourist, the Migrant, and the Anthropologist. In N. Bloch & K. Adams (Eds.), *Intersections of Tourism, Migration, and Exile* (pp. 170–186). Routledge. doi:10.4324/9781003182689-10

Zukin, S. (1991). *Landscapes of Power. From Detroit to Disney World*. University of California Press.

ADDITIONAL READING

Hae, L. (2011). Dilemmas of the Nightlife Fix: Post-Industrialization and the gentrification of nightlife in New York City. *Urban Studies (Edinburgh, Scotland)*, *48*(16), 3444–3460. doi:10.1177/0042098011400772

López-Morales, E., Ruiz-Tagle, J., Santos, O. A. Junior, Blanco, J., & Salinas-Arreortúa, L. (2021). State-led gentrification in three Latin American cities. *Journal of Urban Affairs*, 1–21. doi:10.1080/07352166.2021.1939040

Mellino, M., & Vietti, F. (2019). Dibattito: L'antropologia applicata tra "tecniche di mercato" e "pratiche politiche". Riflessioni sui migranti, Migrantour e Noi. *Antropologia Pubblica*, *5*(1), 123–131.

Schmoll, C., & Semi, G. (2013). Shadow circuits: Urban spaces and mobilities across the Mediterranean. *Identities (Yverdon)*, *20*(4), 377–392. doi:10.1080/1070 289X.2013.822376

Vietti, F., Marletto, E., Marazzini, S., & Carrara, S. (2020). *Migrantour, The world within Cities. Intercultural walks in Bologna, Brussels, Cagliari, Catania, Florence, Genoa, Lisbon, Ljubljana, Milan, Naples, Paris, Pavia, Rome, and Turin*. ACRA.

Wieviorka, M. (1994). Racismo y exclusión [Racism and exclusion]. *Estudios Sociológicos*, *12*(34), 37–47.

KEY TERMS AND DEFINITIONS

Commodification of Diversity: The strategy used by local authorities to transform intercultural areas into tourist destinations aiming to foster economic development.

Intercultural Companion: A person with migrant background living in one of the cities that are part of Migrantour network who has been trained to guide intercultural itineraries in her/his city.

Intercultural Itinerary: A two-hours walk around an intercultural neighborhood or rural area organized by Migrantour in one of the cities that are part of the network. The aim is encouraging participants to walk in the area and interact with people with different origins. It is guided by an intercultural companion.

Post-Fordist Transformation: A concept used to identify the deindustrialization period that has taken place in European cities. It refers, in opposition, to the Fordism, a period started in the early nighties and named after Henry Ford, the inventor of the assembly-line model for industrial production.

Special Rapporteur on the Right to Adequate Housing: A mandate established by the former UN Commission on Human Rights at the beginning of the 2000's with the purpose of further developing strategies of protection of the right to adequate housing around the world. Currently, the mandate is covered by Mr. Balakrishnan Rajagopal.

Top-Down Multiculturalism: A concept created by some authors (Giovanni Semi and Camille Schmoll in particular) to identify an institutional form to promote diversity in a given society. It refers to the use of pleasant multicultural features (such as food or big celebrations) in specific places (restaurants, textile shops, festivals…) to foster interculturalism among part of the population.

Young NEET: Young people Neither in Employment nor Education and Training. It refers to the percentage of young population who is unemployed or inactive and who has not been involved in any form of education (formal or informal) in a given period.

ENDNOTES

[1]   Cf. UN Conference on International Organization. (1945). *United Nations Charter*. San Francisco. Available at: https://www.un.org/en/about-us/un-charter/full-text

[2]   Cf. UNGA. (1948). *Universal Declaration of Human Rights*. Paris. Available at: https://www.un.org/en/about-us/universal-declaration-of-human-rights.

[3]   In *Porta Palazzo* live 5.139 people of foreign origin, corresponding to 50.61% of the total population (Municipal Statistical Office of the City of Turin, 2017); while in *Aurora* neighbourhood live 11.783 people of foreign origin out of a total of 39.151 inhabitants, corresponding to 30% of the population (Municipal Statistical Office of the City of Turin, 2021).

[4]   In *Barriera di Milano* live 17.591 people of foreign origin, out of 50.135 inhabitants, corresponding to 35% of the total population (Municipal Statistical Office of the City of Turin, 2021).

[5]   Italian was the common language spoken by all the people involved in the fieldwork. However, the quotes are here included translated in English to harmonize the reading.

The Migrantour Experience at Porta Palazzo and Barriera di Milano

[6] The project *"Le nostre città invisibili: Incontri e nuove narrazioni del mondo in città* has been implemented between 2018 and 2019 in different cities part of the Migrantour network. The IRC-GloCEd carried out a qualitative evaluation of the effectiveness of intercultural itineraries. The goal was to verify the degree of achievement of the objectives of the project and its impact on the participants and the context.

[7] All trained intercultural companions receive economic compensation for each intercultural itinerary carried out. This is possible thanks to the commercialization of the itineraries: from the beginning, Migrantour wanted to establish an economically self-sustainable approach to be able to cover the compensation of intercultural companions, as well as coordination and administrative expenses.

[8] The most common topics addressed in a training course for intercultural companions are (a) the relationship between migrations and territory; (b) interreligious dialogue; (c) world food and cuisine; (d) museum heritage and intangible heritage; (e) group guiding techniques; (f) group management and public speaking.

[9] "A group of people who can influence the popularity of cultural products, regardless of their intentions. This is possible thanks to their involvement in different fields of cultural production and consumption. Thus, we are speaking about connoisseurs, cultural mediators, marketing bureaus, business associations, tourist boards, parts of national and local governments, etc. (Rath, 2007, p. 8).

[10] The Integration Segment of the United Nations Economic and Social Council (ECOSOC) is organized annually to support UN Member States to achieve the three pillars of sustainable development (economic, social, and environmental). Any Member State, ECOSOC subsidiary body, UN organization, or relevant stakeholder interested in contributing to issues of global concern can participate in the sessions of ECOSOC. For more information please see: https://www.un.org/ecosoc/en/.

[11] "Since 1998, AITR works in Italy for the establishment and respect of culture and the principles of responsible tourism. More information about this issue can be found on their webpage: https://www.aitr.org/documenti-e-materiali/carte-etiche/.

[12] *Mercato Centrale* is a project started in Florence in 2014 (then reproduced in other Italian cities) by a "food entrepreneur" and an Italian company. It aims to promote "open-air" tourism by refurbishing buildings belonging to abandoned historic market areas. When interviewed about urban transformations in Turin (2019), Sociology professor Giovanni Semi defined *Mercato Centrale* as "an intervention for culturally poor. . . . Creating a distinctive pavilion that aims to

bring tourists to a market that is already known to all, is like offending Porta Palazzo. . . . There is no need to redevelop it. Because it is like saying that a place does not exist or does not work". And "the consumer is not the popular class". Interview available at: https://www.lavoroculturale.org/trasformazioni-urbane-il-caso-torino/matteo-lester-viora/2019/.

[13] To reflect on the notion of "top-down multiculturalism", please go back to page 15.

[14] Some people might be forced to take low-paid or low-skilled jobs, or even accept certain forms of exploitation. This, in turn, could create new discriminatory divisions between those who "control" the income and those who are just the "labor force" as well as feed new cultural and social stereotypes (Chang as cited in Rath, 2007, p. 11).

Chapter 7

Human Rights and Workforce Conditions in the Tourism Sector

Osama Khassawneh
The Emirates Academy of Hospitality Management, UAE

Zeynep Gulen Hashmi
(iD) https://orcid.org/0000-0001-6949-6647
National University of Science and Technology, Islamabad, Pakistan

ABSTRACT

In this chapter, the focus is on the various challenges related to workforce conditions in the tourism industry and how human rights can play a role in alleviating these challenges. The chapter draws from a review of literature and offers a global perspective. Topics covered include the treatment of employees in the tourism sector, adherence to human rights and labor standards in the industry, the prevalence of mandatory and forced labor, collective bargaining, the use of child labor, fair treatment for all workers, and employee discrimination. The chapter will feature examples from different countries and conclude with recommendations for improvement.

INTRODUCTION

In today's globalized world, the tourism industry has become an essential part of many countries' economies (Higgins-Desbiolles et al., 2019). However, the industry faces various challenges that threaten the well-being and human rights of its workforce (Gascón, 2019). This chapter focuses on exploring these challenges, their impact on

DOI: 10.4018/978-1-6684-8726-6.ch007

Copyright © 2023, IGI Global. Copying or distributing in print or electronic forms without written permission of IGI Global is prohibited.

workers, and how human rights can play a critical role in alleviating these issues. To provide a comprehensive review of the topic, the chapter draws from a broad range of literature, including academic articles, government reports, and news articles. The analysis takes a global perspective, examining the workforce conditions in different countries and regions worldwide. One of the primary topics covered in the chapter is the treatment of employees in the tourism sector. This includes issues such as low wages, long working hours, and poor working conditions. These problems often lead to high turnover rates, low job satisfaction, and employee burnout (Khassawneh, & Abaker, 2022).

Additionally, the chapter addresses the need for adherence to human rights and labor standards in the industry, such as safe working conditions, the right to form and join trade unions, and the right to fair pay. Another critical issue in the tourism industry is the prevalence of mandatory and forced labor. Many workers in the sector are vulnerable to exploitation due to their immigration status, lack of education, or poverty (Mohammad et al., 2021). The chapter discusses the various forms of forced labor in tourism, including debt bondage, trafficking, and exploitation of migrants. Furthermore, the chapter covers the topic of collective bargaining and the role of unions in protecting workers' rights. The use of child labor is another issue addressed in the chapter, with a focus on its prevalence in developing countries and the negative impact it has on children's health and education. The chapter also emphasizes the need for fair treatment for all workers, regardless of their gender, race, ethnicity, or religion (Mohd. Shamsudin et al., 2022). Discrimination in the tourism industry is a significant issue, with some workers experiencing discrimination in recruitment, promotion, and training opportunities.

To illustrate the various challenges faced by workers in the tourism industry, the chapter features examples from different countries worldwide. These examples demonstrate the complexity and diversity of the issues faced by workers in the sector. Finally, the chapter concludes with recommendations for improvement. These include the need for stronger regulations and enforcement mechanisms, greater awareness of workers' rights among employers and employees, and the need for collaboration among stakeholders to address the challenges faced by workers in the tourism industry. In summary, the chapter provides a comprehensive overview of the various challenges related to workforce conditions in the tourism industry and their impact on workers' human rights. By highlighting the issues and offering recommendations for improvement, the chapter seeks to promote greater understanding and action to address these critical issues.

EMPLOYEES IN THE TOURISM SECTOR

The tourism sector is a vast industry that employs a significant portion of the global workforce. The industry includes a variety of businesses, such as hotels, restaurants, travel agencies, transportation providers, and many more (Riadil, 2020; Bani-Melhem, Abukhait, & Bourini, 2022). The employees working in the tourism sector play a crucial role in shaping the experiences of tourists, and their job responsibilities vary depending on their job position and the specific sector they work in. In this article, we will discuss the employees in the tourism sector and their role in the industry (Belias et al., 2022; Mat, Yaacob, & Melhem, 2015a). The tourism industry is a labor-intensive industry, and it requires a diverse set of skills from its employees (Elbaz & Haddoud, 2017; Abukhait et al., 2023).

Employees in the tourism sector can be categorized into two main groups: front-line employees and support staff (Ram, 2018). Front-line employees include those who directly interact with tourists, such as hotel receptionists, tour guides, restaurant servers, and airline staff (Alegre & Berbegal-Mirabent, 2016). Support staff includes those who work behind the scenes to ensure the smooth operation of the business, such as housekeeping staff, kitchen staff, and maintenance workers (Shafique, Kalyar, & Ahmad, 2018). Front-line employees are the face of the tourism industry, and their interaction with tourists significantly influences their experience. Their job responsibilities include providing information about local attractions and events, making recommendations, answering queries, and ensuring the comfort and safety of the guests (Daniel et al., 2017; Bani-Melhem, Al-Hawari, & Mohd. Shamsudin, 2022). A welcoming and friendly attitude, effective communication skills, and excellent customer service are essential qualities for front-line employees (Robinson et al., 2019).

One of the challenges of working in the tourism industry is the long and irregular working hours. The industry operates 24 hours a day, seven days a week, and employees may have to work during weekends and holidays. This can be challenging for employees who have to balance their work and personal life (Ariza-Montes, 2017). Another challenge that employees in the tourism sector face are the seasonal nature of the industry. Many businesses in the tourism sector experience fluctuations in demand throughout the year, with peak seasons and low seasons (Stamolampros et al., 2019). During peak seasons, businesses may need to hire additional staff to meet the demand, while during low seasons, employees may experience reduced working hours or even temporary layoffs (Fominienė, Mejerytė-Narkevičienė, & Woźniewicz-Dobrzyńska, 2015).

The tourism industry provides several opportunities for career advancement and professional development. Many employees in the tourism sector start their careers in entry-level positions and work their way up to higher positions through experience and training (Yılmazdogan, Secilmis, & Cicek, 2015). The industry offers various training programs and certifications that enable employees to enhance their skills and knowledge and advance their careers (Aynalem, Birhanu, & Tesefay, 2016).

HUMAN RIGHTS AND LABOUR STANDARDS IN THE TOURISM INDUSTRY

The tourism industry is a significant contributor to the global economy, providing employment opportunities to millions of people worldwide (Cole, 2014; Bani-Melhem et al., 2021). However, the industry's growth has been accompanied by concerns regarding human rights and labor standards. This chapter explores the challenges faced by the tourism industry in upholding human rights and labor standards and the initiatives taken to address these challenges (Härkönen, 2020).

Human rights violations in the tourism industry are widespread, and they affect vulnerable groups such as migrant workers, women, and children. Migrant workers are often subjected to exploitative working conditions, including long working hours, low wages, and inadequate accommodation. Women and children are also at risk of exploitation, with reports of sexual harassment and exploitation in the tourism industry (Baum & Hai, 2020; Al-Hawari, Bani-Melhem, & Mohd. Shamsudin, 2021). To address these challenges, international organizations such as the United Nations and the ILO have developed guidelines and standards for the tourism industry (Zeffane & Melhem, 2018). The United Nations Guiding Principles on Business and Human Rights (UNGPs) provides a framework for businesses to respect human rights in their operations, while the ILO Tripartite Declaration of Principles concerning Multinational Enterprises and Social Policy sets out labor standards for businesses.

One of the initiatives taken to promote human rights and labor standards in the tourism industry is the Global Code of Ethics for Tourism. The Global Code of Ethics for Tourism is a set of principles that aims to promote sustainable tourism development while respecting human rights and cultural diversity (Castañeda, 2012). The code encourages tourism businesses to respect the rights of workers, including the right to fair wages, safe working conditions, and freedom of association (Ruiz-Lozano, De-los-Ríos-Berjillos, & Millán-Lara, 2018). Another initiative is the Global Reporting Initiative (GRI) Sustainability Reporting Guidelines (Fennell, 2019). The GRI guidelines provide a framework for businesses to report on their sustainability performance, including their social and environmental impact (Malloy & Fennell, 1998). The guidelines encourage businesses to report on their human rights practices and labor standards, providing transparency and accountability to stakeholders (Riley, 2014; Mat, Yaacob, & Melhem, 2015b).

The tourism industry has also taken steps to promote responsible tourism practices. Responsible tourism refers to tourism that maximizes the benefits to local communities, minimizes negative environmental and social impacts, and promotes sustainable development (Hanafiah et al., 2016). The Responsible Tourism Partnership is an initiative that promotes responsible tourism practices through partnerships between businesses, governments, and civil society organizations (Tecău et al., 2019). Tourism businesses have also implemented their initiatives to promote human rights and labor standards (Kaitano, 2020). For example, some hotels and resorts have implemented fair trade policies, which ensure that workers receive fair wages and working conditions. Others have implemented programs to train and develop their employees, providing opportunities for career advancement (Musavengane, 2019).

MANDATORY AND FORCED LABOUR IN THE TOURISM SECTOR

Mandatory and forced labor is a widespread problem in the tourism industry, with vulnerable groups such as migrant workers, women, and children at particular risk. Migrant workers are often subject to exploitation, including long working hours, low wages, and inadequate accommodation (Baum & Hai, 2019). Women and children are also at risk of exploitation, with reports of sexual harassment and exploitation in the tourism industry (Buckley et al., 2022). The ILO has identified forced labor as one of the most significant challenges facing the global workforce. The ILO estimates that there are over 25 million people worldwide who are victims of forced labor, with the tourism industry being one of the sectors most affected (Kyriazi, 2020).

To tackle the issue of forced labor in the tourism industry, international organizations and tourism businesses have developed policies and initiatives. One such initiative is the Tourism Child Protection Code of Conduct (Nolan & Bott, 2018). The code of conduct provides guidelines for tourism businesses to prevent child sex tourism and child labor in the tourism industry. Businesses that sign up for the code commit to implementing policies and practices that protect children from exploitation and abuse (Yaacob, Mat, & Melhem, 2021). Another initiative is the Global Code of Ethics for Tourism. The code of ethics promotes responsible tourism practices that respect human rights and cultural diversity. The code encourages businesses to respect the rights of workers, including the right to fair wages, safe working conditions, and freedom of association (Ndiuini & Baum, 2021).

Tourism businesses have also implemented their policies to address forced labor in their operations. For example, some hotels and resorts have implemented ethical recruitment policies that ensure that workers are recruited fairly and without coercion. Others have implemented training programs to educate employees on their rights and the risks of exploitation (Akmese, Cetin, & Akmese, 2016). Despite these initiatives, forced labor remains a significant problem in the tourism industry (Moreno de la Santa, 2020). Addressing the issue requires a collaborative effort from all stakeholders, including governments, businesses, civil society organizations, and consumers (Aston et al., 2022).

Governments have a critical role to play in enforcing labor laws and protecting the rights of workers (Dibeh, Fakih, & Marrouch, 2020). Businesses must implement policies and practices that respect human rights and prevent forced labor in their operations (Wen et al., 2020). Civil society organizations can raise awareness of the issue and advocate for the rights of vulnerable groups (Poletti & Sicurelli, 2022). Consumers can also play a role by making informed choices and supporting businesses that prioritize ethical labor practices (Aronowitz, 2019).

COLLECTIVE BARGAINING IN THE TOURISM SECTOR

Collective bargaining is a fundamental right for workers, including those in the tourism sector. Collective bargaining refers to the negotiation process between employers and employees or their representatives to determine wages, working conditions, and other terms of employment (Bagić, 2019). Despite its importance, collective bargaining in the tourism sector faces several challenges, including the casualization of the workforce, weak labor unions, and limited government support (Moreno de la Santa, 2020). The casualization of the workforce is a significant challenge facing collective bargaining in the tourism sector.

The tourism industry is characterized by a high degree of seasonality and variability in demand, which leads to a reliance on casual and temporary workers (Papadopoulos & Ioannou, 2022). These workers often lack job security and are not covered by collective bargaining agreements, making it difficult for labor unions to negotiate on their behalf. The casualization of the workforce also weakens the bargaining power of labor unions, as they are unable to represent a stable and unified workforce. Weak labor unions are another challenge facing collective bargaining in the tourism sector (Godino & Molina Romo, 2019).

Labor unions in the tourism industry face several obstacles, including limited membership, lack of resources, and inadequate legal protection (Aston et al., 2022). Many tourism workers are employed on a casual or temporary basis, making it difficult for labor unions to recruit and retain members. Weak labor unions also struggle to negotiate with employers effectively, as they lack the resources and legal protections needed to engage in collective bargaining (Chan & Warner, 2017; Hayter & Visser, 2021).

Limited government support is a significant challenge facing collective bargaining in the tourism sector (Baum & Hai, 2019). Governments play a crucial role in supporting collective bargaining by ensuring that labor laws are enforced, providing legal protections for workers, and promoting a favorable environment for labor unions to operate (Zeffane & Melhem, 2018). However, in many countries, government support for collective bargaining is limited, with labor laws poorly enforced, weak legal protections for workers, and a hostile environment for labor unions (Abukhait et al., 2023). Despite these challenges, collective bargaining in the tourism sector is essential for promoting decent work and improving working conditions for workers (Aynalem, Birhanu, & Tesefay, 2016).

Collective bargaining agreements can provide workers with job security, fair wages, and safe working conditions (Ram, 2018). Collective bargaining also helps to establish a constructive and cooperative relationship between employers and employees, which can lead to better productivity and efficiency (Higgins-Desbiolle et al., 2019).

To overcome the challenges facing collective bargaining in the tourism sector, several strategies can be employed. These include strengthening labor unions, increasing government support for collective bargaining, and developing innovative approaches to collective bargaining (Mamatzakis, Pegkas, & Staikouras, 2022). For example, labor unions can focus on recruiting and retaining members by offering benefits such as training and education programs (Burroni, Mori, & Bottalico, 2020). Governments can provide legal protections for workers, enforce labor laws, and promote a favorable environment for labor unions to operate (Andersen, 2020). Innovative approaches to collective bargaining, such as industry-wide bargaining or sectoral bargaining, can also help to overcome the challenges facing collective bargaining in the tourism sector (Hayter & Visser, 2021).

CHILD WORKFORCE IN TOURISM SECTOR

Child labor in the tourism sector is a complex issue that requires attention and action from all stakeholders, including governments, tourism businesses, civil society organizations, and consumers. The ILO estimates that there are approximately 152 million child laborers worldwide, with many of them employed in the tourism sector (Cruz Jiménez et al., 2022). Child labor refers to work that is performed by children under the age of 18 and deprives them of their childhood, potential, and dignity. In this article, we will explore the issue of child labor in the tourism sector and the challenges faced in addressing this issue (Baum et al., 2016). The tourism sector is a significant employer worldwide, providing employment opportunities to millions of people, including children.

Child labor in the tourism sector can take many forms, including child prostitution, forced begging, and child labor in hotels and restaurants. Children working in the tourism sector are often subjected to exploitative working conditions, including long working hours, low wages, and inadequate accommodation (Mooney & Baum, 2019). One of the challenges in addressing child labor in the tourism sector is the lack of awareness and understanding of the issue (Elshaer, 2019). Many people are unaware of the extent of child labor in the tourism sector and the negative impacts it has on children's lives. Addressing this challenge requires raising awareness and increasing understanding of the issue among all stakeholders (Cruz Jiménez et al., 2022; Robinson et al., 2022).

Another challenge is the lack of legal protections for children in the tourism sector. Many countries have laws and regulations that prohibit child labor, but these laws are not always enforced effectively. In some cases, children may be employed in the informal sector, making it difficult for authorities to monitor and enforce child labor laws. The nature of the tourism industry, which is characterized by high seasonality and variability in demand, is also a challenge in addressing child labor (Gössling & Schweiggart, 2022). During peak seasons, businesses in the tourism sector may require additional workers to meet the demand, leading to the employment of children to fill these positions. Children may also be employed in the informal sector to provide services to tourists during peak seasons (Karsavuran, 2021).

Tourism businesses have a critical role to play in addressing child labor in the tourism sector. The tourism industry has a responsibility to respect human rights, including the rights of children, and to ensure that its operations do not contribute to child labor (Klein & Smith, 2021). This can be achieved by implementing policies and practices that prevent child labor in their operations, such as fair recruitment practices, monitoring of supply chains, and education and awareness-raising programs (Baum & Hai, 2020).

Governments also have a crucial role to play in addressing child labor in the tourism sector. Governments can enforce child labor laws effectively, provide legal protections for children, and promote a favorable environment for tourism businesses to operate responsibly. Governments can also provide support to vulnerable children and their families, such as access to education, health care, and social services (Ruiz-Lozano, De-los-Ríos-Berjillos, & Millán-Lara, 2018).

Civil society organizations can play an essential role in addressing child labor in the tourism sector by raising awareness, conducting research, and advocating for the rights of children. Civil society organizations can also work with tourism businesses and governments to develop and implement policies and practices that prevent child labor in the tourism sector (Kaitano, 2020).

Consumers also have a role to play in addressing child labor in the tourism sector. Consumers can make informed choices when planning and booking their travel, supporting businesses that prioritize ethical labor practices and avoiding businesses that contribute to child labor (Elshaer, 2019). Consumers can also raise awareness of the issue and advocate for the rights of children by engaging with tourism businesses and governments (Mooney & Baum, 2019).

MIGRANT EMPLOYEES IN THE TOURISM SECTOR

Migrant employees are an essential part of the tourism sector workforce, providing much-needed labor in various areas of the industry, including hotels, restaurants, and transportation. Migrant employees face several challenges, including language barriers, cultural differences, and limited legal protections (Zhou & Chan, 2019). Migrant employees often face language barriers when working in the tourism sector. Many migrant employees may not speak the language of the country where they work, making it difficult for them to communicate with customers and colleagues. This can result in miscommunication, misunderstandings, and decreased job performance (Markova et al., 2016).

Cultural differences are another challenge faced by migrant employees in the tourism sector (Tosun et al., 2021). Migrant employees may come from different cultural backgrounds and may have different beliefs, values, and customs than their colleagues and customers. This can lead to misunderstandings and conflicts, which can affect the work environment and customer experience (Treuren, Manoharan, & Vishnu, 2021). Migrant employees also face limited legal protections in many countries. Migrant employees may be employed on temporary or casual contracts, which do not provide the same legal protections as permanent contracts (Buckley et al., 2020). Migrant employees may also be subject to discrimination and exploitation, including long working hours, low wages, and inadequate working conditions (Lenz, 2021).

One example of the challenges faced by migrant employees in the tourism sector is the case of undocumented workers in the United States. Many undocumented workers are employed in the hospitality industry, including hotels and restaurants (Ndiuini & Baum, 2021). These workers face the risk of deportation and have limited legal protections, making it difficult for them to report labor violations and exploitation (Ioannides, Gyimóthy, & James, 2021). Another example is the case of migrant workers in the Gulf countries. Many migrant workers from Asia and Africa are employed in the hospitality industry in the Gulf countries, including hotels and restaurants (Walmsley, Koens, & Milano, 2022). These workers may face exploitative working conditions, including long working hours, low wages, and inadequate accommodation. Migrant workers in the Gulf countries also face restrictions on their freedom of movement and may be subject to abuse and exploitation by their employers (Okafor, Khalid, & Burzynska, 2022).

Despite these challenges, there are initiatives and policies in place to support migrant employees in the tourism sector. One example is the ILO Fair Recruitment Initiative (Treuren, Manoharan, & Vishnu, 2021). The initiative aims to promote fair recruitment practices that protect migrant workers from exploitation and abuse. The ILO's initiative encourages governments, employers, and labor unions to work together to develop and implement fair recruitment practices that respect the rights of migrant workers (Filimonau & Mika, 2019; Ruiz-Ballesteros & Cáceres-Feria, 2016). Another initiative is the Global Code of Ethics for Tourism, which promotes responsible tourism practices that respect human rights and cultural diversity (Castañeda, 2012). The code encourages tourism businesses to respect the rights of workers, including migrant workers, by providing fair wages, safe working conditions, and freedom of association (Malloy & Fennell, 1998).

Tourism businesses can also take steps to support migrant employees in their operations. For example, businesses can provide language and cultural training to migrant employees, which can help to reduce misunderstandings and conflicts. Businesses can also develop policies and practices that promote fair treatment of migrant employees, such as fair recruitment practices, living wage policies, and policies to prevent discrimination and exploitation (Ruiz-Lozano, De-los-Ríos-Berjillos, & Millán-Lara, 2018).

FAIR WORK FOR ALL EMPLOYEES IN THE TOURISM SECTOR

Fair work for all employees in the tourism sector is essential for promoting decent work and sustainable development. Fair work includes access to decent wages, safe and healthy working conditions, opportunities for career advancement, and protection against discrimination and exploitation (Myhill, Richards, & Sang, 2021). However, fair work for all employees in the tourism sector is often hindered by several challenges, including informal employment, low wages, and weak legal protections.

Informal employment is a significant challenge to fair work in the tourism sector. Many employees in the tourism sector work in the informal economy, meaning they are not registered, do not have formal contracts, and are not covered by labor laws and protections (Djajasinga et al., 2021). Informal employment makes it difficult for employees to access fair wages, safe and healthy working conditions, and

Human Rights and Workforce Conditions in the Tourism Sector

opportunities for career advancement. Informal employment also makes it challenging for employees to organize and negotiate collectively for their rights (Walpole, 2016).

Low wages are another challenge faced by employees in the tourism sector. Many employees in the tourism sector, particularly those in low-skilled jobs, are paid low wages that are often insufficient to cover their basic needs (Achmad & Yulianah, 2022). Low wages also make it challenging for employees to access opportunities for career advancement, as they may not have the financial resources to invest in training and education. Weak legal protections are another challenge to fair work for all employees in the tourism sector (Ioannides, Gyimóthy, & James, 2021).

In many countries, labor laws and protections are weakly enforced, leaving employees vulnerable to exploitation and abuse. Employees may face discrimination, including discrimination based on their gender, race, religion, or sexual orientation. Employees may also be subject to long working hours, inadequate working conditions, and inadequate health and safety protections (Okafor, Khalid, & Burzynska, 2022).

One example of the challenges faced by employees in the tourism sector is the case of hotel housekeepers in the United States. Many hotel housekeepers in the United States are employed in low-paid jobs and face inadequate working conditions, including heavy workloads and inadequate health and safety protections (Ioannides, Gyimóthy, & James, 2021). Hotel housekeepers are often women, immigrants, and people of color, making them particularly vulnerable to discrimination and exploitation (Nicolaides, 2020). Another example is the case of migrant workers in the hospitality industry. Many migrant workers are employed in low-skilled jobs in the hospitality industry, including hotels and restaurants. These workers may face exploitative working conditions, including long working hours, low wages, and inadequate accommodation. Migrant workers may also face restrictions on their freedom of movement and may be subject to abuse and exploitation by their employers (Myhill, Richards, & Sang, 2021).

To address the challenges of fair work for all employees in the tourism sector, several strategies can be employed. One strategy is to promote formal employment in the tourism sector, including the implementation of labor laws and protections that cover all employees (Djajasinga et al., 2021). Another strategy is to promote fair wages in the tourism sector, including living wage policies and wage-setting mechanisms that ensure employees are paid fairly for their work. Training and education programs can also be implemented to provide employees with the skills and knowledge they need to advance in their careers (Gričar, Šugar, & Bojnec, 2021).

Tourism businesses can also take steps to promote fair work for all employees in their operations (Sun et al., 2022). For example, businesses can implement policies and practices that ensure all employees are paid fairly, have access to safe and healthy working conditions, and are protected against discrimination and exploitation. Businesses can also provide training and development opportunities to employees, including career advancement programs and mentoring programs (Vaduva, Echevarria-Cruz, & Takacs Jr, 2020).

EMPLOYEE DISCRIMINATION IN THE TOURISM SECTOR

Employee discrimination in the tourism sector is a pervasive and complex issue that requires attention and action from all stakeholders, including governments, tourism businesses, civil society organizations, and consumers (Ndiuini & Baum, 2021). Discrimination against employees can take many forms, including discrimination based on race, gender, age, religion, sexual orientation, and disability. In this article, we will explore the issue of employee discrimination in the tourism sector and provide examples of the challenges faced (Alagarsamy, Mehrolia, & Aranha, 2020).

One of the challenges in addressing employee discrimination in the tourism sector is the lack of awareness and understanding of the issue (Treuren, Manoharan, & Vishnu, 2021). Many people are unaware of the extent of employment discrimination in the tourism sector and the negative impacts it has on employees' lives (Lenz, 2021). Addressing this challenge requires raising awareness and increasing understanding of the issue among all stakeholders (Klein & Smith, 2021). Another challenge is the lack of legal protections for employees in the tourism sector. Discrimination is often illegal under national and international law, but these laws are not always enforced effectively (Porto & Espinola, 2019).

In some cases, employees may be subject to discrimination that is not covered by existing laws or protections (Obadić, 2016). The nature of the tourism industry, which is characterized by high seasonality and variability in demand, is also a challenge in addressing employee discrimination (Bakker, 2019). During peak seasons, businesses in the tourism sector may require additional workers to meet the demand, leading to the employment of employees to fill these positions. This can create a competitive environment in which discrimination is more likely to occur (Walmsley et al., 2019).

Employee discrimination in the tourism sector can have severe consequences for employees' physical and mental health, career prospects, and job satisfaction (Sun et al., 2022). Discrimination can lead to stress, anxiety, and depression, affecting employees' mental health. Discrimination can also limit employees' career opportunities, as they may be denied promotions or access to training and development opportunities. Discrimination can also lead to decreased job satisfaction, affecting employee morale and productivity (Kortt, Sinnewe, & Pervan, 2018).

One example of the challenges faced by employees in the tourism sector is the case of female employees in the hotel industry. Female employees in the hotel industry may face discrimination based on their gender, including unequal pay, limited career

Human Rights and Workforce Conditions in the Tourism Sector

opportunities, and sexual harassment. Women in the hotel industry are often employed in low-skilled jobs and may face significant barriers to advancement (Goretti et al., 2021). Another example is the case of migrant workers in the hospitality industry. Many migrant workers are employed in the hospitality industry, including hotels and restaurants (Andersen, 2020). These workers may face discrimination based on their race or nationality, including limited access to career opportunities and inadequate working conditions (Burroni, Mori, & Bottalico, 2020).

To tackle the challenges of employment discrimination in the tourism sector, several strategies can be employed. One strategy is to promote diversity and inclusion in the tourism sector, including the implementation of policies and practices that prevent discrimination and promote equal opportunities for all employees (Hayter & Visser, 2021). Training and education programs can also be implemented to provide employees with the skills and knowledge they need to identify and address discrimination (Moreno de la Santa, 2020). Tourism establishments can also take steps to promote non-discrimination in their operations. For example, businesses can implement policies and practices that ensure all employees are treated fairly and have access to equal opportunities for career advancement. Businesses can also provide training and development opportunities to employees, including mentoring programs and diversity training (Yılmazdogan, Secilmis, & Cicek, 2015).

In conclusion, employee discrimination in the tourism sector is a complex issue that requires attention and action from all stakeholders. The challenges faced in addressing employee discrimination in the tourism sector include the lack of awareness and understanding of the issue, the lack of legal protections for employees, and the seasonality and variability of demand in the tourism industry. Addressing these challenges requires a collaborative effort from governments, businesses, and civil society organizations. By promoting diversity and inclusion and implementing policies and practices that prevent discrimination, the tourism sector can benefit from a diverse and talented workforce.

REFERENCES

Abukhait, R., Shamsudin, F. M., Bani-Melhem, S., & Al-Hawari, M. A. (2023). Obsessive–compulsive personality and creative performance: The moderating effect of manager coaching behavior. *Review of Managerial Science*, *17*(1), 375–396. doi:10.100711846-022-00528-6

Achmad, W., & Yulianah, Y. (2022). Corporate social responsibility of the hospitality industry in realizing sustainable tourism development. *Enrichment: Journal of Management*, *12*(2), 1610–1616.

Akmese, H., Cetin, H., & Akmese, K. (2016). Corporate social responsibility reporting: A comparative analysis of tourism and finance sectors of G8 countries. *Procedia Economics and Finance*, *39*, 737–745. doi:10.1016/S2212-5671(16)30273-8

Al-Hawari, M. A., Bani-Melhem, S., & Mohd. Shamsudin, F. (2021). Does employee willingness to take risks affect customer loyalty? A moderated mediation examination of innovative behaviors and decentralization. *International Journal of Contemporary Hospitality Management*, *33*(5), 1746–1767. doi:10.1108/IJCHM-08-2020-0802

Alagarsamy, S., Mehrolia, S., & Aranha, R. H. (2020). The mediating effect of employee engagement: How employee psychological empowerment impacts the employee satisfaction? A study of Maldivian tourism sector. *Global Business Review*. doi:10.1177/0972150920915315

Alegre, I., & Berbegal-Mirabent, J. (2016). Social innovation success factors: Hospitality and tourism social enterprises. *International Journal of Contemporary Hospitality Management*, *28*(6), 1155–1176. doi:10.1108/IJCHM-05-2014-0231

Andersen, I. M. V. (2020). Tourism Employment and Education in a Danish Context. *Tourism Employment in Nordic Countries: Trends, Practices, and Opportunities*, 37-56.

Ariza-Montes, A., Arjona-Fuentes, J. M., Law, R., & Han, H. (2017). Incidence of workplace bullying among hospitality employees. *International Journal of Contemporary Hospitality Management*, *29*(4), 1116–1132. doi:10.1108/IJCHM-09-2015-0471

Aronowitz, A. A. (2019). Regulating business involvement in labor exploitation and human trafficking. *Journal of Labor and Society*, *22*(1), 145–164. doi:10.1111/wusa.12372

Aston, J., Wen, J., Goh, E., & Maurer, O. (2022). Promoting awareness of sex trafficking in tourism and hospitality. *International Journal of Culture, Tourism and Hospitality Research*, *16*(1), 1–6. doi:10.1108/IJCTHR-01-2020-0032

Aynalem, S., Birhanu, K., & Tesefay, S. (2016). Employment opportunities and challenges in tourism and hospitality sectors. *Journal of Tourism & Hospitality (Los Angeles, Calif.)*, *5*(6), 1–5. doi:10.4172/2167-0269.1000257

Bagić, D. (2019). Croatia: stability amidst heterogeneous collective bargaining patterns. In Collective bargaining in Europe: towards an endgame (Vol. 1, pp. 93-108). European Trade Union Institute (ETUI).

Bakker, M. (2019). A conceptual framework for identifying the binding constraints to tourism-driven inclusive growth. *Tourism Planning & Development*, *16*(5), 575–590. doi:10.1080/21568316.2018.1541817

Bani-Melhem, S., Abukhait, R., & Bourini, I. F. (2022). How and when does centralization affect the likelihood of passive leadership? *Leadership and Organization Development Journal*, *43*(4), 533–549. doi:10.1108/LODJ-10-2021-0492

Bani-Melhem, S., Al-Hawari, M. A., & Mohd. Shamsudin, F. (2022). Green innovation performance: A multi-level analysis in the hotel sector. *Journal of Sustainable Tourism*, *30*(8), 1878–1896. doi:10.1080/09669582.2021.1991935

Bani-Melhem, S., Mohd. Shamsudin, F., Mazen Abukhait, R., & Quratulain, S. (2021). Paranoid personality and frontline employee's proactive work behaviours: A moderated mediation model of empathetic leadership and perceived psychological safety. *Journal of Service Theory and Practice*, *31*(1), 113–135. doi:10.1108/JSTP-05-2020-0104

Baum, T., Cheung, C., Kong, H., Kralj, A., Mooney, S., Nguyễn Thị Thanh, H., Ramachandran, S., Dropulić Ružić, M., & Siow, M. L. (2016). Sustainability and the tourism and hospitality workforce: A thematic analysis. *Sustainability (Basel)*, *8*(8), 809. doi:10.3390u8080809

Baum, T., & Hai, N. T. T. (2019). Applying sustainable employment principles in the tourism industry: Righting human rights wrongs? *Tourism Recreation Research*, *44*(3), 371–381. doi:10.1080/02508281.2019.1624407

Baum, T., & Hai, N. T. T. (2020). Hospitality, tourism, human rights and the impact of COVID-19. *International Journal of Contemporary Hospitality Management*, *32*(7), 2397–2407. doi:10.1108/IJCHM-03-2020-0242

Belias, D., Rossidis, I., Papademetriou, C., & Mantas, C. (2022). Job satisfaction as affected by types of leadership: A case study of Greek tourism sector. *Journal of Quality Assurance in Hospitality & Tourism*, *23*(2), 299–317. doi:10.1080/152 8008X.2020.1867695

Buckley, P., Pietropaoli, L., Rosada, A., Harguth, B., & Broom, J. (2022). How has COVID-19 affected migrant workers' vulnerability to human trafficking for forced labour in Southeast Asia? A narrative review'. *Journal of Public Health and Emergency*, *6*, 19. doi:10.21037/jphe-21-108

Buckley, R., Shekari, F., Mohammadi, Z., Azizi, F., & Ziaee, M. (2020). World heritage tourism triggers urban–rural reverse migration and social change. *Journal of Travel Research*, *59*(3), 559–572. doi:10.1177/0047287519853048

Burroni, L., Mori, A., & Bottalico, A. (2020). *Understanding collective bargaining coordination: a network relational approach. The case of Italy*. Academic Press.

Castañeda, Q. (2012). The neoliberal imperative of tourism: Rights and legitimization in the Unwto global code of ethics for tourism. *Practical Anthropology, 34*(3), 47–51. doi:10.17730/praa.34.3.w0251w655647750j

Chan, A. W., & Warner, M. (2017). Employers' associations in Hong Kong: Continuity in the absence of collective bargaining. In Employers' associations in Asia (pp. 102-124). Routledge.

Cole, S. (2014). Tourism and water: From stakeholders to rights holders, and what tourism businesses need to do. *Journal of Sustainable Tourism, 22*(1), 89–106. doi:10.1080/09669582.2013.776062

Cruz Jiménez, G., Serrano-Barquín, R. D. C., Zizumbo Villarreal, L., & Vargas Martínez, E. E. (2022). Child labor and child work in the touristic sector of Cozumel and Valle de Bravo, Mexico. *International Journal of Hospitality & Tourism Administration, 23*(3), 599–622. doi:10.1080/15256480.2020.1805091

Daniel, A. D., Costa, R. A., Pita, M., & Costa, C. (2017). Tourism Education: What about entrepreneurial skills? *Journal of Hospitality and Tourism Management, 30*, 65–72. doi:10.1016/j.jhtm.2017.01.002

Dibeh, G., Fakih, A., & Marrouch, W. (2020). Tourism–growth nexus under duress: Lebanon during the Syrian crisis. *Tourism Economics, 26*(3), 353–370. doi:10.1177/1354816619836338

Djajasinga, N. D., Sulastri, L., Sudirman, A., Sari, A. L., & Rihardi, E. L. (2021, June). Practices in Human Resources and Employee Turnover in the Hospitality Industry. In *2nd Annual Conference on blended learning, educational technology and Innovation (ACBLETI 2020)* (pp. 113-117). Atlantis Press. 10.2991/assehr.k.210615.023

Douglas, S., & Watt, G. (2018). Implications of the Fair Work Commission's modern award review for casuals. *Journal of New Business Ideas and Trends, 16*(2), 30–40.

Elbaz, A. M., & Haddoud, M. Y. (2017). The role of wisdom leadership in increasing job performance: Evidence from the Egyptian tourism sector. *Tourism Management, 63*, 66–76. doi:10.1016/j.tourman.2017.06.008

Elshaer, A. M. (2019). *Labor in the tourism and hospitality industry: Skills, ethics, issues, and rights*. CRC Press. doi:10.1201/9780429465093

Everhart, S. M. (2017). U-Pick-Are Agritourism Workers Exempt from the Wage and Hour Protections of the Fair Labor Standards Act. *U. Md. LJ Race, Religion, Race, Gender & Class, 17*, 29.

Fennell, D. A. (2019). The future of ethics in tourism. *The future of tourism: Innovation and sustainability*, 155-177.

Filimonau, V., & Mika, M. (2019). Return labour migration: An exploratory study of Polish migrant workers from the UK hospitality industry. *Current Issues in Tourism, 22*(3), 357–378. doi:10.1080/13683500.2017.1280778

Fominienė, V. B., Mejerytė-Narkevičienė, K., & Woźniewicz-Dobrzyńska, M. (2015). Employees' career competence for career success: Aspect of human resources management in tourism sector. *Transformations in Business & Economics, 14*, 481–493.

Gascón, J. (2019). Tourism as a right: A "frivolous claim" against degrowth? *Journal of Sustainable Tourism, 27*(12), 1825–1838. doi:10.1080/09669582.2019.1666858

Godino, A., & Molina Romo, Ó. (2019). *Who overcomes collective bargaining? Outsourcing practices, regulatory framework and facility management in Spain.* Academic Press.

Goretti, M. M., Leigh, M. L. Y., Babii, A., Cevik, M. S., Kaendera, S., Muir, M. D. V., ... & Salinas, M. G. (2021). *Tourism in the post-pandemic world: Economic challenges and opportunities for Asia-pacific and the western hemisphere.* Academic Press.

Gössling, S., & Schweiggart, N. (2022). Two years of COVID-19 and tourism: What we learned, and what we should have learned. *Journal of Sustainable Tourism, 30*(4), 915–931. doi:10.1080/09669582.2022.2029872

Gričar, S., Šugar, V., & Bojnec, Š. (2021). The missing link between wages and labour productivity in tourism: Evidence from Croatia and Slovenia. *Ekonomska Istrazivanja, 34*(1), 732–753. doi:10.1080/1331677X.2020.1804427

Hanafiah, M. H., Azman, I., Jamaluddin, M. R., & Aminuddin, N. (2016). Responsible tourism practices and quality of life: Perspective of Langkawi Island communities. *Procedia: Social and Behavioral Sciences, 222*, 406–413. doi:10.1016/j.sbspro.2016.05.194

Härkönen, E. (2020). Human rights and labour conditions in tourism establishments. *Human Rights Issues in Tourism.*

Hayter, S., & Visser, J. (2021). Making collective bargaining more inclusive: The role of extension. *International Labour Review*, *160*(2), 169–195. doi:10.1111/ilr.12191

Higgins-Desbiolles, F., Carnicelli, S., Krolikowski, C., Wijesinghe, G., & Boluk, K. (2019). Degrowing tourism: Rethinking tourism. *Journal of Sustainable Tourism*, *27*(12), 1926–1944. doi:10.1080/09669582.2019.1601732

Ioannides, D., Gyimóthy, S., & James, L. (2021). From liminal labor to decent work: A human-centered perspective on sustainable tourism employment. *Sustainability (Basel)*, *13*(2), 851. doi:10.3390u13020851

Kaitano, D. U. B. E. (2020). Tourism and sustainable development goals in the African context. *International Journal of Economics and Finance Studies*, *12*(1), 88–102.

Karsavuran, Z. (2021). Surviving a major crisis: The case of dismissed tourism and hospitality employees. *Journal of Policy Research in Tourism, Leisure & Events*, *13*(2), 243–265. doi:10.1080/19407963.2020.1787421

Khassawneh, O., & Abaker, M. O. S. M. (2022). Human Resource Management in the United Arab Emirates: Towards a Better Understanding. In *HRM in the Global South: A Critical Perspective* (pp. 103–128). Springer International Publishing. doi:10.1007/978-3-030-98309-3_5

Khuong, M. N., & Nhu, N. V. Q. (2015). The effects of ethical leadership and organizational culture towards employees' sociability and commitment–a study of tourism sector in Ho Chi Minh city. *Vietnam. Journal of Advanced Management Science*, *3*(4). Advance online publication. doi:10.18178/joams.5.4.255-263

Klein, A., & Smith, E. (2021). *Explaining the economic impact of COVID-19: Core industries and the Hispanic workforce*. Academic Press.

Kortt, M. A., Sinnewe, E., & Pervan, S. J. (2018). The gender wage gap in the tourism industry: Evidence from Australia. *Tourism Analysis*, *23*(1), 137–149. doi :10.3727/108354217X15143857878697

Kyriazi, T. (2020). Trafficking in human beings in the tourism industry: trends and approaches. In *Tourism and gender-based violence: challenging inequalities* (pp. 95–110). CABI. doi:10.1079/9781789243215.0095

Lenz, R. (2021). 'Hotel Royal' and Other Spaces of Hospitality: Tourists and Migrants in the Mediterranean. In *Thinking through tourism* (pp. 209–229). Routledge. doi:10.4324/9781003087229-10

Malloy, D. C., & Fennell, D. A. (1998). Codes of ethics and tourism: An exploratory content analysis. *Tourism Management, 19*(5), 453–461. doi:10.1016/S0261-5177(98)00042-9

Mamatzakis, E., Pegkas, P., & Staikouras, C. (2022). Labour market regulations and efficiency in tourism industry. *Tourism Economics.* doi:10.1177/13548166221081522

Markova, E., Anna, P., Williams, A. M., & Shaw, G. (2016). Migrant workers in small London hotels: Employment, recruitment and distribution. *European Urban and Regional Studies, 23*(3), 406–421. doi:10.1177/0969776413513913

Mat, N., Yaacob, N. A., & Melhem, S. B. (2015). Human resource management practices and organizational innovation: A study of four and five star hotels in Malaysia. *Advances in Global Business Research, 12*(1), 596–605.

Mat, N., Yaacob, N. A., & Melhem, S. B. (2015). *Knowledge sharing effect on HRM practices and organisational innovation among Malaysia's Four and Five Star Hotels.* Academic Press.

Mohammad, T., Darwish, T. K., Singh, S., & Khassawneh, O. (2021). Human resource management and organisational performance: The mediating role of social exchange. *European Management Review, 18*(1), 125–136. doi:10.1111/emre.12421

Mohd. Shamsudin, F., Hamouche, S., Abdulmajid Cheikh Ali, D., Bani-Melhem, S., & Jamal Bani-Melhem, A. (2022). Why do employees withhold knowledge? The role of competitive climate, envy and narcissism. *Journal of Knowledge Management.* Advance online publication. doi:10.1108/JKM-02-2022-0133

Mooney, S., & Baum, T. (2019). A sustainable hospitality and tourism workforce research agenda: Exploring the past to create a vision for the future. In *A research agenda for tourism and development* (pp. 189–205). Edward Elgar Publishing. doi:10.4337/9781788112413.00016

Moreno de la Santa, J. G. S. (2020). Tourism as a lever for a more inclusive society. *Worldwide Hospitality and Tourism Themes, 12*(6), 731–738. doi:10.1108/WHATT-07-2020-0071

Musavengane, R. (2019). Small hotels and responsible tourism practice: Hoteliers' perspectives. *Journal of Cleaner Production, 220,* 786–799. doi:10.1016/j.jclepro.2019.02.143

Myhill, K., Richards, J., & Sang, K. (2021). Job quality, fair work and gig work: The lived experience of gig workers. *International Journal of Human Resource Management, 32*(19), 4110–4135. doi:10.1080/09585192.2020.1867612

Ndiuini, A., & Baum, T. (2021). Underemployment and lived experiences of migrant workers in the hotel industry: Policy and industry implications. *Journal of Policy Research in Tourism, Leisure & Events*, *13*(1), 36–58. doi:10.1080/19407963.2020.1743487

Nicolaides, A. (2020). Sustainable ethical tourism (SET) and rural community involvement. *African Journal of Hospitality, Tourism and Leisure*, *9*(1), 1–16.

Nolan, J., & Bott, G. (2018). Global supply chains and human rights: Spotlight on forced labour and modern slavery practices. *Australian Journal of Human Rights*, *24*(1), 44–69. doi:10.1080/1323238X.2018.1441610

Obadić, A. (2016). Gender discrimination and pay gap on tourism labor market. *International Journal of Social, Behavioral, Educational, Economic. Business and Industrial Engineering*, *10*(3), 812–817.

Okafor, L. E., Khalid, U., & Burzynska, K. (2022). The effect of migration on international tourism flows: The role of linguistic networks and common languages. *Journal of Travel Research*, *61*(4), 818–836. doi:10.1177/00472875211008250

Papadopoulos, O., & Ioannou, G. (2022). Working in hospitality and catering in Greece and the UK: Do trade union membership and collective bargaining still matter? *European Journal of Industrial Relations*. doi:10.1177/09596801221104943

Poletti, A., & Sicurelli, D. (2022). The political economy of the EU approach to the Rohingya crisis in Myanmar. *Politics and Governance*, *10*(1), 47–57. doi:10.17645/pag.v10i1.4678

Porto, N., & Espinola, N. (2019). Labor income inequalities and tourism development in Argentina: A regional approach. *Tourism Economics*, *25*(8), 1265–1285. doi:10.1177/1354816619828143

Ram, Y. (2018). Hostility or hospitality? A review on violence, bullying and sexual harassment in the tourism and hospitality industry. *Current Issues in Tourism*, *21*(7), 760–774. doi:10.1080/13683500.2015.1064364

Riadil, I. G. (2020). Tourism industry crisis and its impacts: investigating the Indonesian tourism employees perspectives' in the pandemic of COVID-19. *Jurnal Kepariwisataan: Destinasi. Hospitalitas Dan Perjalanan*, *4*(2), 98–108.

Riley, M. (2014). *Human resource management in the hospitality and tourism industry*. Routledge. doi:10.4324/9781315831565

Robinson, R. N., Martins, A., Solnet, D., & Baum, T. (2019). Sustaining precarity: Critically examining tourism and employment. *Journal of Sustainable Tourism*, *27*(7), 1008–1025. doi:10.1080/09669582.2018.1538230

Robinson, R. N., Martins, A., Solnet, D., & Baum, T. (2021). Sustaining precarity: Critically examining tourism and employment. In *Activating Critical Thinking to Advance the Sustainable Development Goals in Tourism Systems* (pp. 162–179). Routledge. doi:10.4324/9781003140542-10

Ruiz-Ballesteros, E., & Cáceres-Feria, R. (2016). Community-building and amenity migration in community-based tourism development. An approach from southwest Spain. *Tourism Management*, *54*, 513–523. doi:10.1016/j.tourman.2016.01.008

Ruiz-Lozano, M., De-los-Ríos-Berjillos, A., & Millán-Lara, S. (2018). Spanish hotel chains alignment with the Global Code of Ethics for Tourism. *Journal of Cleaner Production*, *199*, 205–213. doi:10.1016/j.jclepro.2018.07.133

Shafique, I. N., Kalyar, M., & Ahmad, B. (2018). The nexus of ethical leadership, job performance, and turnover intention: The mediating role of job satisfaction. *Interdisciplinary Description of Complex Systems: INDECS*, *16*(1), 71–87. doi:10.7906/indecs.16.1.5

Stamolampros, P., Korfiatis, N., Chalvatzis, K., & Buhalis, D. (2019). Job satisfaction and employee turnover determinants in high contact services: Insights from Employees' Online reviews. *Tourism Management*, *75*, 130–147. doi:10.1016/j.tourman.2019.04.030

Sun, Y. Y., Li, M., Lenzen, M., Malik, A., & Pomponi, F. (2022). Tourism, job vulnerability and income inequality during the COVID-19 pandemic: A global perspective. *Annals of Tourism Research Empirical Insights*, *3*(1), 100046. doi:10.1016/j.annale.2022.100046

Tecău, A. S., Brătucu, G., Tescaşiu, B., Chiţu, I. B., Constantin, C. P., & Foris, D. (2019). Responsible tourism—Integrating families with disabled children in tourist destinations. *Sustainability (Basel)*, *11*(16), 4420. doi:10.3390u11164420

Tosun, C., Çalişkan, C., Şahin, S. Z., & Dedeoğlu, B. B. (2021). A critical perspective on tourism employment. *Current Issues in Tourism*, 1–21.

Treuren, G. J., Manoharan, A., & Vishnu, V. (2021). The hospitality sector as an employer of skill discounted migrants. Evidence from Australia. *Journal of Policy Research in Tourism, Leisure & Events*, *13*(1), 20–35. doi:10.1080/19407963.2019.1655859

Vaduva, S., Echevarria-Cruz, S., & Takacs, J. Jr. (2020). The economic and social impact of a university education upon the development of the Romanian tourism industry. *Journal of Hospitality, Leisure, Sport and Tourism Education*, 27, 100270. doi:10.1016/j.jhlste.2020.100270

Walmsley, A., Koens, K., & Milano, C. (2022). Overtourism and employment outcomes for the tourism worker: Impacts to labour markets. *Tourism Review*, 77(1), 1–15. doi:10.1108/TR-07-2020-0343

Walmsley, A., Partington, S., Armstrong, R., & Goodwin, H. (2019). Reactions to the national living wage in hospitality. *Employee Relations*, 41(1), 253–268. doi:10.1108/ER-02-2018-0044

Walpole, K. (2016). How is employees' input and influence over collective agreements shaped by Australia's Fair Work Act? *Labour & Industry: A Journal of the Social and Economic Relations of Work*, 26(3), 220-236.

Wen, J., Klarin, A., Goh, E., & Aston, J. (2020). A systematic review of the sex trafficking-related literature: Lessons for tourism and hospitality research. *Journal of Hospitality and Tourism Management*, 45, 370–376. doi:10.1016/j.jhtm.2020.06.001

Yaacob, N. A., Mat, N., & Melhem, S. B. (2021). Human resource management practices and innovation of hotels in Malaysia. *International Journal of Social Science Research*, 3(4), 17–26.

Yılmazdogan, O. C., Secilmis, C., & Cicek, D. (2015). The effect of corporate social responsibility (CSR) perception on tourism students' intention to work in sector. *Procedia Economics and Finance*, 23, 1340–1346. doi:10.1016/S2212-5671(15)00321-4

Zeffane, R., & Melhem, S. B. (2018). Do feelings of trust/distrust affect employees' turnover intentions? An exploratory study in the United Arab Emirates. *Middle East Journal of Management*, 5(4), 385–408. doi:10.1504/MEJM.2018.095582

Zhou, L., & Chan, E. S. (2019). Motivations of tourism-induced mobility: Tourism development and the pursuit of the Chinese dream. *International Journal of Tourism Research*, 21(6), 824–838. doi:10.1002/jtr.2308

ADDITIONAL READING

Andriotis, K., & Vaughan, D. R. (2004). The tourism workforce and policy: Exploring the assumptions using Crete as the case study. *Current Issues in Tourism, 7*(1), 66–87. doi:10.1080/13683500408667973

Barron, P., Leask, A., & Fyall, A. (2014). Engaging the multi-generational workforce in tourism and hospitality. *Tourism Review, 69*(4), 245–263. doi:10.1108/TR-04-2014-0017

Baum, T., Kralj, A., Robinson, R. N., & Solnet, D. J. (2016). Tourism workforce research: A review, taxonomy and agenda. *Annals of Tourism Research, 60*, 1–22. doi:10.1016/j.annals.2016.04.003

Hipsher, S. A. (2021). Tourism in Thailand: Exploitation or Opportunity? *International Journal of Asian Business and Information Management, 12*(3), 26–42. doi:10.4018/IJABIM.20210701.oa3

Korstanje, M. E. (2020). Problems of Monetary Rewards in Tourist Organizations: Rent-A-Car Sectors in Buenos Aires, Argentina. In *Strategies for Promoting Sustainable Hospitality and Tourism Services* (pp. 70–83). IGI Global. doi:10.4018/978-1-7998-4330-6.ch005

Li, T., Li, Q., & Liu, J. (2021). The spatial mobility of rural tourism workforce: A case study from the micro analytical perspective. *Habitat International, 110*, 102322. doi:10.1016/j.habitatint.2021.102322

Rahimi, R., Hassan, A., & Tekin, O. (2020). Augmented reality apps for tourism destination promotion. In *Destination management and marketing: Breakthroughs in research and practice* (pp. 1066–1077). IGI Global. doi:10.4018/978-1-7998-2469-5.ch059

Saner, R., Yiu, L., & Filadoro, M. (2019). Tourism development in least developed countries: Challenges and opportunities. *Sustainable Tourism: Breakthroughs in Research and Practice*, 94-120.

Sinclair, M. T. (Ed.). (1997). *Gender, work and tourism*. Psychology Press.

Sinclair, M. T. (2005). Gendered work in tourism Comparative perspectives. In *Gender, work and tourism* (pp. 219–233). Routledge. doi:10.4324/9780203991664-14

Uriely, N. (2001). 'Travelling workers' and 'working tourists': Variations across the interaction between work and tourism. *International Journal of Tourism Research, 3*(1), 1–8. doi:10.1002/1522-1970(200101/02)3:1<1::AID-JTR241>3.0.CO;2-M

Van Pelt, M. (2011). Space tourism. In *Space-Based Technologies and Commercialized Development: Economic Implications and Benefits* (pp. 164–177). IGI Global. doi:10.4018/978-1-60960-105-8.ch007

Yiu, L., Saner, R., & Lee, M. R. (2015). Lesotho, a tourism destination: An Analysis of Lesotho's current tourism products and growth potential. In Handbook of research on global hospitality and tourism management (pp. 312-331). IGI Global.

KEY TERMS AND DEFINITIONS

Community-Based Tourism: This represents a type of emerging tourism organized and managed by local community in its integrity.

Human Resource Management: Is the strategic and coherent approach to the effective and efficient management of people in a company.

Job Satisfaction: Or work satisfaction, the term is used for measuring workers´ engagement and contentedness with the desks or jobs.

Labor Relation: This term denotes the relation or relationships between employers and employees.

Tourism Industry: It is a set of subservice sectors organized in the leisure and travel activities. The tourism industry includes a variety of stakeholders and actors such as train or bus station, air industry, hotel industry, travel agents and rent-a-car industry.

Chapter 8

Corporate Social Responsibility and Analysis of Its Social Dimension in Hotels in Malaga

Miriam Stopiakova
EADE University, Spain

Marina Haro-Aragú
iD https://orcid.org/0000-0001-9988-5459
University of Malaga, Spain

Alicia Martin Garcia
iD https://orcid.org/0000-0002-3670-7281
EADE University, Spain

ABSTRACT

The main purpose of this research is to emphasize the importance of corporate social responsibility (CSR) within any hotel in operation. The main objective has focused on the analysis of social activities of CSR of accommodation in the city of Malaga. The basis of this project has been the investigation of the term CSR and its presence in tourism. At the same time, it has focused on the fact of the presence of the Covid-19 pandemic, which has caused many changes in tourism in recent years. As part of the investigation on the current situation of CSR activities in hotels Malaga city, interviews have been carried out with active professionals in the sector, in order to draw correct conclusions. Additionally, this project contributes with the proposal of activities within the social dimension of CSR of a hotel supporting the local community in different areas. It has been possible to reach various conclusions about the positive impact and importance of CSR in the hotel sector together with future lines of research, which can be supported by the results of this work.

DOI: 10.4018/978-1-6684-8726-6.ch008

Copyright © 2023, IGI Global. Copying or distributing in print or electronic forms without written permission of IGI Global is prohibited.

INTRODUCTION

A business that makes nothing but money is a poor business. -Henry Ford-

Entrepreneur Henry Ford, born at the end of the 19th century, already realized at that time that a company that only looks at numbers becomes a company without soul and value. More than 100 years have passed and it is still common to see companies that care about nothing but profit without regard to the affected community, employees, environment or other elements. The list is long and with the growth of technologies and more conscious customers, responsible companies towards society are required. In the quote from Henry Ford (Mansfield News Journal, 1965) this importance of the ethical approach in private organizations is highlighted. Of course the companies are not NGOs (Non-Governmental Organizations) and they have to earn money. But the question is - how? (Sedes Garcia, 2012).

Focused on tourism, this is a sector that is growing rapidly as a result of increasingly fast, accessible and cheap transportation. Areas that decades ago were off-limits to tourists due to complicated transport links are now popular holiday destinations. This trend is unstoppable, as is its impact on the environment, local culture and the community.

Concerns and the resulting interest in the nature and culture of different parts of the Earth have increased environmental concerns and efforts to reduce the impact of tourism on the cultural diversity of countries. Socially responsible tourism has begun to form, focused on sustainable development. This represents the hope of preserving local culture, historical monuments, biodiversity and an uncontaminated environment for future generations.

Therefore, analyzing tourism and the hotel world, we observe that this is a sector in which there is a more complex framework of requirements for sustainability. And sustainability means not only environmental but also social and is developing as a key part of any successful hotel.

Corporate social responsibility (CSR) is, today, a very current and important issue. Specifically, in this research, we are going to focus on its use in tourism, especially in hotels. In recent years there has been more and more talk about its need, but mainly focused on the environment, although the social and economic impacts are also important parts of the CSR strategy that should not be left behind. For this reason, we are going to focus more on social well-being and its integration within the hotels.

The main objective of this research is study the current situation of CSR activities of hotels in Malaga capital and propose actions to improve it.

Being socially conscious also helps a business build a lasting relationship with its community. Furthermore, consumers no longer expect hotels to provide excellent services, but also to help the community in which they operate (Entrepreneur, 2017). In addition to the moral factor, socially conscious companies often create positive work environments and have dynamic ideologies that attract top talent. They, in particular, are likely to choose a company that takes an active role in their community and dedicates some of their resources to helping others.

Malaga has a very fast tourist growth speed in which the number of hotels is increasing every year. According to an analysis by the INE - National Institute of Statistics (EpData, 2022), the number of hotel establishments open in Málaga Municipality has grown from 95 in 2017 to 124 in 2022. It is true that the Covid-19 pandemic has slowed down this trend, but it hasn't stopped it. As we can see in the following graph, growth is once again a reality.

Estimated open hotel establishments in Malaga (Municipality)
The data is from the months of September of each year.

Figure 1. Malaga hotel establishments
Source: INE, www.epdata.es

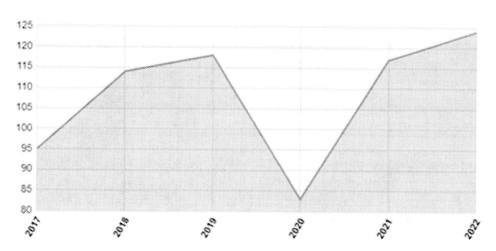

In addition, in the next three years there are projects underway on the Costa del Sol for 12 five-star hotels (Diario Sur, 2021).

Thus, the theme of social responsibility of hotels in Malaga has a relevant importance that requires attention. Although, as we can see in the actions of the hotels, the main focus is, however, towards the environment and how they face this demand, but getting involved with society is also part of the responsible industry. Precisely for this reason, in this research we are going to focus our observation on the issue of social well-being and its importance as part of a successful hotel that is aware of its own social responsibility.

Figure 2. CSR areas
Source: Millie

OBJECTIVES

Corporate social responsibility (CSR) is, today, a very current and important issue. Specifically, in this research, we are going to focus on its use in tourism, especially in hotels. In recent years there has been more and more talk about its need, but mainly focused on the environment, although the social and economic impacts are also important parts of the CSR strategy that should not be left behind. For this reason, we are going to focus more on social well-being and its integration within the hotels.

Main Objective

Study the current situation of CSR activities of hotels in Malaga Capital (focusing mainly on social welfare) and according to the result, propose a proposal for CSR action in accordance with said analysis.

Secondary Objectives

To achieve the main objective, we need to reach the following partial goals:

- *Theoretical objective:*
  - ○ From the theoretical point of view, explain the meaning and strategy of CSR - Corporate Social Responsibility.
- *Analytical objective:*
  - ○ Investigate the current situation on social welfare initiatives as part of CSR in the hotels which have crucial importance in Malaga Capital.

METHODOLOGY

For this investigation several methods will be used with respect to the achievement of the objectives defined in the previous chapter.

The methodology used to carry out this project is based on documentary research, analyzing different sources of information extracted through scientific journals, official web pages, as well as other bibliographic sources.

1. Characteristics of the research object

We are going to focus on the city of Malaga. We chose 4 - 5 hotels based on number of beds, years of operation and representing international chains as well as local accommodations.

2. Data acquisition method and its sources:
   a) Primary - obtained through interviews.
   b) Secondary - library, written publications and Internet resources related to the topic analyzed.
3. Work procedures:
   a) Before beginning, it is necessary to study, in more detail, the issue of Corporate Social Responsibility.
   b) Subsequently, selecting available information from secondary sources, we build the theoretical part of the work.
   c) We analyze CSR activities in selected hotels.
   d) We will investigate the current situation in Malaga Capital.
   e) We created a generic proposal assigned to a hotel in Malaga, whose activity is focused on social welfare and its possible application.

CORPORATE SOCIAL RESPONSIBILITY

Definition

The term corporate social responsibility (CSR) has not been precisely defined for many years. A large number of authors, who deal with this topic, use different definitions and terminology to define it (Dahlsrud, 2008). In the last century we were able to find its various formulations, which spoke mainly of impartiality, commitment, transparency, emphasizing voluntariness and willingness to contribute to the development of quality of life.

Alexander Dahlsrud in his publication How corporate social responsibility is defined: an analysis of 37 definitions explains that this situation is mainly due to the fact that social responsibility is based on the voluntary principle, does not have strictly defined limits and, therefore, provides space for a broad understanding and interpretation of this complex concept (2008).

The European Commission (2001) published the Green Paper entitled Promoting a European framework for corporate social responsibility, which presents CSR as follows: "Being socially responsible does not only mean fully complying with legal obligations, but also going beyond compliance by investing "more" in human capital, the environment and relationships with stakeholders". Next, this document highlights that:

Experience gained from investing in environmentally friendly technologies and business practices suggests that going beyond legal compliance can increase the competitiveness of companies. The application of stricter standards than the requirements of social legislation, for example in terms of training, working conditions or relations between management and workers, can also have a direct impact on productivity. It opens a way to manage change and reconcile social development with increased competitiveness (Libro Verde, 2001).

Clearly, CSR is taking shape and the definition of UNIDO (United Nations Industrial Development Organization), today, the more current explains that: "Corporate Social Responsibility is a management concept through which companies integrate social and environmental concerns in its business operations and in interactions with its stakeholders" (2022).

However, one of the first concepts was developed shortly after World War II, when the modern history of CSR began to be written. Howard R. Bowen is considered the first theorist and father of socially responsible business. In his book Social Responsibilities of the Businessman in 1953 he wrote: "Social responsibility is the commitment of businessmen to follow certain strategies, make decisions or perform activities that are desirable in terms of the objectives and values of our company." According to him, entrepreneurship is expected to create a higher standard of living, expand economic progress, bring order, justice, freedom and personal development (May, Cheney and Roper, 2007, p. 5).

Milton Friedman, Nobel Prize winner in economics (1976), surprised many people with the argument that one cannot strictly talk about CSR since those who acquire responsibilities are people and not an artificial corporation. Those who should be responsible are people and not an artificial corporation (Krause, 2014). In the late 1960s and early 1970s, a series of definitions emerged as a result of social change in Western European societies and the rise of the social sciences (EY Spain, 2021). The turning point in the definition of CSR occurred in 1971, when the CED (Corporation for Economic Development) described the three-level model of CSR in the publication Corporate Social Responsibility:

- **inner circle:** the basic responsibility of the company is to make profit and strive to grow,
- **intermediate circle:** In addition to concentrating on its own business interests, the company must also monitor the changing social dimension between the company and society,
- **outer circle:** duties and activities that the company must fulfill to actively improve its environment, for example poverty or increased environmental pollution (Sbarcea, 2007).

Figure 3. CED definition of the three concentric circles of CSR
Source: Semantic Scholar

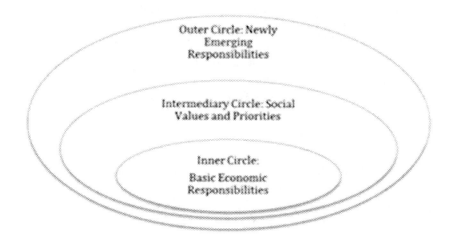

The linking of these three areas is still considered a key CSR model through which companies can operate in accordance with their environment (Sbarcea, March 2007).

The idea of CSR gained momentum with the expansion of large conglomerate corporations and became a popular topic in the 1980s with R. Edward Freeman's Strategic Management: A Stakeholder Approach (May et al., 2007, p. 6). .

In that decade, the theoretical foundations of CSR were finally passed to the real application of this concept. One of the first companies to demonstrate that responsible business can be successful was The Body Shop cosmetics store. Its founder, Anita Roddick, was openly critical of the course of the business, especially the cosmetics industry. Since its inception, the store has supported charitable and social activities in its locality, collaborated with Greenpeace, and products were not tested on animals (Sbarcea, 2007).

In 1997, the GRI (Global Reporting Initiative) standards arrived, which represent the best practices at a global level to publicly report the economic, environmental and social impacts of an organization (GRI, s.f.).

Then comes a dormant period of ten years, until 2010, when more actions begin to be carried out, such as ISO 26000 in September 2010 and the Renewed EU Strategy is also built in October 2011. From there the function of CSR begins to move more and takes another leap upwards. Particularly, when the Directive of 2014/95/UE appears and the specific points in the Spanish legislation begin to change. For example, in the Capital Society Law of 2014, corporate social responsibility is conferred on the boards of directors as a non-delegable responsibility (EY Spain, 2021).

Another push comes in 2019, possibly as a result of the release of a new Business Roundtable Statement, signed by 181 CEOs, redefining the purpose of corporations, away from maximizing shareholder value to promoting an economy that serves all stakeholders, including customers, employees, suppliers, communities and shareholders. This change signaled that social responsibility and sustainability are no longer just a progressive perspective on how to run a business (Business Roundtable, 2019).

In January 2020, just before the Covid-19 pandemic, very active times were arriving and in the same month the OECD Declaration appeared, the DAVOS Manifesto (supporting in some way the economy of the stakeholders thirty years after Freeman) and also the new European New Green Deal. This happens in a short time and CSR becomes very important (EY Spain, 2021).

Triple Bottom Line

The company is not only responsible for generating its own growth and profit, but also for other areas of society that it influences. Triple bottom line speaks of the impact and economic, social and environmental activities of a company, which determine its viability as a responsible company (Henriques and Richardson, 2004). It follows three basic areas in which companies should behave in a socially responsible manner:

Figure 4. Triple Bottom Line
Source: Hatcher+

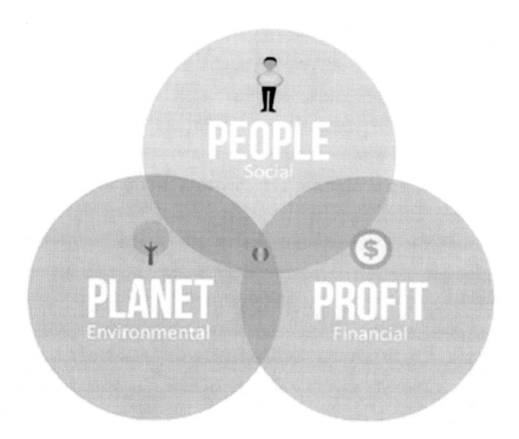

As we can see in the illustration, the triple bottom line describes the social, environmental and economic impact of companies, which is characterized by three elements known in English as 3P (May et al., 2007, p. 75):

- **People** - are equally important because a strong and mutually beneficial relationship with stakeholders (partners, customers, employees, etc.) is essential for any business.

- **Planet** - refers to getting involved in global/local issues and respecting the environment.
- **Profit** - the last item, but just as important as the previous ones. It is a traditional measure and, in most, expressed by the price / profitability. It helps to estimate the financial performance of a company.

Companies with a strong and solid triple bottom line results can move closer to responsibility, sustainable development and success.

CSR, Human Rights, and Tourism

As a result of the Covid-19 pandemic, issues like CSR and human rights have become more important than ever, as stakeholders demand more from global corporate leaders. Often those are faced with making ethical decisions that can affect the well-being of an organization not only nationally but also worldwide (Droll, 2021). John Ruggie in his report *The Corporate Responsibility to Respect Human Rights* reveals that: "The corporate responsibility to respect human rights means to avoid infringing on the rights of others, and addressing adverse impacts that may occur. It applies to all companies in all situations" (2010).

According to Nadácia Integra, globalization has influenced the development of international trade, consumer behavior, company management, and is one of the most important reasons for the increase in the importance of social responsibility in business. One of the consequences of globalization, which motivates doing socially responsible business, is the long-term growing interest in observing human rights. This increase in interest is caused, on the one hand, by information technologies which enable the rapid exchange of information as well as the exchange of norms and cultural patterns. Thanks to this, the Universal Declaration of Human Rights has become a universal norm that regulates mutual relations between individuals, organizations and institutions. On the other hand, corporations that benefit from economic globalization do not always respect human rights in the countries where they operate. It should be noted that many times in the country where the corporation has its headquarters, it respects human rights, but in the country where it has its production, it does not have to respect them (2005, p. 12). For example, during Covid-19 we were used to seeing people wearing masks, but in China, before the pandemic, people were already wearing masks to protect themselves from air pollution caused by many factories. And not having a basic right of free, clean air to breathe is detrimental to people (Schembri, 2021).

Schembri says that, unfortunately, what is considered ethical behavior in one country, it may not be so in another. A global leader or manager must recognize and be sensitive to these differences without compromising the values of the organization.

In her presentation, based on the book *International Business: Competing in the Global Marketplace* (Hill, 2021), names the most common ethical problems faced by companies and organizations involved in global business. Among them are mainly human rights, labor practices, environmental regulations, corruption and moral obligations of companies (2021).

Social pillar of CSR, according to Zelený et al. (2010, p. 86), is focused on two main directions, in terms of the analysis of activities, impacts, results and activities of the organization:

- *The first direction* is oriented to the interior of the organization, it maps the organization's comprehensive social care to its employees.
- *The second direction* is external or beyond the organization, and looks at aspects of the organization's operations and behavior in relation to external stakeholders.

Social area includes mainly interest in human rights, discrimination, equality, employment of people with a deteriorating situation in the labor market (disabled, recently graduated students, single mothers, people who are on the threshold of social - work exclusion), prohibition of child labor, employee health, safety at work, reconciliation of work and family life of employees, contributing to the development of human capital, impact on the local community, charity, support for NGO organizations in the field of community development, etc. (Zelený et al., 2010, p. 86). As we can see, social responsibility carries a wide list of different activities that each company should be interested in. Here it is also necessary to emphasize the activities supporting education, culture and sports in the community in which the company operates.

When we focus on tourism, Sustainable Hospitality Alliance acknowledges this industry has influence on many aspects of human rights, which are basic freedoms all people are entitled to. The travel and tourism industry employs 330 million people worldwide and its responsibility is to ensure respect for the human rights of their employees (2021). The alliance also explains:

"The hospitality industry can be at risk of potential human rights issues. Hotel companies may outsource services, such as cleaning, maintenance and security. The industry also operates under a variety of different business models from owner-operators to franchises. This means that companies can have less control over the employment practices of individual properties or supply chains. Additionally, there is the risk of human trafficking for sexual exploitation taking place in hotels" (2021).

It is fundamental for tourism industry to have procedures in place that enable them to prevent human rights risks: "Addressing human rights issues is a complex process and the industry needs to work together to support the human rights of their colleagues, the workers in the organizations they do business with, and the communities in which they operate" (Sustainable Hospitality Alliance, 2021). And it is precisely the CSR of the companies that plays an irreplaceable role in this process.

CSR IN THE HOTEL SECTOR

The Importance of CSR in Tourism

According to the World Tourism Organization (UNWTO, 2014) "Tourism is one of the industries that originates the most resources, due among other causes to its expansive effect on other sectors and indirect activities, generating economic resources for its area of influence, and multiplying the wealth in the destination" (Romero and Mogollón and Cerro and Fernández, 2017).

The development of CSR in the tourism sector has been carried out as a form of sustainability in recent decades. Setting rigorous labor standards, promoting environmental sustainability, and supporting local communities are important issues for hotel chains (Bohdanowicz and Zientara, April 2009). Holcomb et al. (2007) indicate that there are many studies that have investigated companies in the tourism and hotel sector and show intensive support for CSR activities, which increases their importance compared to other sectors. The observations detected that the main international hotel companies are adopting the integration of social and environmental objectives in their businesses to use them as a basis to develop unique competitive advantages, such as Hilton, Intercontinental and Marriott (Romero and Mogollón and Cerro and Fernández, 2016).

In the analysis, which we have mentioned before, on the behavior of CSR in hotel companies of hotel establishments in Spain from the perspective of their managers, it is established that the influence of CSR on long-term profitability is considered to be less relevant. However, it should be emphasized that the study concludes that CSR has positively affected RevPAR in recent years. On the other hand, trust and reputation achieved through the integration of CSR in the operations of hotel establishments are considered very relevant and especially significant and have obtained the best results in this study (Romero et al., 2017).

According to Carrol (1979), however, the study of the integration of Social Responsibility measures in the hotel activity projects several debates:

- The first would be related to which operational areas should be competent to implement these policies, as well as whether it would be appropriate to apply them.
- The way in which they are communicated or the degree of CSR involvement is also discussed, since in many cases these actions are carried out in hotel facilities in compliance with some legislation. It is questionable whether this leads the hotel company to a real commitment to social responsibility in its ethical and discretionary dimension.

In general, the sector has tendencies to apply CSR measures due to the negative effects of its activities. But hotel companies need to be fully aware of the strategies they implement in their organizations, since the effectiveness of CSR in hotel facilities is closely related to the fact that the steps must be integrated into the company's strategy and with clear objectives to be achieved. And not only in response to the push of stakeholders, or as a common publicity mechanism, fashion, routine, or industry customs (Romero et al., 2016).

Why Involving CSR in the Business and its Benefits

Social responsibility has become a modern business concept that takes into account not only economic goals but also social and environmental ones. Of course, entrepreneurs ask themselves various questions regarding their advantages and benefits for the company. Therefore, it should be noted that CSR is not just about volunteering and sacrificing for a good cause, but can also bring various benefits to the company and in several cases in a non-financial way. The following are according to Nadácia Integra et al. (2005, p. 11):

1. **Allows Risk to be Managed -** a responsible approach to human resource management, product quality control, and environmental standards can protect a company from costly litigation and resulting damage to the company's name/brand.
2. **It helps to increase profits -** compliance with ethical, legal and social standards is perceived by Kotler and Lee (2005, p. 208) as a method that attracts more customers, since consumers prefer to buy from responsible companies.
3. **Helps reduce costs -** this benefit comes from the pressure to use resources efficiently. For example, smaller hotels do simpler things like recycling and saving electricity or water by installing low-consumption light bulbs or water savers in taps and showers. In the case of more ambitious hotels, these measures include the installation of biomass boilers or the use of groundwater for irrigation. Other measures that are usually applied in many hotels are

focused on their guests (placing relevant information in different areas of the hotel) and employees (specific training on sustainability). These initiatives not only minimize the impact of their activity on the environment, but also create significant economic savings for the company, especially if one thinks in the medium-long term (López, 2016).

4. **Allows for better human resource management -** builds on the above benefits as it is a good redistribution of staff roles which can solve the excessive number of employees which means unnecessary salary costs. Employee education and training, resp. career prospects, access to remuneration, anti-discrimination policy, work balance and private time are some of the factors that prevent frequent employee change - fluctuation, which has a positive impact on the quality of services offered.

5. **Supports innovation and brings new business opportunities -** stimulates innovative thinking and management practices. As a result of creating new services for new customers, it generates a long-term competitive advantage (Pavlík and Bělčík, 2010, p. 32).

6. **Helps companies maintain legitimacy -** CSR views the company as a member of a society consisting of stakeholders. The company must have an open dialogue with everyone, which must convince them of the company's correct conduct.

7. **Helps build "trust" and "brand" -** "goodwill" according to Pavlík and Bělčík (2010, p. 31) means customer trust, which is very difficult to build and very easy to destroy. The understanding of the company's responsibility is demonstrated by the quality of the services offered. The standards themselves meet expectations and subsequently build trust in the provider.

8. **Increases attraction for investors -** investment funds prefer to choose opportunities according to financial, economic, social, environmental and ethical factors.

It is evident that the company needs to obtain an economic benefit in the first place to be able to achieve other objectives aimed at the socially responsible company, such as the improvement of society or the protection of the environment.

Measurement and Evaluation of CSR in Tourism

Not only the companies themselves, but especially their stakeholders are interested in demonstrating the credibility of companies by presenting themselves as socially responsible. This interest has created an entire area of social responsibility evaluation. The concept of CSR, like other elements of an organization's performance, needs to be continuously measured, evaluated, analyzed and improved. In principle, there are two types of methods that can be used to assess social responsibility:

1. ***Exact methods of CSR evaluation:***
   - GRI, SA 8000, ISO 26000, etc..
2. ***Benchmarking methods and index***:
   - Measurement based on the analysis of the content of the annual reports,
   - Measurement based on the knowledge obtained from the questionnaires,
   - Pollution indices,
   - Information obtained from credit rating agencies (Kapalková, 2017, p. 35).

There is a series of CSR norms and standards that are developed for each area - environmental, social and economic. Standards are voluntary initiatives that indicate what is right for a company and what activities it should not implement (Kašparová and Kunz, 2013, p. 45). Because there is no uniform definition and interpretation of CSR, there are many standards that adjust it. In this regard, the KATE Center for Ecology and Development (Stuttgart, Germany) summarized the CSR concepts that are applied or could be applied, not only for hotel companies, but in the tourism sector in general (López de Lacalle, 2010):

- EMAS (Eco Management and Audit Scheme - Environmental Management)
- ISO 14001 Environmental Management
- ISO 26000 - Guide on social responsibility
- Social Audit SA 8000
- Sustainability Reporting Guidelines (GRI).
- OECD Guidelines for Multinational Enterprises
- United Nations Norms on Corporate Responsibility
- Transnationals in the field of Human Rights
- United Nations Global Compact "Global Compact"
- Global Code of Ethics for Tourism
- Code of conduct for the protection of children against sexual exploitation
- Code of conduct for the protection of children against sexual exploitation in tourism and the travel industry.

In general, with CSR reporting, the aim is to show initiatives in the field of social responsibility as a source of value creation for the company. In addition, the tourism sector as a whole should not consider responsible management as an expense, but as an investment that pays off in the medium and long term (Guerra and Fernández Pájaro, 2011)..

2.3.1 Return on Investment (ROI) of RSC

Measuring the impact of corporate responsibility activities and putting numbers on these actions is a complicated task and one of the great drawbacks of CSR. Precisely for this reason, Sedes García at the conference on Strategic Management of Corporate Responsibility explains that ROI (Return on Investment) is a topic that has been actively studied in recent years in relation to the measurement and evaluation of CSR activities (2012). Progressively, methodologies aimed at identifying the return on social investments are being developed. One of them is the 5R Framework model (Revenue, Reputation, Recruitment, Retention, Relationships) - an effective tool to measure and report on the ROI of CSR in an organized and strategic way. It can also be used to: "identify new opportunities, prioritize projects and resources, and describe key tactics that will expand and improve your social responsibility program" (Lazovska, 2019).

Figure 5. Framework 5R
Source: SIRSE

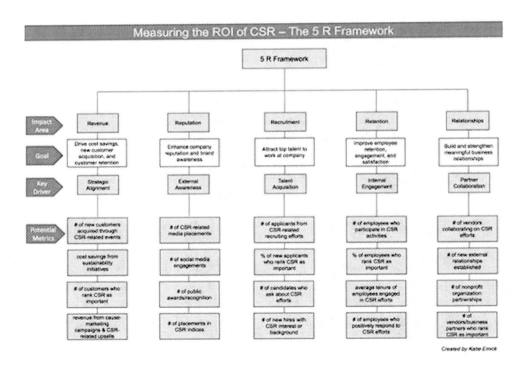

"Greenwashing"

Green sheen, eco bleaching, green image washing, or better known by name *greenwashing*, is:

A misleading practice of companies that outwardly declare their social responsibility and, on the other hand, mislead consumers with false or incomplete information about their products and activities. We talk about greenwashing when a company or organization spends more time and money to declare its business socially responsible through marketing than to implement business practices that reduce the environmental impact of its operations. As an example, we can mention a hotel that declares its interest to protect the environment in front of its guests by leaving them the option of not changing bed linen and towels, but not saving water or electricity at all (Veszprémi Sirotková and Šusterová, 2016, p.69).

Several websites have been created to defend against greenwashing, for example greenwash.earth (2022) or twosides.info (2022). Greenpeace activists are also struggling with it and Forbes or The Guardian magazines dedicate many articles to it. The European Commission also published for the first time the report on Screening of websites in relation to ecological laundering, in which it is stated that: "half of the ecological claims are unfounded" (2021).

Spain and CSR in its Tourism

Spain began to actively build tourism in the 1960s and grew following the pattern of sun and beach tourism focused on the European working class. After joining the EU, Spain has not only continued as a popular European destination but has even become a world leader as a number two tourist destination (Secretaría de Estado de Turismo, 2019).

Covid-19 caused countries to close for tourists or establish certain rules and regulations for travelers between 2019 and 2021. According to data collected in SiteMinder's World Hotel Index after the pandemic, Spain once again became the world leader in tourism and currently is in the first position in the recovery of large destinations due to its number of hotel reservations, which have reached a volume of 117% compared to the data for 2019 (TecnoHotel, 2022).

Table 1. Countries most visited by the World Tourism Organization

Country	Most Recent Year	Most Recent Value (Thousands)
France	2018	89,322.00
Spain	2018	82,773.00
United States	2018	79,745.92
China	2018	62,900.00
Italy	2018	61,567.20

Source: World Tourism Organization via the World Bank

Figure 6. Evolution of hotel reservations
Source: TechnoHotel

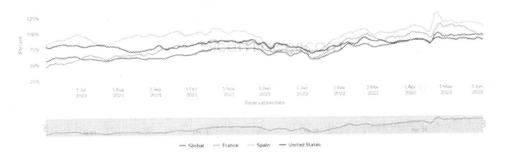

The development of the tourism industry is essential to maintain the established economic system. However, Inventory analysis and carbon footprint of coastal-hotel services: *A Spanish case study* states that if environmental requirements were not taken into account, the country would face a negative effect in the depletion of local environmental resources on which tourism depends (Puiga and Kiliç and Navarro and Albertí and Chacóne, 2017).

At the same time, Spain, with its world leadership position in tourism, must behave as an example to other countries and at the same time be able to maintain, or improve, its position. The Government of Spain, through the Secretary of State for Tourism, prepared the Sustainable Tourism Strategy for Spain 2030, a national tourism agenda to face the challenges of the sector in the medium and long term.

This document states that: "without sustainability, there will simply be no tourism in the future." He then explains that for this reason it is essential to promote the three pillars of sustainability: socioeconomic, environmental and territorial.

Following the aforementioned strategy, the Ministry of Industry, Commerce and Tourism (Mincotur) approved the distribution of the 615 million euros of the recovery funds "Next Generation EU" dedicated to the program of Tourism Sustainability Plans in Destinations, of which Andalusia will to receive a total investment of 72.62 million euros (Europa Press, 2022).

The sustainable tourism growth model is based on the following principles (Secretaría de Estado de Turismo, 2019):

- Socioeconomic growth
- Preservation of natural and cultural values
- Social benefit
- Participation and governance
- Permanent adaptation
- Leadership

The weakest point of the hotels within CSR materializes in the work *Tourism companies in Spain: Socially responsible?* as a delayed integration of responsible business management. And mainly, this is in line with the late implementation of CSR in Spain, not only in tourism but also in other sectors (Guerra and Fernández Pájaro, 2011).

IMPACTS OF COVID-19 ON CSR

At the time when the SDGs were formulated, the possibility of the world being threatened by a deadly virus such as Covid-19 was not considered. This forced countries to rethink such compliance. For example, in one of the World Bank reports it is estimated that between 88 million and 115 million people will fall into extreme poverty due to Covid-19, while the total figure may reach 150 million (World Bank, 2020). The United Nations (UN) estimates that the pandemic could force nearly 490 million people in 70 countries around the world back into defined poverty - such as those without basic housing, clean water and starving children (United Nations, 2021).

In the published report of the United Nations - Shared responsibility global solidarity responding to the socioeconomic impacts of covid-19 (UNDGG, 2020), we can study in detail how the pandemic has affected some of the 17 goals:

Objective 1 - End of poverty. Covid-19 has caused loss of income that leads vulnerable segments of society and families to fall below the poverty line.

Objective 2 - Zero hunger. Food production has been disrupted.

Objective 3 - Health and well-being. Without a doubt, Covid-19 is having devastating effects on health worldwide, especially due to the deaths and sequelae that the disease leaves in some people.

Objective 4 - Quality education. It has caused the closure of many schools. In rural areas, many children have been left without receiving studies due to difficult conditions, lack of connectivity and tools to access virtual learning environments.

Objective 5 - Gender equality. Economic benefits have been put at risk and levels of gender-based violence have increased. Women represent the majority of health and social assistance workers, and have therefore been more exposed to the disease.

Objective 6 - Clean water and sanitation. With the pandemic and preventive measures, the generation of waste that ends up in water sources has increased, which has increased the contamination of rivers and seas.

Objective 7 - Affordable and clean energy. Shortages of supplies and personnel are causing the interruption of access to electricity and the generation of polluting new forms of energy.

Objective 9 - Decent work and economic growth. Economic activities in many sectors of the economy have had to be suspended and with less income or hours of working hours, lower income and unemployment.

Objective 11 - Sustainable cities and communities. The population living in slums faces a higher risk of contracting Covid-19 and different diseases due to the density of the population and poor sanitation conditions.

Objective 13 - Action for the climate. Given the economic slowdown, actions in favor of the climate and sustainability are threatened, however, due to the decrease in the production of transport powered by fossil fuel, the mitigation of polluting emissions into the atmosphere is achieved.

Objective 16 - Peace, justice and strong institutions. The increase in conflicts caused by unemployment and lack of resources threatens the sustainability of institutions and stable and lasting peace. In general we see that the problems caused by the pandemic will stop for a long time.

The impacts of Covid-19 on the SDGs are evident. In relation to this, it is expected that external alliances will increase to achieve the SDGs and, in addition, sustainability objectives will have more importance after this crisis (EY Spain and DIRSE, 2020).

Table 2. Covid affecting the SDGs

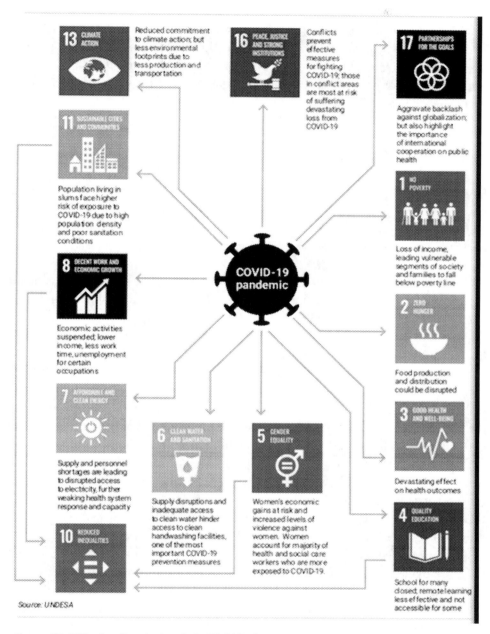

Source: World Tourism Organization via the World Bank

Corporate Social Responsibility and Analysis of Its Social Dimension in Hotels in Malaga

CSR is also considered synonymous with avoiding business risks and is a very important part of an organization today (Mastroeni, July 2020). Covid-19 showed that if you are responsible in the way you act, you can continue doing your business. The pandemic taught companies, for example, how to take care of their employees - because if they are not healthy, who is going to work? You lose productivity, you cannot produce or provide service and consequently you lose money. The business is not sustained and therefore you cannot operate.

APPROACH TO THE SOCIAL DIMENSION

Hotel chains have focused on environmental protection for many years. One of the reasons, possibly, was the pressure from stakeholders, which opened a discussion about the evident impact of hotels on environmental pollution: excessive washing of bed linen and towels, excessive consumption of electricity, etc. Today, it is no longer something extraordinary for hotels to use eco-friendly products and pay close attention to environmental protection. Although, as we have exposed, CSR is not just about that. And as we explained in the previous chapter, the Covid-19 pandemic has brought many changes in the responsibilities of the company.

One of the main conclusions of the first study on the Impact of Covid-19 on CSR/ Sustainability priorities and on the role of its professionals, prepared by the Spanish Association of Social Responsibility Managers (DIRSE) and the Professional Services Firm EY, was that: "the reconstruction after Covid-19 will mean a structural change in the social responsibility of companies" (Diario Responsable, 2020). However, with the Covid-19 crisis, all of society's priorities have changed and they have put us all before reality (Pilnillos, 2020). All sustainability issues will increase in relevance, although their relative weight will change. In this sense, while before Covid-19, the mitigation of climate change and energy efficiency occupied importance in the top 7 relevant topics, after Covid-19 no topic related to the environment appears in that top 7. Today, it is led by the issues of employee health and safety (which have grown by 42%) and customers (+41%) (EY and DIRSE, 2020).

According to the results of the research published in the article "A true friend becomes evident on a rainy day: corporate social responsibility practices of the best hotels during the COVID-19 pandemic", 50% of the hotels organized CSR activities for the community and 76% for its employees and 87% for its customers. Based on these results, where the 100 hotels in the world were examined using the content analysis method, this research also provided key practical implications for hotel managers to effectively implement CSR practices in the pandemic period (Gürlek, 2021).

Sustainability involves a whole series of actions related to the "health" of our planet, but also to our society and good governance.

Figure 7. Growth / importance of health and well-being after Covid-19
Source: EY, DIRSE

Figure 8. Growth / importance of cultural change and social action after Covid-19
Source: EY, DIRSE

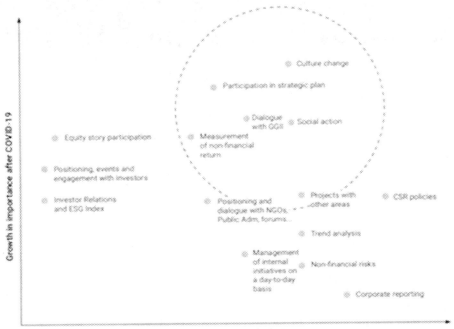

HOTELS IN MÁLAGA AND THE PRESENCE OF SOCIAL ACTIVITIES

At the beginning of this research we have mentioned that Malaga has a very fast tourist growth rate with the increase in hotels open every year. As explained before, one of the important parts of any successful hotel today is sustainability. And that means not only mitigating environmental impacts but also being conscious in the social sphere which, among other things, helps the hotel to build a lasting relationship with its community.

Corporate Social Responsibility and Analysis of Its Social Dimension in Hotels in Malaga

Commitment to the community is one of the key pillars of corporate social responsibility, along with concern for the workplace, the marketplace and the environment. Community involvement can take many forms. For example, some companies choose (Invest Northern Ireland, n.d.):

- support a local charity with financial contributions,
- sponsor a local event,
- organize cleaning events,
- volunteer at local schools or community projects.

For most companies, it makes business sense to get involved in community-based CSR related to their product or service. This allows you to use your experience and show the human face of your business at the same time. For example, some restaurants or hotels provide food to local homeless groups, while some builders provide free labor and materials for community projects.

In addition to improving community relations, engaging your staff in CSR can help motivate them and foster their personal and professional development.

In the introduction we have already mentioned that companies are not NGOs and it is understandable that the benefits that social responsibility can bring are questioned.

The advantages of community participation for hotels are several. For example:

- Local people are an important source of sales. Getting involved in the community allows you to capitalize on word of mouth marketing. Recommendations from other local vendors can be a great help in getting guests to the hotel. Getting involved in community events and projects can boost community relationships. This also supports growing the hotel brand and builds brand recognition, which can help in marketing to the local population. While they may not always need a room, your hotel can still provide a place for people to meet, eat, or host business or family events. It is an easy way to mobilize the local population to take advantage of the facilities you offer and helps generate income for other facilities you offer (Preno, n.d.).
- Demonstrating commitment to the community can also enhance a hotel's reputation and, in turn, make it easier to recruit or retain employees..
- A good relationship with local authorities can also help if they prefer to award contracts to companies with a history of community involvement (Invest Northern Ireland, n.d.).

In the next part we are going to observe the current situation in the best-known hotels in Malaga City. We will focus on activities or social events and if they get involved in them. The objective is to find out if they take actions to benefit the community that surrounds them, for those who live in that area or the employees who work in these hotels.

Information in the Media

First, we have focused on communication channels and instruments that allow any external person or stakeholder to obtain information. We follow different media with the intention of observing possible information related to projects or social activities of hotels in Malaga City.

<u>**Online Press**</u> (Examples)
- Gastrosuma 2021 (Annex 2): More than 2,100 menus that arrived on Christmas Eve to the most vulnerable families in Malaga city thanks to the initiative 'A solidarity menu from the Malaga hospitality industry for Christmas' in which catering establishments such as **Only You**, **Hotel Malaga Premium**, **Gran Hotel Miramar** or **Hotel Molina Larios** (Gurmé Malaga, 2021).
- Hoteles Santos (the chain of which is the **Gran Hotel Miramar**) created its Sustainability and CSR Committee to reinforce its social and environmental commitment, which was communicated by the press in March of this year. The policy is developed in three areas. Except for the environmental focus, he talks about social action (where he tries to ensure that all his decisions, especially at a strategic level, go hand in hand with the most committed social action possible) and CSR awareness, aimed at employees, customers and suppliers (Europa Press, 2022).
- The **Soho Boutique Hotels** group joins as a new sponsor of the Museo Carmen Thyssen Málaga, after the collaboration agreement that connects the museum with the business world and allows it to continue its activity and projects (Málaga Actualidad, 2022).

<u>**Internet**</u> (Official web pages of hotel establishments)
Web pages of 13 hotels that operate in the center of Malaga have been analyzed. Although some of them have information on their websites, they are more general and none of them specifies a specific project focused on the local community of Malaga. However, when we started looking for the references, we found very little information. In most cases, it is data without particular details. And if they do, they are solely focused on the environment.

Corporate Social Responsibility and Analysis of Its Social Dimension in Hotels in Malaga

Table 3. Information on CSR on the web pages: Málaga Capital Hotels

Hotel	Actividades Sociales	Actividades Ambientales
Soho Boutique Hotels	X	X
Vincci Seleccion Posada del Patio	✓	✓
AC Palacio Málaga by Marriott	X	X
Gran Hotel Miramar	X	✓
Room Mate Larios / Valeria	X	X
Hotel NH Malaga	✓	✓
Barceló Málaga	✓	✓
Ilunion Málaga	✓	X
Hotel Málaga Centro	X	X
Ibis Hotel by Accor	✓	✓
Palacio Solecio	X	X
Parador de Málaga Gibralfaro	X	X
Only You Hotel Málaga	X	X

Source: authors

Social networks (Facebook, Instagram, LinkedIn)

In the case of Facebook and Instagram, there are "Stories" (publications visible for only 24 hours) so it cannot be concluded if there is content on social projects in these media. Despite the fact that we have not observed any highly visible project published and communicated by social networks in permanent publications.

The fact that hotels in Malaga are focused almost solely on environmental protection and social issues are left in the background also demonstrates the event of the Hotel Sustainability Conference in Malaga at the beginning of 2022. The concern of tourism companies is increasing, although still focusing only on ecological problems. There is talk about sustainability but only in relation to the environment (Fluixa Ferra, 2022).

For comparison, a prominent example is the Riu Hotels & Resort chain, which in March 2022 launched the new Riusponsible project with its own website riu.com/riusponsible where it publishes and communicates all CSR projects in a very clear and detailed manner. In addition, it informs not only about environmental activities, but also social and charitable ones.

PROPOSAL

There are a number of arguments for becoming a socially responsible hotel. From the moment it starts its activities, the company becomes part of the community that surrounds it. A socially responsible business strives to create good neighborly relations and participates in solving local problems. This effort tends to be rewarded in the form of positive acceptance by the local community, which generates potential customers and future employees (Kapalková, 2017, p. 67).

From the point of view of the companies that operate in tourism, these businesses, through their activities in the area, significantly help to improve the locality and increase its prosperity. They make it attractive not only for visitors but also for the population of the city. In addition, an important aspect is that they create jobs in the region. However, it is necessary to take into account the opinions of the community in the area in which a hotel operates, its impact on changes in the nature of the natural environment due to poorly located and insensitively constructed buildings.

The growth of tourist attendance can generate negative impacts not only on the environment but also by changing its cultural identity or architectural personality due to constant construction, increased noise and air pollution due to excessive traffic without the necessary infrastructure.

To this end, cooperation and building a relationship and mutual understanding are needed. Businesses must support the community in which they operate in their interests. Therefore, many more activities should be developed in Malaga by the hotels.

For this reason, it was decided to design a project that can later be implemented by any hotel, since it is not expensive.

Project: Podcast SPEAKeamos?

A socially responsible company is a company that does things beyond the legislative requirements, outside of its commercial obligations. One of these activities can also be help and support in the field of mental health.

Thinking of Malaga, it is a place of sun and sand where most months of the year the population dresses in summer clothes and the cult of the slim body is more present than in other places. Therefore, knowledge of the subject of eating disorders is very important, particularly among adolescents. Despite this, today, this issue is still somewhat taboo and if the knowledge about this disease is more widespread, it can prevent its development in many cases. Furthermore, the reality of eating disorders is much more complex than stereotypes make it out to be. For all these reasons, instead of making a typical web page with information, the proposal is to create a podcast focused on eating disorders.

Logo:

Figure 9. Logo design: Podcast SPEAKeamos?
Source: Authors, Canva

The first part of the name comes from the word "speak" expressing people with eating disorders, although they talk about the problem, in many cases they feel that they are not understood.

Objectives:

- Create a podcast that looks at eating disorders from all angles (body, diet, diagnosis, treatment) in interviews with experts.
- Education, prevention and support to the local community on the issue of eating disorders.
- Collaboration with the Eating Disorders Unit (UTCA) and its support.

With the podcast there are also opportunities to develop prevention and create more activities and social gatherings dealing with the issue of eating disorders, such as conferences in schools or balanced diet workshops.

Example of the Programming of Topics for 1 year - 12 topics:

- January - Fine line between a healthy diet, a disturbed relationship with food and an eating disorder.
- February - Interview with the psychologist: causes of eating disorders.
- March - It's not just extremely skinny people who suffer from eating disorders.
- April - The signs that my daughter / son suffers from an eating disorder.
- May - Forms of support for the person with an eating disorder.
- June - Interview with a person who has suffered mental anorexia.
- July - How to gain healthy self-esteem and healthy self-love.
- August - What parents should watch out for to prevent an eating disorder in their daughter or son.
- September - Interview with the doctor: how we react to eating disorders or alternating diets.
- October - Family and social relationships during recovery from an eating disorder.
- November - Life after overcoming an eating disorder.
- December - A healthy relationship with food: why is it so important?

Launch of the podcast

Why Podcast?

Podcast can help insert the brand into conversations in a culturally relevant way and will drive awareness. It is also tracking metrics such as consideration and engagement (Dua, 2016).

In Figures

The study, prepared in 2021 by the consultancy Prodigioso Volcán in collaboration with the market research company SEIM, surveyed 769 Internet users between the ages of 18 and 74 who used the internet. One of the conclusions about podcasts is that podcast consumption continues its unstoppable growth in Spain. In 2021, almost 18 million people signed up for this format in the country.

According to this study, 53% of the Spanish Internet user population reproduced these audios during the year 2021. This means that podcast consumption exceeded half of the Internet user population. Regarding consumption by generations, in the case of podcasts, the average age of consumption is 42 years (NOBBOT, 2022).

Alonso, head of studios for Southern and Eastern Europe at Spotify states: "The podcast has been fully established in Spain, as the consumption figures reflect" (IPMARK, 2021).

Objective Group

The population of Malaga of all ages.

Periodicity and Duration

Monthly - commit to at least 9 - 12 months to build listener awareness and loyalty. According to Špronglová, 2 podcasts per month lasting 20 - 30 minutes are recommended at first to win over the audience. Periodicity and topicality is very important - avoid preparing recordings many months before its publication (2022).

Depending on the audience results of the first episodes, there is the possibility of developing more digital content, including Vodcasts that have a greater impact.

Transmission Channels

The Swedish multimedia services company Spotify continues to establish itself as the most used platform in Spain for these services. For its part, iVoox, the Spanish online listening service, is the second most used platform (NOBBOT, 2022).

Collaboration with one of the local radio stations such as Onda Color, Cope or Canal Málaga and transmission of a link to the social networks of the schools and institutes of Málaga can also be considered.

Table 4. Most used podcast platforms in Spain in 2021

Source: NOBBOT

Communication Channels

Social networks such as Facebook, Instagram, Linkedin.

Recording Location

Hotel facilities. Some episodes can be turned into the above mentioned "Vodcast".

CONCLUSION

CSR is a present reality. And when you think about it, to a certain extent, you do things that governments don't do or where they fail on issues like homelessness, LGBT people, older people, education, health, etc. (Diskusie Zdvorilo, 2020). If CSR is done well, it is no longer just "cosmetic" and can be integrated into the business strategy. Because if a company does things wrong and does not convey trust, it is counterproductive (Mastroeni, 2021). Before the arrival of Covid-19, 68% of Booking.com and Exodus Travel customers were hopeful that their travel money would return to the local community (Travelabs Online Talk, 2020), (Exhib. Based on the information provided in Chapter 4, it can be concluded that this percentage has increased due to the pandemic situation. It has been detected that environmental issues have been left a step behind and from this it can be deduced that the dimension of social well-being has taken on great importance.

One of the main objectives of this research is to study the current situation of CSR activities in hotels in Malaga Capital (focusing mainly on social issues) and according to the result, propose a proposal for social action. Different media were followed to analyze these hotels. As a result, not much relevant information on support or development of social projects was found. On the other hand, there is no doubt that certain activities are taking place, although they are not sufficiently communicated.

The disclosure of positive information is important to the public, but even here the so-called "middle ground" must be found. It is argued that if a company does not provide information about itself, it does not act with the same credibility as a company that provides too much positive information about itself. However, if there is only minimal awareness of social activities among the people of a certain region, that can be considered a great pity because good deeds should be spread.

The hotel sector is aware of the positive impact of CSR on the creation of value and reputation in hotel accommodation and being sustainable should no longer be an option. Within the approach of the proposal focused on social welfare, a project focused on creating its own podcast is proposed, applicable to any hotel. It has focused on various problems, especially on help in the field of mental health (Speak*eamos*? Project).

It is expected that the hotels in Malaga Capital will continue on the path of more awareness towards their surroundings.

Limitations in Research and Future Lines of Research

In the course of the investigation several obstacles have been encountered. More significant was the not very clear difference between CSR and sustainability. Many authors use the term "sustainability" but are really talking about CSR or the other way around. In general, there are many publications with different opinions on the aforementioned terms and that is confusing. Another limitation was related to online information on the CSR strategies of the hotels in Malaga Capital. It has been found to be very small and it may be that it does not sufficiently reflect reality. Additionally, it was observed that the operational status of some hotels is still in post-Covid-19 mode. That means they operate differently as in normal circumstances. The proposal for future lines of research is to extend the research to the entire province of Malaga and compare the different areas of hotel involvement in CSR activities. The investigation can continue up to the national level with the purpose of contrasting the regions of Spain, or a comparison can also be made with another country.

REFERENCES

Banco Mundial. (October 7th, 2020). *Debido a la pandemia de COVID-19, el número de personas que viven en la pobreza extrema habrá aumentado en 150 millones para 2021.* (Due to th Pandemic COVID19- the number of poor people has been triplicated). Banco Mundial. https://www.bancomundial.org/es/news/press-release/2020/10/07/covid-19-to-add-as-many-as-150-million-extreme-poor-by-2021

Bohdanowicz, P. & Zientara, P. (April 1st, 2019). Hotel Companies' Contribution to Improving the Quality of Life of Local Communities and the Well-Being of Their Employees. *SAGE Journals*. doi:10.1057/thr.2008.46

Bowen, H. R. (2013). *Social Responsibilities of Businessmen*. University of Iowa Press. doi:10.2307/j.ctt20q1w8f

Business Roundtable. (August 19th, 2019). *Business Roundtable Redefines the Purpose of a Corporation to Promote 'An Economy That Serves All Americans'*. Business Roundtable. https://businessroundtable.org/business-roundtable-redefines-the-purpose-of-acorporation-to-promote-an-economy-that-serves-all-americanshttps://ec.europa.eu/commission/presscorner/detail/es/ip_21_269

Dahlsrud, A. (2006). How corporate social responsibility is defined: An analysis of 37 definitions. *InterScience. Corporate Social Responsibility and Environmental Management, 15*(1), 1–13. doi:10.1002/csr.132

Diario Responsable. (June 16th, 2020). Rumbo a la nueva normalidad, retos y cambios de la RSE. [Towards the new Normal]. *Diario Responsable*. https://diarioresponsable.com/noticias/29517-rumbo-a-la-nueva-normalidad-retos-y-cambios-de-la-rse. https://youtube.com/watch?v=p2u6x2FCxVs

Dua, T. (October 20th, 2016). InterContinental launches its own podcast series. *Digiday*. https://digiday.com/marketing/marketing-content-driven-intercontinental-hotels-launches-podcast/

EpData. (May 24th, 2022). Málaga - La ocupación de los hoteles en el municipio, en datos y gráficos. [Occupation in hotels of the Province] EpData. https://www.epdata.es/datos/ocupacion-hotelera-hoteles-datos-graficos-municipios/143/malaga/4282

Europa Press. (January 13th, 2022). El BOE oficializa la distribución en Andalucía de 72,6 millones para Planes de Sostenibilidad Turística en Destinos. [The BOE makes official the Sustainabel programs]. *Europa Press*. https://europapress.es/andalucia/noticia-boe-oficializa-distribucion-andalucia-726-millones-planes-sostenibilidad-turistica-destinos-20220113135307.html

Europa Press. (March 29th, 2022). Hoteles Santos crea su Comité de Sostenibilidad y RSC para reforzar su compromiso social y medioambiental. [Hotels Santos creates a Comitee for Sustainability]. *Europa Press*. https://europapress.es/epsocial/responsables/noticia-hoteles-santos-crea-comite-sostenibilidad-rsc-reforzar-compromiso-social-medioambiental-20220329103821.html

EY Spain y DIRSE (2020). *Impacto del Covid-19 en las prioridades de la RSC / Sostenibilidad y en el rol de sus profesionales.* [Impacts and priorities of RSC befores COVID-19]. https://dirse.es/wp-content/uploads/2020/06/200622-Impacto-COVID-19_RSC_Sostenibilidas-v8.pdf

Fluixa Ferra, C. (February 17th, 2022). Aterrizan en Málaga las Jornadas de Sostenibilidad Hotelera. [Sustainable programs in Malaga] *Hosteltur.* https://hosteltur.com/comunidad/nota/028386_aterrizan-en-malaga-las-jornadas-de-sostenibilidad-hotelera.html

García, I. (August 30th, 2017). Definición de Stakeholders. *Economía Simple.* https://economiasimple.net/glosario/stakeholders

GNUDS Grupo de las Naciones Unidas para el Desarrollo Sostenible. (March 2020). *Responsabilidad compartida, solidaridad global: Respuesta a los impactos socioeconómicos de la Covid-19*. Naciones Unidas. https://un.org/sites/un2.un.org/files/articlefile/eosg_covid-19_socioeconomic_report-2005791s.pdf

González, F. (n.d.). Podcast para destinos y hoteles. [Postcast for destinations and hotels] *El Blog de Andalucía Lab.* https://andalucialab.org/blog/podcast-para-destinos-hoteles/

GRI. (n.d.). *How to use the GRI Standards*. Global Reporting. https://globalreporting.org/how-to-use-the-gri-standards/gri-standards-spanish-transltions/

Guerra, A., & Fernández Pájaro, E. (2011, August). Empresas turísticas en España: ¿Socialmente responsable? (Tourist enterprises in Spain: are they sustainable? *Cultur*, *02*, 43–60.

Gürlek, M., & Kılıç, I. (2021, February 7th). A true friend becomes apparent on a rainy day: Corporate social responsibility practices of top hotels during the COVID-19 pandemic. *Current Issues in Tourism*, *24*(7), 905–918. doi:10.1080/13683500.2021.1883557

Gurmé Málaga. (December 27th, 2021). Más de 2.100 menús solidarios para las familias más vulnerables de Málaga. [More than 2100 menus and culinary option for more vulnerable people in Malaga]. *ABC*. https://abc.es/gurme/malaga/abci-mas-de-2-100-menus-solidarios-para-las-familias-mas-vulnerables-de-malaga-202112271015_noticia.html

Henriques, A., & Richardson, J. (2004). *The Triple Bottom Line: Does It All Add Up?* Earthscan.

Heuvel, J. (2005). *Diensten Marketing (Services marketing)*. The Netherlands Wolters Noordhoff Groningen.

Integra Foundation and Pontis Foundation and PANET. (2005). *Socially responsible business*. Integra Foundation. https://nadaciapontis.sk/wpcontent/uploads/2019/01/text_zodpovedne_podnikanie.pdf

Invest Northern Ireland. (n.d.). *Corporate social responsibility: local community*. Nibusinessinfo. https://nibusinessinfo.co.uk/content/corporate-social-responsibility-local-community

IPMARK. (September 15th, 2021). El 38% de los oyentes de podcasts se 'engancharon' en la cuarentena. (An estimate 38% followers in Postcast engaged themselves during the lockdown). *IPMARK*. https://ipmark.com/el-38-de-los-oyentes-de-podcasts-se-engancharon-en-la-cuarentena/

Kapalková, D. (2017). Corporate Social Responsibility in the Hotel industry [Master's Dissertation, The Institute of Hospitality Management in Prague 8, Ltd.]. VŠHE Information system. https://is.vsh.cz/th/hf4su/Diplomova_praca.pdf

Kašparová, K., & Kunz, V. (2013). *Modern approaches to corporate social responsibility and CSR reporting*. Grada Publishing.

Kotler. (2010). *Marketing for hospitality and tourism*. Pearson Education.

Kotler, P., & Lee, N. R. (2005). *Corporate Social Responsibility: Doing the Most Good For Your Company and Your Cause*. Wiley.

Krause, M. (June 30th, 2014). Milton Friedman escandaliza: la responsabilidad social de los empresarios es aumentar sus ganancias. [Milton Friedman trembles: the social responsabilities of businessmen is amassing profits]. *El foro y el bazar*. https://bazar.ufm.edu/milton-friedman-escandaliza-la-responsabilidad-social-delos-empresarios-es-aumentar-sus-ganancias

Kunz, V. (2012). *Corporate Social Responsibility*. Grada Publishing.

Lazovska, D. (2019, October 10). *Las 5 Rs de la RSE (The 5 Rs of CSR)*. ExpokNews; Expok. https://www.expoknews.com/las-5-r-de-la-rse/

López, M. (October 18th, 2016). Por qué invertir en RSC en un hotel. [Why RSC in a hotel]. *Hosteltur*. https://hosteltur.com/comunidad/005121_por-que-invertir-en-rsc-en-un-hotel.html

López de Lacalle, R. (January 13th, 2010). ¿Qué es la RSC y cómo se puede relacionar con el turismo justo? La experiencia española. [What is RSC and how it can be related to tourism?: The Spanish experience]. *Portal de América*. https://portaldeamerica.com/index.php/columnistas/anteriores-columnistas/item/135-%C2%BFqu%C3%A9-es-la-rsc-y-c%C3%B3mo-se-puede-relacionar-con-el-turismo-justo

Málaga Actualidad. (March 31st, 2022). Soho Boutique Hotels se incorpora como patrocinador del Museo Carmen Thyssen Málaga. [Soho Boutique Hotels promotes Carmen Thyssen Museum] *Málaga Actualidad*. http://malagactualidad.es/teletipos/item/41506-soho-boutique-hotels-se-incorpora-como-patrocinador-del-museo-carmen-thyssen-malaga.html

Mastroeni, L. (Anfitrión). (July 30th, 2020). Responsabilidad Social Empresarial #RSE In *Entre Compas Podcast*. (Nro. 3) [Social Corporate Responsibility] [Episodio de podcast]. https://www.listennotes.com/es/podcasts/entre-compas-podcast/s3-responsabilidad-social-p3Y9L4HSOTq/

May, S. K., Cheney, G., & Roper, J. (2007). *The Debate over Corporate Social Responsibility*. Oxford University Press.

McKinsey. (2011). *The business of sustainability survey*. McKinsey & Company. https://mckinsey.com/business-functions/sustainability/our-insights/the-business-of-sustainability-mckinsey-global-survey-results

Mercado (January 12th, 2003). La responsabilidad moral de las empresas. [Moral Ethics in corporations] *Mercado*. https://mercado.com.ar/management-marketing/la-responsabilidad-moral-de-las-empresas/

Naciones Unidas. (n.d.). *Sustainable Development*. UN. https://un.org/sustainabledevelopment/es/

NOBBOT. (February 3rd, 2022). El consumo de podcast crece en España y Spotify es la plataforma más usada. (Postcast Consumption in Spain and Spotify). *NOBBOT*. https://www.nobbot.com/tecnologia/aplicaciones-moviles-tecnologia/podcast-espana-spotify/

OCDE (2016). *Principios de Gobierno Corporativo de la OCDE y del G20*. [Principles for Corporate Governance in OCDE and G20]. OCDE. doi:10.1787/9789264259171-es

Pavlík, M., Bělčík, M., Srpová, J., Kunz, V., & Kužel, S. (2010). Corporate Social Responsibility: CSR. In *Practice And How To Go On With It*. Grada Publishing.

Preno (n.d.). *How the local community can help grow your hotel brand and presence*. Preno HQ. https://prenohq.com/blog/local-community-and-hotel-brand/

Puiga, R., Kiliç, E., Navarro, A., Albertí, J., & Chacóne, L. (2017). Inventory analysis and carbon footprint of coastland-hotel services: A Spanish case study. *The Science of the Total Environment*, *595*, 244–254. doi:10.1016/j.scitotenv.2017.03.245 PMID:28384580

Reich, R. (2007). *Supercapitalism - The transformation of business democracy, and everyday life*. Random House.

Romero, J. M., Mogollón, J. M., Cerro, A. M., & Fernández, J. A. (2016). El impacto de la RSC en la industria hotelera: Estado del arte. [The impacts of social responsability in the hospitality industry: an state of the art]. In Jiménez Caballero, J. L. (Ed.), El turismo y la experiencia del cliente: IX jornadas de investigación en turismo (pp. 409 - 435). FTF, University of Sevilla.

Romero, J. M., Mogollón, J. M., Cerro, A. M., & Fernández, J. A. (2017). Aproximación al estudio del comportamiento de la RSC en las empresas hoteleras. [Approaching Social Corporate Responsability in hotels] *Turismo & Desenvolvimento, 27/28*, 159- 170. https://proa.ua.pt/index.php/rtd/article/view/8387/5939

Ruggie, J. (May 15th, 2010). *The Corporate Responsibility to Respect Human Rights*. Harvard Law School Forum on Corporate Governance. https://corpgov. law.harvard.edu/2010/05/15/the-corporate-responsibility-to-respect-human-rights/#:~:text=The%20corporate%20responsibility%20to%20respect%20 human%20rights%20means%20to%20avoid,all%20companies%20in%20all%20 situations

Sbarcea, K. (March 27th, 2007). The Evolution of CSR. *ThinkingShift*. https:// thinkingshift.wordpress.com/2007/03/27/the-evolution-of-csr/

Secretaría de Estado de Turismo. (January 2019). *Estrategia de Turismo Sostenible de España 2030. Gobierno de España.* Secretaría de Estado de Turismo.[https:// turismo.gob.es/es-es/estrategia-turismo-sostenible/Documents/directrices-estrategia-turismo-sostenible.pdf

Sedes García, J. M. [EOI Escuela de Organización Industrial] (March 14th, 2012). *Gestión Estratégica de la Responsabilidad Corporativa* [Video]. (EOI School). YouTube. https://youtube.com/watch?v=-FKzPKsmg4o

Spain, E. Y. (June 16th, 2021). *Impacto del COVID-19 en las prioridades de la RSC y Sostenibilidad y en el rol de sus profesionales* [Video]. [effects of COVID-19 and the priorities of RSC for sustainability and the role of the professionals]. YouTube. https://youtube.com/watch?v=7pKPaw9Vdl0

Sustainable Hospitality Alliance. (n.d.). *Human rights*. Sustainable Hospitality Alliance. https://sustainablehospitalityalliance.org/our-work/human-rights/

TecnoHotel. (June 3rd, 2022). España vuelve a ser líder del turismo con un nivel de reservas hoteleras al 117%. [Spain takes the lead on the industry with a booking percentage of 117%]. *TecnoHotel*. https://tecnohotelnews.com/2022/06/espana-lider-turismo-global-nivel-reservas-hoteleras/

Travelabs Online Talk [Anula Galewska] (April 24th, 2020). *How sustainability and CSR will help your tourism business recover quicker* [Video]. YouTube. https://youtube.com/watch?v=a9-2_ATvsDU

UNIDO. (n.d.). *What is CSR?* United Nations Industrial Development Organization. https://unido.org/our-focus/advancing-economic-competitiveness/competitive-trade-capacities-and-corporate-responsibility/corporate-social-responsibility-market-integration/what-csr

United Nations. (2021). *Comprehensive response to Covid-19: Update 2021*. UN Sustainable Development Group. https://unsdg.un.org/sites/default/files/2021-12/un-comprehensive-response-covid-19-2021.pdf

UNODC. (n.d.). *Corruption and integrity & Ethics*. UNODC United Nations Office on Drugs and Crime. https://unodc.org/e4j/en/secondary/corruption-integrity-ethics.html

Veszprémi Sirotková, A. & Šusterová, V. (2016). Social responsibility and its enforcement in business. Tourism Economics and Business, *8*, (1/29), 64 - 70.

ADDITIONAL READING

Arnaudov, K., & Koseska, E. (2012). Business ethics and social responsibility in tourist organizations in terms of changing environment. *Procedia: Social and Behavioral Sciences*, *44*, 387–397. doi:10.1016/j.sbspro.2012.05.043

Coles, T., Fenclova, E., & Dinan, C. (2013). Tourism and corporate social responsibility: A critical review and research agenda. *Tourism Management Perspectives*, *6*, 122–141. doi:10.1016/j.tmp.2013.02.001

Dwyer, L., Jago, L., Deery, M., & Fredline, L. (2007). Corporate responsibility as essential to sustainable tourism yield. *Tourism Review International*, *11*(2), 155–166. doi:10.3727/154427207783948946

Font, X., & Lynes, J. (2018). Corporate social responsibility in tourism and hospitality. *Journal of Sustainable Tourism*, *26*(7), 1027–1042. doi:10.1080/0966 9582.2018.1488856

Henderson, J. C. (2007). Corporate social responsibility and tourism: Hotel companies in Phuket, Thailand, after the Indian Ocean tsunami. *International Journal of Hospitality Management*, *26*(1), 228–239. doi:10.1016/j.ijhm.2006.02.001

Hughes, E., & Scheyvens, R. (2016). Corporate social responsibility in tourism post-2015: A development first approach. *Tourism Geographies*, *18*(5), 469–482. doi:10.1080/14616688.2016.1208678

Martínez, P., Pérez, A., & Rodriguez del Bosque, I. (2013). Measuring corporate social responsibility in tourism: Development and validation of an efficient measurement scale in the hospitality industry. *Journal of Travel & Tourism Marketing*, *30*(4), 365–385. doi:10.1080/10548408.2013.784154

Miller, G. (2001). Corporate responsibility in the UK tourism industry. *Tourism Management*, *22*(6), 589–598. doi:10.1016/S0261-5177(01)00034-6

Seraphin, H., Korstanje, M., & Gowreesunkar, V. (2020). Diaspora and ambidextrous management of tourism in post-colonial, post-conflict and post-disaster destinations. *Journal of Tourism and Cultural Change*, *18*(2), 113–132. doi:10.1080/14766825 .2019.1582658

Tamajón, L. G., & Font, X. (2013). Corporate social responsibility in tourism small and medium enterprises evidence from Europe and Latin America. *Tourism Management Perspectives*, *7*, 38–46. doi:10.1016/j.tmp.2013.03.002

KEY TERMS AND DEFINITIONS

Podcast: This is the preparation of audios and their distributions using RSS files.

Responsibility: This is understood as a moral solidarity for others that include corporate and individual liability for the acts.

Social Corporate Responsibility: This is a international private business self regulation which aims to protect the communal interests.

Tourism: This is defined as a set of service sectors that contribute to the leisure activities or outdoor recreation.

Vulnerability: This is an state of fragility or unprotection that involves peoples or communities.

Glossary

4.0 Industry: Industry 4.0 has emerged from the overlap between the financialization of the economy and an exacerbated neoliberalism, intensifying the use of digital technologies in production systems and the replacement of human labor (Antunes, 2019).

Boredom: Is a mental state of restlessness due to lack of interest in an activity. It could also be caused by doing repeated work.

Commodification of Diversity: The strategy used by local authorities to transform intercultural areas into tourist destinations aiming to foster economic development.

Community-Based Tourism: This represents a type of emerging tourism organized and managed by local community in its integrity.

Conspicuous Consumption: Conspicuous consumption has typically analyzed how people spend money on products that signal status (Bellezza et al., 2017).

COVID-19: Is a pandemic which was caused by Corona virus first detected in the Wuhan province of China in the early phase of 2020.

Cyber Fordism: Cyber Fordism is a production model that preserves flexibility and the search for quality as well as cost reduction, like classic Fordism, but requires new interfaces between man and machine and between machines, marked by reduced human labor and increased automation (Paes-De-Paula, Paes, 2021).

Dark Tourism: Is an emerging nice of tourism which consists in the visit to spaces of mass death or suffering.

Fatigue: Is a feeling of continued tiredness, could be mental or physical or both generally experienced by human beings due to extreme physical activity or mental stress.

Glossary

Global Citizenship: The term global citizenship denotes the commitment to avoid the increase of world poverty and the destruction of ancient cultures and the natural environment, and also the complexity of individual connections with international law and overlapping political institutions in a globalized world (Carter, 2001).

Heritage: Is a full range of inherited traditions, objects or monuments that belong to our cultural background.

Heritage Management: Should be seen as the application of techniques aimed at conserving cultural resources.

Human Resource Management: Is the strategic and coherent approach to the effective and efficient management of people in a company.

Human Rights: A set of rights which belonging to every person has oriented to protect its integrity.

Intercultural Companion: A person with migrant background living in one of the cities that are part of Migrantour network who has been trained to guide intercultural itineraries in her/his city.

Intercultural Itinerary: A two-hours walk around an intercultural neighborhood or rural area organized by Migrantour in one of the cities that are part of the network. The aim is encouraging participants to walk in the area and interact with people with different origins. It is guided by an intercultural companion.

Job Satisfaction: Or work satisfaction, the term is used for measuring workers´ engagement and contentedness with the desks or jobs.

Labor Relation: This term denotes the relation or relationships between employers and employees.

Podcast: This is the preparation of audios and their distributions using RSS files.

Post-Fordist Transformation: A concept used to identify the deindustrialization period that has taken place in European cities. It refers, in opposition, to the Fordism, a period started in the early nighties and named after Henry Ford, the inventor of the assembly-line model for industrial production.

Glossary

Poverty: Is a state of having few material possessions or facing low income.

Responsibility: This is understood as a moral solidarity for others that include corporate and individual liability for the acts.

Revenge Travel: Is a phenomenon where people seek to travel post the period of forced lockdown and travel restrictions which were caused due to pandemic from 2020 to 2022.

Safety-Security Tourism: Is a set of conditions, prerequisite, legal dispositions, and instruments orchestrated to protect tourists and their integrities.

Social Corporate Responsibility: This is a international private business self regulation which aims to protect the communal interests.

Social Rights: Social rights are rights of citizens to receive services such as food, health care, housing, and social security (Landau, 2012, p. 190).

Special Rapporteur on the Right to Adequate Housing: A mandate established by the former UN Commission on Human Rights at the beginning of the 2000's with the purpose of further developing strategies of protection of the right to adequate housing around the world. Currently, the mandate is covered by Mr. Balakrishnan Rajagopal.

Sustainability: Is a practice of ensuring ecological balance along with social being so that the future generations do not suffer.

Top-Down Multiculturalism: A concept created by some authors (Giovanni Semi and Camille Schmoll in particular) to identify an institutional form to promote diversity in a given society. It refers to the use of pleasant multicultural features (such as food or big celebrations) in specific places (restaurants, textile shops, festivals…) to foster interculturalism among part of the population.

Tourism: Is a subservice sector, commercial activity or industry dedicated to organize tours and travels following pleasure for travels.

Tourism Consumption: Includes the consumption of tourist experiences and products located in a specific destination or territory.

Glossary

Tourism Industry: It is a set of subservice sectors organized in the leisure and travel activities. The tourism industry includes a variety of stakeholders and actors such as train or bus station, air industry, hotel industry, travel agents and rent-a-car industry.

Trauma: Is a pervasive psychological problem derived from an exposure to severe incidents or events emotionally disturbing for the subject.

Violence: Is an atypical behavior oriented to hurt, harm, or kill someone or something.

Vulnerability: This is an state of fragility or unprotection that involves peoples or communities.

Water Access: Is a basic right endorsed to all citizens without distinction of class, ethnicity, or nationality.

Water Justice: Is seen as a set of actions, laws and regulations orchestrated to ensure the equal access to water for all citizens.

Young NEET: Young people Neither in Employment nor Education and Training. It refers to the percentage of young population who is unemployed or inactive and who has not been involved in any form of education (formal or informal) in a given period.

Compilation of References

A bibliometric review of research on COVID-19 and tourism: Reflections for moving forward. (n.d.). Academic Press.

Abhishek, B., Zohre, M., Manisha, A., Zilmiyah, K., & Gerardine, D.-T. (2022). Post COVID-19: Cautious or courageous travel behaviour? *Asia Pacific Journal of Tourism Research*, 581–600.

Abukhait, R., Shamsudin, F. M., Bani-Melhem, S., & Al-Hawari, M. A. (2023). Obsessive–compulsive personality and creative performance: The moderating effect of manager coaching behavior. *Review of Managerial Science*, *17*(1), 375–396. doi:10.100711846-022-00528-6

Achmad, W., & Yulianah, Y. (2022). Corporate social responsibility of the hospitality industry in realizing sustainable tourism development. *Enrichment: Journal of Management*, *12*(2), 1610–1616.

Akmese, H., Cetin, H., & Akmese, K. (2016). Corporate social responsibility reporting: A comparative analysis of tourism and finance sectors of G8 countries. *Procedia Economics and Finance*, *39*, 737–745. doi:10.1016/S2212-5671(16)30273-8

Alagarsamy, S., Mehrolia, S., & Aranha, R. H. (2020). The mediating effect of employee engagement: How employee psychological empowerment impacts the employee satisfaction? A study of Maldivian tourism sector. *Global Business Review*. doi:10.1177/0972150920915315

Alarcón, D. M., & Cole, S. (2019). No sustainability for tourism without gender equality. *Journal of Sustainable Tourism*, *27*(7), 903–919. doi:10.1080/09669582.2019.1588283

Alegre, I., & Berbegal-Mirabent, J. (2016). Social innovation success factors: Hospitality and tourism social enterprises. *International Journal of Contemporary Hospitality Management*, *28*(6), 1155–1176. doi:10.1108/IJCHM-05-2014-0231

Al-Hawari, M. A., Bani-Melhem, S., & Mohd. Shamsudin, F. (2021). Does employee willingness to take risks affect customer loyalty? A moderated mediation examination of innovative behaviors and decentralization. *International Journal of Contemporary Hospitality Management*, *33*(5), 1746–1767. doi:10.1108/IJCHM-08-2020-0802

Andersen, I. M. V. (2020). Tourism Employment and Education in a Danish Context. *Tourism Employment in Nordic Countries: Trends, Practices, and Opportunities*, 37-56.

Compilation of References

Andersen, L., & Dowdell, E. B. (2019). Access to clean water and urinary tract infections in Haitian women. *Public Health Nursing (Boston, Mass.)*, *36*(6), 800–805. doi:10.1111/phn.12660 PMID:31465129

Andreen, W. L. (2011). Water resources planning and management Water law and the search for sustainability: a comparative analysis. In R. Q. Grafton & K. Hussey (Eds.), *Water Resources Planning and Management* (1st ed., pp. 115–174). Cambridge University Press. doi:10.1017/CBO9780511974304.011

Apriando, T. (2015). *Izin Lingkungan Banyak Kejanggalan, Warga Karangwuni Gugat Apartemen Uttara*. Mongabay. https://www.mongabay.co.id/2015/12/23/izin-lingkungan-banyak-kejanggalan-warga-karangwuni-gugat-apartemen-uttara/

Ariza-Montes, A., Arjona-Fuentes, J. M., Law, R., & Han, H. (2017). Incidence of workplace bullying among hospitality employees. *International Journal of Contemporary Hospitality Management*, *29*(4), 1116–1132. doi:10.1108/IJCHM-09-2015-0471

Arku, F. S. (2010). Time savings from easy access to clean water. *Progress in Development Studies*, *10*(3), 233–246. doi:10.1177/146499340901000303

Aronowitz, A. A. (2019). Regulating business involvement in labor exploitation and human trafficking. *Journal of Labor and Society*, *22*(1), 145–164. doi:10.1111/wusa.12372

Aston, J., Wen, J., Goh, E., & Maurer, O. (2022). Promoting awareness of sex trafficking in tourism and hospitality. *International Journal of Culture, Tourism and Hospitality Research*, *16*(1), 1–6. doi:10.1108/IJCTHR-01-2020-0032

Aynalem, S., Birhanu, K., & Tesefay, S. (2016). Employment opportunities and challenges in tourism and hospitality sectors. *Journal of Tourism & Hospitality (Los Angeles, Calif.)*, *5*(6), 1–5. doi:10.4172/2167-0269.1000257

Bagić, D. (2019). Croatia: stability amidst heterogeneous collective bargaining patterns. In Collective bargaining in Europe: towards an endgame (Vol. 1, pp. 93-108). European Trade Union Institute (ETUI).

Baillat, A. (2013). *Corruption and the human right to water and sanitation: Human right-based approach to tackling corruption in the water sector*. Water Integrity Network, Berlin and WaterLex. https://www.waterlex.org/new/wp-content/uploads/2013/12/2013-WaterLex-WIN_Corruption-and-the-HRWS-.pdf

Bakar, N. A., & Rosbi, S. (2020). Effect of Coronavirus disease (COVID-19) to tourism industry. *International Journal of Advanced Engineering Research and Science*, *7*(4), 189–193. doi:10.22161/ijaers.74.23

Bakker, M. (2019). A conceptual framework for identifying the binding constraints to tourism-driven inclusive growth. *Tourism Planning & Development*, *16*(5), 575–590. doi:10.1080/21568316.2018.1541817

Baldacchino, G. (2006). Warm versus cold water island tourism: A review of policy implications. *Island Studies Journal*, *1*(2), 183–200. doi:10.24043/isj.193

Bali Water Project. (2017). *IDEP was invited by the bali hotel association to present the bali water protection program to a pool of hotel environmental and engineering-managers.* https://baliwaterprotection.net/idep-was-invited-by-the-bali-hotel-association-to-present-the-bali-water-protection-program-to-a-pool-of-hotel-environmental-and-engineering-managers/

Banco Mundial. (October 7th, 2020). *Debido a la pandemia de COVID-19, el número de personas que viven en la pobreza extrema habrá aumentado en 150 millones para 2021.* (Due to th Pandemic COVID19- the number of poor people has been triplicated). Banco Mundial. https://www.bancomundial.org/es/news/press-release/2020/10/07/covid-19-to-add-as-many-as-150-million-extreme-poor-by-2021

Bani-Melhem, S., Abukhait, R., & Bourini, I. F. (2022). How and when does centralization affect the likelihood of passive leadership? *Leadership and Organization Development Journal*, *43*(4), 533–549. doi:10.1108/LODJ-10-2021-0492

Bani-Melhem, S., Al-Hawari, M. A., & Mohd. Shamsudin, F. (2022). Green innovation performance: A multi-level analysis in the hotel sector. *Journal of Sustainable Tourism*, *30*(8), 1878–1896. doi:10.1080/09669582.2021.1991935

Bani-Melhem, S., Mohd. Shamsudin, F., Mazen Abukhait, R., & Quratulain, S. (2021). Paranoid personality and frontline employee's proactive work behaviours: A moderated mediation model of empathetic leadership and perceived psychological safety. *Journal of Service Theory and Practice*, *31*(1), 113–135. doi:10.1108/JSTP-05-2020-0104

Barros, A., Monz, C., & Pickering, C. (2015). Is tourism damaging ecosystems in the Andes? Current knowledge and an agenda for future research. *Ambio*, *44*(2), 82–98. doi:10.100713280-014-0550-7 PMID:25201299

Bauman, Z. (2013). *Liquid fear.* John Wiley & Sons.

Baum, T., Cheung, C., Kong, H., Kralj, A., Mooney, S., Nguyễn Thị Thanh, H., Ramachandran, S., Dropulić Ružić, M., & Siow, M. L. (2016). Sustainability and the tourism and hospitality workforce: A thematic analysis. *Sustainability (Basel)*, *8*(8), 809. doi:10.3390u8080809

Baum, T., & Hai, N. T. T. (2019). Applying sustainable employment principles in the tourism industry: Righting human rights wrongs? *Tourism Recreation Research*, *44*(3), 371–381. doi:10.1080/02508281.2019.1624407

Baum, T., & Hai, N. T. T. (2020). Hospitality, tourism, human rights and the impact of COVID-19. *International Journal of Contemporary Hospitality Management*, *32*(7), 2397–2407. doi:10.1108/IJCHM-03-2020-0242

Becken, S. (2014). Water equity–Contrasting tourism water use with that of the local community. *Water Resources and Industry*, *7*, 9–22. doi:10.1016/j.wri.2014.09.002

Compilation of References

Belias, D., Rossidis, I., Papademetriou, C., & Mantas, C. (2022). Job satisfaction as affected by types of leadership: A case study of Greek tourism sector. *Journal of Quality Assurance in Hospitality & Tourism*, *23*(2), 299–317. doi:10.1080/1528008X.2020.1867695

Bianchi, R. V., & Stephenson, M. L. (2013). Deciphering tourism and citizenship in a globalized world. *Tourism Management*, *39*, 10–20. doi:10.1016/j.tourman.2013.03.006

Bianchi, R. V., Stephenson, M. L., & Hannam, K. (2020). The contradictory politics of the right to travel: Mobilities, borders & tourism. *Mobilities*, *15*(2), 290–306. doi:10.1080/17450101.2020.1723251

Bianchi, R., & Stephenson, M. (2014). *Tourism and citizenship: Rights, freedoms and responsibilities in the global order*. Routledge. doi:10.4324/9781134594535

Blake, A., Arbache, J. S., Sinclair, M. T., & Teles, V. (2008). Tourism and poverty relief. *Annals of Tourism Research*, *35*(1), 107–126. doi:10.1016/j.annals.2007.06.013

Bohdanowicz, P. & Zientara, P. (April 1st, 2019). Hotel Companies' Contribution to Improving the Quality of Life of Local Communities and the Well-Being of Their Employees. *SAGE Journals*. doi:10.1057/thr.2008.46

Bohoslavsky, J. P., Martín, L., & Justo, J. (2015). The state duty to protect from business-related human rights violations in water and sanitation services: Regulatory and BITS implications. *International Law. Revista Colombiana de Derecho Internacional*, *26*, 63–116. doi:10.11144/Javeriana.il15-26.sdpb

Bolaños, C. (2019). Conflictos socioambientales por la gestión del agua: el caso de la comunidad de Playa Potrero, Guanacaste. In F. Alpízar (Ed.), Agua y poder en Costa Rica 1980-2017 (pp. 193–238). Centro de Investigación y Estudios Políticos (CIEP), Universidad de Costa Rica.

Bowen, H. R. (2013). *Social Responsibilities of Businessmen*. University of Iowa Press. doi:10.2307/j.ctt20q1w8f

Bowman, M. S., & Pezzullo, P. C. (2009). What's so 'dark about 'dark tourism'?: Death, tours, and performance. *Tourist Studies*, *9*(3), 187–202. doi:10.1177/1468797610382699

Brooks, D. B. (2007). Human rights to water in North Africa and the Middle East: What is new and what is not; what is important and what is not. *International Journal of Water Resources Development*, *23*(2), 227–241. doi:10.1080/07900620601097075

Brooks, R. K., Webster, R. K., Smith, L. E., Woodland, L., Wessely, S., Greenberg, N., & Rubin, G. J. (2020, March). The psychological impact of quarantine and how to reduce it: Rapid review of the evidence. *Lancet*, *395*(10227), 912–920. doi:10.1016/S0140-6736(20)30460-8 PMID:32112714

Buckley, P., Pietropaoli, L., Rosada, A., Harguth, B., & Broom, J. (2022). How has COVID-19 affected migrant workers' vulnerability to human trafficking for forced labour in Southeast Asia? A narrative review'. *Journal of Public Health and Emergency*, *6*, 19. doi:10.21037/jphe-21-108

Buckley, R., Shekari, F., Mohammadi, Z., Azizi, F., & Ziaee, M. (2020). World heritage tourism triggers urban–rural reverse migration and social change. *Journal of Travel Research*, *59*(3), 559–572. doi:10.1177/0047287519853048

Burroni, L., Mori, A., & Bottalico, A. (2020). *Understanding collective bargaining coordination: a network relational approach. The case of Italy.* Academic Press.

Business Roundtable. (August 19th, 2019). *Business Roundtable Redefines the Purpose of a Corporation to Promote 'An Economy That Serves All Americans'.* Business Roundtable. https://businessroundtable.org/business-roundtable-redefines-the-purpose-of-acorporation-to-promote-an-economy-that-serves-all-americanshttps://ec.europa.eu/commission/presscorner/detail/es/ip_21_269

Butt, B. (2016). Conservation, Neoliberalism, and Human Rights in Kenya's Arid Lands. *Humanity*, *7*(1), 91–110. doi:10.1353/hum.2016.0009

Caldeira, A. M., Seabra, C., & AlAshry, M. S. (2022). Contrasting the COVID-19 Effects on Tourism Safety Perceptions and Coping Behavior among Young People during Two Pandemic Waves: Evidence from Egypt. *Sustainability*. https://doi.org/https://doi.org/10.3390/su14127492

Camară, G. (2022). The COVID-19 Pandemic and the Enhanced Marginalisation of Marginal Tourist Destinations. *COVID-19 and Marginalisation of People and Places*, 117–129. https://doi.org/https://doi.org/10.1007/978-3-031-11139-6_9

Campón-Cerro, A. M., Di-Clemente, E., Hernández-Mogollón, J. M., & Folgado-Fernández, J. A. (2020). Healthy water-based tourism experiences: Their contribution to quality of life, satisfaction and loyalty. *International Journal of Environmental Research and Public Health*, *17*(6), 1961. doi:10.3390/ijerph17061961 PMID:32192098

Cañada, E. (2019). Conflictos por el agua en Guanacaste, Costa Rica: Respuestas al desarrollo turístico. *Anuario de Estudios Centroamericanos*, *45*, 323–344. doi:10.15517/aeca.v45i0.37666

Caprón, G., & González Arellano, S. (2006). Las Escalas de la segregación y de la fragmentación urbana. *Trace (México, DF)*, (49), 65–75. doi:10.22134/trace.49.2006.469

Castañeda, Q. (2012). The neoliberal imperative of tourism: Rights and legitimization in the Unwto global code of ethics for tourism. *Practical Anthropology*, *34*(3), 47–51. doi:10.17730/praa.34.3.w0251w655647750j

Cazcarro, I., Hoekstra, A. Y., & Chóliz, J. S. (2014). The water footprint of tourism in Spain. *Tourism Management*, *40*, 90–101. doi:10.1016/j.tourman.2013.05.010

Chan, A. W., & Warner, M. (2017). Employers' associations in Hong Kong: Continuity in the absence of collective bargaining. In Employers' associations in Asia (pp. 102-124). Routledge.

Chief, K. (2020). Water in the Native World. *Journal of Contemporary Water Research & Education*, *169*(1), 1–7. doi:10.1111/j.1936-704X.2020.03328.x

Compilation of References

Choudhary, N., Brewis, A., Wutich, A., & Udas, P. B. (2020). Sub-optimal household water access is associated with greater risk of intimate partner violence against women: Evidence from Nepal. *Journal of Water and Health*, *18*(4), 579–594. doi:10.2166/wh.2020.024 PMID:32833684

Cingolani, P. (2018). È tutto etnico quel che conta? Conflitto per le risorse e narrazioni della diversità a Barriera di Milano. In Torino, un profilo etnografico (pp. 91-113). Meltemi.

Cohen, E. H. (2011). Educational dark tourism at an populo site: The Holocaust Museum in Jerusalem. *Annals of Tourism Research*, *38*(1), 193–209. doi:10.1016/j.annals.2010.08.003

Cole, S., & Eriksson, J. (2010). Tourism and human rights. *Tourism and inequality: Problems and prospects*, 107-125.

Cole, S. (2012). A political ecology of water equity and tourism. A Case Study from Bali. *Annals of Tourism Research*, *39*(2), 1221–1241. doi:10.1016/j.annals.2012.01.003

Cole, S. (2014). Tourism and water: From stakeholders to rights holders, and what tourism businesses need to do. *Journal of Sustainable Tourism*, *22*(1), 89–106. doi:10.1080/09669582 .2013.776062

Cole, S. (2017). Water worries: An intersectional feminist political ecology of tourism and water in Labuan Bajo, Indonesia. *Annals of Tourism Research*, *67*, 14–24. doi:10.1016/j.annals.2017.07.018

Cole, S. K. G., Mullor, E. C., Ma, Y., & Sandang, Y. (2020). "Tourism, water, and gender"—An international review of an unexplored nexus. *WIREs. Water*, *7*(4), 1–16. doi:10.1002/wat2.1442

Cole, S., & Browne, M. (2015). Tourism and Water Inequity in Bali: A Social-Ecological Systems Analysis. *Human Ecology: an Interdisciplinary Journal*, *43*(3), 439–450. doi:10.100710745-015-9739-z

Cole, S., & Ferguson, L. (2015). Towards a gendered political economy of water and tourism. *Tourism Geographies*, *17*(4), 511–528. doi:10.1080/14616688.2015.1065509

Cole, S., Wardana, A., & Dharmiasih, W. (2021). Making an impact on Bali's water crisis: Research to mobilize NGOs, the tourism industry and policy makers. *Annals of Tourism Research*, *87*, 103119. doi:10.1016/j.annals.2020.103119

Coller, X. (2005). *Estudio de Casos*. Centro de Investigaciones Sociológicas.

Collins-Kreiner, N. (2016). Dark tourism as/is pilgrimage. *Current Issues in Tourism*, *19*(12), 1185–1189. doi:10.1080/13683500.2015.1078299

Comaroff, J. L., & Comaroff, J. (2009). *Ethnicity, Inc.* University of Chicago Press. doi:10.7208/chicago/9780226114736.001.0001

Cordoba-Azcarrate, M. (2020). *Stuck with Tourism: space, power and labor in contemporary Yucatan*. University of California Press. doi:10.1525/9780520975552

Córdova, N. I. (2008). Between Freedom of Speech and Cultural Diversity of Expression: Bureaucratizing the Multicultural Imagination. In W. Binford & S. Basu (Eds.), *The Role of Freedom of Expression in a Multicultural and Democratic Society* (pp. 215–239). Willamette University.

Cosmopolitan tourists: the most resilient travellers in the face of COVID-19. (n.d.). Academic Press.

Croes, R., & Vanegas, M. Sr. (2008). Cointegration and causality between tourism and poverty reduction. *Journal of Travel Research, 47*(1), 94–103. doi:10.1177/0047287507312429

Cruz Jiménez, G., Serrano-Barquín, R. D. C., Zizumbo Villarreal, L., & Vargas Martínez, E. E. (2022). Child labor and child work in the touristic sector of Cozumel and Valle de Bravo, Mexico. *International Journal of Hospitality & Tourism Administration, 23*(3), 599–622. doi:10.1080/15256480.2020.1805091

Dahlsrud, A. (2006). How corporate social responsibility is defined: An analysis of 37 definitions. *InterScience. Corporate Social Responsibility and Environmental Management, 15*(1), 1–13. doi:10.1002/csr.132

Daniel, A. D., Costa, R. A., Pita, M., & Costa, C. (2017). Tourism Education: What about entrepreneurial skills? *Journal of Hospitality and Tourism Management, 30*, 65–72. doi:10.1016/j.jhtm.2017.01.002

Das, Nayak, & Naik. (2023). An impact study on COVID-19 and tourism sustainability: intelligent solutions, issues and future challenges. *World Review of Science, Technology and Sustainable Development, 19*, 92–119. doi:10.1504/WRSTSD.2021.10038456

De Kadt, E. (1979a). *Tourism: Passport to Development. In Perspectives on the social and cultural effects of tourism in developing countries.* Oxford University Press.

De Kadt, E. (1979b). Social planning for tourism in the developing countries. *Annals of Tourism Research, 6*(1), 36–48. doi:10.1016/0160-7383(79)90093-8

De Martini Ugolotti, P. (2018). "No sleep 'till Parco Dora": Parkour e i paradossi di una città rigenerata, tra eterotopie e governo della differenza. In Torino, un profilo etnografico (pp. 159-178). Meltemi.

Dell'Orto, G. (2022, August 20). *On Chile rivers, Native spirituality and development clash | AP News*. https://apnews.com/article/sacred-rivers-religion-chile-7112a8bff283516c44799840c7b47df3

Deng, S., Wang, W., Xie, P., Chao, Y., & Zhu, J. (2020). Perceived severity of COVID-19 and post-pandemic consumption willingness: The roles of boredom and sensation-seeking. *Frontiers in Psychology, 11*, 11. doi:10.3389/fpsyg.2020.567784 PMID:33041933

Deva, S. (2020). From business or human rights to business and human rights: What next? *Research Handbook on Human Rights and Business, 2015*, 1–21. doi:10.4337/9781786436405.00005

Compilation of References

Diario Responsable. (June 16th, 2020). Rumbo a la nueva normalidad, retos y cambios de la RSE. [Towards the new Normal]. *Diario Responsable.* https://diarioresponsable.com/noticias/29517-rumbo-a-la-nueva-normalidad-retos-y-cambios-de-la-rse. https://youtube.com/watch?v=p2u6x2FCxVs

Dibeh, G., Fakih, A., & Marrouch, W. (2020). Tourism–growth nexus under duress: Lebanon during the Syrian crisis. *Tourism Economics, 26*(3), 353–370. doi:10.1177/1354816619836338

Dietrich, L., Koalick, M., & Leisinger, M. (2017). *Human Rights Assessments in the Tourism Sector: A data collection guide for practitioners.* Institut für nachhaltigen Tourismus GmbH (Inatour). https://www.humanrights-in-tourism.net/file/1153/download?token=DTQXcBXi

Djajasinga, N. D., Sulastri, L., Sudirman, A., Sari, A. L., & Rihardi, E. L. (2021, June). Practices in Human Resources and Employee Turnover in the Hospitality Industry. In *2nd Annual Conference on blended learning, educational technology and Innovation (ACBLETI 2020)* (pp. 113-117). Atlantis Press. 10.2991/assehr.k.210615.023

Donnelly, J. (1984). Cultural relativism and universal human rights. *Human Rights Quarterly, 6*(4), 400. doi:10.2307/762182

Donnelly, J. (2013). *Universal Human Rights in Theory and Practice.* Cornell University Press. doi:10.7591/9780801467493

Douglas, S., & Watt, G. (2018). Implications of the Fair Work Commission's modern award review for casuals. *Journal of New Business Ideas and Trends, 16*(2), 30–40.

Dua, T. (October 20th, 2016). InterContinental launches its own podcast series. *Digiday.* https://digiday.com/marketing/marketing-content-driven-intercontinental-hotels-launches-podcast/

Duong, L. H., Phan, Q. D., Nguyen, T. T., Huynh, D. V., Truong, T. T., & Duong, K. Q. (2022). Understanding Tourists' Behavioral Intention and Destination Support in Post-pandemic Recovery: The Case of the Vietnamese Domestic Market. *Sustainability (Basel), 14*(16), 9969. doi:10.3390u14169969

Elbaz, A. M., & Haddoud, M. Y. (2017). The role of wisdom leadership in increasing job performance: Evidence from the Egyptian tourism sector. *Tourism Management, 63*, 66–76. doi:10.1016/j.tourman.2017.06.008

Eliakimu, E. S., & Mans, L. (2022). Addressing Inequalities Toward Inclusive Governance for Achieving One Health: A Rapid Review. *Frontiers in Public Health, 9*, 755285. Advance online publication. doi:10.3389/fpubh.2021.755285 PMID:35127612

Elshaer, A. M. (2019). *Labor in the tourism and hospitality industry: Skills, ethics, issues, and rights.* CRC Press. doi:10.1201/9780429465093

EpData. (May 24th, 2022). Málaga - La ocupación de los hoteles en el municipio, en datos y gráficos. [Occupation in hotels of the Province] EpData. https://www.epdata.es/datos/ocupacion-hotelera-hoteles-datos-graficos-municipios/143/malaga/4282

Epler-Wood, M. (2017). *Sustainable Tourism on a Finite Planet* (1st ed.). Routledge., doi:10.4324/9781315439808

Equality in Tourism. (2015). *Stroma Cole's Bali presentation on tourism-related water shortages.* http://equalityintourism.org/stroma-coles-bali-presentation-on-tourism-related-water-shortages-in-bali/

Eriksson, J., Noble, R., Pattullo, P., Barnett, T., Eriksson, J., Noble, R., Pattullo, P., & Barnett, T. (2009). *Putting Tourism to Rights.* https://www.tourismconcern.org.uk/wp-content/uploads/2014/10/LowRes_Putting-Tourism-to-Rights_A-report-by-TourismConcern2.pdf

Europa Press. (January 13th, 2022). El BOE oficializa la distribución en Andalucía de 72,6 millones para Planes de Sostenibilidad Turística en Destinos. [The BOE makes official the Sustainabel programs]. *Europa Press.* https://europapress.es/andalucia/noticia-boe-oficializa-distribucion-andalucia-726-millones-planes-sostenibilidad-turistica-destinos-20220113135307.html

Europa Press. (March 29th, 2022). Hoteles Santos crea su Comité de Sostenibilidad y RSC para reforzar su compromiso social y medioambiental. [Hotels Santos creates a Comitee for Sustainability]. *Europa Press.* https://europapress.es/epsocial/responsables/noticia-hoteles-santos-crea-comite-sostenibilidad-rsc-reforzar-compromiso-social-medioambiental-20220329103821.html

Everhart, S. M. (2017). U-Pick-Are Agritourism Workers Exempt from the Wage and Hour Protections of the Fair Labor Standards Act. *U. Md. LJ Race, Religion, Race, Gender & Class, 17,* 29.

EY Spain y DIRSE (2020). *Impacto del Covid-19 en las prioridades de la RSC / Sostenibilidad y en el rol de sus profesionales.* [Impacts and priorities of RSC befores COVID-19]. https://dirse.es/wp-content/uploads/2020/06/200622-Impacto-COVID-19_RSC_Sostenibilidas-v8.pdf

Fantini, E. (2019). An introduction to the human right to water: Law, politics, and beyond. *WIREs. Water, 7*(November), 1–8. doi:10.1002/wat2.1405

Faruk, S., & Carlos, C. (2022). A scenario planning framework for (post-)pandemic tourism in European destinations. *European Planning Studies, 30*(12).

Fatma, & Mehmet. (2021). The effect of COVID-19 pandemic on domestic tourism: A DEMATEL method analysis on quarantine decisions. *International Journal of Hospitality Management, 92.* PMID:33519015

Fayissa, B., Nsiah, C., & Tadasse, B. (2008). Impact of tourism on economic growth and development in Africa. *Tourism Economics, 14*(4), 807–818. doi:10.5367/000000008786440229

Feng, W. J., & Lan, X. (2021). Revenge travel: Nostalgia and desire for leisure travel post COVID-19. *Journal of Travel & Tourism Marketing,* 935–955.

Fennell, D. A. (2019). The future of ethics in tourism. *The future of tourism: Innovation and sustainability,* 155-177.

Compilation of References

Filimonau, V., & Mika, M. (2019). Return labour migration: An exploratory study of Polish migrant workers from the UK hospitality industry. *Current Issues in Tourism, 22*(3), 357–378. doi:10.1080/13683500.2017.1280778

Fluixa Ferra, C. (February 17th, 2022). Aterrizan en Málaga las Jornadas de Sostenibilidad Hotelera. [Sustainable programs in Malaga] *Hosteltur.* https://hosteltur.com/comunidad/nota/028386_aterrizan-en-malaga-las-jornadas-de-sostenibilidad-hotelera.html

Fominienė, V. B., Mejerytė-Narkevičienė, K., & Woźniewicz-Dobrzyńska, M. (2015). Employees' career competence for career success: Aspect of human resources management in tourism sector. *Transformations in Business & Economics, 14*, 481–493.

Fonseca, L. M., Domingues, J. P., & Dima, A. M. (2020). Mapping the Sustainable Development Goals Relationships. *Sustainability (Basel), 12*(8), 3359. doi:10.3390u12083359

Foroudi, P. H., Tabaghdehi, S. A., & Marvi, R. (2021). The gloom of the COVID-19 shock in the hospitality industry: A study of consumer risk perception and adaptive belief in the dark cloud of a pandemic. *International Journal of Hospitality Management, 92*, 102717. doi:10.1016/j.ijhm.2020.102717 PMID:36919037

Freeman, M. (2011). *Human Rights: An Interdisciplinary Approach* (4th ed.). Polity Press.

Freire-Medeiros, B. (2014). *Touring poverty.* Routledge. doi:10.4324/9780203840719

Frezzo, M. (2014). *The sociology of human rights.* John Wiley & Sons.

García, I. (August 30th, 2017). Definición de Stakeholders. *Economía Simple.* https://economiasimple.net/glosario/stakeholders

Gascón, J. (2019). Tourism as a right: A "frivolous claim" against degrowth? *Journal of Sustainable Tourism, 27*(12), 1825–1838. doi:10.1080/09669582.2019.1666858

George, B. P., & Varghese, V. (2007). Human Rights in Tourism: Conceptualization and Stakeholder Perspectives. *Electronic Journal of Business Ethics and Organization Studies, 12*(2), 40–48.

Ghosh, R. (n.d.). What Is Revenge Travel? India Today.

Gismero-González, E., Bermejo-Toro, L., Cagigal, V., Roldán, A., Martínez-Beltrán, M. J., & Halty, L. (2020). Emotional Impact of COVID-19 Lockdown Among the Spanish Population. *Frontiers in Psychology, 11*, 11. doi:10.3389/fpsyg.2020.616978 PMID:33391136

Gleick, P. (1998). The human right to water. *Water Policy, 1*(5), 487–503. doi:10.1016/S1366-7017(99)00008-2

Global Sustainable Tourism Council. (2016). *GSTC Hotel Criteria.* https://www.gstcouncil.org/wp-content/uploads/2015/11/GSTC-Hotel_Industry_Criteria_with_hotel_indicators_21-Dec-2016_Final.pdf

GNUDS Grupo de las Naciones Unidas para el Desarrollo Sostenible. (March 2020). *Responsabilidad compartida, solidaridad global: Respuesta a los impactos socioeconómicos de la Covid-19.* Naciones Unidas. https://un.org/sites/un2.un.org/files/articlefile/eosg_covid-19_socioeconomic_report-200579 1s.pdf

Godino, A., & Molina Romo, Ó. (2019). *Who overcomes collective bargaining? Outsourcing practices, regulatory framework and facility management in Spain.* Academic Press.

González, F. (n.d.). Podcast para destinos y hoteles. [Postcast for destinations and hotels] *El Blog de Andalucía Lab.* https://andalucialab.org/blog/podcast-para-destinos-hoteles/

Goretti, M. M., Leigh, M. L. Y., Babii, A., Cevik, M. S., Kaendera, S., Muir, M. D. V., ... & Salinas, M. G. (2021). *Tourism in the post-pandemic world: Economic challenges and opportunities for Asia-pacific and the western hemisphere.* Academic Press.

Gössling, S. (2006). Tourism and water. In *Tourism and global environmental change* (pp. 180–194). Routledge. doi:10.4324/9780203011911-12

Gössling, S., Hall, C. M., & Scott, D. (2015). *Tourism and water* (Vol. 2). Channel View Publications. doi:10.21832/9781845415006

Gössling, S., & Schweiggart, N. (2022). Two years of COVID-19 and tourism: What we learned, and what we should have learned. *Journal of Sustainable Tourism, 30*(4), 915–931. doi:10.108 0/09669582.2022.2029872

Götzmann, N. (2017). Human Rights Impact Assessment of Business Activities: Key Criteria for Establishing a Meaningful Practice. *Business and Human Rights Journal, 2*(1), 87–108. doi:10.1017/bhj.2016.24

GRI. (n.d.). *How to use the GRI Standards.* Global Reporting. https://globalreporting.org/how-to-use-the-gri-standards/gri-standards-spanish-transltions/

Gričar, S., Šugar, V., & Bojnec, Š. (2021). The missing link between wages and labour productivity in tourism: Evidence from Croatia and Slovenia. *Ekonomska Istrazivanja, 34*(1), 732–753. doi: 10.1080/1331677X.2020.1804427

Guerra, A., & Fernández Pájaro, E. (2011, August). Empresas turísticas en España: ¿Socialmente responsable? (Tourist enterprises in Spain: are they sustainable? *Cultur, 02*, 43–60.

Gürlek, M., & Kılıç, I. (2021, February 7th). A true friend becomes apparent on a rainy day: Corporate social responsibility practices of top hotels during the COVID-19 pandemic. *Current Issues in Tourism, 24*(7), 905–918. doi:10.1080/13683500.2021.1883557

Gurmé Málaga. (December 27th, 2021). Más de 2.100 menús solidarios para las familias más vulnerables de Málaga. [More than 2100 menus and culinary option for more vulnerable people in Malaga]. *ABC.* https://abc.es/gurme/malaga/abci-mas-de-2-100-menus-solidarios-para-las-familias-mas-vulnerables-de-malaga-202112271015_noticia.html

Compilation of References

Gu, Y., Onggo, B. S., Kunc, M. H., & Bayer, S. (2022). Small Island Developing States (SIDS) COVID-19 post-pandemic tourism recovery: A system dynamics approach. *Current Issues in Tourism*, *25*(9), 1481–1508. doi:10.1080/13683500.2021.1924636

Hadjikakou, M., Chenoweth, J., & Miller, G. (2012). Water and tourism. In A. Holden & D. Fennell (Eds.), *The Routledge handbook of tourism and the environment* (1st ed., pp. 457–468). Routledge. https://www.taylorfrancis.com/books/e/9780203121108/chapters/10.4324/9780203121108-52

Hanafiah, M. H., Azman, I., Jamaluddin, M. R., & Aminuddin, N. (2016). Responsible tourism practices and quality of life: Perspective of Langkawi Island communities. *Procedia: Social and Behavioral Sciences*, *222*, 406–413. doi:10.1016/j.sbspro.2016.05.194

Härkönen, E. (2020). Human rights and labour conditions in tourism establishments. *Human Rights Issues in Tourism*.

Harris, L. M., McKenzie, S., Rodina, L., Shah, S., & Wilson, N. (2017). Water Justice: Concepts, debates and research agendas. In R. Holifield, J. Chakraborty, & G. Walker (Eds.), *Handbook of Environmental Justice* (1st ed.). Routledge.

Harrison, D., & Schipani, S. (2009). Tourism in the Lao people's democratic republic. *Tourism in Southeast Asia: Challenges and new directions*, 165-188.

Hashimoto, A., Harkonen, E., & Nkyi, E. (2020). *Human Rights Issues in Tourism*. Routledge. doi:10.4324/9781351033862

Hayter, S., & Visser, J. (2021). Making collective bargaining more inclusive: The role of extension. *International Labour Review*, *160*(2), 169–195. doi:10.1111/ilr.12191

Henriques, A., & Richardson, J. (2004). *The Triple Bottom Line: Does It All Add Up?* Earthscan.

Hernández Peñaloza, N., Zizumbo Villarreal, L., & Torregrosa Martí, T. (2017). Agua y turismo como instrumentos de acumulación de capital, el caso de Benidorm, España. *Teoría y Praxis*, *13*(21), 31–53. doi:10.22403/UQROOMX/TYP21/02

Heuvel, J. (2005). *Diensten Marketing (Services marketing)*. The Netherlands Wolters Noordhoff Groningen.

Higgins Desbiolles, F., & Blanchard, L. (2010). *Context of Human Rights, Justic e and Peace. In Tourism, progress and peace*. CABI.

Higgins-Desbiolles, F., Carnicelli, S., Krolikowski, C., Wijesinghe, G., & Boluk, K. (2019). Degrowing tourism: Rethinking tourism. *Journal of Sustainable Tourism*, *27*(12), 1926–1944. doi:10.1080/09669582.2019.1601732

Higgins-Desbiolles, F., & Whyte, K. P. (2015). Tourism and human rights. In *The Routledge handbook of tourism and sustainability* (pp. 123–134). Routledge.

Hof, A., & Blázquez-Salom, M. (2015). Changing tourism patterns, capital accumulation, and urban water consumption in Mallorca, Spain: A sustainability fix? *Journal of Sustainable Tourism*, *23*(5), 770–796. doi:10.1080/09669582.2014.991397

Holden, A. (2013). *Tourism, poverty and development*. Routledge. doi:10.4324/9780203861547

Hoogendoorn, G., Letsatsi, N., Malleka, T., & Booyens, I. (2020). Tourist and resident perspectives on 'slum tourism': The case of the Vilakazi precinct, Soweto. *GeoJournal*, *85*(4), 1133–1149. doi:10.100710708-019-10016-2

Hooper, G., & Lennon, J. (2016). *Dark tourism*. Taylor & Francis. doi:10.4324/9781315575865

Hull, H. F. (2005). SARS control and psychological effects of quarantine, Toronto, Canada. *Emerging Infectious Diseases*, *11*(2), 354–355. doi:10.3201/eid1102.040760 PMID:15759346

Human Rights Council. (2010). *Human rights and access to safe drinking water and sanitation*. Pub. L. No. A/HRC/RES/15/9 (2010). https://ap.ohchr.org/documents/dpage_e.aspx?si=A/HRC/RES/15/9

Ignatieff, M. (2011). Human rights as idolatry. In *Human rights as politics and idolatry* (pp. 53–98). Princeton University Press.

Institute for Human Rights and Business. (2011). *More than resources: Water, Business and Human Rights*. https://www.ihrb.org/pdf/More_than_a_resource_Water_business_and_human_rights.pdf

Integra Foundation and Pontis Foundation and PANET. (2005). *Socially responsible business*. Integra Foundation. https://nadaciapontis.sk/wpcontent/uploads/2019/01/text_zodpovedne_podnikanie.pdf

Invest Northern Ireland. (n.d.). *Corporate social responsibility: local community*. Nibusinessinfo. https://nibusinessinfo.co.uk/content/corporate-social-responsibility-local-community

Ioannides, D., Gyimóthy, S., & James, L. (2021). From liminal labor to decent work: A human-centered perspective on sustainable tourism employment. *Sustainability (Basel)*, *13*(2), 851. doi:10.3390u13020851

IPMARK. (September 15th, 2021). El 38% de los oyentes de podcasts se 'engancharon' en la cuarentena. (An estimate 38% followers in Postcast engaged themselves during the lockdown). *IPMARK*. https://ipmark.com/el-38-de-los-oyentes-de-podcasts-se-engancharon-en-la-cuarentena/

Isaac, R. K., Çakmak, E., & Butler, R. (Eds.). (2019). *Tourism and hospitality in conflict-ridden destinations*. Routledge. doi:10.4324/9780429463235

Ivanov, S., & Webster, C. (2007). Measuring the impact of tourism on economic growth. *Tourism Economics*, *13*(3), 379–388. doi:10.5367/000000007781497773

Jackson, S. (2016). *Indigenous Peoples and Water Justice in a Globalizing World* (K. Conca & E. Weinthal, Eds., Vol. 1). Oxford University Press. doi:10.1093/oxfordhb/9780199335084.013.5

Compilation of References

Jennings, G. (2007). *Water-based tourism, sport, leisure, and recreation experiences*. Routledge. doi:10.4324/9780080468310

Kaitano, D. U. B. E. (2020). Tourism and sustainable development goals in the African context. *International Journal of Economics and Finance Studies*, *12*(1), 88–102.

Kapalková, D. (2017). Corporate Social Responsibility in the Hotel industry [Master's Dissertation, The Institute of Hospitality Management in Prague 8, Ltd.]. VŠHE Information system. https://is.vsh.cz/th/hf4su/Diplomova_praca.pdf

Karim, K. M. R., Emmelin, M., Resurreccion, B. P., & Wamala, S. (2012). Water Development Projects and Marital Violence: Experiences from Rural Bangladesh. *Health Care for Women International*, *33*(3), 200–216. doi:10.1080/07399332.2011.603861 PMID:22325022

Karsavuran, Z. (2021). Surviving a major crisis: The case of dismissed tourism and hospitality employees. *Journal of Policy Research in Tourism, Leisure & Events*, *13*(2), 243–265. doi:10.1080/19407963.2020.1787421

Kašparová, K., & Kunz, V. (2013). *Modern approaches to corporate social responsibility and CSR reporting*. Grada Publishing.

Keet, A. (2012). Discourse, betrayal, critique: The renewal of human rights education. In *Safe spaces* (pp. 5–27). Brill. doi:10.1007/978-94-6091-936-7_2

Khassawneh, O., & Abaker, M. O. S. M. (2022). Human Resource Management in the United Arab Emirates: Towards a Better Understanding. In *HRM in the Global South: A Critical Perspective* (pp. 103–128). Springer International Publishing. doi:10.1007/978-3-030-98309-3_5

Khuong, M. N., & Nhu, N. V. Q. (2015). The effects of ethical leadership and organizational culture towards employees' sociability and commitment–a study of tourism sector in Ho Chi Minh city. *Vietnam. Journal of Advanced Management Science*, *3*(4). Advance online publication. doi:10.18178/joams.5.4.255-263

Kiper, V. O., Saraç, Ö., & Batman, O. (2022). Drought Tourism: Adopting Tourism for Water Scarcity. In E. Christou & A. Fotiadis (Eds.), *Restarting tourism, travel and hospitality* (1st ed., pp. 248–257). School of Economics and Business, International Hellenic University.

Klein, A., & Smith, E. (2021). *Explaining the economic impact of COVID-19: Core industries and the Hispanic workforce*. Academic Press.

Knox, J. H. (2015). Human Rights, Environmental Protection, and the Sustainable Development Goals. *Washington International Law Journal*, *24*(3), 517–536.

Korstanje, M. E. (2016). *The rise of thana-capitalism and tourism*. Routledge. doi:10.4324/9781315457482

Korstanje, M. E. (2017). *Terrorism, Tourism and the end of Hospitality in the West*. Palgrave Macmillan.

Korstanje, M. E. (2018). *The mobilities paradox: A critical analysis*. Edward Elgar Publishing. doi:10.4337/9781788113311

Korstanje, M. E. (2020). *The dark tourist: Consuming dark spaces in the periphery. In Tourism, terrorism and security*. Emerald. doi:10.1108/9781838679057

Korstanje, M. E., & Baker, D. (2018). Politics of dark tourism: The case of Cromanon and ESMA, Buenos Aires, Argentina. In *The Palgrave Handbook of Dark Tourism Studies* (pp. 533–552). Palgrave Macmillan. doi:10.1057/978-1-137-47566-4_22

Korstanje, M. E., & George, B. (2021). *Mobility and globalization in the aftermath of COVID-19: Emerging new geographies in a locked world*. Palgrave Macmillan. doi:10.1007/978-3-030-78845-2

Korstanje, M. E., & Ivanov, S. H. (2012). Tourism as a form of new psychological resilience: The inception of dark tourism. *SSRN*, *6*(4), 56–71. doi:10.2139srn.2168400

Korstanje, M. E., & Olsen, D. H. (2011). The discourse of risk in horror movies posts 9/11: Hospitality and hostility in perspective. *International Journal of Tourism Anthropology*, *1*(3), 304–317. doi:10.1504/IJTA.2011.043712

Korstanje, M. E., & Tarlow, P. (2012). Being lost: Tourism, risk and vulnerability in the post-'9/11'entertainment industry. *Journal of Tourism and Cultural Change*, *10*(1), 22–33. doi:10.1080/14766825.2011.639455

Kortt, M. A., Sinnewe, E., & Pervan, S. J. (2018). The gender wage gap in the tourism industry: Evidence from Australia. *Tourism Analysis*, *23*(1), 137–149. doi:10.3727/108354217X15143857878697

Kotler. (2010). *Marketing for hospitality and tourism*. Pearson Education.

Kotler, P., & Lee, N. R. (2005). *Corporate Social Responsibility: Doing the Most Good For Your Company and Your Cause*. Wiley.

Krause, M. (June 30th, 2014). Milton Friedman escandaliza: la responsabilidad social de los empresarios es aumentar sus ganancias. [Milton Friedman trembles: the social responsabilities of businessmen is amassing profits]. *El foro y el bazar*. https://bazar.ufm.edu/milton-friedman-escandaliza-la-responsabilidad-social-delos-empresarios-es-aumentar-sus-ganancias

Kunz, V. (2012). *Corporate Social Responsibility*. Grada Publishing.

Kyriazi, T. (2020). Trafficking in human beings in the tourism industry: trends and approaches. In *Tourism and gender-based violence: challenging inequalities* (pp. 95–110). CABI. doi:10.1079/9781789243215.0095

Lazovska, D. (2019, October 10). *Las 5 Rs de la RSE (The 5 Rs of CSR)*. ExpokNews; Expok. https://www.expoknews.com/las-5-r-de-la-rse/

Compilation of References

Lenz, R. (2021). 'Hotel Royal'and Other Spaces of Hospitality: Tourists and Migrants in the Mediterranean. In *Thinking through tourism* (pp. 209–229). Routledge. doi:10.4324/9781003087229-10

Levy, D., & Sznaider, N. (2006). Sovereignty transformed: Sociology of human rights 1. *The British Journal of Sociology*, *57*(4), 657–676. doi:10.1111/j.1468-4446.2006.00130.x PMID:17168943

Light, D. (2017). Progress in dark tourism and thanatourism research: An uneasy relationship with heritage tourism. *Tourism Management*, *61*, 275–301. doi:10.1016/j.tourman.2017.01.011

Lischer, S. K. (2019). Narrating atrocity: Genocide memorials, dark tourism, and the politics of memory. *Review of International Studies*, *45*(5), 805–827. doi:10.1017/S0260210519000226

Liu, C. L., Jeon, C. Y., Song, W. G., & Yang, H. W. (2022). The COVID-19 Pandemic and Its Impact on Tourism: The Effect of Tourism Knowledge on Risk Perception, Attitude, and Intention. *Journal of Quality Assurance in Hospitality & Tourism*, 1–17. doi:10.1080/152800 8X.2022.2077887

Logie, C. H., Okumu, M., Latif, M., Musoke, D. K., Odong Lukone, S., Mwima, S., & Kyambadde, P. (2021). Exploring resource scarcity and contextual influences on wellbeing among young refugees in Bidi Bidi refugee settlement, Uganda: Findings from a qualitative study. *Conflict and Health*, *15*(1), 3. doi:10.118613031-020-00336-3 PMID:33413546

López de Lacalle, R. (January 13th, 2010). ¿Qué es la RSC y cómo se puede relacionar con el turismo justo? La experiencia española. [What is RSC and how it can be related to tourism?: The Spanish experience]. *Portal de América*. https://portaldeamerica.com/index.php/columnistas/anteriores-columnistas/item/135-%C2%BFqu%C3%A9-es-la-rsc-y-c%C3%B3mo-se-puede-relacionar-con-el-turismo-justo

López, M. (October 18th, 2016). Por qué invertir en RSC en un hotel. [Why RSC in a hotel]. *Hosteltur*. https://hosteltur.com/comunidad/005121_por-que-invertir-en-rsc-en-un-hotel.html

Málaga Actualidad. (March 31st, 2022). Soho Boutique Hotels se incorpora como patrocinador del Museo Carmen Thyssen Málaga. [Soho Boutique Hotels promotes Carmen Thyssen Museum] *Málaga Actualidad*. http://malagactualidad.es/teletipos/item/41506-soho-boutique-hotels-se-incorpora-como-patrocinador-del-museo-carmen-thyssen-malaga.html

Malloy, D. C., & Fennell, D. A. (1998). Codes of ethics and tourism: An exploratory content analysis. *Tourism Management*, *19*(5), 453–461. doi:10.1016/S0261-5177(98)00042-9

Mamatzakis, E., Pegkas, P., & Staikouras, C. (2022). Labour market regulations and efficiency in tourism industry. *Tourism Economics*. doi:10.1177/13548166221081522

Mariolis, T., Rodousakis, N., & Soklis, G. (2021). The COVID-19 multiplier effects of tourism on the Greek economy. *Tourism Economics*, *27*(8), 1848–1855. doi:10.1177/1354816620946547

Markova, E., Anna, P., Williams, A. M., & Shaw, G. (2016). Migrant workers in small London hotels: Employment, recruitment and distribution. *European Urban and Regional Studies*, *23*(3), 406–421. doi:10.1177/0969776413513913

Martínez Carazo, P. C. (2006). El método de estudio de caso: estrategia metodológica de la investigación científica. Pensamiento & Gestión, (20), 65-193.

Martini, A., & Buda, D. M. (2020). Dark tourism and affect: Framing places of death and disaster. *Current Issues in Tourism, 23*(6), 679–692. doi:10.1080/13683500.2018.1518972

Massey, D. S., & Denton, N. A. (1988). The Dimensions of Residential Segregation. *Social Forces, 67*(2), 281–315. doi:10.2307/2579183

Mastroeni, L. (Anfitrión). (July 30th, 2020). Responsabilidad Social Empresarial #RSE In *Entre Compas Podcast*. (Nro. 3) [Social Corporate Responsibility] [Episodio de podcast]. https://www.listennotes.com/es/podcasts/entre-compas-podcast/s3-responsabilidad-social-p3Y9L4HSOTq/

Mat, N., Yaacob, N. A., & Melhem, S. B. (2015). *Knowledge sharing effect on HRM practices and organisational innovation among Malaysia's Four and Five Star Hotels*. Academic Press.

Mat, N., Yaacob, N. A., & Melhem, S. B. (2015). Human resource management practices and organizational innovation: A study of four and five star hotels in Malaysia. *Advances in Global Business Research, 12*(1), 596–605.

May, S. K., Cheney, G., & Roper, J. (2007). *The Debate over Corporate Social Responsibility*. Oxford University Press.

McIntyre, O. (2019). The Emergence of Standards Regarding the Right of Access to Water and Sanitation. In S. J. Turner, D. L. Shelton, J. Razzaque, O. McIntyre, & J. R. May (Eds.), *Environmental Rights: The Oxford Handbook of International Environmental Law* (1st ed., pp. 147–173). Cambridge University Press. doi:10.1017/9781108612500.007

Mckay, T. J. (2014). White water adventure tourism on the Ash River, South Africa. *African Journal for Physical, Health Education, Recreation & Dance, 20*(1), 1–15.

McKinsey. (2011). *The business of sustainability survey*. McKinsey & Company. https://mckinsey.com/business-functions/sustainability/our-insights/the-business-of-sustainability-mckinsey-global-survey-results

Mercado (January 12th, 2003). La responsabilidad moral de las empresas. [Moral Ethics in corporations] *Mercado*. https://mercado.com.ar/management-marketing/la-responsabilidad-moral-de-las-empresas/

Miles, S. (2014). Battlefield sites as dark tourism attractions: An analysis of experience. *Journal of Heritage Tourism, 9*(2), 134–147. doi:10.1080/1743873X.2013.871017

Miller, D. S., Gonzalez, C., & Hutter, M. (2017). Phoenix tourism within dark tourism: Rebirth, rebuilding and rebranding of tourist destinations following disasters. *Worldwide Hospitality and Tourism Themes, 9*(2), 196–215. doi:10.1108/WHATT-08-2016-0040

Compilation of References

Moayerian, N., McGehee, N. G., & Stephenson, M. O. Jr. (2022). Community cultural development: Exploring the connections between collective art making, capacity building and sustainable community-based tourism. *Annals of Tourism Research, 93*, 103355. doi:10.1016/j.annals.2022.103355

Mohammad, T., Darwish, T. K., Singh, S., & Khassawneh, O. (2021). Human resource management and organisational performance: The mediating role of social exchange. *European Management Review, 18*(1), 125–136. doi:10.1111/emre.12421

Mohd. Shamsudin, F., Hamouche, S., Abdulmajid Cheikh Ali, D., Bani-Melhem, S., & Jamal Bani-Melhem, A. (2022). Why do employees withhold knowledge? The role of competitive climate, envy and narcissism. *Journal of Knowledge Management.* Advance online publication. doi:10.1108/JKM-02-2022-0133

Mooney, S., & Baum, T. (2019). A sustainable hospitality and tourism workforce research agenda: Exploring the past to create a vision for the future. In *A research agenda for tourism and development* (pp. 189–205). Edward Elgar Publishing. doi:10.4337/9781788112413.00016

Moreno de la Santa, J. G. S. (2020). Tourism as a lever for a more inclusive society. *Worldwide Hospitality and Tourism Themes, 12*(6), 731–738. doi:10.1108/WHATT-07-2020-0071

Morinville, C., & Rodina, L. (2013). Rethinking the Human Right to Water: Water access and dispossession in Botswana's Central Kalahari game reserve. *Geoforum, 49*, 150–159. doi:10.1016/j.geoforum.2013.06.012

Municipal Statistical Office of the City of Turin. (n.d.). *Dati statistici: stranieri per sesso, età, circoscrizione, quartiere, provenienza.* Turin: Municipal Statistical Office. Found on: http://www.comune.torino.it/statistica/dati/

Murie, A., & Musterd, S. (2004). Social Exclusion and Opportunity Structures in European Cities and Neighbourhood Matters. *Urban Studies (Edinburgh, Scotland), 41*(8), 1441–1459. doi:10.1080/0042098042000226948

Musavengane, R. (2019). Small hotels and responsible tourism practice: Hoteliers' perspectives. *Journal of Cleaner Production, 220*, 786–799. doi:10.1016/j.jclepro.2019.02.143

Myhill, K., Richards, J., & Sang, K. (2021). Job quality, fair work and gig work: The lived experience of gig workers. *International Journal of Human Resource Management, 32*(19), 4110–4135. doi:10.1080/09585192.2020.1867612

Naciones Unidas. (n.d.). *Sustainable Development.* UN. https://un.org/sustainabledevelopment/es/

Ndiuini, A., & Baum, T. (2021). Underemployment and lived experiences of migrant workers in the hotel industry: Policy and industry implications. *Journal of Policy Research in Tourism, Leisure & Events, 13*(1), 36–58. doi:10.1080/19407963.2020.1743487

Neef, A. (2019). *Tourism, Land Grabs and Displacement: A Study with Particular Focus on the Global South.* Academic Press.

Nicolaides, A. (2020). Sustainable ethical tourism (SET) and rural community involvement. *African Journal of Hospitality, Tourism and Leisure*, *9*(1), 1–16.

NOBBOT. (February 3rd, 2022). El consumo de podcast crece en España y Spotify es la plataforma más usada. (Postcast Consumption in Spain and Spotify). *NOBBOT.* https://www.nobbot.com/tecnologia/aplicaciones-moviles-tecnologia/podcast-espana-spotify/

Noble, R., Smith, P., Pattullo, P., Brown, M., Cole, S., Slade, L., Latchford, R., Niang, D., & Gama, A. de. (2012). *Water equity in tourism: a human right, a global responsibility.* Tourism Concern research report.

Nofre, J., Giordano, E., Eldridge, A., Martins, J. C., & Sequera, J. (2018). Tourism, nightlife, and planning: Challenges and opportunities for community liveability in La Barceloneta. *Tourism Geographies*, *20*(3), 377–396. doi:10.1080/14616688.2017.1375972

Nolan, J., & Bott, G. (2018). Global supply chains and human rights: Spotlight on forced labour and modern slavery practices. *Australian Journal of Human Rights*, *24*(1), 44–69. doi:10.1080/1323238X.2018.1441610

Obadić, A. (2016). Gender discrimination and pay gap on tourism labor market. *International Journal of Social, Behavioral, Educational, Economic. Business and Industrial Engineering*, *10*(3), 812–817.

OCDE (2016). *Principios de Gobierno Corporativo de la OCDE y del G20.* [Principles for Corporate Governance in OCDE and G20]. OCDE. doi:10.1787/9789264259171-es

OHCHR. (2014). *Contribution to the 2014 United Nations Economic and Social Council (ECOSOC) Integration Segment.* United Nations.

Ojeda, D. (2016). Los paisajes del despojo: Propuestas para un análisis desde las reconfiguraciones socioespaciales. *Revista Colombiana de Antropología*, *52*(2), 19–43. doi:10.22380/2539472X38

Ojeda, D., Petzl, J., Quiroga, C., Ana Catalina, R., & Juan Guillermo, R. (2015). Paisajes del despojo cotidiano: Acaparamiento de tierra y agua en Montes de María, Colombia. *Revista de Estudios Sociales*, *54*(54), 107–119. doi:10.7440/res54.2015.08

Okafor, L. E., Khalid, U., & Burzynska, K. (2022). The effect of migration on international tourism flows: The role of linguistic networks and common languages. *Journal of Travel Research*, *61*(4), 818–836. doi:10.1177/00472875211008250

Orden-Mejía, M., Carvache-Franco, M., Huertas, A., Carvache-Franco, W., Landeta-Bejarano, N., & Carvache-Franco. (2022). Post-COVID-19 Tourists' Preferences, Attitudes and Travel Expectations: A Study in Guayaquil, Ecuador. *International Journal of Environmental Research and Public Health.*

Pablo-Romero, M. D. P., & Molina, J. A. (2013). Tourism and economic growth: A review of empirical literature. *Tourism Management Perspectives*, *8*, 28–41. doi:10.1016/j.tmp.2013.05.006

Compilation of References

Papadopoulos, O., & Ioannou, G. (2022). Working in hospitality and catering in Greece and the UK: Do trade union membership and collective bargaining still matter? *European Journal of Industrial Relations*. doi:10.1177/09596801221104943

Pavlík, M., Bělčík, M., Srpová, J., Kunz, V., & Kužel, S. (2010). Corporate Social Responsibility: CSR. In *Practice And How To Go On With It*. Grada Publishing.

Pitts, C. (2016). The United Nations' Protect, Respect, Remedy' Framework and Guiding Principles. In D. Baumann-Pauly & J. Nolan (Eds.), *Business and Human Rights from Principles to Practice* (1st ed., pp. 51–63). Routledge.

Poletti, A., & Sicurelli, D. (2022). The political economy of the EU approach to the Rohingya crisis in Myanmar. *Politics and Governance*, *10*(1), 47–57. doi:10.17645/pag.v10i1.4678

Porto, N., & Espinola, N. (2019). Labor income inequalities and tourism development in Argentina: A regional approach. *Tourism Economics*, *25*(8), 1265–1285. doi:10.1177/1354816619828143

Post-pandemic tourism: The desired wave of recovery in India. (n.d.). Academic Press.

Powell, R., & Kennell, J. (2016). Dark cities? Developing a methodology for researching dark tourism in European cities. In *Tourism and culture in the age of innovation* (pp. 303–319). Springer. doi:10.1007/978-3-319-27528-4_21

Preno (n.d.). *How the local community can help grow your hotel brand and presence*. Preno HQ. https://prenohq.com/blog/local-community-and-hotel-brand/

Puiga, R., Kiliç, E., Navarro, A., Albertí, J., & Chacóne, L. (2017). Inventory analysis and carbon footprint of coastland-hotel services: A Spanish case study. *The Science of the Total Environment*, *595*, 244–254. doi:10.1016/j.scitotenv.2017.03.245 PMID:28384580

Quintão, C., Andrade, P., & Almeida, F. (2021). How to Improve the Validity and Reliability of a Case Study Approach? *Journal of Interdisciplinary Studies in Education*, *9*(2), 264–275.

Raine, R. (2013). A dark tourist spectrum. *International Journal of Culture, Tourism and Hospitality Research*, *7*(3), 242–256. doi:10.1108/IJCTHR-05-2012-0037

Ram, Y. (2018). Hostility or hospitality? A review on violence, bullying and sexual harassment in the tourism and hospitality industry. *Current Issues in Tourism*, *21*(7), 760–774. doi:10.108 0/13683500.2015.1064364

Rath, J. (2007). *The transformation of ethnic Neighborhoods into Places of Leisure and Consumption*. Working Paper 144. Institute for Migration and Ethic Studies. University of Amsterdam.

Reich, R. (2007). *Supercapitalism - The transformation of business democracy, and everyday life*. Random House.

Riadil, I. G. (2020). Tourism industry crisis and its impacts: investigating the Indonesian tourism employees perspectives' in the pandemic of COVID-19. *Jurnal Kepariwisataan: Destinasi. Hospitalitas Dan Perjalanan*, *4*(2), 98–108.

Riley, M. (2014). *Human resource management in the hospitality and tourism industry*. Routledge. doi:10.4324/9781315831565

Rivera, Gutierrez, & Roxas. (2022). Re-thinking Governance in Tourism: Harnessing Tourism's post-COVID-19 Economic Potential. *Journal of Quality Assurance in Hospitality & Tourism*.

Robinson, R. N., Martins, A., Solnet, D., & Baum, T. (2019). Sustaining precarity: Critically examining tourism and employment. *Journal of Sustainable Tourism*, *27*(7), 1008–1025. doi:10.1080/09669582.2018.1538230

Robinson, R. N., Martins, A., Solnet, D., & Baum, T. (2021). Sustaining precarity: Critically examining tourism and employment. In *Activating Critical Thinking to Advance the Sustainable Development Goals in Tourism Systems* (pp. 162–179). Routledge. doi:10.4324/9781003140542-10

Romero, J. M., Mogollón, J. M., Cerro, A. M., & Fernández, J. A. (2016). El impacto de la RSC en la industria hotelera: Estado del arte. [The impacts of social responsability in the hospitality industry: an state of the art]. In Jiménez Caballero, J. L. (Ed.), El turismo y la experiencia del cliente: IX jornadas de investigación en turismo (pp. 409 - 435). FTF, University of Sevilla.

Romero, J. M., Mogollón, J. M., Cerro, A. M., & Fernández, J. A. (2017). Aproximación al estudio del comportamiento de la RSC en las empresas hoteleras. [Approaching Social Corporate Responsability in hotels] *Turismo & Desenvolvimento*, *27/28*, 159- 170. https://proa.ua.pt/index. php/rtd/article/view/8387/5939

Roxas, J. P. R., & Gutierrez, E. L. M. (2022). Bootstrapping tourism post-COVID-19: A systems thinking approach. *Tourism and Hospitality Research*, *22*(1), 86–101. doi:10.1177/14673584211038859

Ruggie, J. (May 15th, 2010). *The Corporate Responsibility to Respect Human Rights*. Harvard Law School Forum on Corporate Governance. https://corpgov.law.harvard.edu/2010/05/15/ the-corporate-responsibility-to-respect-human-rights/#:~:text=The%20corporate%20 responsibility%20to%20respect%20human%20rights%20means%20to%20avoid,all%20 companies%20in%20all%20situations

Ruggie, J. G. (2008). Protect, Respect and Remedy: A Framework for Business and Human Rights. *Innovations: Technology, Governance, Globalization*, *3*(2), 189–212. doi:10.1162/ itgg.2008.3.2.189

Ruiz-Ballesteros, E., & Cáceres-Feria, R. (2016). Community-building and amenity migration in community-based tourism development. An approach from southwest Spain. *Tourism Management*, *54*, 513–523. doi:10.1016/j.tourman.2016.01.008

Compilation of References

Ruiz-Lozano, M., De-los-Ríos-Berjillos, A., & Millán-Lara, S. (2018). Spanish hotel chains alignment with the Global Code of Ethics for Tourism. *Journal of Cleaner Production, 199*, 205–213. doi:10.1016/j.jclepro.2018.07.133

Salvia, A. L., Leal Filho, W., Brandli, L. L., & Griebeler, J. S. (2019). Assessing research trends related to Sustainable Development Goals: Local and global issues. *Journal of Cleaner Production, 208*, 841–849. doi:10.1016/j.jclepro.2018.09.242

Sandang, Y. (2022). *Hotels and the human right to water: prospect and challenges in Yogyakarta, Indonesia* [Doctoral dissertation]. Faculty of Environment and Technology, University of the West of England.

Sandang, Y., & Cole, S. (2022). Using a human rights approach to improve hotels' water use and sustainability. *Journal of Sustainable Tourism*, 1–19. doi:10.1080/09669582.2022.2108041

Santoro, M. A. (2015). Business and Human Rights in Historical Perspective. *Journal of Human Rights, 14*(2), 155–161. doi:10.1080/14754835.2015.1025945

Sather-Wagstaff, J. (2015). Heritage and memory. In *The Palgrave handbook of contemporary heritage research* (pp. 191–204). Palgrave Macmillan. doi:10.1057/9781137293565_12

Sather-Wagstaff, J. (2016a). *Heritage that hurts: Tourists in the memoryscapes of September 11*. Routledge. doi:10.4324/9781315427539

Sather-Wagstaff, J. (2016b). Making polysense of the world: Affect, memory, heritage. In *Heritage, affect and emotion* (pp. 30–48). Routledge.

Sbarcea, K. (March 27th, 2007). The Evolution of CSR. *ThinkingShift*. https://thinkingshift. wordpress.com/2007/03/27/the-evolution-of-csr/

Scheyvens, R., & Cheer, J. M. (2021). Tourism, the SDGs and partnerships. *Journal of Sustainable Tourism, 0*(0), 1–11. doi:10.1080/09669582.2021.1982953

Seaton, A. V. (1996). Guided by the dark: From thanatopsis to thanatourism. *International Journal of Heritage Studies, 2*(4), 234–244. doi:10.1080/13527259608722178

Secretaría de Estado de Turismo. (January 2019). *Estrategia de Turismo Sostenible de España 2030. Gobierno de España*. Secretaría de Estado de Turismo.[https://turismo.gob.es/es-es/estrategia-turismo-sostenible/Documents/directrices-estrategia-turismo-sostenible.pdf

Sedes García, J. M. [EOI Escuela de Organización Industrial] (March 14th, 2012). *Gestión Estratégica de la Responsabilidad Corporativa* [Video]. (EOI School). YouTube. https://youtube.com/watch?v=-FKzPKsmg4o

Semi, G. (2009). Il mercato come spazio di relazione e di conflittualità interetnica. In Migrazioni (pp. 637-652). Einaudi.

Semi, G. (2015). *Gentrification. Tutte le città come Disneyland*. Il Mulino.

Séraphin, H., & Korstanje, M. E. (2020). Ethical comments revolving around post-disaster marketing. In *Sustainable destination branding and marketing: strategies for tourism development* (pp. 73–81). CABI. doi:10.1079/9781786394286.0073

Seraphin, H., & Korstanje, M. E. (2021). Neither Passive nor Powerless: Reframing Tourism Development in a Postcolonial, Post-conflict and Post-disaster Destination Context. In *Progress in Ethical Practices of Businesses* (pp. 117–135). Springer. doi:10.1007/978-3-030-60727-2_7

Shafique, I. N., Kalyar, M., & Ahmad, B. (2018). The nexus of ethical leadership, job performance, and turnover intention: The mediating role of job satisfaction. *Interdisciplinary Description of Complex Systems: INDECS, 16*(1), 71–87. doi:10.7906/indecs.16.1.5

Sharma, G. D., Thomas, A., & Paul, J. (2021). Reviving tourism industry post-COVID-19: A resilience-based framework. *Tourism Management Perspectives, 37*, 100786. doi:10.1016/j.tmp.2020.100786 PMID:33391988

Sharpley, R. (2006). Travels to the edge of darkness: Towards a typology of "dark tourism". In *Taking tourism to the limits* (pp. 239–250). Routledge.

Sigala, M. (2020). Tourism and COVID-19: Impacts and implications for advancing and resetting industry and research. *Journal of Business Research, 117*, 312–321. doi:10.1016/j.jbusres.2020.06.015 PMID:32546875

Škare, M., Soriano, D. R., & Porada-Rochoń, M. (2021). Impact of COVID-19 on the travel and tourism industry. *Technological Forecasting and Social Change, 163*, 120469. doi:10.1016/j.techfore.2020.120469 PMID:35721368

Skoll, G. R., & Korstanje, M. (2014). Urban heritage, gentrification, and tourism in Riverwest and El Abasto. *Journal of Heritage Tourism, 9*(4), 349–359. doi:10.1080/1743873X.2014.890624

Sorenson, S. B., Morssink, C., & Campos, P. A. (2011). Safe access to safe water in low-income countries: Water fetching in current times. *Social Science & Medicine, 72*(9), 1522–1526. doi:10.1016/j.socscimed.2011.03.010 PMID:21481508

Soulard, J., Stewart, W., Larson, M., & Samson, E. (2022). Dark Tourism and Social Mobilization: Transforming Travelers After Visiting a Holocaust Museum. *Journal of Travel Research.*

Spain, E. Y. (June 16th, 2021). *Impacto del COVID-19 en las prioridades de la RSC y Sostenibilidad y en el rol de sus profesionales* [Video]. [effects of COVID-19 and the priorities of RSC for sustainability and the role of the professionals]. YouTube. https://youtube.com/watch?v=7pKPaw9Vdl0

Special Rapporteur on the right to adequate housing. (2021). *Discrimination in the context of housing - Report A/76/408*. General Assembly, 76th Session.

Special Rapporteur on the right to adequate housing. (2022). *Spatial segregation and the right to adequate housing - Report A/HRC/49/48*. Human Rights Council, 49th Session.

Compilation of References

Spicer, N., Parlee, B., Chisaakay, M., & Lamalice, D. (2020). Drinking Water Consumption Patterns: An Exploration of Risk Perception and Governance in Two First Nations Communities. *Sustainability (Basel)*, *12*(17), 6851. doi:10.3390u12176851

Staddon, C., Appleby, T., & Grant, E. (2012). A Right to Water? Geographico-legal perspectives. In F. Sultana & A. Loftus (Eds.), The Right to Water: Politics, governance and social struggles (pp. 61–77). Earthscan, Taylor & Francis.

Stamolampros, P., Korfiatis, N., Chalvatzis, K., & Buhalis, D. (2019). Job satisfaction and employee turnover determinants in high contact services: Insights from Employees' Online reviews. *Tourism Management*, *75*, 130–147. doi:10.1016/j.tourman.2019.04.030

Stone, P. R. (2012). Dark tourism and significant other death: Towards a model of mortality mediation. *Annals of Tourism Research*, *39*(3), 1565–1587. doi:10.1016/j.annals.2012.04.007

Stone, P. R., Hartmann, R., Seaton, A. V., Sharpley, R., & White, L. (Eds.). (2018). *The Palgrave handbook of dark tourism studies* (pp. 335–354). Palgrave Macmillan. doi:10.1057/978-1-137-47566-4

Stone, P., & Sharpley, R. (2008). Consuming dark tourism: A thanatological perspective. *Annals of Tourism Research*, *35*(2), 574–595. doi:10.1016/j.annals.2008.02.003

Strauß, S. (2011). Water Conflicts among Different User Groups in South Bali, Indonesia. *Human Ecology: an Interdisciplinary Journal*, *39*(1), 69–79. doi:10.100710745-011-9381-3

Sun, Y. Y., Li, M., Lenzen, M., Malik, A., & Pomponi, F. (2022). Tourism, job vulnerability and income inequality during the COVID-19 pandemic: A global perspective. *Annals of Tourism Research Empirical Insights*, *3*(1), 100046. doi:10.1016/j.annale.2022.100046

Sustainable Hospitality Alliance. (n.d.). *Human rights*. Sustainable Hospitality Alliance. https://sustainablehospitalityalliance.org/our-work/human-rights/

Sustainable or a butterfly effect in global tourism? Nexus of pandemic fatigue, covid-19-branded destination safety, travel stimulus incentives, and post-pandemic revenge travel. (n.d.). Academic Press.

Tallman, P. S., Collins, S., Salmon-Mulanovich, G., Rusyidi, B., Kothadia, A., & Cole, S. (2023). Water insecurity and gender-based violence: A global review of the evidence. *WIREs. Water*, *10*(1). Advance online publication. doi:10.1002/wat2.1619

Tarlow, P. (2007). Dark tourism–the appealing 'dark'side of tourism and more. In *Niche tourism* (pp. 61–72). Routledge.

Tarlow, P. (2014). *Tourism security: strategies for effectively managing travel risk and safety.* Elsevier.

Tecău, A. S., Brătucu, G., Tescaşiu, B., Chiţu, I. B., Constantin, C. P., & Foris, D. (2019). Responsible tourism—Integrating families with disabled children in tourist destinations. *Sustainability (Basel)*, *11*(16), 4420. doi:10.3390u11164420

TecnoHotel. (June 3rd, 2022). España vuelve a ser líder del turismo con un nivel de reservas hoteleras al 117%. [Spain takes the lead on the industry with a booking percentage of 117%]. *TecnoHotel*. https://tecnohotelnews.com/2022/06/espana-lider-turismo-global-nivel-reservas-hoteleras/

Tirado Bennasar, D. (2014). Water consumption, tourism. In J. Jafari & H. Xiao (Eds.), *Encyclopedia of Tourism*. Springer. doi:10.1007/978-3-319-01669-6_313-1

Torres, E. N., Ridderstaat, J., & Wei, W. (2021). Negative affectivity and people's return intentions to hospitality and tourism activities: The early stages of COVID-19. *Journal of Hospitality and Tourism Management*, *49*, 89–100. doi:10.1016/j.jhtm.2021.08.021

Tosun, C., Çalişkan, C., Şahin, S. Z., & Dedeoğlu, B. B. (2021). A critical perspective on tourism employment. *Current Issues in Tourism*, 1–21.

Travelabs Online Talk [Anula Galewska] (April 24th, 2020). *How sustainability and CSR will help your tourism business recover quicker* [Video]. YouTube. https://youtube.com/watch?v=a9-2_ATvsDU

Treuren, G. J., Manoharan, A., & Vishnu, V. (2021). The hospitality sector as an employer of skill discounted migrants. Evidence from Australia. *Journal of Policy Research in Tourism, Leisure & Events*, *13*(1), 20–35. doi:10.1080/19407963.2019.1655859

Tumarkin, M. (2001). 'Wishing you weren't here...': Thinking about trauma, place and the port Arthur massacre. *Journal of Australian Studies*, *25*(67), 196–205. doi:10.1080/14443050109387653

Tumarkin, M. (2019). Twenty years of thinking about traumascapes. *Fabrications*, *29*(1), 4–20. doi:10.1080/10331867.2018.1540077

Tumarkin, M. M. (2005). *Traumascapes: The power and fate of places transformed by tragedy*. Melbourne Univ. Publishing.

Tzanelli, R. (2015). On avatar's (2009) semiotechnologies: From cinematic utopias to chinese heritage tourism. *Tourism Analysis*, *20*(3), 269–282. doi:10.3727/108354215X14356694891771

Tzanelli, R. (2016). *Thanatourism and cinematic representations of risk: Screening the end of tourism*. Routledge. doi:10.4324/9781315624105

Tzanelli, R. (2018). Slum tourism: A review of state-of-the-art scholarship. *Tourism, Culture & Communication*, *18*(2), 149–155. doi:10.3727/109830418X15230353469528

Tzanelli, R. (2021). Post-viral tourism's antagonistic tourist imaginaries. *Journal of Tourism Futures*, *7*(3), 377–389. doi:10.1108/JTF-07-2020-0105

Tzanelli, R., & Korstanje, M. E. (2016). Tourism in the European economic crisis: Mediatised worldmaking and new tourist imaginaries in Greece. *Tourist Studies*, *16*(3), 296–314. doi:10.1177/1468797616648542

Compilation of References

Tzanelli, R., & Korstanje, M. E. (2019). On killing the 'toured object': Anti-terrorist fantasy, touristic edgework and morbid consumption in the illegal settlements in West Bank, Palestine. In *Tourism and hospitality in conflict-ridden destinations* (pp. 71–83). Routledge.

UNIDO. (n.d.). *What is CSR?* United Nations Industrial Development Organization. https://unido.org/our-focus/advancing-economic-competitiveness/competitive-trade-capacities-and-corporate-responsibility/corporate-social-responsibility-market-integration/what-csr

United Nations. (2015). *The 17 Goals | Sustainable Development.* https://sdgs.un.org/goals

United Nations. (2021). *Comprehensive response to Covid-19: Update 2021.* UN Sustainable Development Group. https://unsdg.un.org/sites/default/files/2021-12/un-comprehensive-response-covid-19-2021.pdf

UNODC. (n.d.). *Corruption and integrity & Ethics.* UNODC United Nations Office on Drugs and Crime. https://unodc.org/e4j/en/secondary/corruption-integrity-ethics.html

UN-Water Decade Programme on Advocacy and Communication and Water Supply and Sanitation Collaborative Council. (n.d.). *The Human Right to Water and Sanitation Media Brief.*

Vaduva, S., Echevarria-Cruz, S., & Takacs, J. Jr. (2020). The economic and social impact of a university education upon the development of the Romanian tourism industry. *Journal of Hospitality, Leisure, Sport and Tourism Education, 27*, 100270. doi:10.1016/j.jhlste.2020.100270

Vargas-Llovera, M. D. (2020). ¿Somos racistas? Caminando a través de los conceptos de racismo, exclusión y segregación urbana y social. In Racismo, etnicidad e identidad en el siglo XXI (pp. 79-99). AnthropiQa 2.0.

Veszprémi Sirotková, A. & Šusterová, V. (2016). Social responsibility and its enforcement in business. Tourism Economics and Business, *8*, (1/29), 64 - 70.

Vietti, F. (2022). The Tourist, the Migrant, and the Anthropologist. In N. Bloch & K. Adams (Eds.), *Intersections of Tourism, Migration, and Exile* (pp. 170–186). Routledge. doi:10.4324/9781003182689-10

Wachyuni, S. S., & Kusumaningrum, D. A. (2020). The Effect of COVID-19 Pandemic: How are the Future Tourist Behavior? *J. Educ. Soc. Behav. Sci., 33*, 67–76. doi:10.9734/jesbs/2020/v33i430219

Walmsley, A., Koens, K., & Milano, C. (2022). Overtourism and employment outcomes for the tourism worker: Impacts to labour markets. *Tourism Review, 77*(1), 1–15. doi:10.1108/TR-07-2020-0343

Walmsley, A., Partington, S., Armstrong, R., & Goodwin, H. (2019). Reactions to the national living wage in hospitality. *Employee Relations, 41*(1), 253–268. doi:10.1108/ER-02-2018-0044

Walpole, K. (2016). How is employees' input and influence over collective agreements shaped by Australia's Fair Work Act? *Labour & Industry: A Journal of the Social and Economic Relations of Work, 26*(3), 220-236.

Warren, C., & Becken, S. (2017). Saving energy and water in tourist accommodation: A systematic literature review (1987–2015). *International Journal of Tourism Research, 19*(3), 289–303. doi:10.1002/jtr.2112

Wen, J., Klarin, A., Goh, E., & Aston, J. (2020). A systematic review of the sex trafficking-related literature: Lessons for tourism and hospitality research. *Journal of Hospitality and Tourism Management, 45*, 370–376. doi:10.1016/j.jhtm.2020.06.001

Winkler, I. (2014). *The human right to water: significance, legal status and implications for water allocation.* Hart Publishing.

Yaacob, N. A., Mat, N., & Melhem, S. B. (2021). Human resource management practices and innovation of hotels in Malaysia. *International Journal of Social Science Research, 3*(4), 17–26.

Yao, Y., Zhao, X., Ren, L., & Jia, G. (2023). Compensatory travel in the post COVID-19 pandemic era: How does boredom stimulate intentions? *Journal of Hospitality and Tourism Management, 54*, 56–64. doi:10.1016/j.jhtm.2022.12.003

Yeh, S. S. (2021). Tourism recovery strategy against COVID-19 pandemic. *Tourism Recreation Research, 46*(2), 188–194. doi:10.1080/02508281.2020.1805933

Yılmazdogan, O. C., Secilmis, C., & Cicek, D. (2015). The effect of corporate social responsibility (CSR) perception on tourism students' intention to work in sector. *Procedia Economics and Finance, 23*, 1340–1346. doi:10.1016/S2212-5671(15)00321-4

Zeffane, R., & Melhem, S. B. (2018). Do feelings of trust/distrust affect employees' turnover intentions? An exploratory study in the United Arab Emirates. *Middle East Journal of Management, 5*(4), 385–408. doi:10.1504/MEJM.2018.095582

Zhou, L., & Chan, E. S. (2019). Motivations of tourism-induced mobility: Tourism development and the pursuit of the Chinese dream. *International Journal of Tourism Research, 21*(6), 824–838. doi:10.1002/jtr.2308

Zukin, S. (1991). *Landscapes of Power. From Detroit to Disney World.* University of California Press.

Related References

To continue our tradition of advancing information science and technology research, we have compiled a list of recommended IGI Global readings. These references will provide additional information and guidance to further enrich your knowledge and assist you with your own research and future publications.

Abdul Razak, R., & Mansor, N. A. (2021). Instagram Influencers in Social Media-Induced Tourism: Rethinking Tourist Trust Towards Tourism Destination. In M. Dinis, L. Bonixe, S. Lamy, & Z. Breda (Eds.), *Impact of New Media in Tourism* (pp. 135-144). IGI Global. https://doi.org/10.4018/978-1-7998-7095-1.ch009

Abir, T., & Khan, M. Y. (2022). Importance of ICT Advancement and Culture of Adaptation in the Tourism and Hospitality Industry for Developing Countries. In C. Ramos, S. Quinteiro, & A. Gonçalves (Eds.), *ICT as Innovator Between Tourism and Culture* (pp. 30–41). IGI Global. https://doi.org/10.4018/978-1-7998-8165-0.ch003

Abtahi, M. S., Behboudi, L., & Hasanabad, H. M. (2017). Factors Affecting Internet Advertising Adoption in Ad Agencies. *International Journal of Innovation in the Digital Economy*, 8(4), 18–29. doi:10.4018/IJIDE.2017100102

Afenyo-Agbe, E., & Mensah, I. (2022). Principles, Benefits, and Barriers to Community-Based Tourism: Implications for Management. In I. Mensah & E. Afenyo-Agbe (Eds.), *Prospects and Challenges of Community-Based Tourism and Changing Demographics* (pp. 1–29). IGI Global. doi:10.4018/978-1-7998-7335-8.ch001

Agbo, V. M. (2022). Distributive Justice Issues in Community-Based Tourism. In I. Mensah & E. Afenyo-Agbe (Eds.), *Prospects and Challenges of Community-Based Tourism and Changing Demographics* (pp. 107–129). IGI Global. https://doi.org/10.4018/978-1-7998-7335-8.ch005

Agrawal, S. (2017). The Impact of Emerging Technologies and Social Media on Different Business(es): Marketing and Management. In O. Rishi & A. Sharma (Eds.), *Maximizing Business Performance and Efficiency Through Intelligent Systems* (pp. 37–49). Hershey, PA: IGI Global. doi:10.4018/978-1-5225-2234-8.ch002

Ahmad, A., & Johari, S. (2022). Georgetown as a Gastronomy Tourism Destination: Visitor Awareness Towards Revisit Intention of Nasi Kandar Restaurant. In M. Valeri (Ed.), *New Governance and Management in Touristic Destinations* (pp. 71–83). IGI Global. https://doi.org/10.4018/978-1-6684-3889-3.ch005

Alkhatib, G., & Bayouq, S. T. (2021). A TAM-Based Model of Technological Factors Affecting Use of E-Tourism. *International Journal of Tourism and Hospitality Management in the Digital Age*, 5(2), 50–67. https://doi.org/10.4018/IJTHMDA.20210701.oa1

Altinay Ozdemir, M. (2021). Virtual Reality (VR) and Augmented Reality (AR) Technologies for Accessibility and Marketing in the Tourism Industry. In C. Eusébio, L. Teixeira, & M. Carneiro (Eds.), *ICT Tools and Applications for Accessible Tourism* (pp. 277-301). IGI Global. https://doi.org/10.4018/978-1-7998-6428-8.ch013

Anantharaman, R. N., Rajeswari, K. S., Angusamy, A., & Kuppusamy, J. (2017). Role of Self-Efficacy and Collective Efficacy as Moderators of Occupational Stress Among Software Development Professionals. *International Journal of Human Capital and Information Technology Professionals*, 8(2), 45–58. doi:10.4018/IJHCITP.2017040103

Aninze, F., El-Gohary, H., & Hussain, J. (2018). The Role of Microfinance to Empower Women: The Case of Developing Countries. *International Journal of Customer Relationship Marketing and Management*, 9(1), 54–78. doi:10.4018/IJCRMM.2018010104

Antosova, G., Sabogal-Salamanca, M., & Krizova, E. (2021). Human Capital in Tourism: A Practical Model of Endogenous and Exogenous Territorial Tourism Planning in Bahía Solano, Colombia. In V. Costa, A. Moura, & M. Mira (Eds.), *Handbook of Research on Human Capital and People Management in the Tourism Industry* (pp. 282–302). IGI Global. https://doi.org/10.4018/978-1-7998-4318-4.ch014

Arsenijević, O. M., Orčić, D., & Kastratović, E. (2017). Development of an Optimization Tool for Intangibles in SMEs: A Case Study from Serbia with a Pilot Research in the Prestige by Milka Company. In M. Vemić (Ed.), *Optimal Management Strategies in Small and Medium Enterprises* (pp. 320–347). Hershey, PA: IGI Global. doi:10.4018/978-1-5225-1949-2.ch015

Related References

Aryanto, V. D., Wismantoro, Y., & Widyatmoko, K. (2018). Implementing Eco-Innovation by Utilizing the Internet to Enhance Firm's Marketing Performance: Study of Green Batik Small and Medium Enterprises in Indonesia. *International Journal of E-Business Research, 14*(1), 21–36. doi:10.4018/IJEBR.2018010102

Asero, V., & Billi, S. (2022). New Perspective of Networking in the DMO Model. In M. Valeri (Ed.), *New Governance and Management in Touristic Destinations* (pp. 105–118). IGI Global. https://doi.org/10.4018/978-1-6684-3889-3.ch007

Atiku, S. O., & Fields, Z. (2017). Multicultural Orientations for 21st Century Global Leadership. In N. Baporikar (Ed.), *Management Education for Global Leadership* (pp. 28–51). Hershey, PA: IGI Global. doi:10.4018/978-1-5225-1013-0.ch002

Atiku, S. O., & Fields, Z. (2018). Organisational Learning Dimensions and Talent Retention Strategies for the Service Industries. In N. Baporikar (Ed.), *Global Practices in Knowledge Management for Societal and Organizational Development* (pp. 358–381). Hershey, PA: IGI Global. doi:10.4018/978-1-5225-3009-1.ch017

Atsa'am, D. D., & Kuset Bodur, E. (2021). Pattern Mining on How Organizational Tenure Affects the Psychological Capital of Employees Within the Hospitality and Tourism Industry: Linking Employees' Organizational Tenure With PsyCap. *International Journal of Tourism and Hospitality Management in the Digital Age, 5*(2), 17–28. https://doi.org/10.4018/IJTHMDA.2021070102

Ávila, L., & Teixeira, L. (2018). The Main Concepts Behind the Dematerialization of Business Processes. In M. Khosrow-Pour, D.B.A. (Ed.), Encyclopedia of Information Science and Technology, Fourth Edition (pp. 888-898). Hershey, PA: IGI Global. https://doi.org/ doi:10.4018/978-1-5225-2255-3.ch076

Ayorekire, J., Mugizi, F., Obua, J., & Ampaire, G. (2022). Community-Based Tourism and Local People's Perceptions Towards Conservation: The Case of Queen Elizabeth Conservation Area, Uganda. In I. Mensah & E. Afenyo-Agbe (Eds.), *Prospects and Challenges of Community-Based Tourism and Changing Demographics* (pp. 56–82). IGI Global. https://doi.org/10.4018/978-1-7998-7335-8.ch003

Baleiro, R. (2022). Tourist Literature and the Architecture of Travel in Olga Tokarczuk and Patti Smith. In R. Baleiro & R. Pereira (Eds.), *Global Perspectives on Literary Tourism and Film-Induced Tourism* (pp. 202-216). IGI Global. https://doi.org/10.4018/978-1-7998-8262-6.ch011

Barat, S. (2021). Looking at the Future of Medical Tourism in Asia. *International Journal of Tourism and Hospitality Management in the Digital Age, 5*(1), 19–33. https://doi.org/10.4018/IJTHMDA.2021010102

Barbosa, C. A., Magalhães, M., & Nunes, M. R. (2021). Travel Instagramability: A Way of Choosing a Destination? In M. Dinis, L. Bonixe, S. Lamy, & Z. Breda (Eds.), *Impact of New Media in Tourism* (pp. 173-190). IGI Global. https://doi.org/10.4018/978-1-7998-7095-1.ch011

Bari, M. W., & Khan, Q. (2021). Pakistan as a Destination of Religious Tourism. In E. Alaverdov & M. Bari (Eds.), *Global Development of Religious Tourism* (pp. 1-10). IGI Global. https://doi.org/10.4018/978-1-7998-5792-1.ch001

Bartens, Y., Chunpir, H. I., Schulte, F., & Voß, S. (2017). Business/IT Alignment in Two-Sided Markets: A COBIT 5 Analysis for Media Streaming Business Models. In S. De Haes & W. Van Grembergen (Eds.), *Strategic IT Governance and Alignment in Business Settings* (pp. 82–111). Hershey, PA: IGI Global. doi:10.4018/978-1-5225-0861-8.ch004

Bashayreh, A. M. (2018). Organizational Culture and Organizational Performance. In W. Lee & F. Sabetzadeh (Eds.), *Contemporary Knowledge and Systems Science* (pp. 50–69). Hershey, PA: IGI Global. doi:10.4018/978-1-5225-5655-8.ch003

Bechthold, L., Lude, M., & Prügl, R. (2021). Crisis Favors the Prepared Firm: How Organizational Ambidexterity Relates to Perceptions of Organizational Resilience. In A. Zehrer, G. Glowka, K. Schwaiger, & V. Ranacher-Lackner (Eds.), *Resiliency Models and Addressing Future Risks for Family Firms in the Tourism Industry* (pp. 178–205). IGI Global. https://doi.org/10.4018/978-1-7998-7352-5.ch008

Bedford, D. A. (2018). Sustainable Knowledge Management Strategies: Aligning Business Capabilities and Knowledge Management Goals. In N. Baporikar (Ed.), *Global Practices in Knowledge Management for Societal and Organizational Development* (pp. 46–73). Hershey, PA: IGI Global. doi:10.4018/978-1-5225-3009-1.ch003

Bekjanov, D., & Matyusupov, B. (2021). Influence of Innovative Processes in the Competitiveness of Tourist Destination. In J. Soares (Ed.), *Innovation and Entrepreneurial Opportunities in Community Tourism* (pp. 243–263). IGI Global. https://doi.org/10.4018/978-1-7998-4855-4.ch014

Bharwani, S., & Musunuri, D. (2018). Reflection as a Process From Theory to Practice. In M. Khosrow-Pour, D.B.A. (Ed.), Encyclopedia of Information Science and Technology, Fourth Edition (pp. 1529-1539). Hershey, PA: IGI Global. doi:10.4018/978-1-5225-2255-3.ch132

Bhatt, G. D., Wang, Z., & Rodger, J. A. (2017). Information Systems Capabilities and Their Effects on Competitive Advantages: A Study of Chinese Companies. *Information Resources Management Journal*, *30*(3), 41–57. doi:10.4018/IRMJ.2017070103

Related References

Bhushan, M., & Yadav, A. (2017). Concept of Cloud Computing in ESB. In R. Bhadoria, N. Chaudhari, G. Tomar, & S. Singh (Eds.), *Exploring Enterprise Service Bus in the Service-Oriented Architecture Paradigm* (pp. 116–127). Hershey, PA: IGI Global. doi:10.4018/978-1-5225-2157-0.ch008

Bhushan, S. (2017). System Dynamics Base-Model of Humanitarian Supply Chain (HSCM) in Disaster Prone Eco-Communities of India: A Discussion on Simulation and Scenario Results. *International Journal of System Dynamics Applications, 6*(3), 20–37. doi:10.4018/IJSDA.2017070102

Binder, D., & Miller, J. W. (2021). A Generations' Perspective on Employer Branding in Tourism. In V. Costa, A. Moura, & M. Mira (Eds.), *Handbook of Research on Human Capital and People Management in the Tourism Industry* (pp. 152–174). IGI Global. https://doi.org/10.4018/978-1-7998-4318-4.ch008

Birch Freeman, A. A., Mensah, I., & Antwi, K. B. (2022). Smiling vs. Frowning Faces: Community Participation for Sustainable Tourism in Ghanaian Communities. In I. Mensah & E. Afenyo-Agbe (Eds.), *Prospects and Challenges of Community-Based Tourism and Changing Demographics* (pp. 83–106). IGI Global. https://doi. org/10.4018/978-1-7998-7335-8.ch004

Biswas, A., & De, A. K. (2017). On Development of a Fuzzy Stochastic Programming Model with Its Application to Business Management. In S. Trivedi, S. Dey, A. Kumar, & T. Panda (Eds.), *Handbook of Research on Advanced Data Mining Techniques and Applications for Business Intelligence* (pp. 353–378). Hershey, PA: IGI Global. doi:10.4018/978-1-5225-2031-3.ch021

Boragnio, A., & Faracce Macia, C. (2021). "Taking Care of Yourself at Home": Use of E-Commerce About Food and Care During the COVID-19 Pandemic in the City of Buenos Aires. In M. Korstanje (Ed.), *Socio-Economic Effects and Recovery Efforts for the Rental Industry: Post-COVID-19 Strategies* (pp. 45–71). IGI Global. https://doi.org/10.4018/978-1-7998-7287-0.ch003

Borges, V. D. (2021). Happiness: The Basis for Public Policy in Tourism. In A. Perinotto, V. Mayer, & J. Soares (Eds.), *Rebuilding and Restructuring the Tourism Industry: Infusion of Happiness and Quality of Life* (pp. 1–25). IGI Global. https:// doi.org/10.4018/978-1-7998-7239-9.ch001

Bücker, J., & Ernste, K. (2018). Use of Brand Heroes in Strategic Reputation Management: The Case of Bacardi, Adidas, and Daimler. In A. Erdemir (Ed.), *Reputation Management Techniques in Public Relations* (pp. 126–150). Hershey, PA: IGI Global. doi:10.4018/978-1-5225-3619-2.ch007

Buluk Eşitti, B. (2021). COVID-19 and Alternative Tourism: New Destinations and New Tourism Products. In M. Demir, A. Dalgıç, & F. Ergen (Eds.), *Handbook of Research on the Impacts and Implications of COVID-19 on the Tourism Industry* (pp. 786–805). IGI Global. https://doi.org/10.4018/978-1-7998-8231-2.ch038

Bureš, V. (2018). Industry 4.0 From the Systems Engineering Perspective: Alternative Holistic Framework Development. In R. Brunet-Thornton & F. Martinez (Eds.), *Analyzing the Impacts of Industry 4.0 in Modern Business Environments* (pp. 199–223). Hershey, PA: IGI Global. doi:10.4018/978-1-5225-3468-6.ch011

Buzady, Z. (2017). Resolving the Magic Cube of Effective Case Teaching: Benchmarking Case Teaching Practices in Emerging Markets – Insights from the Central European University Business School, Hungary. In D. Latusek (Ed.), *Case Studies as a Teaching Tool in Management Education* (pp. 79–103). Hershey, PA: IGI Global. doi:10.4018/978-1-5225-0770-3.ch005

Camillo, A. (2021). *Legal Matters, Risk Management, and Risk Prevention: From Forming a Business to Legal Representation*. IGI Global. doi:10.4018/978-1-7998-4342-9.ch004

Căpusneanu, S., & Topor, D. I. (2018). Business Ethics and Cost Management in SMEs: Theories of Business Ethics and Cost Management Ethos. In I. Oncioiu (Ed.), *Ethics and Decision-Making for Sustainable Business Practices* (pp. 109–127). Hershey, PA: IGI Global. doi:10.4018/978-1-5225-3773-1.ch007

Chan, R. L., Mo, P. L., & Moon, K. K. (2018). Strategic and Tactical Measures in Managing Enterprise Risks: A Study of the Textile and Apparel Industry. In K. Strang, M. Korstanje, & N. Vajjhala (Eds.), *Research, Practices, and Innovations in Global Risk and Contingency Management* (pp. 1–19). Hershey, PA: IGI Global. doi:10.4018/978-1-5225-4754-9.ch001

Charlier, S. D., Burke-Smalley, L. A., & Fisher, S. L. (2018). Undergraduate Programs in the U.S: A Contextual and Content-Based Analysis. In J. Mendy (Ed.), *Teaching Human Resources and Organizational Behavior at the College Level* (pp. 26–57). Hershey, PA: IGI Global. doi:10.4018/978-1-5225-2820-3.ch002

Chumillas, J., Güell, M., & Quer, P. (2022). The Use of ICT in Tourist and Educational Literary Routes: The Role of the Guide. In C. Ramos, S. Quinteiro, & A. Gonçalves (Eds.), *ICT as Innovator Between Tourism and Culture* (pp. 15–29). IGI Global. https://doi.org/10.4018/978-1-7998-8165-0.ch002

Related References

Dahlberg, T., Kivijärvi, H., & Saarinen, T. (2017). IT Investment Consistency and Other Factors Influencing the Success of IT Performance. In S. De Haes & W. Van Grembergen (Eds.), *Strategic IT Governance and Alignment in Business Settings* (pp. 176–208). Hershey, PA: IGI Global. doi:10.4018/978-1-5225-0861-8.ch007

Damnjanović, A. M. (2017). Knowledge Management Optimization through IT and E-Business Utilization: A Qualitative Study on Serbian SMEs. In M. Vemić (Ed.), *Optimal Management Strategies in Small and Medium Enterprises* (pp. 249–267). Hershey, PA: IGI Global. doi:10.4018/978-1-5225-1949-2.ch012

Daneshpour, H. (2017). Integrating Sustainable Development into Project Portfolio Management through Application of Open Innovation. In M. Vemić (Ed.), *Optimal Management Strategies in Small and Medium Enterprises* (pp. 370–387). Hershey, PA: IGI Global. doi:10.4018/978-1-5225-1949-2.ch017

Daniel, A. D., & Reis de Castro, V. (2018). Entrepreneurship Education: How to Measure the Impact on Nascent Entrepreneurs. In A. Carrizo Moreira, J. Guilherme Leitão Dantas, & F. Manuel Valente (Eds.), *Nascent Entrepreneurship and Successful New Venture Creation* (pp. 85–110). Hershey, PA: IGI Global. doi:10.4018/978-1-5225-2936-1.ch004

David, R., Swami, B. N., & Tangirala, S. (2018). Ethics Impact on Knowledge Management in Organizational Development: A Case Study. In N. Baporikar (Ed.), *Global Practices in Knowledge Management for Societal and Organizational Development* (pp. 19–45). Hershey, PA: IGI Global. doi:10.4018/978-1-5225-3009-1.ch002

De Uña-Álvarez, E., & Villarino-Pérez, M. (2022). Fostering Ecocultural Resources, Identity, and Tourism in Inland Territories (Galicia, NW Spain). In G. Fernandes (Ed.), *Challenges and New Opportunities for Tourism in Inland Territories: Ecocultural Resources and Sustainable Initiatives* (pp. 1-16). IGI Global. https://doi.org/10.4018/978-1-7998-7339-6.ch001

Delias, P., & Lakiotaki, K. (2018). Discovering Process Horizontal Boundaries to Facilitate Process Comprehension. *International Journal of Operations Research and Information Systems*, *9*(2), 1–31. doi:10.4018/IJORIS.2018040101

Denholm, J., & Lee-Davies, L. (2018). Success Factors for Games in Business and Project Management. In *Enhancing Education and Training Initiatives Through Serious Games* (pp. 34–68). Hershey, PA: IGI Global. doi:10.4018/978-1-5225-3689-5.ch002

Deshpande, M. (2017). Best Practices in Management Institutions for Global Leadership: Policy Aspects. In N. Baporikar (Ed.), *Management Education for Global Leadership* (pp. 1–27). Hershey, PA: IGI Global. doi:10.4018/978-1-5225-1013-0.ch001

Deshpande, M. (2018). Policy Perspectives for SMEs Knowledge Management. In N. Baporikar (Ed.), *Knowledge Integration Strategies for Entrepreneurship and Sustainability* (pp. 23–46). Hershey, PA: IGI Global. doi:10.4018/978-1-5225-5115-7.ch002

Dezdar, S. (2017). ERP Implementation Projects in Asian Countries: A Comparative Study on Iran and China. *International Journal of Information Technology Project Management*, 8(3), 52–68. doi:10.4018/IJITPM.2017070104

Domingos, D., Respício, A., & Martinho, R. (2017). Reliability of IoT-Aware BPMN Healthcare Processes. In C. Reis & M. Maximiano (Eds.), *Internet of Things and Advanced Application in Healthcare* (pp. 214–248). Hershey, PA: IGI Global. doi:10.4018/978-1-5225-1820-4.ch008

Dosumu, O., Hussain, J., & El-Gohary, H. (2017). An Exploratory Study of the Impact of Government Policies on the Development of Small and Medium Enterprises in Developing Countries: The Case of Nigeria. *International Journal of Customer Relationship Marketing and Management*, 8(4), 51–62. doi:10.4018/IJCRMM.2017100104

Durst, S., Bruns, G., & Edvardsson, I. R. (2017). Retaining Knowledge in Smaller Building and Construction Firms. *International Journal of Knowledge and Systems Science*, 8(3), 1–12. doi:10.4018/IJKSS.2017070101

Edvardsson, I. R., & Durst, S. (2017). Outsourcing, Knowledge, and Learning: A Critical Review. *International Journal of Knowledge-Based Organizations*, 7(2), 13–26. doi:10.4018/IJKBO.2017040102

Edwards, J. S. (2018). Integrating Knowledge Management and Business Processes. In M. Khosrow-Pour, D.B.A. (Ed.), Encyclopedia of Information Science and Technology, Fourth Edition (pp. 5046-5055). Hershey, PA: IGI Global. doi:10.4018/978-1-5225-2255-3.ch437

Eichelberger, S., & Peters, M. (2021). Family Firm Management in Turbulent Times: Opportunities for Responsible Tourism. In A. Zehrer, G. Glowka, K. Schwaiger, & V. Ranacher-Lackner (Eds.), *Resiliency Models and Addressing Future Risks for Family Firms in the Tourism Industry* (pp. 103–124). IGI Global. https://doi.org/10.4018/978-1-7998-7352-5.ch005

Related References

Eide, D., Hjalager, A., & Hansen, M. (2022). Innovative Certifications in Adventure Tourism: Attributes and Diffusion. In R. Augusto Costa, F. Brandão, Z. Breda, & C. Costa (Eds.), *Planning and Managing the Experience Economy in Tourism* (pp. 161-175). IGI Global. https://doi.org/10.4018/978-1-7998-8775-1.ch009

Ejiogu, A. O. (2018). Economics of Farm Management. In *Agricultural Finance and Opportunities for Investment and Expansion* (pp. 56–72). Hershey, PA: IGI Global. doi:10.4018/978-1-5225-3059-6.ch003

Ekanem, I., & Abiade, G. E. (2018). Factors Influencing the Use of E-Commerce by Small Enterprises in Nigeria. *International Journal of ICT Research in Africa and the Middle East*, 7(1), 37–53. doi:10.4018/IJICTRAME.2018010103

Ekanem, I., & Alrossais, L. A. (2017). Succession Challenges Facing Family Businesses in Saudi Arabia. In P. Zgheib (Ed.), *Entrepreneurship and Business Innovation in the Middle East* (pp. 122–146). Hershey, PA: IGI Global. doi:10.4018/978-1-5225-2066-5.ch007

El Faquih, L., & Fredj, M. (2017). Ontology-Based Framework for Quality in Configurable Process Models. *Journal of Electronic Commerce in Organizations*, 15(2), 48–60. doi:10.4018/JECO.2017040104

Faisal, M. N., & Talib, F. (2017). Building Ambidextrous Supply Chains in SMEs: How to Tackle the Barriers? *International Journal of Information Systems and Supply Chain Management*, 10(4), 80–100. doi:10.4018/IJISSCM.2017100105

Fernandes, T. M., Gomes, J., & Romão, M. (2017). Investments in E-Government: A Benefit Management Case Study. *International Journal of Electronic Government Research*, 13(3), 1–17. doi:10.4018/IJEGR.2017070101

Figueira, L. M., Honrado, G. R., & Dionísio, M. S. (2021). Human Capital Management in the Tourism Industry in Portugal. In V. Costa, A. Moura, & M. Mira (Eds.), *Handbook of Research on Human Capital and People Management in the Tourism Industry* (pp. 1–19). IGI Global. doi:10.4018/978-1-7998-4318-4.ch001

Gao, S. S., Oreal, S., & Zhang, J. (2018). Contemporary Financial Risk Management Perceptions and Practices of Small-Sized Chinese Businesses. In I. Management Association (Ed.), Global Business Expansion: Concepts, Methodologies, Tools, and Applications (pp. 917-931). Hershey, PA: IGI Global. doi:10.4018/978-1-5225-5481-3.ch041

Garg, R., & Berning, S. C. (2017). Indigenous Chinese Management Philosophies: Key Concepts and Relevance for Modern Chinese Firms. In B. Christiansen & G. Koc (Eds.), *Transcontinental Strategies for Industrial Development and Economic Growth* (pp. 43–57). Hershey, PA: IGI Global. doi:10.4018/978-1-5225-2160-0.ch003

Gencer, Y. G. (2017). Supply Chain Management in Retailing Business. In U. Akkucuk (Ed.), *Ethics and Sustainability in Global Supply Chain Management* (pp. 197–210). Hershey, PA: IGI Global. doi:10.4018/978-1-5225-2036-8.ch011

Gera, R., Arora, S., & Malik, S. (2021). Emotional Labor in the Tourism Industry: Strategies, Antecedents, and Outcomes. In V. Costa, A. Moura, & M. Mira (Eds.), *Handbook of Research on Human Capital and People Management in the Tourism Industry* (pp. 73–91). IGI Global. https://doi.org/10.4018/978-1-7998-4318-4.ch004

Giacosa, E. (2018). The Increasing of the Regional Development Thanks to the Luxury Business Innovation. In L. Carvalho (Ed.), *Handbook of Research on Entrepreneurial Ecosystems and Social Dynamics in a Globalized World* (pp. 260–273). Hershey, PA: IGI Global. doi:10.4018/978-1-5225-3525-6.ch011

Glowka, G., Tusch, M., & Zehrer, A. (2021). The Risk Perception of Family Business Owner-Manager in the Tourism Industry: A Qualitative Comparison of the Intra-Firm Senior and Junior Generation. In A. Zehrer, G. Glowka, K. Schwaiger, & V. Ranacher-Lackner (Eds.), *Resiliency Models and Addressing Future Risks for Family Firms in the Tourism Industry* (pp. 126–153). IGI Global. https://doi.org/10.4018/978-1-7998-7352-5.ch006

Glykas, M., & George, J. (2017). Quality and Process Management Systems in the UAE Maritime Industry. *International Journal of Productivity Management and Assessment Technologies*, 5(1), 20–39. doi:10.4018/IJPMAT.2017010102

Glykas, M., Valiris, G., Kokkinaki, A., & Koutsoukou, Z. (2018). Banking Business Process Management Implementation. *International Journal of Productivity Management and Assessment Technologies*, 6(1), 50–69. doi:10.4018/IJPMAT.2018010104

Gomes, J., & Romão, M. (2017). The Balanced Scorecard: Keeping Updated and Aligned with Today's Business Trends. *International Journal of Productivity Management and Assessment Technologies*, 5(2), 1–15. doi:10.4018/IJPMAT.2017070101

Gomes, J., & Romão, M. (2017). Aligning Information Systems and Technology with Benefit Management and Balanced Scorecard. In S. De Haes & W. Van Grembergen (Eds.), *Strategic IT Governance and Alignment in Business Settings* (pp. 112–131). Hershey, PA: IGI Global. doi:10.4018/978-1-5225-0861-8.ch005

Related References

Goyal, A. (2021). Communicating and Building Destination Brands With New Media. In M. Dinis, L. Bonixe, S. Lamy, & Z. Breda (Eds.), *Impact of New Media in Tourism* (pp. 1-20). IGI Global. https://doi.org/10.4018/978-1-7998-7095-1.ch001

Grefen, P., & Turetken, O. (2017). Advanced Business Process Management in Networked E-Business Scenarios. *International Journal of E-Business Research, 13*(4), 70–104. doi:10.4018/IJEBR.2017100105

Guasca, M., Van Broeck, A. M., & Vanneste, D. (2021). Tourism and the Social Reintegration of Colombian Ex-Combatants. In J. da Silva, Z. Breda, & F. Carbone (Eds.), *Role and Impact of Tourism in Peacebuilding and Conflict Transformation* (pp. 66-86). IGI Global. https://doi.org/10.4018/978-1-7998-5053-3.ch005

Haider, A., & Saetang, S. (2017). Strategic IT Alignment in Service Sector. In S. Rozenes & Y. Cohen (Eds.), *Handbook of Research on Strategic Alliances and Value Co-Creation in the Service Industry* (pp. 231–258). Hershey, PA: IGI Global. doi:10.4018/978-1-5225-2084-9.ch012

Hajilari, A. B., Ghadaksaz, M., & Fasghandis, G. S. (2017). Assessing Organizational Readiness for Implementing ERP System Using Fuzzy Expert System Approach. *International Journal of Enterprise Information Systems, 13*(1), 67–85. doi:10.4018/IJEIS.2017010105

Haldorai, A., Ramu, A., & Murugan, S. (2018). Social Aware Cognitive Radio Networks: Effectiveness of Social Networks as a Strategic Tool for Organizational Business Management. In H. Bansal, G. Shrivastava, G. Nguyen, & L. Stanciu (Eds.), *Social Network Analytics for Contemporary Business Organizations* (pp. 188–202). Hershey, PA: IGI Global. doi:10.4018/978-1-5225-5097-6.ch010

Hall, O. P. Jr. (2017). Social Media Driven Management Education. *International Journal of Knowledge-Based Organizations, 7*(2), 43–59. doi:10.4018/IJKBO.2017040104

Hanifah, H., Halim, H. A., Ahmad, N. H., & Vafaei-Zadeh, A. (2017). Innovation Culture as a Mediator Between Specific Human Capital and Innovation Performance Among Bumiputera SMEs in Malaysia. In N. Ahmad, T. Ramayah, H. Halim, & S. Rahman (Eds.), *Handbook of Research on Small and Medium Enterprises in Developing Countries* (pp. 261–279). Hershey, PA: IGI Global. doi:10.4018/978-1-5225-2165-5.ch012

Hartlieb, S., & Silvius, G. (2017). Handling Uncertainty in Project Management and Business Development: Similarities and Differences. In Y. Raydugin (Ed.), *Handbook of Research on Leveraging Risk and Uncertainties for Effective Project Management* (pp. 337–362). Hershey, PA: IGI Global. doi:10.4018/978-1-5225-1790-0.ch016

Hass, K. B. (2017). Living on the Edge: Managing Project Complexity. In Y. Raydugin (Ed.), *Handbook of Research on Leveraging Risk and Uncertainties for Effective Project Management* (pp. 177–201). Hershey, PA: IGI Global. doi:10.4018/978-1-5225-1790-0.ch009

Hawking, P., & Carmine Sellitto, C. (2017). Developing an Effective Strategy for Organizational Business Intelligence. In M. Tavana (Ed.), *Enterprise Information Systems and the Digitalization of Business Functions* (pp. 222–237). Hershey, PA: IGI Global. doi:10.4018/978-1-5225-2382-6.ch010

Hawking, P., & Sellitto, C. (2017). A Fast-Moving Consumer Goods Company and Business Intelligence Strategy Development. *International Journal of Enterprise Information Systems*, *13*(2), 22–33. doi:10.4018/IJEIS.2017040102

Hawking, P., & Sellitto, C. (2017). Business Intelligence Strategy: Two Case Studies. *International Journal of Business Intelligence Research*, *8*(2), 17–30. doi:10.4018/IJBIR.2017070102

Hee, W. J., Jalleh, G., Lai, H., & Lin, C. (2017). E-Commerce and IT Projects: Evaluation and Management Issues in Australian and Taiwanese Hospitals. *International Journal of Public Health Management and Ethics*, *2*(1), 69–90. doi:10.4018/IJPHME.2017010104

Hernandez, A. A. (2018). Exploring the Factors to Green IT Adoption of SMEs in the Philippines. *Journal of Cases on Information Technology*, *20*(2), 49–66. doi:10.4018/JCIT.2018040104

Hollman, A., Bickford, S., & Hollman, T. (2017). Cyber InSecurity: A Post-Mortem Attempt to Assess Cyber Problems from IT and Business Management Perspectives. *Journal of Cases on Information Technology*, *19*(3), 42–70. doi:10.4018/JCIT.2017070104

Ibrahim, F., & Zainin, N. M. (2021). Exploring the Technological Impacts: The Case of Museums in Brunei Darussalam. *International Journal of Tourism and Hospitality Management in the Digital Age*, *5*(1), 1–18. https://doi.org/10.4018/IJTHMDA.2021010101

Igbinakhase, I. (2017). Responsible and Sustainable Management Practices in Developing and Developed Business Environments. In Z. Fields (Ed.), *Collective Creativity for Responsible and Sustainable Business Practice* (pp. 180–207). Hershey, PA: IGI Global. doi:10.4018/978-1-5225-1823-5.ch010

Related References

Iwata, J. J., & Hoskins, R. G. (2017). Managing Indigenous Knowledge in Tanzania: A Business Perspective. In P. Jain & N. Mnjama (Eds.), *Managing Knowledge Resources and Records in Modern Organizations* (pp. 198–214). Hershey, PA: IGI Global. doi:10.4018/978-1-5225-1965-2.ch012

Jain, P. (2017). Ethical and Legal Issues in Knowledge Management Life-Cycle in Business. In P. Jain & N. Mnjama (Eds.), *Managing Knowledge Resources and Records in Modern Organizations* (pp. 82–101). Hershey, PA: IGI Global. doi:10.4018/978-1-5225-1965-2.ch006

James, S., & Hauli, E. (2017). Holistic Management Education at Tanzanian Rural Development Planning Institute. In N. Baporikar (Ed.), *Management Education for Global Leadership* (pp. 112–136). Hershey, PA: IGI Global. doi:10.4018/978-1-5225-1013-0.ch006

Janošková, M., Csikósová, A., & Čulková, K. (2018). Measurement of Company Performance as Part of Its Strategic Management. In R. Leon (Ed.), *Managerial Strategies for Business Sustainability During Turbulent Times* (pp. 309–335). Hershey, PA: IGI Global. doi:10.4018/978-1-5225-2716-9.ch017

Jean-Vasile, A., & Alecu, A. (2017). Theoretical and Practical Approaches in Understanding the Influences of Cost-Productivity-Profit Trinomial in Contemporary Enterprises. In A. Jean Vasile & D. Nicolò (Eds.), *Sustainable Entrepreneurship and Investments in the Green Economy* (pp. 28–62). Hershey, PA: IGI Global. doi:10.4018/978-1-5225-2075-7.ch002

Joia, L. A., & Correia, J. C. (2018). CIO Competencies From the IT Professional Perspective: Insights From Brazil. *Journal of Global Information Management*, 26(2), 74–103. doi:10.4018/JGIM.2018040104

Juma, A., & Mzera, N. (2017). Knowledge Management and Records Management and Competitive Advantage in Business. In P. Jain & N. Mnjama (Eds.), *Managing Knowledge Resources and Records in Modern Organizations* (pp. 15–28). Hershey, PA: IGI Global. doi:10.4018/978-1-5225-1965-2.ch002

K., I., & A, V. (2018). Monitoring and Auditing in the Cloud. In K. Munir (Ed.), *Cloud Computing Technologies for Green Enterprises* (pp. 318-350). Hershey, PA: IGI Global. https://doi.org/ doi:10.4018/978-1-5225-3038-1.ch013

Kabra, G., Ghosh, V., & Ramesh, A. (2018). Enterprise Integrated Business Process Management and Business Intelligence Framework for Business Process Sustainability. In A. Paul, D. Bhattacharyya, & S. Anand (Eds.), *Green Initiatives for Business Sustainability and Value Creation* (pp. 228–238). Hershey, PA: IGI Global. doi:10.4018/978-1-5225-2662-9.ch010

Kaoud, M. (2017). Investigation of Customer Knowledge Management: A Case Study Research. *International Journal of Service Science, Management, Engineering, and Technology*, *8*(2), 12–22. doi:10.4018/IJSSMET.2017040102

Katuu, S. (2018). A Comparative Assessment of Enterprise Content Management Maturity Models. In N. Gwangwava & M. Mutingi (Eds.), *E-Manufacturing and E-Service Strategies in Contemporary Organizations* (pp. 93–118). Hershey, PA: IGI Global. doi:10.4018/978-1-5225-3628-4.ch005

Khan, M. Y., & Abir, T. (2022). The Role of Social Media Marketing in the Tourism and Hospitality Industry: A Conceptual Study on Bangladesh. In C. Ramos, S. Quinteiro, & A. Gonçalves (Eds.), *ICT as Innovator Between Tourism and Culture* (pp. 213–229). IGI Global. https://doi.org/10.4018/978-1-7998-8165-0.ch013

Kinnunen, S., Ylä-Kujala, A., Marttonen-Arola, S., Kärri, T., & Baglee, D. (2018). Internet of Things in Asset Management: Insights from Industrial Professionals and Academia. *International Journal of Service Science, Management, Engineering, and Technology*, *9*(2), 104–119. doi:10.4018/IJSSMET.2018040105

Klein, A. Z., Sabino de Freitas, A., Machado, L., Freitas, J. C. Jr, Graziola, P. G. Jr, & Schlemmer, E. (2017). Virtual Worlds Applications for Management Education. In L. Tomei (Ed.), *Exploring the New Era of Technology-Infused Education* (pp. 279–299). Hershey, PA: IGI Global. doi:10.4018/978-1-5225-1709-2.ch017

Kővári, E., Saleh, M., & Steinbachné Hajmásy, G. (2022). The Impact of Corporate Digital Responsibility (CDR) on Internal Stakeholders' Satisfaction in Hungarian Upscale Hotels. In M. Valeri (Ed.), *New Governance and Management in Touristic Destinations* (pp. 35–51). IGI Global. https://doi.org/10.4018/978-1-6684-3889-3.ch003

Kożuch, B., & Jabłoński, A. (2017). Adopting the Concept of Business Models in Public Management. In M. Lewandowski & B. Kożuch (Eds.), *Public Sector Entrepreneurship and the Integration of Innovative Business Models* (pp. 10–46). Hershey, PA: IGI Global. doi:10.4018/978-1-5225-2215-7.ch002

Kumar, J., Adhikary, A., & Jha, A. (2017). Small Active Investors' Perceptions and Preferences Towards Tax Saving Mutual Fund Schemes in Eastern India: An Empirical Note. *International Journal of Asian Business and Information Management*, *8*(2), 35–45. doi:10.4018/IJABIM.2017040103

Related References

Latusi, S., & Fissore, M. (2021). Pilgrimage Routes to Happiness: Comparing the Camino de Santiago and Via Francigena. In A. Perinotto, V. Mayer, & J. Soares (Eds.), *Rebuilding and Restructuring the Tourism Industry: Infusion of Happiness and Quality of Life* (pp. 157–182). IGI Global. https://doi.org/10.4018/978-1-7998-7239-9.ch008

Lavassani, K. M., & Movahedi, B. (2017). Applications Driven Information Systems: Beyond Networks toward Business Ecosystems. *International Journal of Innovation in the Digital Economy, 8*(1), 61–75. doi:10.4018/IJIDE.2017010104

Lazzareschi, V. H., & Brito, M. S. (2017). Strategic Information Management: Proposal of Business Project Model. In G. Jamil, A. Soares, & C. Pessoa (Eds.), *Handbook of Research on Information Management for Effective Logistics and Supply Chains* (pp. 59–88). Hershey, PA: IGI Global. doi:10.4018/978-1-5225-0973-8.ch004

Lechuga Sancho, M. P., & Martín Navarro, A. (2022). Evolution of the Literature on Social Responsibility in the Tourism Sector: A Systematic Literature Review. In G. Fernandes (Ed.), *Challenges and New Opportunities for Tourism in Inland Territories: Ecocultural Resources and Sustainable Initiatives* (pp. 169–186). IGI Global. https://doi.org/10.4018/978-1-7998-7339-6.ch010

Lederer, M., Kurz, M., & Lazarov, P. (2017). Usage and Suitability of Methods for Strategic Business Process Initiatives: A Multi Case Study Research. *International Journal of Productivity Management and Assessment Technologies, 5*(1), 40–51. doi:10.4018/IJPMAT.2017010103

Lee, I. (2017). A Social Enterprise Business Model and a Case Study of Pacific Community Ventures (PCV). In V. Potocan, M. Üngan, & Z. Nedelko (Eds.), *Handbook of Research on Managerial Solutions in Non-Profit Organizations* (pp. 182–204). Hershey, PA: IGI Global. doi:10.4018/978-1-5225-0731-4.ch009

Leon, L. A., Seal, K. C., Przasnyski, Z. H., & Wiedenman, I. (2017). Skills and Competencies Required for Jobs in Business Analytics: A Content Analysis of Job Advertisements Using Text Mining. *International Journal of Business Intelligence Research, 8*(1), 1–25. doi:10.4018/IJBIR.2017010101

Levy, C. L., & Elias, N. I. (2017). SOHO Users' Perceptions of Reliability and Continuity of Cloud-Based Services. In M. Moore (Ed.), *Cybersecurity Breaches and Issues Surrounding Online Threat Protection* (pp. 248–287). Hershey, PA: IGI Global. doi:10.4018/978-1-5225-1941-6.ch011

Levy, M. (2018). Change Management Serving Knowledge Management and Organizational Development: Reflections and Review. In N. Baporikar (Ed.), *Global Practices in Knowledge Management for Societal and Organizational Development* (pp. 256–270). Hershey, PA: IGI Global. doi:10.4018/978-1-5225-3009-1.ch012

Lewandowski, M. (2017). Public Organizations and Business Model Innovation: The Role of Public Service Design. In M. Lewandowski & B. Kożuch (Eds.), *Public Sector Entrepreneurship and the Integration of Innovative Business Models* (pp. 47–72). Hershey, PA: IGI Global. doi:10.4018/978-1-5225-2215-7.ch003

Lhannaoui, H., Kabbaj, M. I., & Bakkoury, Z. (2017). A Survey of Risk-Aware Business Process Modelling. *International Journal of Risk and Contingency Management*, 6(3), 14–26. doi:10.4018/IJRCM.2017070102

Li, J., Sun, W., Jiang, W., Yang, H., & Zhang, L. (2017). How the Nature of Exogenous Shocks and Crises Impact Company Performance?: The Effects of Industry Characteristics. *International Journal of Risk and Contingency Management*, 6(4), 40–55. doi:10.4018/IJRCM.2017100103

Lopez-Fernandez, M., Perez-Perez, M., Serrano-Bedia, A., & Cobo-Gonzalez, A. (2021). Small and Medium Tourism Enterprise Survival in Times of Crisis: "El Capricho de Gaudí. In D. Toubes & N. Araújo-Vila (Eds.), *Risk, Crisis, and Disaster Management in Small and Medium-Sized Tourism Enterprises* (pp. 103–129). IGI Global. doi:10.4018/978-1-7998-6996-2.ch005

Mahajan, A., Maidullah, S., & Hossain, M. R. (2022). Experience Toward Smart Tour Guide Apps in Travelling: An Analysis of Users' Reviews on Audio Odigos and Trip My Way. In R. Augusto Costa, F. Brandão, Z. Breda, & C. Costa (Eds.), *Planning and Managing the Experience Economy in Tourism* (pp. 255-273). IGI Global. https://doi.org/10.4018/978-1-7998-8775-1.ch014

Malega, P. (2017). Small and Medium Enterprises in the Slovak Republic: Status and Competitiveness of SMEs in the Global Markets and Possibilities of Optimization. In M. Vemić (Ed.), *Optimal Management Strategies in Small and Medium Enterprises* (pp. 102–124). Hershey, PA: IGI Global. doi:10.4018/978-1-5225-1949-2.ch006

Malewska, K. M. (2017). Intuition in Decision-Making on the Example of a Non-Profit Organization. In V. Potocan, M. Üngan, & Z. Nedelko (Eds.), *Handbook of Research on Managerial Solutions in Non-Profit Organizations* (pp. 378–399). Hershey, PA: IGI Global. doi:10.4018/978-1-5225-0731-4.ch018

Related References

Maroofi, F. (2017). Entrepreneurial Orientation and Organizational Learning Ability Analysis for Innovation and Firm Performance. In N. Baporikar (Ed.), *Innovation and Shifting Perspectives in Management Education* (pp. 144–165). Hershey, PA: IGI Global. doi:10.4018/978-1-5225-1019-2.ch007

Marques, M., Moleiro, D., Brito, T. M., & Marques, T. (2021). Customer Relationship Management as an Important Relationship Marketing Tool: The Case of the Hospitality Industry in Estoril Coast. In M. Dinis, L. Bonixe, S. Lamy, & Z. Breda (Eds.), Impact of New Media in Tourism (pp. 39-56). IGI Global. https://doi.org/ doi:10.4018/978-1-7998-7095-1.ch003

Martins, P. V., & Zacarias, M. (2017). A Web-based Tool for Business Process Improvement. *International Journal of Web Portals*, *9*(2), 68–84. doi:10.4018/ IJWP.2017070104

Matthies, B., & Coners, A. (2017). Exploring the Conceptual Nature of e-Business Projects. *Journal of Electronic Commerce in Organizations*, *15*(3), 33–63. doi:10.4018/JECO.2017070103

Mayer, V. F., Fraga, C. C., & Silva, L. C. (2021). Contributions of Neurosciences to Studies of Well-Being in Tourism. In A. Perinotto, V. Mayer, & J. Soares (Eds.), *Rebuilding and Restructuring the Tourism Industry: Infusion of Happiness and Quality of Life* (pp. 108–128). IGI Global. https://doi.org/10.4018/978-1-7998-7239-9.ch006

McKee, J. (2018). Architecture as a Tool to Solve Business Planning Problems. In M. Khosrow-Pour, D.B.A. (Ed.), Encyclopedia of Information Science and Technology, Fourth Edition (pp. 573-586). Hershey, PA: IGI Global. doi:10.4018/978-1-5225-2255-3.ch050

McMurray, A. J., Cross, J., & Caponecchia, C. (2018). The Risk Management Profession in Australia: Business Continuity Plan Practices. In N. Bajgoric (Ed.), *Always-On Enterprise Information Systems for Modern Organizations* (pp. 112–129). Hershey, PA: IGI Global. doi:10.4018/978-1-5225-3704-5.ch006

Meddah, I. H., & Belkadi, K. (2018). Mining Patterns Using Business Process Management. In R. Hamou (Ed.), *Handbook of Research on Biomimicry in Information Retrieval and Knowledge Management* (pp. 78–89). Hershey, PA: IGI Global. doi:10.4018/978-1-5225-3004-6.ch005

Melian, A. G., & Camprubí, R. (2021). The Accessibility of Museum Websites: The Case of Barcelona. In C. Eusébio, L. Teixeira, & M. Carneiro (Eds.), *ICT Tools and Applications for Accessible Tourism* (pp. 234–255). IGI Global. https://doi.org/10.4018/978-1-7998-6428-8.ch011

Related References

Mendes, L. (2017). TQM and Knowledge Management: An Integrated Approach Towards Tacit Knowledge Management. In D. Jaziri-Bouagina & G. Jamil (Eds.), *Handbook of Research on Tacit Knowledge Management for Organizational Success* (pp. 236–263). Hershey, PA: IGI Global. doi:10.4018/978-1-5225-2394-9.ch009

Menezes, V. D., & Cavagnaro, E. (2021). Communicating Sustainable Initiatives in the Hotel Industry: The Case of the Hotel Jakarta Amsterdam. In F. Brandão, Z. Breda, R. Costa, & C. Costa (Eds.), *Handbook of Research on the Role of Tourism in Achieving Sustainable Development Goals* (pp. 224-234). IGI Global. https://doi.org/10.4018/978-1-7998-5691-7.ch013

Menezes, V. D., & Cavagnaro, E. (2021). Communicating Sustainable Initiatives in the Hotel Industry: The Case of the Hotel Jakarta Amsterdam. In F. Brandão, Z. Breda, R. Costa, & C. Costa (Eds.), *Handbook of Research on the Role of Tourism in Achieving Sustainable Development Goals* (pp. 224-234). IGI Global. https://doi.org/10.4018/978-1-7998-5691-7.ch013

Mitas, O., Bastiaansen, M., & Boode, W. (2022). If You're Happy, I'm Happy: Emotion Contagion at a Tourist Information Center. In R. Augusto Costa, F. Brandão, Z. Breda, & C. Costa (Eds.), *Planning and Managing the Experience Economy in Tourism* (pp. 122-140). IGI Global. https://doi.org/10.4018/978-1-7998-8775-1.ch007

Mnjama, N. M. (2017). Preservation of Recorded Information in Public and Private Sector Organizations. In P. Jain & N. Mnjama (Eds.), *Managing Knowledge Resources and Records in Modern Organizations* (pp. 149–167). Hershey, PA: IGI Global. doi:10.4018/978-1-5225-1965-2.ch009

Mokoqama, M., & Fields, Z. (2017). Principles of Responsible Management Education (PRME): Call for Responsible Management Education. In Z. Fields (Ed.), *Collective Creativity for Responsible and Sustainable Business Practice* (pp. 229–241). Hershey, PA: IGI Global. doi:10.4018/978-1-5225-1823-5.ch012

Monteiro, A., Lopes, S., & Carbone, F. (2021). Academic Mobility: Bridging Tourism and Peace Education. In J. da Silva, Z. Breda, & F. Carbone (Eds.), *Role and Impact of Tourism in Peacebuilding and Conflict Transformation* (pp. 275-301). IGI Global. https://doi.org/10.4018/978-1-7998-5053-3.ch016

Muniapan, B. (2017). Philosophy and Management: The Relevance of Vedanta in Management. In P. Ordóñez de Pablos (Ed.), *Managerial Strategies and Solutions for Business Success in Asia* (pp. 124–139). Hershey, PA: IGI Global. doi:10.4018/978-1-5225-1886-0.ch007

Related References

Murad, S. E., & Dowaji, S. (2017). Using Value-Based Approach for Managing Cloud-Based Services. In A. Turuk, B. Sahoo, & S. Addya (Eds.), *Resource Management and Efficiency in Cloud Computing Environments* (pp. 33–60). Hershey, PA: IGI Global. doi:10.4018/978-1-5225-1721-4.ch002

Mutahar, A. M., Daud, N. M., Thurasamy, R., Isaac, O., & Abdulsalam, R. (2018). The Mediating of Perceived Usefulness and Perceived Ease of Use: The Case of Mobile Banking in Yemen. *International Journal of Technology Diffusion*, *9*(2), 21–40. doi:10.4018/IJTD.2018040102

Naidoo, V. (2017). E-Learning and Management Education at African Universities. In N. Baporikar (Ed.), *Management Education for Global Leadership* (pp. 181–201). Hershey, PA: IGI Global. doi:10.4018/978-1-5225-1013-0.ch009

Naidoo, V., & Igbinakhase, I. (2018). Opportunities and Challenges of Knowledge Retention in SMEs. In N. Baporikar (Ed.), *Knowledge Integration Strategies for Entrepreneurship and Sustainability* (pp. 70–94). Hershey, PA: IGI Global. doi:10.4018/978-1-5225-5115-7.ch004

Naumov, N., & Costandachi, G. (2021). Creativity and Entrepreneurship: Gastronomic Tourism in Mexico. In J. Soares (Ed.), *Innovation and Entrepreneurial Opportunities in Community Tourism* (pp. 90–108). IGI Global. https://doi.org/10.4018/978-1-7998-4855-4.ch006

Nayak, S., & Prabhu, N. (2017). Paradigm Shift in Management Education: Need for a Cross Functional Perspective. In N. Baporikar (Ed.), *Management Education for Global Leadership* (pp. 241–255). Hershey, PA: IGI Global. doi:10.4018/978-1-5225-1013-0.ch012

Nedelko, Z., & Potocan, V. (2017). Management Solutions in Non-Profit Organizations: Case of Slovenia. In V. Potocan, M. Üngan, & Z. Nedelko (Eds.), *Handbook of Research on Managerial Solutions in Non-Profit Organizations* (pp. 1–22). Hershey, PA: IGI Global. doi:10.4018/978-1-5225-0731-4.ch001

Nedelko, Z., & Potocan, V. (2017). Priority of Management Tools Utilization among Managers: International Comparison. In V. Wang (Ed.), *Encyclopedia of Strategic Leadership and Management* (pp. 1083–1094). Hershey, PA: IGI Global. doi:10.4018/978-1-5225-1049-9.ch075

Nedelko, Z., Raudeliūnienė, J., & Črešnar, R. (2018). Knowledge Dynamics in Supply Chain Management. In N. Baporikar (Ed.), *Knowledge Integration Strategies for Entrepreneurship and Sustainability* (pp. 150–166). Hershey, PA: IGI Global. doi:10.4018/978-1-5225-5115-7.ch008

Nguyen, H. T., & Hipsher, S. A. (2018). Innovation and Creativity Used by Private Sector Firms in a Resources-Constrained Environment. In S. Hipsher (Ed.), *Examining the Private Sector's Role in Wealth Creation and Poverty Reduction* (pp. 219–238). Hershey, PA: IGI Global. doi:10.4018/978-1-5225-3117-3.ch010

Obicci, P. A. (2017). Risk Sharing in a Partnership. In *Risk Management Strategies in Public-Private Partnerships* (pp. 115–152). Hershey, PA: IGI Global. doi:10.4018/978-1-5225-2503-5.ch004

Obidallah, W. J., & Raahemi, B. (2017). Managing Changes in Service Oriented Virtual Organizations: A Structural and Procedural Framework to Facilitate the Process of Change. *Journal of Electronic Commerce in Organizations, 15*(1), 59–83. doi:10.4018/JECO.2017010104

Ojo, O. (2017). Impact of Innovation on the Entrepreneurial Success in Selected Business Enterprises in South-West Nigeria. *International Journal of Innovation in the Digital Economy, 8*(2), 29–38. doi:10.4018/IJIDE.2017040103

Okdinawati, L., Simatupang, T. M., & Sunitiyoso, Y. (2017). Multi-Agent Reinforcement Learning for Value Co-Creation of Collaborative Transportation Management (CTM). *International Journal of Information Systems and Supply Chain Management, 10*(3), 84–95. doi:10.4018/IJISSCM.2017070105

Olivera, V. A., & Carrillo, I. M. (2021). Organizational Culture: A Key Element for the Development of Mexican Micro and Small Tourist Companies. In J. Soares (Ed.), *Innovation and Entrepreneurial Opportunities in Community Tourism* (pp. 227–242). IGI Global. doi:10.4018/978-1-7998-4855-4.ch013

Ossorio, M. (2022). Corporate Museum Experiences in Enogastronomic Tourism. In R. Augusto Costa, F. Brandão, Z. Breda, & C. Costa (Eds.), Planning and Managing the Experience Economy in Tourism (pp. 107-121). IGI Global. https://doi.org/ doi:10.4018/978-1-7998-8775-1.ch006

Ossorio, M. (2022). Enogastronomic Tourism in Times of Pandemic. In G. Fernandes (Ed.), *Challenges and New Opportunities for Tourism in Inland Territories: Ecocultural Resources and Sustainable Initiatives* (pp. 241–255). IGI Global. https://doi.org/10.4018/978-1-7998-7339-6.ch014

Özekici, Y. K. (2022). ICT as an Acculturative Agent and Its Role in the Tourism Context: Introduction, Acculturation Theory, Progress of the Acculturation Theory in Extant Literature. In C. Ramos, S. Quinteiro, & A. Gonçalves (Eds.), *ICT as Innovator Between Tourism and Culture* (pp. 42–66). IGI Global. https://doi.org/10.4018/978-1-7998-8165-0.ch004

Related References

Pal, K. (2018). Building High Quality Big Data-Based Applications in Supply Chains. In A. Kumar & S. Saurav (Eds.), *Supply Chain Management Strategies and Risk Assessment in Retail Environments* (pp. 1–24). Hershey, PA: IGI Global. doi:10.4018/978-1-5225-3056-5.ch001

Palos-Sanchez, P. R., & Correia, M. B. (2018). Perspectives of the Adoption of Cloud Computing in the Tourism Sector. In J. Rodrigues, C. Ramos, P. Cardoso, & C. Henriques (Eds.), *Handbook of Research on Technological Developments for Cultural Heritage and eTourism Applications* (pp. 377–400). Hershey, PA: IGI Global. doi:10.4018/978-1-5225-2927-9.ch018

Papadopoulou, G. (2021). Promoting Gender Equality and Women Empowerment in the Tourism Sector. In F. Brandão, Z. Breda, R. Costa, & C. Costa (Eds.), Handbook of Research on the Role of Tourism in Achieving Sustainable Development Goals (pp. 152-174). IGI Global. https://doi.org/ doi:10.4018/978-1-7998-5691-7.ch009

Papp-Váry, Á. F., & Tóth, T. Z. (2022). Analysis of Budapest as a Film Tourism Destination. In R. Baleiro & R. Pereira (Eds.), *Global Perspectives on Literary Tourism and Film-Induced Tourism* (pp. 257-279). IGI Global. https://doi.org/10.4018/978-1-7998-8262-6.ch014

Patiño, B. E. (2017). New Generation Management by Convergence and Individual Identity: A Systemic and Human-Oriented Approach. In N. Baporikar (Ed.), *Innovation and Shifting Perspectives in Management Education* (pp. 119–143). Hershey, PA: IGI Global. doi:10.4018/978-1-5225-1019-2.ch006

Patro, C. S. (2021). Digital Tourism: Influence of E-Marketing Technology. In M. Dinis, L. Bonixe, S. Lamy, & Z. Breda (Eds.), *Impact of New Media in Tourism* (pp. 234-254). IGI Global. https://doi.org/10.4018/978-1-7998-7095-1.ch014

Pawliczek, A., & Rössler, M. (2017). Knowledge of Management Tools and Systems in SMEs: Knowledge Transfer in Management. In A. Bencsik (Ed.), *Knowledge Management Initiatives and Strategies in Small and Medium Enterprises* (pp. 180–203). Hershey, PA: IGI Global. doi:10.4018/978-1-5225-1642-2.ch009

Pejic-Bach, M., Omazic, M. A., Aleksic, A., & Zoroja, J. (2018). Knowledge-Based Decision Making: A Multi-Case Analysis. In R. Leon (Ed.), *Managerial Strategies for Business Sustainability During Turbulent Times* (pp. 160–184). Hershey, PA: IGI Global. doi:10.4018/978-1-5225-2716-9.ch009

Perano, M., Hysa, X., & Calabrese, M. (2018). Strategic Planning, Cultural Context, and Business Continuity Management: Business Cases in the City of Shkoder. In A. Presenza & L. Sheehan (Eds.), *Geopolitics and Strategic Management in the Global Economy* (pp. 57–77). Hershey, PA: IGI Global. doi:10.4018/978-1-5225-2673-5.ch004

Pereira, R., Mira da Silva, M., & Lapão, L. V. (2017). IT Governance Maturity Patterns in Portuguese Healthcare. In S. De Haes & W. Van Grembergen (Eds.), *Strategic IT Governance and Alignment in Business Settings* (pp. 24–52). Hershey, PA: IGI Global. doi:10.4018/978-1-5225-0861-8.ch002

Pérez-Uribe, R. I., Torres, D. A., Jurado, S. P., & Prada, D. M. (2018). Cloud Tools for the Development of Project Management in SMEs. In R. Perez-Uribe, C. Salcedo-Perez, & D. Ocampo-Guzman (Eds.), *Handbook of Research on Intrapreneurship and Organizational Sustainability in SMEs* (pp. 95–120). Hershey, PA: IGI Global. doi:10.4018/978-1-5225-3543-0.ch005

Petrisor, I., & Cozmiuc, D. (2017). Global Supply Chain Management Organization at Siemens in the Advent of Industry 4.0. In L. Saglietto & C. Cezanne (Eds.), *Global Intermediation and Logistics Service Providers* (pp. 123–142). Hershey, PA: IGI Global. doi:10.4018/978-1-5225-2133-4.ch007

Pierce, J. M., Velliaris, D. M., & Edwards, J. (2017). A Living Case Study: A Journey Not a Destination. In N. Silton (Ed.), *Exploring the Benefits of Creativity in Education, Media, and the Arts* (pp. 158–178). Hershey, PA: IGI Global. doi:10.4018/978-1-5225-0504-4.ch008

Pipia, S., & Pipia, S. (2021). Challenges of Religious Tourism in the Conflict Region: An Example of Jerusalem. In E. Alaverdov & M. Bari (Eds.), *Global Development of Religious Tourism* (pp. 135-148). IGI Global. https://doi.org/10.4018/978-1-7998-5792-1.ch009

Poulaki, P., Kritikos, A., Vasilakis, N., & Valeri, M. (2022). The Contribution of Female Creativity to the Development of Gastronomic Tourism in Greece: The Case of the Island of Naxos in the South Aegean Region. In M. Valeri (Ed.), *New Governance and Management in Touristic Destinations* (pp. 246–258). IGI Global. https://doi.org/10.4018/978-1-6684-3889-3.ch015

Radosavljevic, M., & Andjelkovic, A. (2017). Multi-Criteria Decision Making Approach for Choosing Business Process for the Improvement: Upgrading of the Six Sigma Methodology. In J. Stanković, P. Delias, S. Marinković, & S. Rochhia (Eds.), *Tools and Techniques for Economic Decision Analysis* (pp. 225–247). Hershey, PA: IGI Global. doi:10.4018/978-1-5225-0959-2.ch011

Related References

Radovic, V. M. (2017). Corporate Sustainability and Responsibility and Disaster Risk Reduction: A Serbian Overview. In M. Camilleri (Ed.), *CSR 2.0 and the New Era of Corporate Citizenship* (pp. 147–164). Hershey, PA: IGI Global. doi:10.4018/978-1-5225-1842-6.ch008

Raghunath, K. M., Devi, S. L., & Patro, C. S. (2018). Impact of Risk Assessment Models on Risk Factors: A Holistic Outlook. In K. Strang, M. Korstanje, & N. Vajjhala (Eds.), *Research, Practices, and Innovations in Global Risk and Contingency Management* (pp. 134–153). Hershey, PA: IGI Global. doi:10.4018/978-1-5225-4754-9.ch008

Raman, A., & Goyal, D. P. (2017). Extending IMPLEMENT Framework for Enterprise Information Systems Implementation to Information System Innovation. In M. Tavana (Ed.), *Enterprise Information Systems and the Digitalization of Business Functions* (pp. 137–177). Hershey, PA: IGI Global. doi:10.4018/978-1-5225-2382-6.ch007

Rao, Y., & Zhang, Y. (2017). The Construction and Development of Academic Library Digital Special Subject Databases. In L. Ruan, Q. Zhu, & Y. Ye (Eds.), *Academic Library Development and Administration in China* (pp. 163–183). Hershey, PA: IGI Global. doi:10.4018/978-1-5225-0550-1.ch010

Ravasan, A. Z., Mohammadi, M. M., & Hamidi, H. (2018). An Investigation Into the Critical Success Factors of Implementing Information Technology Service Management Frameworks. In K. Jakobs (Ed.), *Corporate and Global Standardization Initiatives in Contemporary Society* (pp. 200–218). Hershey, PA: IGI Global. doi:10.4018/978-1-5225-5320-5.ch009

Rezaie, S., Mirabedini, S. J., & Abtahi, A. (2018). Designing a Model for Implementation of Business Intelligence in the Banking Industry. *International Journal of Enterprise Information Systems*, *14*(1), 77–103. doi:10.4018/IJEIS.2018010105

Richards, V., Matthews, N., Williams, O. J., & Khan, Z. (2021). The Challenges of Accessible Tourism Information Systems for Tourists With Vision Impairment: Sensory Communications Beyond the Screen. In C. Eusébio, L. Teixeira, & M. Carneiro (Eds.), *ICT Tools and Applications for Accessible Tourism* (pp. 26–54). IGI Global. https://doi.org/10.4018/978-1-7998-6428-8.ch002

Rodrigues de Souza Neto, V., & Marques, O. (2021). Rural Tourism Fostering Welfare Through Sustainable Development: A Conceptual Approach. In A. Perinotto, V. Mayer, & J. Soares (Eds.), *Rebuilding and Restructuring the Tourism Industry: Infusion of Happiness and Quality of Life* (pp. 38–57). IGI Global. https://doi.org/10.4018/978-1-7998-7239-9.ch003

Romano, L., Grimaldi, R., & Colasuonno, F. S. (2017). Demand Management as a Success Factor in Project Portfolio Management. In L. Romano (Ed.), *Project Portfolio Management Strategies for Effective Organizational Operations* (pp. 202–219). Hershey, PA: IGI Global. doi:10.4018/978-1-5225-2151-8.ch008

Rubio-Escuderos, L., & García-Andreu, H. (2021). Competitiveness Factors of Accessible Tourism E-Travel Agencies. In C. Eusébio, L. Teixeira, & M. Carneiro (Eds.), *ICT Tools and Applications for Accessible Tourism* (pp. 196–217). IGI Global. https://doi.org/10.4018/978-1-7998-6428-8.ch009

Rucci, A. C., Porto, N., Darcy, S., & Becka, L. (2021). Smart and Accessible Cities?: Not Always – The Case for Accessible Tourism Initiatives in Buenos Aries and Sydney. In C. Eusébio, L. Teixeira, & M. Carneiro (Eds.), *ICT Tools and Applications for Accessible Tourism* (pp. 115–145). IGI Global. https://doi.org/10.4018/978-1-7998-6428-8.ch006

Ruhi, U. (2018). Towards an Interdisciplinary Socio-Technical Definition of Virtual Communities. In M. Khosrow-Pour, D.B.A. (Ed.), Encyclopedia of Information Science and Technology, Fourth Edition (pp. 4278-4295). Hershey, PA: IGI Global. doi:10.4018/978-1-5225-2255-3.ch371

Ryan, L., Catena, M., Ros, P., & Stephens, S. (2021). Designing Entrepreneurial Ecosystems to Support Resource Management in the Tourism Industry. In V. Costa, A. Moura, & M. Mira (Eds.), *Handbook of Research on Human Capital and People Management in the Tourism Industry* (pp. 265–281). IGI Global. https://doi.org/10.4018/978-1-7998-4318-4.ch013

Sabuncu, I. (2021). Understanding Tourist Perceptions and Expectations During Pandemic Through Social Media Big Data. In M. Demir, A. Dalgıç, & F. Ergen (Eds.), *Handbook of Research on the Impacts and Implications of COVID-19 on the Tourism Industry* (pp. 330–350). IGI Global. https://doi.org/10.4018/978-1-7998-8231-2.ch016

Safari, M. R., & Jiang, Q. (2018). The Theory and Practice of IT Governance Maturity and Strategies Alignment: Evidence From Banking Industry. *Journal of Global Information Management, 26*(2), 127–146. doi:10.4018/JGIM.2018040106

Sahoo, J., Pati, B., & Mohanty, B. (2017). Knowledge Management as an Academic Discipline: An Assessment. In B. Gunjal (Ed.), *Managing Knowledge and Scholarly Assets in Academic Libraries* (pp. 99–126). Hershey, PA: IGI Global. doi:10.4018/978-1-5225-1741-2.ch005

Related References

Saini, D. (2017). Relevance of Teaching Values and Ethics in Management Education. In N. Baporikar (Ed.), *Management Education for Global Leadership* (pp. 90–111). Hershey, PA: IGI Global. doi:10.4018/978-1-5225-1013-0.ch005

Sambhanthan, A. (2017). Assessing and Benchmarking Sustainability in Organisations: An Integrated Conceptual Model. *International Journal of Systems and Service-Oriented Engineering*, 7(4), 22–43. doi:10.4018/IJSSOE.2017100102

Sambhanthan, A., & Potdar, V. (2017). A Study of the Parameters Impacting Sustainability in Information Technology Organizations. *International Journal of Knowledge-Based Organizations*, 7(3), 27–39. doi:10.4018/IJKBO.2017070103

Sánchez-Fernández, M. D., & Manríquez, M. R. (2018). The Entrepreneurial Spirit Based on Social Values: The Digital Generation. In P. Isaias & L. Carvalho (Eds.), *User Innovation and the Entrepreneurship Phenomenon in the Digital Economy* (pp. 173–193). Hershey, PA: IGI Global. doi:10.4018/978-1-5225-2826-5.ch009

Sanchez-Ruiz, L., & Blanco, B. (2017). Process Management for SMEs: Barriers, Enablers, and Benefits. In M. Vemić (Ed.), *Optimal Management Strategies in Small and Medium Enterprises* (pp. 293–319). Hershey, PA: IGI Global. doi:10.4018/978-1-5225-1949-2.ch014

Sanz, L. F., Gómez-Pérez, J., & Castillo-Martinez, A. (2018). Analysis of the European ICT Competence Frameworks. In V. Ahuja & S. Rathore (Eds.), *Multidisciplinary Perspectives on Human Capital and Information Technology Professionals* (pp. 225–245). Hershey, PA: IGI Global. doi:10.4018/978-1-5225-5297-0.ch012

Sarvepalli, A., & Godin, J. (2017). Business Process Management in the Classroom. *Journal of Cases on Information Technology*, 19(2), 17–28. doi:10.4018/JCIT.2017040102

Saxena, G. G., & Saxena, A. (2021). Host Community Role in Medical Tourism Development. In M. Singh & S. Kumaran (Eds.), *Growth of the Medical Tourism Industry and Its Impact on Society: Emerging Research and Opportunities* (pp. 105–127). IGI Global. https://doi.org/10.4018/978-1-7998-3427-4.ch006

Saygili, E. E., Ozturkoglu, Y., & Kocakulah, M. C. (2017). End Users' Perceptions of Critical Success Factors in ERP Applications. *International Journal of Enterprise Information Systems*, 13(4), 58–75. doi:10.4018/IJEIS.2017100104

Saygili, E. E., & Saygili, A. T. (2017). Contemporary Issues in Enterprise Information Systems: A Critical Review of CSFs in ERP Implementations. In M. Tavana (Ed.), *Enterprise Information Systems and the Digitalization of Business Functions* (pp. 120–136). Hershey, PA: IGI Global. doi:10.4018/978-1-5225-2382-6.ch006

Related References

Schwaiger, K. M., & Zehrer, A. (2021). The COVID-19 Pandemic and Organizational Resilience in Hospitality Family Firms: A Qualitative Approach. In A. Zehrer, G. Glowka, K. Schwaiger, & V. Ranacher-Lackner (Eds.), *Resiliency Models and Addressing Future Risks for Family Firms in the Tourism Industry* (pp. 32–49). IGI Global. https://doi.org/10.4018/978-1-7998-7352-5.ch002

Scott, N., & Campos, A. C. (2022). Cognitive Science of Tourism Experiences. In R. Augusto Costa, F. Brandão, Z. Breda, & C. Costa (Eds.), Planning and Managing the Experience Economy in Tourism (pp. 1-21). IGI Global. https://doi.org/ doi:10.4018/978-1-7998-8775-1.ch001

Seidenstricker, S., & Antonino, A. (2018). Business Model Innovation-Oriented Technology Management for Emergent Technologies. In M. Khosrow-Pour, D.B.A. (Ed.), Encyclopedia of Information Science and Technology, Fourth Edition (pp. 4560-4569). Hershey, PA: IGI Global. doi:10.4018/978-1-5225-2255-3.ch396

Selvi, M. S. (2021). Changes in Tourism Sales and Marketing Post COVID-19. In M. Demir, A. Dalgıç, & F. Ergen (Eds.), *Handbook of Research on the Impacts and Implications of COVID-19 on the Tourism Industry* (pp. 437–460). IGI Global. doi:10.4018/978-1-7998-8231-2.ch021

Senaratne, S., & Gunarathne, A. D. (2017). Excellence Perspective for Management Education from a Global Accountants' Hub in Asia. In N. Baporikar (Ed.), *Management Education for Global Leadership* (pp. 158–180). Hershey, PA: IGI Global. doi:10.4018/978-1-5225-1013-0.ch008

Sensuse, D. I., & Cahyaningsih, E. (2018). Knowledge Management Models: A Summative Review. *International Journal of Information Systems in the Service Sector*, *10*(1), 71–100. doi:10.4018/IJISSS.2018010105

Seth, M., Goyal, D., & Kiran, R. (2017). Diminution of Impediments in Implementation of Supply Chain Management Information System for Enhancing its Effectiveness in Indian Automobile Industry. *Journal of Global Information Management*, *25*(3), 1–20. doi:10.4018/JGIM.2017070101

Seyal, A. H., & Rahman, M. N. (2017). Investigating Impact of Inter-Organizational Factors in Measuring ERP Systems Success: Bruneian Perspectives. In M. Tavana (Ed.), *Enterprise Information Systems and the Digitalization of Business Functions* (pp. 178–204). Hershey, PA: IGI Global. doi:10.4018/978-1-5225-2382-6.ch008

Shaqrah, A. A. (2018). Analyzing Business Intelligence Systems Based on 7s Model of McKinsey. *International Journal of Business Intelligence Research*, *9*(1), 53–63. doi:10.4018/IJBIR.2018010104

Related References

Sharma, A. J. (2017). Enhancing Sustainability through Experiential Learning in Management Education. In N. Baporikar (Ed.), *Management Education for Global Leadership* (pp. 256–274). Hershey, PA: IGI Global. doi:10.4018/978-1-5225-1013-0.ch013

Shetty, K. P. (2017). Responsible Global Leadership: Ethical Challenges in Management Education. In N. Baporikar (Ed.), *Innovation and Shifting Perspectives in Management Education* (pp. 194–223). Hershey, PA: IGI Global. doi:10.4018/978-1-5225-1019-2.ch009

Sinthupundaja, J., & Kohda, Y. (2017). Effects of Corporate Social Responsibility and Creating Shared Value on Sustainability. *International Journal of Sustainable Entrepreneurship and Corporate Social Responsibility*, 2(1), 27–38. doi:10.4018/IJSECSR.2017010103

Škarica, I., & Hrgović, A. V. (2018). Implementation of Total Quality Management Principles in Public Health Institutes in the Republic of Croatia. *International Journal of Productivity Management and Assessment Technologies*, 6(1), 1–16. doi:10.4018/IJPMAT.2018010101

Skokic, V. (2021). How Small Hotel Owners Practice Resilience: Longitudinal Study Among Small Family Hotels in Croatia. In A. Zehrer, G. Glowka, K. Schwaiger, & V. Ranacher-Lackner (Eds.), *Resiliency Models and Addressing Future Risks for Family Firms in the Tourism Industry* (pp. 50–73). IGI Global. doi:10.4018/978-1-7998-7352-5.ch003

Smuts, H., Kotzé, P., Van der Merwe, A., & Loock, M. (2017). Framework for Managing Shared Knowledge in an Information Systems Outsourcing Context. *International Journal of Knowledge Management*, 13(4), 1–30. doi:10.4018/IJKM.2017100101

Sousa, M. J., Cruz, R., Dias, I., & Caracol, C. (2017). Information Management Systems in the Supply Chain. In G. Jamil, A. Soares, & C. Pessoa (Eds.), *Handbook of Research on Information Management for Effective Logistics and Supply Chains* (pp. 469–485). Hershey, PA: IGI Global. doi:10.4018/978-1-5225-0973-8.ch025

Spremic, M., Turulja, L., & Bajgoric, N. (2018). Two Approaches in Assessing Business Continuity Management Attitudes in the Organizational Context. In N. Bajgoric (Ed.), *Always-On Enterprise Information Systems for Modern Organizations* (pp. 159–183). Hershey, PA: IGI Global. doi:10.4018/978-1-5225-3704-5.ch008

Steenkamp, A. L. (2018). Some Insights in Computer Science and Information Technology. In *Examining the Changing Role of Supervision in Doctoral Research Projects: Emerging Research and Opportunities* (pp. 113–133). Hershey, PA: IGI Global. doi:10.4018/978-1-5225-2610-0.ch005

Stipanović, C., Rudan, E., & Zubović, V. (2022). Reaching the New Tourist Through Creativity: Sustainable Development Challenges in Croatian Coastal Towns. In M. Valeri (Ed.), *New Governance and Management in Touristic Destinations* (pp. 231–245). IGI Global. https://doi.org/10.4018/978-1-6684-3889-3.ch014

Tabach, A., & Croteau, A. (2017). Configurations of Information Technology Governance Practices and Business Unit Performance. *International Journal of IT/Business Alignment and Governance, 8*(2), 1–27. doi:10.4018/IJITBAG.2017070101

Talaue, G. M., & Iqbal, T. (2017). Assessment of e-Business Mode of Selected Private Universities in the Philippines and Pakistan. *International Journal of Online Marketing, 7*(4), 63–77. doi:10.4018/IJOM.2017100105

Tam, G. C. (2017). Project Manager Sustainability Competence. In *Managerial Strategies and Green Solutions for Project Sustainability* (pp. 178–207). Hershey, PA: IGI Global. doi:10.4018/978-1-5225-2371-0.ch008

Tambo, T. (2018). Fashion Retail Innovation: About Context, Antecedents, and Outcome in Technological Change Projects. In I. Management Association (Ed.), Fashion and Textiles: Breakthroughs in Research and Practice (pp. 233-260). Hershey, PA: IGI Global. https://doi.org/ doi:10.4018/978-1-5225-3432-7.ch010

Tantau, A. D., & Frățilă, L. C. (2018). Information and Management System for Renewable Energy Business. In *Entrepreneurship and Business Development in the Renewable Energy Sector* (pp. 200–244). Hershey, PA: IGI Global. doi:10.4018/978-1-5225-3625-3.ch006

Teixeira, N., Pardal, P. N., & Rafael, B. G. (2018). Internationalization, Financial Performance, and Organizational Challenges: A Success Case in Portugal. In L. Carvalho (Ed.), *Handbook of Research on Entrepreneurial Ecosystems and Social Dynamics in a Globalized World* (pp. 379–423). Hershey, PA: IGI Global. doi:10.4018/978-1-5225-3525-6.ch017

Teixeira, P., Teixeira, L., Eusébio, C., Silva, S., & Teixeira, A. (2021). The Impact of ICTs on Accessible Tourism: Evidence Based on a Systematic Literature Review. In C. Eusébio, L. Teixeira, & M. Carneiro (Eds.), *ICT Tools and Applications for Accessible Tourism* (pp. 1–25). IGI Global. doi:10.4018/978-1-7998-6428-8.ch001

Related References

Trad, A., & Kalpić, D. (2018). The Business Transformation Framework, Agile Project and Change Management. In M. Khosrow-Pour, D.B.A. (Ed.), Encyclopedia of Information Science and Technology, Fourth Edition (pp. 620-635). Hershey, PA: IGI Global. https://doi.org/ doi:10.4018/978-1-5225-2255-3.ch054

Trad, A., & Kalpić, D. (2018). The Business Transformation and Enterprise Architecture Framework: The Financial Engineering E-Risk Management and E-Law Integration. In B. Sergi, F. Fidanoski, M. Ziolo, & V. Naumovski (Eds.), *Regaining Global Stability After the Financial Crisis* (pp. 46–65). Hershey, PA: IGI Global. doi:10.4018/978-1-5225-4026-7.ch003

Trengereid, V. (2022). Conditions of Network Engagement: The Quest for a Common Good. In R. Augusto Costa, F. Brandão, Z. Breda, & C. Costa (Eds.), *Planning and Managing the Experience Economy in Tourism* (pp. 69-84). IGI Global. https://doi.org/10.4018/978-1-7998-8775-1.ch004

Turulja, L., & Bajgoric, N. (2018). Business Continuity and Information Systems: A Systematic Literature Review. In N. Bajgoric (Ed.), *Always-On Enterprise Information Systems for Modern Organizations* (pp. 60–87). Hershey, PA: IGI Global. doi:10.4018/978-1-5225-3704-5.ch004

Vargas-Hernández, J. G. (2017). Professional Integrity in Business Management Education. In N. Baporikar (Ed.), *Management Education for Global Leadership* (pp. 70–89). Hershey, PA: IGI Global. doi:10.4018/978-1-5225-1013-0.ch004

Varnacı Uzun, F. (2021). The Destination Preferences of Foreign Tourists During the COVID-19 Pandemic and Attitudes Towards: Marmaris, Turkey. In M. Demir, A. Dalgıç, & F. Ergen (Eds.), *Handbook of Research on the Impacts and Implications of COVID-19 on the Tourism Industry* (pp. 285–306). IGI Global. https://doi.org/10.4018/978-1-7998-8231-2.ch014

Vasista, T. G., & AlAbdullatif, A. M. (2017). Role of Electronic Customer Relationship Management in Demand Chain Management: A Predictive Analytic Approach. *International Journal of Information Systems and Supply Chain Management, 10*(1), 53–67. doi:10.4018/IJISSCM.2017010104

Vieru, D., & Bourdeau, S. (2017). Survival in the Digital Era: A Digital Competence-Based Multi-Case Study in the Canadian SME Clothing Industry. *International Journal of Social and Organizational Dynamics in IT, 6*(1), 17–34. doi:10.4018/IJSODIT.2017010102

Vijayan, G., & Kamarulzaman, N. H. (2017). An Introduction to Sustainable Supply Chain Management and Business Implications. In M. Khan, M. Hussain, & M. Ajmal (Eds.), *Green Supply Chain Management for Sustainable Business Practice* (pp. 27–50). Hershey, PA: IGI Global. doi:10.4018/978-1-5225-0635-5.ch002

Vlachvei, A., & Notta, O. (2017). Firm Competitiveness: Theories, Evidence, and Measurement. In A. Vlachvei, O. Notta, K. Karantininis, & N. Tsounis (Eds.), *Factors Affecting Firm Competitiveness and Performance in the Modern Business World* (pp. 1–42). Hershey, PA: IGI Global. doi:10.4018/978-1-5225-0843-4.ch001

Wang, C., Schofield, M., Li, X., & Ou, X. (2017). Do Chinese Students in Public and Private Higher Education Institutes Perform at Different Level in One of the Leadership Skills: Critical Thinking?: An Exploratory Comparison. In V. Wang (Ed.), *Encyclopedia of Strategic Leadership and Management* (pp. 160–181). Hershey, PA: IGI Global. doi:10.4018/978-1-5225-1049-9.ch013

Wang, J. (2017). Multi-Agent based Production Management Decision System Modelling for the Textile Enterprise. *Journal of Global Information Management*, 25(4), 1–15. doi:10.4018/JGIM.2017100101

Wiedemann, A., & Gewald, H. (2017). Examining Cross-Domain Alignment: The Correlation of Business Strategy, IT Management, and IT Business Value. *International Journal of IT/Business Alignment and Governance*, 8(1), 17–31. doi:10.4018/IJITBAG.2017010102

Wolf, R., & Thiel, M. (2018). Advancing Global Business Ethics in China: Reducing Poverty Through Human and Social Welfare. In S. Hipsher (Ed.), *Examining the Private Sector's Role in Wealth Creation and Poverty Reduction* (pp. 67–84). Hershey, PA: IGI Global. doi:10.4018/978-1-5225-3117-3.ch004

Yablonsky, S. (2018). Innovation Platforms: Data and Analytics Platforms. In *Multi-Sided Platforms (MSPs) and Sharing Strategies in the Digital Economy: Emerging Research and Opportunities* (pp. 72–95). Hershey, PA: IGI Global. doi:10.4018/978-1-5225-5457-8.ch003

Yaşar, B. (2021). The Impact of COVID-19 on Volatility of Tourism Stocks: Evidence From BIST Tourism Index. In M. Demir, A. Dalgıç, & F. Ergen (Eds.), *Handbook of Research on the Impacts and Implications of COVID-19 on the Tourism Industry* (pp. 23–44). IGI Global. https://doi.org/10.4018/978-1-7998-8231-2.ch002

Related References

Yusoff, A., Ahmad, N. H., & Halim, H. A. (2017). Agropreneurship among Gen Y in Malaysia: The Role of Academic Institutions. In N. Ahmad, T. Ramayah, H. Halim, & S. Rahman (Eds.), *Handbook of Research on Small and Medium Enterprises in Developing Countries* (pp. 23–47). Hershey, PA: IGI Global. doi:10.4018/978-1-5225-2165-5.ch002

Zacher, D., & Pechlaner, H. (2021). Resilience as an Opportunity Approach: Challenges and Perspectives for Private Sector Participation on a Community Level. In A. Zehrer, G. Glowka, K. Schwaiger, & V. Ranacher-Lackner (Eds.), *Resiliency Models and Addressing Future Risks for Family Firms in the Tourism Industry* (pp. 75–102). IGI Global. https://doi.org/10.4018/978-1-7998-7352-5.ch004

Zanin, F., Comuzzi, E., & Costantini, A. (2018). The Effect of Business Strategy and Stock Market Listing on the Use of Risk Assessment Tools. In *Management Control Systems in Complex Settings: Emerging Research and Opportunities* (pp. 145–168). Hershey, PA: IGI Global. doi:10.4018/978-1-5225-3987-2.ch007

Zgheib, P. W. (2017). Corporate Innovation and Intrapreneurship in the Middle East. In P. Zgheib (Ed.), *Entrepreneurship and Business Innovation in the Middle East* (pp. 37–56). Hershey, PA: IGI Global. doi:10.4018/978-1-5225-2066-5.ch003

About the Contributors

Maximiliano E. Korstanje is editor in chief of International Journal of Safety and Security in Tourism (UP Argentina) and Editor in Chief Emeritus of International Journal of Cyber Warfare and Terrorism (IGI-Global US). Korstanje is Senior Researchers in the Department of Economics at University of Palermo, Argentina. In 2015 he was awarded as Visiting Research Fellow at School of Sociology and Social Policy, University of Leeds, UK and the University of La Habana Cuba. In 2017 is elected as Foreign Faculty Member of AMIT, Mexican Academy in the study of Tourism, which is the most prominent institutions dedicated to tourism research in Mexico. He had a vast experience in editorial projects working as advisory member of Elsevier, Routledge, Springer, IGI global and Cambridge Scholar publishing. Korstanje had visited and given seminars in many important universities worldwide. He has also recently been selected to take part of the 2018 Albert Nelson Marquis Lifetime Achievement Award. a great distinction given by Marquis Who´s Who in the world.

Vanessa (Gaitree) Gowreesunkar is an Associate Professor with varied research interests in tourism. She is a citizen of Mauritius with a PhD cutting across three disciplines namely Tourism Management, Communication and Marketing. Vanessa is the Associate Editor of the Emerald International Journal of Tourism Cities and the Vice President of the International Tourism Studies Association. she is also assuming the role of observer at the World Tourism Network (). With over a decade of experience in teaching, training and research, Vanessa has brought her contributions in various international universities and educational institutions. She currently serves as Associate Professor at the Anant National University in India. Previously, she was assuming the role of Head of Department for Hospitality and Tourism at the University of Africa. Vanessa is an editorial board member of several scientific journals, and has published in Scopus-Indexed journals. Vanessa is the main editor of a number of international text books and she has authored/co-authored several book chapters. She is the review editor of Frontier in Sustainable Tourism. Vanessa has been conferred various awards for her contribution in research in Mauritius, India and Africa. She is an elected member of the ICOMOS International Cultural

About the Contributors

Tourism Committee and a specialist member of the World Commission on Protected Areas and Tourism and Protected Areas . She is member of Planet Happiness. Vanessa plays key role in a number of community empowerment initiatives; from 2010 to 2015, she assumed the role of Vice President and from 2015 to 2017, as President, at the African Network for Policy, Research and Advocacy for Sustainability, a regional Non-Governmental Organisation affiliated with the African Union. As a co-founder , she spearheaded a number of community-based initiatives and research activities in the field of island tourism, women empowerment, informal tourism economy, community-based tourism and sustainable development. Vanessa occupied the position of Cluster Secretary for the woman and gender cluster from 2015 to 2018 and that of Deputy Chair for the African Union ECOSOCC Tourism cluster of African Union Economic and Social Council.

***

Charul Agrawal has a PhD in Administration from the Federal University of Rio Grande do Sul, with emphasis on Organizational Studies. Master's in Administration from the Federal University of Espírito Santo, with emphasis in Organizational Management. Bachelor's degree in Social Communication from PUCMinas, with emphasis in Advertising. Professional experience as Temporary Professor at the School of Administration of the Federal University of Rio Grande do Sul. Currently, in post-doctoral training in the Graduate Program in Administration at FACC at the Federal University of Juiz de Fora.

Stroma Cole is a senior lecturer in international tourism development at the University of Westminster. Stroma combines her academic career with action research and consultancy. With research interests in gender, responsible tourism development, Human Rights, and the links between tourism and the SDGs, she is an activist researcher critiquing the consequences of tourism development. Stroma is an Associate Editor for Annals of Tourism Research and on the editorial board at Journal of Sustainable Tourism and Tourism Geographies. She is a director of Equality in Tourism, an international charity seeking to increase gender equality in tourism.

Taranjeet Duggal is a Professor at Amity Business School with 22 years of teaching and research experience in the area of HRM, Organizational Behaviour, and behavioral science . As a facilitator & Coach, she had conducted Faculty Development Programmes, corporate trainings and workshops in topics related to self Emotional Intelligence, positive attitude, motivation, team building, transaction Analyziz psychometric profiling, etc

About the Contributors

Marina Haro Aragú is a PhD student in Tourism. She completed the Master's Degree in Tourism Management and Planning, as well as the Master's Degree in Teaching with an English specialty. She is currently Front Office Manager of the Soho Boutique Equitativa Hotel in Malaga.

Zeynep Gulen Hashmi is an award-winning scholar-practitioner with more than twenty-six years of experience in the hospitality industry. She is a holder of the Socrates "Best Manager of the Year 2016" award from UK. Her doctoral specialization lies in tourism and hotel sustainability strategies, change management and action research. Her publications are on systemic collaborative challenges of our time, such as collaboration for tourism and sustainability, linkage between corporate well-being and societal well-being as well as sustainable luxury management. Currently, she is teaching various hospitality and tourism courses at the Emirates Academy of Hospitality Management in Dubai. Dr. Zeynep Gulen Hashmi may be contacted at gulen.hashmi@eahm.ae or at gulen.hashmi@bsl-lausanne.ch ORCID ID: 0000-0001-6949-6647

Adriana Offredi Rodriguez is a PhD student in Politics, Policies and International Relations at the Institute of Government and Public Policies (IGOP) of the Autonomous University of Barcelona. She holds a Master's Degree in Social Policy and Community Action from UAB and a Degree in Law from the University of Turin. Her research interests are mainly linked to Social and Public Policies, Migrations, Gender, Urbanism, Community Action, and Tourism. In previous years, she has been part of different projects of national and international relevance in Spain and Italy. She has also worked as an international aid worker in European and Asian Countries and is involved in various activities of social inclusion of migrants and refugees.

Marcela Oliveira has a PhD in Sciences for Development, Sustainability and Tourism at the University of Guadalajara, Centro Universitario de la Costa. Master in Economic and Social Sciences from the Universidad Autónoma de Sinaloa, Mexico. B.A. in Tourism from the Federal University of Juiz de Fora. Member of the Latin American Center of Excellence in Tourism (CELAT); of the Economic and Social Observatory of Tourism (OEST), and Critical Realism, Collective Action and Work (REACT) - Federal University of Juiz de Fora. He has experience in Tourism, with emphasis on Public Policies, Social Participation. In Social Sciences she focuses on Tourism Development, Collective Action and Power Relations.

About the Contributors

Mariana Pimentel has a PhD in Social Sciences - Federal University of Juiz de Fora/ UFJF (2016). Master's Degree in Administration - Federal University of Minas Gerais/ UFMG (2011). Bachelor in Tourism / UFMG (2006). Professor and researcher at UFJF, of the undergraduate degrees in Tourism and Human Sciences. Vice-leader of the Social and Economic Observatory of Tourism / OEST and member of the Latin American Center of Tourismology / CELAT. Federal University of Juiz de Fora, Institute of Human Sciences, Department of Tourism. R. José Lourenço Kelmer, Campus Universitário, CEP: 36036-330, Juiz de Fora/MG, Brazil.

Thiago Pimentel is an associate professor at Federal University of Juiz de Fora/ UFJF. Post doctorate in Sociology (Social Theory & Critical Realism) at the Federal University of Rio de Janeiro (2019), with supervision of Frédéric Vandenberghe. PhD in Social Sciences (Sociology) from UFJF (2012). Master in Administration (2008) and Bachelor in Integrated Tourism Planning (2006) both from the Federal University of Minas Gerais. Permanent Professor of the Graduate Programs in Social Sciences/PPGCSO (master & doctorate), in Administration/PPGA (academic master's) and in Public Administration (professional master's) at UFJF. Regular collaborator in the Postgraduate Programs in Sustainable Development at the University of Guadalajara/UdG (Mexico) and in Social Sciences at the Autonomous University of Sinaloa/UAS (Mexico). Regular Member of International Scientific Associations (ISA - International Sociological Association, and member of the Board of Directors of the International Sociological Association, in its Research Committee 17 (Sociology of Organizations); AIEST - International Association of Scientific Experts in Tourism, IPPA - International Public Policy Association, CLACSO, COMECSO, AMECIP) and national (ANPAD, SBEO, ANPTUR, COODTUR). Visiting scholar at Université du Quebec a Montreal (UQAM / Canada), Arizona State University (USA), Universidad de Guadalajara (México), Universidad Autónoma de Sinaloa (Mexico), Universidad de la Habana (Cuba), UTE and UNEMI (Ecuador), UNED (Costa Rica) among others. Professor at the Interdisciplinary Bachelor in Humanities/ BACH and Bachelor in Tourism, both at UFJF. Former coordinator of the Interdisciplinary Degree in Humanities/BACH, president of its academic council, and of its structuring teaching nucleus. Editor in chief of the journal Anais Brasileiros de Estudos Turísticos/ABET and of the journal Revista Latinoamericana de Turismologia/RELAT. Leader of the research groups Critical Realism, Collective Action and Work (sociology area CNPq/UFJF). Founder and director of the Latin American Center of Tourism - CELAT; and director of the Social and Economic Observatory

About the Contributors

of Tourism/OEST (tourism area CNPq/UFJF) and the Laboratory of Tourism Planning/LAPLANTUR. Former Counselor of the State Council of Tourism from the Minas Gerais-CET/SETUR/MG. Former vice-president of the Municipal Council of Tourism/COMTUR of the city of Juiz de Fora/MG and leader of its committee on Research, Information and Culture. Consultant for international (CONACYT), national (CNPq, Fapemig) and local (Research Advisory Committee - UFJF) funding agencies. Member of editorial board and also reviewer in international and national scientific journals in the areas of sociology, public and business administration, and tourism. Working subjects: of Sociology, Administration/Public Policies and Tourism, with emphasis on the following research lines and thematic fields (1) Social Theory - Critical Realism; Sociology of Organizations and Professions, Collective Action; Institutional Theory; (2) Administration Public and Social Management, Universities and Higher Education; Autonomous Forms of Self/Co-Management; Public Policies on Work, Leisure and Tourism; University and Research Centers; (3) Tourism - Sociology of Tourism; Management, Planning and Governance in Tourism Destinations; Public Policies in Tourism, Tourism Indicators, Leisure Policies. Authors of interest: (critical realism) Roy Bhaskar, Margaret Archer, Frédéric Vandenberghe; (social theory) Pierre Bourdieu, Anthony Giddens, Georges Gurvitch; (organizational/institutional theory) Michel Crozier, Erhard Friedberg, DiMaggio & Powell, Neil Flegstein; (social movements) Sidney Tarrow, Alberto Melucci, Alain Touraine; (public policy) Pierre Muller, Aguillar Villanueva, March & Olsen, Thomas Dye. Courses Taught: Social and Sociological Theory, Epistemology, Theory/Sociology of Organizations, Public Policies, Critical Realism, Discourse Analysis; Tourism Theory.

Yesaya Sandang is a lecturer at the Faculty of Interdisciplinary Studies-Universitas Kristen Satya Wacana. He researches the intersection of law, tourism, and human rights, particularly by using socio-legal approaches. Yesaya is also an activist and affiliated with communities' development and human rights NGOs in Indonesia.

Miriam Stopiakova was born in Piešťany, Slovakia. She obtained master degree in Marketing in University of Ss. Cyril and Methodius (Trnava) and in Hotel Management in EADE University (Málaga). During her studies she wrote various thesis related to CSR in tourism. She has worked in hotels in China, Argentina, Slovakia and Spain.

About the Contributors

João Vieira is a PhD candidate in Social Sciences at the Federal University of Juiz de Fora - UFJF. He has a Master's degree from the Graduate Program in Rural Extension from the Federal University of Viçosa - UFV (2019). Specialization in Urban and Environmental Law from the Pontifical Catholic University of Minas Gerais - PUC-MG (2017). Bachelor of History from the Federal University of Viçosa - UFV (2016) and Bachelor of Law from the School of Biological and Health Sciences - UNIVIÇOSA (2014). He is currently Secretary of Agriculture, Livestock and Environment of the Municipality of Paula Cândido. President of the Tourism Council of Paula Cândido - CONTUR (2021-2023). President of the Council for the Defense of the Environment of Paula Cândido - CODEMA (2022-2024). Member of the Municipal Council of Cultural Policies of Paula Cândido (2021-2023). Member of the Council for Cultural Heritage of Paula Cândido. (2021-2023).

Index

4.0 Industry 57

A

Adequate Housing 114, 124, 126

B

Boredom 72, 74, 79-80, 86, 88, 90-91

C

Child Workforce in Tourism 135
Collective Bargaining 129-130, 134-135, 142, 144-146, 148
Commodification of Diversity 122, 125
Community-Based Tourism 33, 149, 152
Conspicuous Consumption 40, 49, 57
COVID 72-73, 75-87, 91, 173, 186
COVID-19 5, 10, 70, 75-77, 79, 83-84, 87-91, 98, 143, 145-146, 148-149, 153, 155, 160, 162, 169, 171-172, 174-176, 184, 186-187, 191
CSR 150, 153-154, 156-160, 162-169, 171, 174, 177-179, 184-186, 188-191
Cyber Fordism 46, 57

D

Dark Consumption 59, 61, 66
Dark Tourism 59-60, 62-71
Democracy 40, 190

E

Economic Development 19, 36, 42-43, 53, 55, 125, 159
Equality 1, 5, 15, 21-22, 25-26, 28, 31, 40-41, 163, 172

F

Fatigue 72, 74, 76, 79, 86, 90-91
Forced Labor 129-130, 133-134

G

Global Citizenship 37, 39-40, 48-50, 53, 57, 99

H

Heritage 61-64, 68-71, 96-97, 101-102, 124, 127, 143
Heritage Management 61-62, 71
HOTEL 19, 25, 28, 31, 81, 85, 131, 139-141, 143, 146, 148-149, 152-157, 163-167, 169-170, 174, 176-180, 184-186, 188-190, 192
HR and Labour Standards in Tourism 129
Human Enrichment and Fulfillment 39-40
Human Resource Management 146-148, 150, 152, 165-166
Human Rights 1, 4-19, 21-25, 27, 29-36, 40-42, 44, 48, 50-51, 54, 59-61, 64-68, 71, 90, 92-95, 97-98, 100, 103, 107, 110, 113-114, 118, 121-124, 126, 129-130, 132-134, 136, 138, 143, 145,

Index

148, 162-164, 167, 190-191
Human Rights to Water 13-15, 18, 22-24, 29
Human Suffering 59, 65

I

Intercultural Companion 125
Intercultural Itinerary 92, 103-106, 110,
112, 118, 125, 127
Interculturalism 92-93, 98, 118, 120, 122,
126

J

Job Satisfaction 130, 140, 143, 149, 152

L

Labor Relation 152

M

Migrant Employees 137-138
Migrations 92, 97, 101, 107, 111, 127

P

Podcast 153, 180-187, 189, 193
Post-Fordist Transformation 126
Poverty 1-6, 8-10, 12, 22-23, 57, 64, 130,
159, 171-172

R

Responsible Tourism 54, 92-93, 97, 101,
108, 121, 127, 133, 138, 145, 147,
149, 154
Revenge Travel 72, 74, 76, 87-88, 90-91
Right to Adequate Housing 114, 124, 126

S

Safety-Security Tourism 8-9, 12
SDGs 13, 15, 21, 25, 27, 34, 171-173
Social Corporate Responsibility 189, 193
social dimension 116, 159, 174
Social Rights 43, 46, 53, 58
Special Rapporteur 113, 124, 126

T

Top-Down Multiculturalism 108, 110,
126, 128
Tourism Consumption 12, 49, 66, 92-93,
97-98, 100, 121-123
Tourism Development 2, 11, 14, 16-18, 22,
36, 132, 141, 148-151
Tourism Employees 129, 148
Tourism Industry 13-14, 16, 18, 25-27,
30, 76, 86-87, 89, 91, 129-134, 136,
140-141, 143, 146-148, 150, 152,
163-164, 170, 192
Travel and Tourism 42, 55, 72-73, 79, 84,
86, 89, 163

V

Violence 7-9, 12, 20, 22, 26, 29, 32, 34,
59-60, 64, 114, 146, 148, 172
Vulnerability 3, 68, 86, 114, 143, 149, 193

W

Water Access 17, 29, 33, 35
Water Justice 31-32, 35

Y

Young NEET 96, 126

Recommended Reference Books

IGI Global's reference books are available in three unique pricing formats:
Print Only, E-Book Only, or Print + E-Book.

Order direct through IGI Global's Online Bookstore at **www.igi-global.com** or through your preferred provider.

ISBN: 9781799887096
EISBN: 9781799887119
© 2022; 413 pp.
List Price: US$ **250**

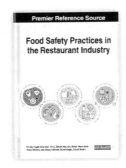

ISBN: 9781799874157
EISBN: 9781799874164
© 2022; 334 pp.
List Price: US$ **240**

ISBN: 9781668440230
EISBN: 9781668440254
© 2022; 320 pp.
List Price: US$ **215**

ISBN: 9781799889502
EISBN: 9781799889526
© 2022; 263 pp.
List Price: US$ **240**

ISBN: 9781799885283
EISBN: 9781799885306
© 2022; 587 pp.
List Price: US$ **360**

ISBN: 9781668455906
EISBN: 9781668455913
© 2022; 2,235 pp.
List Price: US$ **1,865**

Do you want to stay current on the latest research trends, product announcements, news, and special offers?
Join IGI Global's mailing list to receive customized recommendations, exclusive discounts, and more.
Sign up at: **www.igi-global.com/newsletters**.

Publisher of Timely, Peer-Reviewed Inclusive Research Since 1988

www.igi-global.com   Sign up at www.igi-global.com/newsletters   facebook.com/igiglobal   twitter.com/igiglobal

Ensure Quality Research is Introduced to the Academic Community

Become an Evaluator for IGI Global Authored Book Projects

  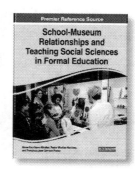 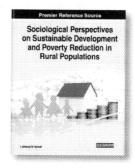

The overall success of an authored book project is dependent on quality and timely manuscript evaluations.

Applications and Inquiries may be sent to:
development@igi-global.com

Applicants must have a doctorate (or equivalent degree) as well as publishing, research, and reviewing experience. Authored Book Evaluators are appointed for one-year terms and are expected to complete at least three evaluations per term. Upon successful completion of this term, evaluators can be considered for an additional term.

If you have a colleague that may be interested in this opportunity, we encourage you to share this information with them.

Easily Identify, Acquire, and Utilize Published Peer-Reviewed Findings in Support of Your Current Research

IGI Global OnDemand

Purchase Individual IGI Global OnDemand Book Chapters and Journal Articles

For More Information:
www.igi-global.com/e-resources/ondemand/

Browse through 150,000+ Articles and Chapters!

Find specific research related to your current studies and projects that have been contributed by international researchers from prestigious institutions, including:

- Accurate and Advanced Search
- Affordably Acquire Research
- Instantly Access Your Content
- Benefit from the InfoSci Platform Features

It really provides an excellent entry into the research literature of the field. *It presents a manageable number of* highly relevant sources *on topics of interest to a wide range of researchers. The sources are* scholarly, but also accessible *to 'practitioners'.*

- Ms. Lisa Stimatz, MLS, University of North Carolina at Chapel Hill, USA

Interested in Additional Savings?

Subscribe to
IGI Global OnDemand *Plus*

Learn More

Acquire content from over 128,000+ research-focused book chapters and 33,000+ scholarly journal articles for as low as US$ 5 per article/chapter (original retail price for an article/chapter: US$ 37.50).

7,300+ E-BOOKS.
ADVANCED RESEARCH.
INCLUSIVE & AFFORDABLE.

IGI Global e-Book Collection

- Flexible Purchasing Options (Perpetual, Subscription, EBA, etc.)
- Multi-Year Agreements with No Price Increases Guaranteed
- No Additional Charge for Multi-User Licensing
- No Maintenance, Hosting, or Archiving Fees
- Continually Enhanced & Innovated Accessibility Compliance Features (WCAG)

Handbook of Research on Digital Transformation, Industry Use Cases, and the Impact of Disruptive Technologies
ISBN: 9781799877127
EISBN: 9781799877141

Handbook of Research on New Investigations in Artificial Life, AI, and Machine Learning
ISBN: 9781799886860
EISBN: 9781799886877

Handbook of Research on Future of Work and Education
ISBN: 9781799882756
EISBN: 9781799882770

Research Anthology on Physical and Intellectual Disabilities in an Inclusive Society (4 Vols.)
ISBN: 9781668435427
EISBN: 9781668435434

Innovative Economic, Social, and Environmental Practices for Progressing Future Sustainability
ISBN: 9781799895909
EISBN: 9781799895923

Applied Guide for Event Study Research in Supply Chain Management
ISBN: 9781799889694
EISBN: 9781799889717

Mental Health and Wellness in Healthcare Workers
ISBN: 9781799888130
EISBN: 9781799888147

Clean Technologies and Sustainable Development in Civil Engineering
ISBN: 9781799898108
EISBN: 9781799898122

Request More Information, or Recommend the IGI Global e-Book Collection to Your Institution's Librarian

For More Information or to Request a Free Trial, Contact IGI Global's e-Collections Team: eresources@igi-global.com | 1-866-342-6657 ext. 100 | 717-533-8845 ext. 100

Are You Ready to Publish Your Research

IGI Global offers book authorship and editorship opportunities across 11 subject areas, including business, computer science, education, science and engineering, social sciences, and more!

Benefits of Publishing with IGI Global:

- Free one-on-one editorial and promotional support.
- Expedited publishing timelines that can take your book from start to finish in less than one (1) year.
- Choose from a variety of formats, including Edited and Authored References, Handbooks of Research, Encyclopedias, and Research Insights.
- Utilize IGI Global's eEditorial Discovery® submission system in support of conducting the submission and double-blind peer review process.
- IGI Global maintains a strict adherence to ethical practices due in part to our full membership with the Committee on Publication Ethics (COPE).
- Indexing potential in prestigious indices such as Scopus®, Web of Science™, PsycINFO®, and ERIC – Education Resources Information Center.
- Ability to connect your ORCID iD to your IGI Global publications.
- Earn honorariums and royalties on your full book publications as well as complimentary content and exclusive discounts.

Join Your Colleagues from Prestigious Institutions, Including: Australian National University, Massachusetts Institute of Technology, Johns Hopkins University, Harvard University, Columbia University in the City of New York

Learn More at: www.igi-global.com/publish
or by Contacting the Acquisitions Department at: acquisition@igi-global.com

Individual Article & Chapter Downloads
US$ 29.50/each

Easily Identify, Acquire, and Utilize Published Peer-Reviewed Findings in Support of Your Current Research

- Browse Over **170,000+ Articles & Chapters**
- **Accurate & Advanced** Search
- Affordably Acquire **International Research**
- **Instantly Access** Your Content
- Benefit from the **InfoSci® Platform Features**

THE UNIVERSITY *of* NORTH CAROLINA *at* CHAPEL HILL

" *It really provides an excellent entry into the research literature of the field. It presents a manageable number of highly relevant sources on topics of interest to a wide range of researchers. The sources are scholarly, but also accessible to 'practitioners'.* "

- Ms. Lisa Stimatz, MLS, University of North Carolina at Chapel Hill, USA

Interested in Additional Savings?

Subscribe to
IGI Global OnDemand *Plus*

Learn More

Acquire content from over 128,000+ research-focused book chapters and 33,000+ scholarly journal articles for as low as US$ 5 per article/chapter (original retail price for an article/chapter: US$ 37.50).